THE DEADLY SIN OF TERRORISM

THE DEADLY SIN OF TERRORISM

Its Effect on Democracy and Civil Liberty in —— Six Countries ——

Edited by *David A. Charters*

Published under the Auspices of the Centre for Conflict Studies, University of New Brunswick

Contributions in Political Science, Number 340
Bernard K. Johnpoll, *Series Editor*

GREENWOOD PRESS
Westport, Connecticut • London

Library of Congress Cataloging-in-Publication Data

The Deadly sin of terrorism : its effect on democracy and civil
   liberty in six countries / edited by David A. Charters.
        p. cm.—(Contributions in political science, ISSN 0147–1066
 ; no. 340)
    "Published under the auspices of the Centre for Conflict Studies,
University of New Brunswick."
    Includes bibliographical references (p.   ) and index.
    ISBN 0–313–28964–6 (alk. paper)
    1. Terrorism. 2. Terrorism—Prevention. 3. Civil rights.
   4. Democracy. I. Charters, David. II. Series.
   HV6431.D43 1994
   303.6′25—dc20   93–31604

British Library Cataloguing in Publication Data is available.

Library of Congress Catalog Card Number: 93–31604
ISBN: 0–313–28964–6
ISSN: 0147–1066

First published in 1994

Greenwood Press, 88 Post Road West, Westport CT 06881
An imprint of Greenwood Publishing Group, Inc.

Printed in the United States of America

The paper used in this book complies with the
Permanent Paper Standard issued by the National
Information Standards Organization (Z39.48–1984).

10 9 8 7 6 5 4 3 2

Contents

Preface

In its annual report, *Patterns of Global Terrorism: 1992*, published at the end of April 1993, the U.S. State Department stated that in 1992 the number of international terrorist incidents had fallen to a seventeen-year low. This represents the continuation of a trend that began in 1989 and, if sustained, bodes well for the future. But it hardly seems the most auspicious time to produce a book on responses to the threat of international terrorism.

In fact, there are several valid reasons for publishing such a study at this time. First, as the World Trade Center bombing in February 1993 and the apparently related plots uncovered in June 1993 demonstrate, the problem is still with us— all over the world. Second, the "new world disorder" of the post–Cold War period has added a whole new panoply of conflicts and sources of political violence to those longstanding issues left over from the earlier era, which continue to fuel international terrorism. In short, the current downward trend is not irreversible.

The third and final point is that we may benefit from both the reduced threat and the distance in time from the worst years by trying to gain a sense of perspective on that period. As this book sets out to demonstrate, academic research on terrorism has matured to the point where it can contribute to such understanding. If we utilize the present wisely, to learn from experience, we might better prepare ourselves for the next time international terrorism challenges the security and liberty of democratic states. And that is a sound reason for this book at this time.

Acknowledgments

By its very nature, an edited volume represents a collective effort, and this one is no exception. My thanks go first to the authors, for their work and for their patience with the lengthy editing process. If this volume makes an original and useful contribution to the study of political violence, the credit must go to them.

Many others had a hand in the production of the volume: Deborah Stapleford and Marion Jagoe stoically word-processed successive drafts. Linda Hansen meticulously created the index. Ronda Hallihan of Cummings Imagesetting typeset the camera-ready proofs effectively and efficiently. I am grateful for all of their efforts. Mildred Vasan and Karen Davis of Greenwood Press deserve special commendation for perseverance. I hope that their faith in the project—or at least their patience with it—is justified by the final product.

Finally, I owe a special debt of gratitude to the Donner Canadian Foundation, which provided a major grant to support this project. Without that funding, this project would not have been possible. The foundation has accepted graciously my explanations for the book's long gestation. I can only hope that they feel the final version was worth the wait.

David A. Charters
Centre for Conflict Studies
University of New Brunswick
April 1994

Introduction

> The seventh and deadliest sin of terrorism is that it saps the will of a civilized society to defend itself.
>
> Paul Johnson[1]
> in Benjamin Netanyahu, ed., *International Terrorism: Challenge and Response*

Paul Johnson's comment, published in 1980, reflected a sense of alarm that was widely shared at that time. For more than ten years, domestic and international terrorism had raged across Europe and the Middle East. One government after another had capitulated to the demands of terrorist groups. Diplomats, business people, soldiers, heads of state, and innocent bystanders had been killed or maimed. No state, however small or far removed from the world's trouble spots, seemed immune. In the early 1980s, the problem only appeared to get worse. Under the circumstances, it is not surprising that many felt democracy itself might not survive the onslaught.

Yet fourteen years later the democracies of Europe and North America remain in existence. While they suffer from many problems, Johnson's worst fears have not been realized: None has succumbed to international terrorism. That said, the democracies did not survive unscathed. Some enacted or renewed special powers, security forces expanded their jurisdictions, and most states increased protection around certain installations and important persons. So it might be argued that in these and other ways the democracies emerged subtly less free. In other words, the real danger from international terrorism was not that democracies would fail to defend themselves, but rather that they would (and did) do so far too well—and, in so doing, became less democratic.

The aim of this study is to examine in comparative context the extent to which this process occurred in six democratic states. In particular, it attempts to show

how these countries achieved (or failed to achieve) a balance between effective countermeasures against international terrorism and the protection of democratic practices and civil liberties.

Before going further, it is necessary to clarify terminology. As Thomas H. Mitchell points out, defining terrorism is important for policy-makers and for scholars of the subject. Defining a problem provides a common terminology and a frame of reference for understanding and responding to it; as such, it limits misjudgment in the making of policy.[2] This study advances from the assumption that terrorism is not a monolithic phenomenon; as historian Walter Laqueur observes, "there is no such thing as pure, unalloyed, unchanging terrorism, . . . there are many forms of terrorism."[3] He adds that these many forms defy categorization under a single, all-encompassing, universally accepted definition.[4] However, as he and others point out, it is possible to develop or adopt a "working" concept that embraces the essential common characteristics of the phenomenon. It may not be academically perfect,[5] but it is probably adequate for conveying the necessary common frame of reference. For the purpose of this study, the following definition has been accepted: "[Terrorism is] . . . the purposeful act or the threat of the act of violence to create fear and/or compliant behaviour in a victim, and/or audiences of the act or threat."[6]

Since the focus of this study is international terrorism, it is necessary to expand this definition to include that dimension. Edward F. Mickolus and his colleagues include under the rubric of international terrorism, "activities involving agents— terrorists, government participants, citizens or institutions—from two or more nations . . . originating in one nation and terminating in another . . . [or] involving the demands made of a nation other than the one where the incident occurs."[7] In other words, the perpetrators, the targets, the effects, or the consequences transcend international frontiers. While these formulations might not satisfy all critics, they appear to be reasonable compromises. More important, the terrorist activities described in the case studies clearly fit these criteria and illustrate the multifaceted nature of terrorism.

Turning now to the comparative dimension of this study, it must be acknowledged at the outset that any attempt to compare the political, legislative, legal, police, and other policies and practices of six countries raises a number of methodological issues: What can be compared? Is comparative analysis possible? What kind of framework can be employed? While challenging, these issues do not pose insurmountable problems.[8]

First, democratic states can be compared, even while acknowledging their differences. There are indeed varieties of democracy, and the varieties are well represented in this volume. Each political culture is unique, and each functions and responds to challenges in ways peculiar to itself. But they all have a number of features in common: multiparty political cultures, elected legislatures, responsible government, rule of law, institutionalized structures and procedures for law enforcement, domestic and foreign policy, and a heritage of fundamental democratic principles and civil rights, such as freedom of speech and freedom of the press. The extent to which those things were influenced or altered either by terrorism or by the response to it is something that can be determined and compared. In the first chapter, which precedes the case studies, Grant Wardlaw provides a philosophical framework for examining these issues. He suggests some general principles, which are intended to link effectiveness to the democratic practices and traditions that the countermeasures are supposed to protect. As such, they comprise useful criteria for comparative assessment of the performance of the countries studied by extrapolating from the evidence provided in the cases studies.

Second, the kinds of countermeasures undertaken, even if somewhat different in form and practice from country to country, are sufficiently similar and common to permit comparison. In the case studies of the individual countries that follow, each author examines four key aspects of the problem: the nature of the international terrorist threat(s) to the country concerned, the political and social settings in which responses were developed, the range of countermeasures and other resources employed and their effectiveness, and the impact of these countermeasures on the democratic character of the state. The countermeasures examined include special powers, negotiations with terrorist groups, international collaborative measures, intelligence methods, target-hardening, and military/para-military actions. In considering the impact of these measures on the democratic character of the state, the case studies will assess the extent to which they imposed limits on individual rights or restrictions on the media, widened the intrusive investigative powers of police and other security forces, and modified law enforcement and judicial procedures—to the detriment of democracy and civil liberties.

Employing Wardlaw's criteria, the conclusions address three basic issues: the impact of international terrorism on these countries, the effectiveness of the countermeasures employed, and the extent to which those countermeasures preserved or eroded fundamental democratic practices and traditions. In relation both to their effectiveness and to their impact on democracy, the various countermeasures are assessed in a comparative manner: The relative merits of each are considered, commonalities and anomalies of experience and results are identified, and some general conclusions are drawn as to their wider appropriateness for democratic counter-terrorism policies. Obviously, the differences in political cultures will ensure that the results or the impact of specific policies and actions will be unique to the country concerned. Even so, in a comparative assessment, uniqueness and commonality may be equally significant, with much to be learned from each. The limitations of the analytical method, however, mean that the conclusions drawn should be considered instructive, but suggestive rather than definitive.

NOTES

1. Paul Johnson, "The Seven Deadly Sins of Terrorism," in Benjamin Netanyahu, ed., *International Terrorism: Challenge and Response* (Jerusalem: Jonathan Institute, 1980), p. 20.

2. Thomas H. Mitchell, "Defining the Problem," in David A. Charters, ed., *Democratic Responses to International Terrorism* (Dobbs Ferry, N.Y.: Transnational Publishers, 1991), pp. 9, 12–13.

3. Walter Laqueur, *The Age of Terrorism* (Boston: Little Brown, 1987), p. 145.

4. Ibid., pp. 142–49.

5. The most rigorous attempt at defining terrorism may be found in Alex P. Schmid and Albert J. Jongman, *Political Terrorism: A New Guide to Actors, Authors, Concepts, Data Bases, Theories and Literature* (New Brunswick, N.J.: Transaction Books, 1988), p. 28.

6. Michael Stohl, "Demystifying Terrorism: The Myths and Realities of Contemporary Political Terrorism," in Michael Stohl, ed., *The Politics of Terrorism,* 3d ed. (New York: Marcel Dekker, 1988), p. 3.

7. Edward F. Mickolus, Todd Sandler, and Jean M. Murdock, *International Terrorism in the 1980s: A Chronology of Events.* vol. 2, 1984–1987 (Ames: Iowa State University Press, 1989), pp. xi–xii.

8. For a thorough discussion of the potential and limitations of comparative studies of terrorism, see Ted Robert Gurr, "Empirical Research on Political Terrorism: The State of the Art and How It Might Be Improved," in Robert O. Slater and Michael Stohl, eds., *Current Perspectives on International Terrorism* (London: Macmillan, 1988), pp. 115–48.

1

The Democratic Framework

Grant Wardlaw

This study reflects an understanding that democratic states have, over the past two decades, accumulated enough experience dealing with terrorism to allow scholars to assess how effective their policies have been and what impact they have had on the fabric of democracy. The range of problems faced, measures introduced, and outcomes has been sufficiently broad to permit the assessment to take a comparative approach.

One feature of the debate over counter-terrorism has struck many observers: Decision-makers and even so-called informed observers frequently approach the problem in an analytically simple manner, which can easily inflate the threat posed by terrorism[1] and lead to serious consideration or actual adoption of similarly terrorist methods as a means of reacting to it. A central problem for democracies lies in accurately assessing the nature and extent of the terrorist threat facing them and in constructing rational, appropriate, and consistent countermeasures that deal with the threat without fundamentally undermining or changing the democratic practices and traditions that the measures are designed to protect.

A central weakness of much of the debate about how to deal with terrorism is that many of the contributions are clouded by political posturing, moral confusion, and wishful thinking.[2] In particular, the search for simple solutions has contributed to the proposal, and in some cases adoption, of naive, dangerous, and even terrorist countermeasures by countries that have been terrorist targets. This is apparent in several of the case studies that follow.

In order to arrive at policies that are appropriate for democratic states and as effective as it is possible to be (given the realities of the nature of terrorism, the limits on the powers of democratic governments, and the restraints imposed by being part of the international community), it is vital for governments first to distinguish among types and levels of terrorist threats. Even where it has been clear that some incidents, groups, or even campaigns pose less of a real threat than others (except, of course, to the immediate victims), many governments have been unwilling to distinguish among them. Instead, they have tended to portray all acts of terrorism as being equally dangerous to states or to the international system.[3] Moreover, there has been a continuing expansion of the term terrorism into a meaningless "catchall" that encompasses anything from minor crime to acts of international warfare.[4]

This failure has grossly exaggerated the threat posed by terrorism to democratic societies and frequently has inflamed public reaction to particular incidents to the point at which governments may find their politically feasible options severely limited, if not virtually predetermined in some cases. Some of the blame for this inflated threat perception can be laid squarely on the media, which have exploited the terrorist image. Terrorist incidents are often deliberately stage-managed by the terrorists and publicized by the media *as* spectaculars (the hijacking of TWA Flight 847 being a case in point). The perceptions that flow from sensational coverage of such events are responsible in part for the widespread belief that terrorism poses a significant challenge to the survival of democracies that are the target of terrorist attack. Of course, it is unfair to place all the blame on the media for inaccurate views about the nature of terrorism.[5] Politicians and government leaders have usually spoken the loudest during the terrorist debate, and their contribution is often simplistic and alarmist. Sadly, too, the academic community—especially the crop of self-appointed "experts" who are the darlings of TV talk shows—must shoulder some of the blame. Willing or not, they are victims of a medium that values the visual over the cerebral and that is not oriented to exploring complex and contradictory issues at length.

The great challenge is to try to divorce oneself from the human tragedy and the barbarism that is terrorism in order to assess objectively just what damage is being done away from the scene of the horror and what measures need to be instituted as a consequence. It is this type of analysis that is needed if counter-terrorism responses are to be measured and appropriate—and that is attempted in this volume.

It is important to stress that those who believe that the seriousness of the terrorist threat is overrated are by no means claiming that terrorism is not a problem that needs to be taken seriously.[6] However, much of the debate about methods of responding to terrorism has become unfocused because of the failure to distinguish one sort of threat from another, to determine which vital interests (if any) are threatened and in what way, and to communicate the results of these analyses to the public properly. By failing to make these distinctions and to carry their consequences through into policy-making, it is all too easy to trap oneself into believing that terrorism is a more potent threat than it really is. The danger lies in the possibility of doing the terrorists' job for them by taking unnecessary steps in an attempt to counter the perceived threat and thereby fundamentally altering the nature of democracy.

While terrorism is abhorrent and immoral, it can seldom if ever be a real threat to democratic states. The illusion of strength is all-important to terrorism. The shock effect of attacks, the impossibility of securing the multiplicity of targets, and the fact that governments are usually surprised by terrorism and forced into a reactive/defensive posture reinforce the media-induced images of power and invincibility, which in turn add to the essential element of fear, which is the real source of terrorist leverage.

But that power is an illusion. Terrorists are not superhuman. Democratic societies are vulnerable to attack in the sense that there are many attractive targets and the freedoms that are the core of democracy make it more difficult to monitor and control terrorists. However, this does not seem to have created vulnerabilities of a fundamental nature. Terrorism alone has never succeeded in destroying the essence of any democratic state and certainly has not caused the collapse of such a state. It is difficult to see how it could do so except where terrorism is merely one facet of a more fundamental social upheaval, such as an insurrection or a revolution enjoying some significant popular support.[7]

Indeed, if the experience of the last decades tells us anything, it is that democracies are remarkably resilient when faced with a serious terrorist threat. In fact, it appears that rather than weakening a democratic society, terrorism may instead increase internal cohesion and public support for the government in its efforts to suppress terrorism. This support may include giving up freedoms with little or no resistance (the October Crisis in Canada being a case in point).

As Walter Laqueur has pointed out, there is thus a paradox inherent in the terrorism equation: The more successful the terrorists are, the nearer they come to ultimate defeat. "As long as terrorism is no more than a nuisance, a democracy will rightly resist any attempt to curtail its traditional freedoms. Once terrorism becomes more than a nuisance, once the normal functioning of society is affected, there will be overwhelming pressure on the government to defeat them by all available means."[8] The reality is that the democratic state (indeed, probably any state) is always more powerful than the terrorists and will prevail sufficiently to prevent them from ever really undermining the social order. In fact, the problem is that the state can be too powerful. By overreacting or by failing to pull back after weakening or defeating the terrorists, the state itself may subvert democracy if it employs severe countermeasures.

The case studies that follow will show that democratic societies can succeed in reducing terrorism to manageable proportions without betraying the values that set them apart from other political systems. Although some of the democracies at times failed to define the threat properly, or instituted unnecessary measures, or occasionally allowed official agencies to step outside the law, the general tenor of the evidence is that they tried to balance the threat and response in such a way as to avoid fundamental changes to democratic forms. Where such changes have occurred, they have generally been in the context of larger shifts in social structures and norms, with terrorism being only the instant cause for changes that probably would have occurred anyway. This does not necessarily make the changes any more desirable or palatable, but it does reduce the importance of terrorism as a cause.

Before turning to the case studies, it may be useful to suggest some general principles that should guide counter-terrorism policy-making in democratic states. These will provide a context for drawing conclusions about the relative and the comparative merits of the courses of action pursued by the several nations studied.

First and foremost must be a genuine and public commitment to the rule of law. This is what sets democracies apart from other systems and is what the policies are designed to protect. It is often tempting to believe that adherence to law ties democracies' hands and forces them into a position of weakness. There may be some cases of extreme threat in which this might occur, but in the threat range democracies face, terrorism alone is unlikely to produce sufficient justification for stepping outside the bounds of the law. Further, it is practically unwise, since in open societies such actions invariably come to public attention; they can be seized upon by terrorists for propaganda purposes and can have divisive and corrosive effects on public opinion. Actions must be seen to be legal to be worthy of public support.

The element of public commitment in this regard is of great importance. Governments must make it clear that they will not turn a blind eye to illegality on the part of officials and will not allow them to overstep the law. This makes it much more difficult for governments to blur the boundaries of adherence to legal norms. It also serves to put security officials on notice. If there are limitations on current powers that seem to diminish the effectiveness of the response, then the government should make it clear to security authorities that it will present the case for increased powers and argue it in the appropriate legislative forum. Security authorities should enjoy the wholehearted support of government, but at the price of understanding that their powers are only those contained in the law and that any excursions outside the law will be punished.

The second principle is that each state must settle on a definition of terrorism. This is a contentious issue, which many see as unresolvable. But it is precisely the lack of precision over definition that allows counter-terrorism policy to go off the rails: to encompass activities that many would not consider terrorism and to promote unnecessary laws on the basis of an inflated threat. There must be at least an attempt to delimit what each country is going to define for itself as terrorism.[9]

The issue of definition is closely related to threat assessments and the psychological climate that surrounds them. Experience suggests that many nations would benefit from a more sophisticated analytical approach to terrorism—one that differentiates between different types, assigns varying degrees of threat, and produces individualized countermeasures.[10] The idea of a firmly stated general policy against terrorism may be inherently faulty—terrorism must be countered in a discriminating, case-by-case manner. While each country needs sophisticated, well-exercised, and well-led counter-terrorist machinery, its policy must not be set in concrete; modification must be possible in order to cope with an infinite range of possibilities and opportunities.[11]

The issue of how strictly a state should delineate its counter-terrorism policy is bound up with the issue of the language with which terrorism is discussed. The third principle is that language should not run ahead of the facts or options. The credibility of a nation's counter-terrorism policy will depend on a close coincidence between words and deeds. Rhetoric may be an inevitable part of the democratic process, but it must not be shown that it is devoid of content. A series of empty threats merely expressed to assuage public anxieties is a dangerous phenomenon, which may either embolden the terrorists or cause so much embarrassment to a government as eventually to force it to act in an excessive manner in response to the next incident.

It ought to be noted that the warnings against overreaction should not be taken as instructions for a government to be unconcerned about terrorism. Failure to act resolutely in the face of a terrorist campaign will surely do considerable damage. At the extreme, irresolute responses may result in small, ruthless bands being able to dictate government policy. At the very least, public confidence in the ability of legitimate governments to provide for the security of their citizens will be undermined, with the very real possibility that a domestic crisis will be precipitated. Moreover, it is when confidence in the government's will or ability to protect its citizens fails that vigilante counter-terror may arise to fill the perceived gap in public security.

What democracies must strive for is a balance. That balance is easier to discover if governments and their publics realize that democracies are not fragile in the face of terrorist attack and that they can defend themselves. Rather than inflating the terrorist bogey, democracies ought to realize that experience shows that the number of terrorists is limited and can probably be contained and reduced by government policies. Christopher Hewitt's study demonstrated that as the number of terrorists in prison increased, the level of violence decreased.[12] More and more terrorists are being captured, tried, and imprisoned. They are not invincible, and more publicity needs to be given to the counter-terrorist success stories.

A fourth principle is that governments should realize (and educate their publics to understand) that there is no simple solution to terrorism, no ideal outcome that can realistically be expected in all cases. The reality is that—given the ordering of values relevant in a particular crisis (e.g., the relative precedence of national security and personal security values); given the ideological, psychological, and other differences between different terrorists and different incidents; and given the domestic and international pressures on a target state—there will always be a vast range of possible and actual (as opposed to ideal) outcomes of a terrorist incident. In many, if not most, cases, the outcomes will not be "clean"; that is, there will not be a clear victory for the government (and not usually for the terrorists). The appreciation that solutions will of necessity often be compromises between the desirable and the attainable will greatly enlarge the range of options open to the government and should dissuade it from the crusading zeal that is the genesis of excess. A lowering, rather than a heightening, of expectations thus might be the most appropriate public stance for government leaders.[13]

A corollary to this is that governments should not devote too much obvious high-level attention to the particular terrorist problem. The senior levels of government must be involved, but not to the extent that whole departments are paralyzed during a terrorist incident[14] or that terrorist incidents occupy large amounts of the personal attention of heads of state. This only accords the terrorists more leverage and increases the pressure on governments to do something, often creating a mentality that leads to extralegal solutions.[15]

Within the framework of an approach that emphasizes precision of definition, refinement of threat assessment, adherence to the rule of law, and acceptance of the imperfection of any counter-terrorism strategy, a strong case can be made that democratic states can withstand a terrorist assault without fundamentally altering the nature of their societies. The following chapters will show how well some specific states have measured up to the challenge and will reveal some valuable lessons for other states. The bottom line for the democracies is to remember not only whom they are fighting, but what they are fighting for.

NOTES

1. In a January 1987 broadcast address, then Vice-President George Bush said, "Terrorism ranks as one of the greatest modern day threats to democracy in our hemisphere," Quoted in *Department of State Bulletin* (April 1987), p. 4. British historian Paul Johnson, in "The Seven Deadly Sins of Terrorism," in Benjamin Netanayahu, ed., *International Terrorism: Challenge and Response* (Jerusalem: Jonathan Institute, 1980), pp. 12–13, stated that "it is almost impossible to exaggerate the threat which terrorism holds for our civilization. It is . . . more serious than the risk of nuclear war . . . or global pollution . . . the threat of terrorism is not being contained . . . it is, on the contrary increasing steadily."

2. A good example of wishful thinking is President Ronald Reagan's January 1981 promise of "swift and effective retribution" in response to terrorism. Leading terrorism experts in the U.S. State Department had grave misgivings about making such a public commitment. See David C. Martin and John Walcott, *Best Laid Plans: The Inside Story of America's War Against Terrorism* (New York: Harper and Row, 1988), pp. 43, 45.

3. See, for example, Neil C. Livingstone and Terrell E. Arnold, eds., *Fighting Back: Winning the War Against Terrorism* (Lexington, Mass.: Lexington Books, 1986), pp. 2–5.

4. This is one of the methodological problems of works such as Uri Ra'anan et al., eds., *Hydra of Carnage: The International Linkages of Terrorism and Other Low-Intensity Operations—the Witnesses Speak* (Lexington, Mass.: Lexington Books, 1986), and of the concept "narcoterrorism," which is emotive, but simplistic and potentially misleading. On this subject, see Grant Wardlaw, "Linkages Between Illegal Drugs Traffic and Terrorism," *Conflict Quarterly* 6, no. 3 (Summer 1988), pp. 5–8, 11–12, 22–24.

5. See Ronald D. Crelinsten, "Terrorism and the Media: Problems, Solutions and Counter-Problems," in David A. Charters, ed., *Democratic Responses to International Terrorism* (Dobbs Ferry, N.Y.: Transnational Publishers, 1991), chap. 9.

6. See Walter Laqueur, "Reflections on Terrorism," *Foreign Affairs* 6, no. 1 (Fall 1986), pp. 86–87.

7. The one exception might be Uruguay, and there democracy was destroyed by the *response* to the terrorist threat. Yet even in this case it is not entirely clear whether terrorism

alone caused the crisis in government that then led to military intervention.

8. Laqueur, "Reflections," p. 95.

9. Even this is easier said than done; between 1977 and 1986, various agencies in the US government produced at least ten different definitions. See Alex P. Schmid and Albert J. Jongman, *Political Terrorism: A New Guide to Actors, Authors, Concepts, Data Bases, Theories and Literature* (New Brunswick, N.J.: Transaction Books, 1988), pp. 32–33.

10. For a discussion of some analytical/methodological options, see Grant Wardlaw, *Political Terrorism: Theory, Tactics, and Counter-measures*, 2d ed. (Cambridge: Cambridge University Press, 1989), pp. 138–45, 161–74.

11. Charters, *Democratic Responses*, pp. 350-51.

12. Christopher Hewitt, *The Effectiveness of Anti-terrorist Policies* (Lanham, Md.: University Press of America, 1984), p. 47.

13. Charters, *Democratic Responses*, pp. 351-52.

14. The normal procedure to avoid such paralysis is to create special crisis management centers and teams. See G. Davidson Smith, "Counter-terrorism Contingency Planning and Incident Management," in Charters, *Democratic Responses*, chap. 5.

15. The pressure on President Reagan to "do something" about the hostages in Lebanon clearly led to the ill-fated "arms for hostages" deal; see Martin and Walcott, *Best Laid Plans*, pp. 323–61.

2

Great Britain and the Response to International Terrorism

Bruce W. Warner

INTRODUCTION

Great Britain experienced nearly 250 incidents of international terrorism at home and abroad in the period from 1970 to 1992.[1] The perpetrators ranged from domestic anarchists through various Middle Eastern groups and states to Irish terrorists outside the UK. These incidents posed no direct threat to the United Kingdom. The threat that did exist was indirect, but insidious. Such activity not only contravened British laws and endangered innocent bystanders, but also contained the potential to disrupt British relations with nations whose citizens were targets in Great Britain. More important for this study, some have argued that the response to the threat endangered the civil liberties of every British citizen.

THE THREAT

The tactics employed by international terrorists in Great Britain included simple petrol bombings, more sophisticated explosive bombings, assassinations, and the seizure of diplomatic missions. Few of the targets attacked were British or had a direct British connection. In fact, Britain's first encounter with international terrorism in the period under study came with assaults by the First of May Group on Spanish and Italian government facilities and the Spanish national air carrier in 1970.

Middle Eastern terrorism proved the most persistent variety of non-Irish international terrorism in Great Britain. Most of this was related directly to the Palestinian-Israeli conflict. Israeli analyst Ariel Merari notes that the Palestine Liberation Organization (PLO), as an organization, has usually refrained from international terrorism since 1974, and attacks conducted since then are primarily the work of Palestinian splinter groups.[2] This assessment applies to Great Britain.

Indeed, concurrent with attacks on Jewish/Israeli targets was the internecine feuding between the splinter groups and the more moderate, mainstream PLO factions, which the extremists labeled "reactionary." The feud was exacerbated by the Syrian-backed split within the PLO in 1983.

Prior to the period of "restraint," however, Black September (the "plausibly deniable" covert action arm of *Al-Fatah*) carried out a letter-bomb campaign against Jewish targets in England and Scotland. The only exception to this pattern of activity was an assassination attempt on the Jordanian ambassador in 1971, part of Black September's reprisals against Jordan for its expulsion of the PLO in September 1970.[3]

Abu Nidal's *Fatah*–The Revolutionary Council (*Fatah*–RC) was one of the dissident factions that attacked both Jewish/Israeli and Palestinian targets. In January 1978, the *Fatah*–RC assassinated the PLO representative in London and, in June 1982, attempted to assassinate the Israeli ambassador.[4]

The involvement of agents of particular states in support of or actual participation in political violence represented yet another strand of Middle Eastern terrorism in the UK. During the 1970s, Iraqi agents were suspected of attempting to assassinate several Iraqi dissidents in Britain. However, the extent of Iraq's role, if any, in the seizure of the Iranian embassy in London in April-May 1980 is uncertain.[5]

Likewise, in early 1980, Libyan leader Muammar Qaddafi warned Libyan exiles that they would face "revolutionary justice" if they did not return to Libya. Not long afterward, three Libyans were murdered in Great Britain, and there was an attempt to poison the family of a fourth. Libya was also suspected in a series of bombings in March 1984. The following month, a staff member of the Libyan People's Bureau (embassy) in London killed a woman police constable while firing on a group of anti-Qaddafi demonstrators, prompting Britain to sever diplomatic relations. Libya has also supplied large quantities of weapons to the Provisional Irish Republican Army (PIRA), and Libyan agents have been identified by Britain and the United States as the perpetrators of the bombing of Pan Am Flight 103 in December 1988.[6]

The final strand of Middle Eastern terrorism in Great Britain arose from the milieu of Islamic fundamentalism. In 1989, tension heightened in Britain's Muslim community as controversy developed over publication of Salman Rushdie's *The Satanic Verses*. Along with large-scale demonstrations, several bookshops were bombed. Five Arabs were arrested in May 1990 in connection with threats to kill Rushdie, and two were expelled. By mid-1990, twenty persons had been expelled from Britain since Khomeini issued the call for Rushdie's murder.[7]

Since the motives of Middle Eastern and other groups had little to do directly with Britain, and since many of the targets attacked existed in other states, why was the UK chosen as a stage for these incidents? Three points in particular stand out. First, since London is the capital and a major international city in its own right, it is a "target-rich environment." Second, terrorist attacks in Britain, and London in particular, are assured of global news coverage because it is a major media center.

Finally, some terrorists considered Britain a "soft target." Two examples illustrate this perception. When the terrorists who seized the Iranian embassy in 1980 were recruited in Iraq, they were assured that the British police were unarmed and would not hurt them.[8] Similarly, one Libyan claimed, "If one of your countrymen killed a man in Libya he would be shot in a matter of days. Here the assassins know that if they do get caught it will be a jail sentence of ten years at most. Then they will go home to a hero's welcome."[9] The validity of this perception of Britain will be examined later.

No analysis of the British response to international terrorism would be complete without reference to the "Irish Dimension," since the conflict in Northern Ireland has influenced Great Britain's response to terrorism in general. Its impact was visible in three broad areas: First, the conflict itself spilled over into the UK itself, with Republican groups carrying out some 300 terrorist attacks there and more than forty on British targets overseas. Second, Irish Republican attacks on the UK "mainland" (the most prevalent form of political violence during the 1970s) were significant for this study because, although domestic in origin, they led to the introduction of emergency powers, which were later extended to deal with international terrorism. Third, and finally, the Northern Ireland conflict provided the British intelligence services and security forces with operational experience and skills (such as physical security and bomb disposal) that could be applied to the problem of international terrorism.

As well as experiencing international terrorism within the British Isles, Great Britain was the target of attacks overseas. Diplomatic posts and personnel, airline and tourist offices, businessmen, and other visible signs of the British presence became the targets of a number of different groups and causes. From November 1981 to November 1986, a total of nineteen British citizens died as the result of terrorism outside the UK.[10] Irish Republican terrorists and Middle Eastern groups were the major perpetrators of attacks on British targets overseas. Irish Republican terrorism accounted for forty two attacks (over 28 percent of the total). The congruence with the incidence of international terrorism in the UK itself is noteworthy; over 23 percent were committed by groups linked to the Middle East. The majority of these occurred in the mid-1980s. Most were the work of Abu Nidal's *Fatah*–RC under its cover name of the Revolutionary Organization of Socialist Muslims (ROSM).[11] Armenian groups carried out the third largest number of attacks: just six incidents in the period from September 1979 to January 1980. They confined their attacks to the bombing of British airline and tourist offices.

Irish groups were equally selective in their operations, but over a much longer period and with a different emphasis. The attacks were restricted to diplomats (two ambassadors were assassinated, one each in Dublin and The Hague), other official representatives, and British military personnel (and their families) and installations. The means employed have ranged from letter bombs and explosive bombings to assassinations by firearms.

The motives for Irish Republican attacks abroad were, of course, directly related to their campaign objectives in Northern Ireland: Attacks on military and official targets in Europe were intended to increase pressure on Britain to withdraw from Northern Ireland. Following the assassination of a British colonel in West Germany in March 1980, the PIRA warned "all British soldiers and administrators that there will be no sanctuary from their war of oppression in Ireland."[12] A similar message appeared in May 1988 following the killings in Holland. The Provisionals explained their motivation for attacks on the British forces in Europe in more detail in *Republican News* in 1980: "we intend to keep Ireland on their minds so that it haunts them and they want to do something about not wanting to go back."[13] The PIRA went on to place the attacks in a broader context, noting that

Overseas attacks also have a prestige value and internationalise the war in Ireland . . . we have kept Ireland in the world headlines. . . . Sooner or later an expression of discontent, possibly from the English people rather than the Army, will snowball and the British government's ability to stay, which we are sapping, will snap completely.[14]

Irish terrorism had a similar magnitude overseas, relative to other forms, as it did in Great Britain itself. Traditionally, Irish attacks in Europe were peripheral to those in England, which had a higher priority. It has been suggested that the Provisionals attacked targets in Europe when it was too hard for them to operate in Great Britain, although this is impossible to prove conclusively. But the magnitude of attacks in Europe at the end of the 1980s suggests that the PIRA may have changed its priorities.

The British government attached special significance to the possible involvement of foreign groups. During the 1970s, radical left-wing groups in Europe formed support organizations for the PIRA, and the British suspected that such groups in Europe provided material assistance to both the PIRA and the Irish National Liberation Army (INLA) in attacks on the continent. In late 1979, the Garda (the Irish police) concluded that a PIRA cell operating in Europe was receiving assistance from sympathizers in Belgium, Holland, and West Germany. In December 1981, West German Interior Minister Gerhardt Baum claimed that he possessed evidence of growing links between German left-wing terrorists and Irish terrorists.[15] Many of the attacks that occurred in Europe were suspected of having been joint operations with left-wing groups such as the Dutch Red Cells or the West German Revolutionary Cells. Others, such as the 2 November 1981 bombing in France by the Bobby Sands Group, were proxy operations. The years 1987–1990 were especially bad for attacks on the British military in Europe. This was demonstrated clearly in the almost simultaneous attacks on 1 May 1988, which killed three British servicemen and injured three others in Holland and West Germany. There were also barracks bombings from 1987 to 1990 in West Germany.

While less active than Irish Republican terrorists, Middle Eastern groups employed a far wider range of tactics and attacked a broader range of British targets. The Abu Nidal organization, under the cover name of the ROSM, attacked British diplomats and missions, assassinated official representatives, kidnapped journalists, and bombed hotels housing ordinary British tourists. All of the group's attacks on British targets stemmed from the fact that three members of the group (one of whom was a relative of Abu Nidal), captured in London after the assassination attempt on the Israeli ambassador in 1982, were sentenced to long prison terms. Within days of their conviction, the organization began to make public threats to harm British interests if they were not released. In a message to Agence France Presse in Bucharest, an anonymous spokesman demanded their freedom or promised that British "judges will learn what revolutionary justice is."[16] The same message was given to *The Times* (London) correspondent Robert Fisk in a personal meeting with spokesman Abd al-Rahman Isa in Damascus in March 1983. This objective of freeing jailed members of the group encompassed all states holding their members, not just the UK.

Attacks on British interests in the Middle East followed later in 1983 and expanded to include targets in both Europe and Asia in 1984. In an interview with *Der Spiegel* in October 1985, Abu Nidal stated that his organization harbored "great enmity towards the Thatcher government," and because British intelligence was cooperating with the Israelis, his group worked with all the forces opposed to the British, including the PIRA.[17]

THE RESPONSE

Political Setting

The international terrorist events discussed in this chapter occurred in a unique political setting. Those features that bear directly on this study include, first, the fact that Britain is a liberal democracy that functions *without a written constitution.* Political authority and practice, civil rights, and the law derive their legitimacy from a mixture of historical precedents, legislation, common (i.e., case) law, custom, and tradition. This means that power, law, and rights exist in an inherently flexible political culture and are subject to interpretation by the government, the police, and the courts.

The importance of this lies in the second distinct feature of British politics: the power of the executive branch. Although Britain has a bicameral parliament, with both elected and unelected houses, the real power lies in the office of the prime minister, the leader of the governing party in the House of Commons. The prime minister exercises authority through several influential channels: the cabinet ministers, drawn from the elected party members and sometimes from the House of Lords; the Cabinet Office, staffed by appointed advisors; and a complex array of committees, managed by senior civil servants, which transmit executive branch decisions to the departments and agencies of government. The prime minister and cabinet members are accountable to Parliament; the others are not. One of the key features of the British form of cabinet government is its freedom to exercise *unlegislated authority.* The cabinet's directives, instructions, and regulations transmitted to the departments and agencies are the prerogative of cabinet. They can be issued under orders-in-council, which carry the same authority as parliamentary legislation, but do not require prior parliamentary approval and do not receive detailed scrutiny.[18]

This executive freedom is particularly notable in the field of internal security. For example, in a terrorist-related emergency, the armed forces can be deployed within the UK or overseas on ministerial order, without reference to Parliament. Until recently, the entire intelligence community operated without legislated authority. Successive governments steadfastly refused even to acknowledge the existence of the intelligence services; questions in Parliament went unanswered, and there was little scrutiny of intelligence activities outside the highly secretive committee system. Since 1989, MI5—the domestic security service—has operated under a legislated mandate, but that still provides no independent parliamentary oversight. MI5's relations with, for example, police Special Branches, which have the law enforcement role in counter-terrorism, are still governed by secret internal regulations and customs, not by legislation.[19]

Through much of the period under study, the power of the executive branch was enhanced by the third influential factor: the character of Prime Minister Margaret Thatcher, who served from 1979 to 1990. Confident, articulate, forceful, and direct, born to power with the appearance of a sense of mission and moral conviction, the "Iron Lady" displayed several aspects of her personality and convictions that had a direct impact on British counter-terrorism policies.[20] First, her strong opposition to socialist doctrines in any form placed her firmly against "revolutionary" movements. Second, her stubbornness and firm conviction in the rightness of her policies made it unlikely that she would bow to terrorist threats or pressure. Third, Mrs. Thatcher's wholehearted commitment to traditional notions of democratic freedom and free enterprise ensured that she would find a "soul mate" in her US counterpart, President Ronald Reagan. The Anglo-American "Special Relationship" was secure during Thatcher's tenure, a fact that benefited both states on the issue of countering terrorism.

Anti-terrorism Policy

How, then, did this political setting translate into British anti-terrorism policy? Paul Wilkinson identifies the key features of British policy as:

1. "a firm political will to uphold the rule of law and democratic government and to defeat terrorism";
2. "absolute refusal to surrender to terrorist extortion and demands";
3. "determination to act in accord with domestic and international law";
4. "treatment of convicted terrorists as common criminals with no special privileges, pardons or amnesty"; and

5. "the promotion of national and international measures to combat terrorists by minimizing their rewards and maximizing their losses."[21]

These policy guidelines produced specific countermeasures, including emergency legal powers, the strengthening of police and intelligence capabilities, the use of the armed forces at home and abroad, target-hardening, and international cooperative efforts. In these policies and their manifestations, one can discern the influence of British political culture. Mrs. Thatcher's character is visible in the determination to uphold the law, to defeat and not to submit to terrorism. The strength of the executive branch shows itself in the use of the various security forces without reference to Parliament. The treatment of terrorists as common criminals is an expression of Britain's common law tradition. And the vulnerable status of British civil liberties under an unwritten constitution became readily apparent with the application of emergency powers, the Prevention of Terrorism Act.

Emergency Legislation

The Prevention of Terrorism (Temporary Provisions) Act 1974 (PTA), introduced in November 1974 and since superseded by new legislation in 1976, 1984, and 1989, is the sole piece of "emergency" legislation introduced in Great Britain in response to terrorism in the mainland UK. Beyond this, law enforcement officials rely on the ordinary criminal law. The PTA introduced extended powers of arrest and detention, forcible removal (exclusion) of suspected terrorists from Great Britain, proscription of organizations, and several new offenses relating to support for terrorists. But the British government specifically rejected proposals to create an offense of terrorism itself. Originally formulated to apply solely to those connected with Irish terrorism in Great Britain, the powers of arrest and detention (part II, section 12) were extended in the 1984 act to apply to other international terrorists. The 1984 act also widened the ambit of sections 10 and 11 of part I (which created new offenses relating to support of terrorism in general). These sections were revised to apply to the support of Irish terrorism anywhere in the world, not just the UK.[22] The 1984 PTA lapsed at the end of five years and was replaced by a new act. There is no limit on the time span of the 1989 legislation, and the powers are renewable annually, in whole or in part, by a statutory instrument subject to positive resolution by Parliament.

There have been relatively few prosecutions under the PTA. Only two organizations have been proscribed: the PIRA and the INLA.[23] The exclusion power was applied only to those suspected of involvement in Irish terrorism[24] and was not extended to other groups, since it was felt that powers under the Immigration Act were sufficient to accomplish the same purpose.

Nevertheless, although the PTA has been applied in a discreet fashion and enjoyed solid bipartisan support from its initial passage in 1974 until 1983 (when the Labour Party, which first introduced it, voted against renewal), it has been the subject of considerable controversy. The harsh character of the powers and their violation of fundamental democratic liberties have been acknowledged even by those law lords (Shackleton, Jellicoe, and Viscount Colville) who carried out the required reviews of the legislation prior to each renewal. Moreover, while insisting that the PTA was effective against terrorism, they acknowledged that it was difficult to *prove* the effectiveness of the powers—that they had materially or statistically reduced or deterred the threat of terrorism in the UK in a manner that could not have been achieved through normal due process.[25]

The inability to demonstrate the PTA's effectiveness led critics to mount a twofold attack on the arrest provisions of section 12 (section 14 of the 1989 act). First, they argued that ordinary powers of arrest were sufficient in instances where a crime has been committed, and that in the majority of cases where charges were laid the additional arrest powers under section 12 were superfluous. Second, critics asserted that the large number of arrests compared to the small number of actual charges laid confirmed their suspicion that most arrests were to intimidate and assist in the gathering of low-level intelligence. In this regard, Viscount Colville's 1987 review stated that "the statistics give some prima facie cause for concern."[26]

The PTA notwithstanding, British sentencing of terrorists, international or domestic, was closely tied to the policy that terrorist acts are, first and foremost, crimes at common law, whatever their motivation, and should be treated as such. It means that there is no special attention paid to the political motivation of the offenders. This was illustrated in the comments of a senior appeal court judge in 1983. Five Tanzanians had been convicted of a hijacking the previous year and were appealing for a reduction in their sentences on the grounds that they were fleeing an oppressive regime. In dismissing the appeal, Lord Justice Lawton noted that it was very dangerous for the courts to attempt to assess political motivation, although he admitted that the appeal court was not categorically dismissing consideration of such factors.[27]

However, in 1989 and 1991, the freeing of those convicted in the Guildford and Birmingham pub bombings of the early 1970s highlighted the risk to civil liberties posed by the PTA. In 1989, the four people charged with the Guildford bombings were freed, following sustained pressure on the government, when it became clear that their 1975 convictions had been based on confessions coerced by the police and were not substantiated by sufficient corroborating evidence. Similarly, in 1991, the "Birmingham Six" had their convictions reversed by the court of appeal. The legitimacy of their convictions had been undermined considerably by a British television broadcast, that featured an interview with an individual who claimed credibly to have placed one of the bombs. Clearly, in the hysteria that followed those incidents, pressure for "results" caused standards of police behavior and investigative practices to lapse, resulting in the conviction of innocent persons.[28] Most other convictions, including those involving non-Irish international terrorists, have not been similarly challenged. Nevertheless, as the Birmingham Six were released, the home secretary announced a royal commission review of aspects of the judicial process.

In 1983, Lord Jellicoe, noting the increase of international terrorism in Great Britain, which by then rivaled Irish-related terrorism, recommended that section 12 powers be extended to cover international terrorists. In justifying this extension, he asserted, first, that the powers had proven useful against Irish terrorism. Second, he noted that some criticized the powers on the grounds that they were aimed in a discriminatory manner at Irish people; an extension to cover other types of terrorism would resolve this problem.[29]

The application of section 12 to other types of terrorism generated more concern than any other part of the 1984 act. The major fear was that the powers would be used against groups like the African National Congress, which legally maintained offices in London, but were considered terrorist organizations by some states. This view was supported by the fact that, while Lord Jellicoe's recommendation had been that the powers be restricted to acts of international terrorism committed in the UK, the government had not made this territorial restriction in the 1984 act.

The National Council for Civil Liberties (NCCL) expressed concern that "the power could be used indiscriminately, or more systematically on the basis of colour or other prejudice (for example against Libyans or Middle Eastern Arabs), to detain people from overseas in order to obtain information."[30] In response, the government issued a circular advising the police to restrict their use of the powers of arrest and detention to those cases where there was a prospect of a charge before the courts or of deportation. Prior to and during the 1991 Gulf War, the British government detained about 170 Arabs in the UK, mostly Iraqi nationals, on the grounds that they could be national security risks. They were all served with deportation notices. About eighty left the UK voluntarily. But it appears that this case was handled under the Immigration Act, not the PTA.[31]

On the recommendation of Lord Colville, the government introduced a new part (III) in the 1989 act. It is intended to ensure disclosure of terrorist funds held in the UK and to block their transfer.[32]

The conflicts that arose over the PTA's impact on the media and freedom of expression highlighted its potential to affect the lives of ordinary British citizens and the dilemmas inherent in the democratic response to terrorism. A number of broadcasts about Northern Ireland, which, the government asserted, gave publicity to proscribed organizations, brought the government and the media into conflict. No media organization or person was ever prosecuted under section 11 (section 18 in the 1989 act), but the BBC canceled one program in 1985 under pressure from the government. A 1988 ban on broadcasting interviews with representatives of Republican and Loyalist extremist groups does not appear to have inhibited routine reporting on the Northern Ireland conflict or coverage of non-Irish international terrorism in the UK or overseas. But such measures do have a chilling effect on democratic discourse, thereby undermining—to a degree—the moral high ground from which this otherwise democratic state deals with the terrorism problem.

These restrictions were offset, in part, by the efforts of senior police officers to develop closer relations with the news media. Commissioner Robert Mark and his successor, David McNee, negotiated two "gentlemen's agreements" with the media that formalized relations and discussed a reporting moratorium in cases involving kidnapping or hostage-taking. This was not an attempt to muzzle or manipulate the media. Rather, the agreements were voluntary statements of principle, which did not sacrifice the freedom of the press. The trade-off with the press was increased access to information after an event in exchange for restraint during the event in the interests of saving lives. The North Atlantic Assembly recommended this approach in a report that states, "The practical answer to media coverage problems probably lies in closer media-to-government working relations rather than government-imposed restraint."[33]

The PTA has been characterized both as "draconian" and as "one of the most restrained legislative measures against terrorism in the Western World."[34] At the heart of these comments are the notion of balance and the conviction of its proponents that the PTA is a measured, necessary response to the terrorist threat. Yet they have no doubt as to its character. The home secretary admitted in 1983 that "its powers are unwelcome and make sad inroads into our cherished traditions of civil liberties."[35] Nonetheless, successive governments, of both major parties, have renewed the measures on the basis of perceived necessity.

Negotiation

Since 1970, the British position on negotiation with terrorists has been clear and unequivocal: no negotiation for *substantive* concessions. In June 1970, the British ambassador to Uruguay, Geoffrey Jackson, aware that he might be a kidnap target, consulted with the Foreign and Commonwealth Office (FCO). It was agreed that in such an event the government would immediately announce that it would not submit to blackmail in any circumstances, pay ransom, or pressure the Uruguayan authorities to do so. Jackson was kidnapped, but eventually released without concession. This same strategy was followed when another British diplomat, James Cross, was kidnapped by Quebec separatists that same year. In 1983, Britain dismissed unofficial approaches from both Iraq and Libya to exchange imprisoned British businessmen for convicted Arab terrorists in British prisons.[36] This position was also made clear to both France and West Germany when they released convicted terrorists under similar pressure in the 1980s.

This stance has caused some conflict with the activities of private security companies involved in the lucrative kidnap and ransom end of the insurance business. In 1984, Control Risks Ltd., a London-based firm, informed neither the Irish nor the British authorities when it bowed to the wishes of the company concerned and paid £2 million to the PIRA in return for the release of a kidnapped supermarket executive. When this was revealed in 1985, it created a public outcry, and there were calls in Parliament for the prosecution of Control Risks under section 10(2) of the PTA for soliciting funds for the Provisionals.[37] Although no charges were laid, this case aptly illustrates the dilemma that arises when counter-terrorism policy collides with the free market.

British policy on negotiation was most severely tested with regard to the three British hostages, including Anglican church envoy Reverend Terry Waite, held by the pro-Iranian *Hizb'Allah* in Lebanon. In August 1988, a senior Iranian official came to London for talks with the Archbishop of Canterbury on the matter, and a senior FCO first secretary flew to Teheran for similar discussions.[38] The government claimed that it was not negotiating, as the talks were not with those directly in control of the hostages, but rather with parties believed to have some influence with the kidnappers. Despite the break in relations occasioned by the Rushdie affair in March 1989, the changed atmosphere in the region following the 1991 Gulf War and the kidnappers' apparent conclusion that the hostages no longer had any bargaining value led to the release of almost all of the Western hostages, including Terry Waite, by the end of 1991.

The British experience suggests that one of a government's best weapons against terrorism is a firm policy of granting no major concessions and negotiating only over peripheral issues, such as the provision of food and water. At the same time, as Dr. Richard L. Clutterbuck notes, it is unrealistic for governments to assume that either families or corporations will follow such a line when one of their own is at risk.[39]

Intelligence

Intelligence is the key to developing appropriate anti-terrorist measures.[40] In Great Britain, this is the province of the police and the security/intelligence services. The military role is peripheral and consists primarily of input from Northern Ireland, which may figure in intelligence about PIRA bombing campaigns on the mainland. This would be channeled through the Royal Ulster Constabulary Special Branch to the counterparts on the UK mainland.

There are three levels of organizations gathering anti-terrorist intelligence in Great Britain. Since May 1992, MI5, the security service, has been designated the lead agency—at least for intelligence on Irish terrorism. Apparently, there are two investigative sections, F3 and F5, which study the "hard" targets of terrorism and the related area of arms and explosives movements. In pursuit of intelligence on such targets, MI5 is authorized in certain circumstances to employ informers, infiltrate groups, open mail, plant listening devices, and tap telephones, but has no powers of arrest or detention.[41]

Next to MI5, with which it has an almost symbiotic relationship, is the Metropolitan Police Special Branch and the provincial Special Branches (SBs). As of 1984, there were 1,316 SB officers in the UK.[42] The number assigned to Irish terrorism has fluctuated according to the level of threat and other manpower demands. Other sections within the SB are responsible for covering non-Irish international terrorism.

Like MI5, the SB employs informers and infiltrators, and some individuals detained under the PTA have alleged that SB officers tried to coerce them into becoming informers. The Kenneth Lennon case was probably the most controversial example. Lennon identified for the SB several people in Provisional Sinn Fein who were later convicted of armed robbery. Lennon himself was murdered by "persons unknown" shortly after telling the NCCL that he thought the SB might kill him and make it look like an IRA execution. A deputy commissioner investigated the affair, rejected the claim that Lennon had been blackmailed into becoming an informer, and concluded that the SB had no role in his death, either directly or indirectly.[43]

Finally, at the sharp end of anti-terrorist intelligence, is the Anti-Terrorist Squad (ATS) or SO-13 (previously C-13) of the Metropolitan Police. This body was formed in January 1971 as the Bomb Squad, as a temporary response to the Angry Brigade bombings. In 1972, the first IRA bombing persuaded Commissioner Robert Mark to make the Bomb Squad permanent. Many of the officers involved were members of the SB. In the mid-1970s, the Bomb Squad had expanded to investigate other forms of terrorist activity and became C-13.[44]

The ATS has a twofold role. Its personnel respond to bombing incidents, and where there are live devices, the squad's explosive ordnance disposal officers assist in their dismantling. In those situations where a bomb has exploded or a shooting has taken place, they carefully examine the site in a search for evidence. In this, they work closely with the Home Office, the Royal Arsenal at Woolwich, and other police forensic scientists in an effort to build up a composite of the type of bomb or weapon used and who used it. Intelligence gathered in this way helps to establish a criminal case against the perpetrators. One source wrote in 1979 that "The Branch and the Anti-Terrorist Squad, whilst having separate and defined areas of responsibilities, often combine forces on a particular investigation."[45]

By the mid-1980s, reports indicated that this cooperative atmosphere had given way to an attempt by the SB to absorb C-13. Following the Brighton bombing of 1984, it was believed that senior SB officers had failed in an attempt to organize a takeover of C-13 at the same time that MI5 was trying to wrest control of anti-IRA operations in Great Britain from the SB. Just over four months later, the rumors were so prevalent that Scotland Yard formally announced that there were no plans to merge C-13 with the SB. The only change that did occur was the placement of both bodies under the same administrative head, a deputy assistant commissioner, a change designed to improve liaison. The idea of merging the two organizations was based on a misperception of their respective roles. SO-13 does not come into operation until the actual commission of a crime, and then it attempts to build a case leading to criminal prosecution. The SB has a much wider role and targets individuals or groups who may not yet have committed an offense but who are suspected of subversive or violent intent. The overlap of the two bodies was explained by the head of SO-13 as follows: "In the vast majority of cases, we rely on Special Branch for intelligence information as our collator source . . . if we get information we automatically pass it over to them, and if they have something operational, they hand it over to us."[46]

Largely as the result of continued PIRA activity, institutionalized cooperation between the SB and SO-13 was achieved in mid-1990. The head of SO-13 assumed responsibility for IRA inquiries throughout Great Britain. The squad was given the power to monitor and direct operations by local Criminal Investigation Department chiefs as well as the ability to direct SB intelligence activity. Two years later, however, the apparent inability of these arrangements to provide adequate intelligence on IRA terrorism in the UK led to the transfer of responsibility to MI5.[47]

In 1984, in the aftermath of Brighton, some light was thrown on the use of anti-terrorism intelligence. In late October, the home secretary announced new central arrangements both for assessing terrorist intentions and capabilities and for coordinating the necessary countermeasures. Unofficially baptized the TIGER (Terrorism Intelligence Gathering Evaluation and Review/Research) Committee by the media, this body was intended to channel information from the SB "and other security agencies and to coordinate counter-measures."[48] Chaired by a Home Office deputy secretary, the TIGER Committee is composed of civil servants from the Home Office, the Foreign and Commonwealth Office, SO-13, MI5, MI6 and the Ministry of Defence. But one problem remains: Such committees—and there are four that deal with intelligence matters (not all related to terrorism)—can only give advice.[49] There is no certainty that the advice will be followed—a point that reinforces the maxim that the best intelligence is of no value if it is not used properly.

Military/Para-military Measures

The military response to international terrorism in Great Britain operated on two levels and was informed by the wealth of experience the British military has gained in counterinsurgency operations throughout the world and from two decades of conflict in Northern Ireland.[50] At one level was a defensive military response, under the rubric of military aid to the civil power. Rarely employed, it was most clearly evident in the periodic security exercises at Heathrow Airport and was more a show of force and resolve than a specific response to a possible attack.

The second level involved the use of military special forces offensively in counter-revolutionary warfare (CRW).[51] The rescue of hostages by the Special Air Service Regiment (SAS), which ended the Iranian embassy siege in 1980, is probably the most dramatic example. However, other specialist units have also been involved. In the late 1970s, for example, the Ministry of Defence, local police, and other government departments planned and carried out several anti-terrorism exercises designed to protect North Sea oil and gas installations.[52] The first publicly reported anti-terrorist exercise involving the SAS occurred in April 1973 at Stansted Airport, where it played out a scenario involving a hijacked aircraft. Such exercises continued into the 1980s. In 1975, the unit was called back to Stansted when a real hijacking occurred, but it was resolved without resort to force. That same year the mere presence of the regiment's anti-terrorist unit was sufficient to persuade four PIRA bombers and hostage-takers to surrender during the Balcombe Street siege in London.[53]

There are four squadrons of the regular SAS but only one was committed at any one time to what the army refers to as CRW tasks. Each squadron has three sub-units (troops), with one on instant standby, and the second on follow-up, while the third is stood down. The capabilities of the CRW troop were clearly demonstrated at the Iranian embassy siege in 1980. Once the authorities became aware that terrorists had seized a foreign mission with both foreign and British hostages, the CRW troop on instant standby was flown to London. From 1 May, assisted by intelligence gathered by various electronic devices employed by C-7, Scotland Yard's Technical Support Branch, they built up an operational plan in preparation for an assault. Overall authority during this period was in the hands of the civil authority, the police, as they negotiated with the terrorists. But when the gunmen executed their first hostage, the police commander on the scene recommended the use of the SAS and received permission from the home secretary. At 7:07 p.m. the deputy assistant commissioner of the Metropolitan Police passed control of the operation *in writing* to the senior army officer present. The SAS went in, and eleven minutes later five of the six terrorists were dead and all but one of the hostages rescued alive. At 7:50 p.m. control was returned to the police.[54]

The Gibraltar incident of March 1988 was the most controversial SAS counter-terrorism operation. Three unarmed PIRA activists were shot dead by an SAS team following them, in the belief they were planning to bomb a British military parade in Gibraltar. A coroner's inquest cleared the soldiers of any unlawful conduct, bringing in a verdict of lawful killing. But the incident raised troubling questions, which the inquest left unanswered. The operation had been planned the previous month, following several weeks of surveillance by Spanish and British authorities. The rules of engagement, worked out by the Cabinet Office Permanent Secretaries Group on Internal Security and the Joint Intelligence Committee (JIC), were that once the PIRA team entered British territory in Gibraltar, they were not to be allowed back into Spain. The JIC, once it collated all available information, determined that a bombing was imminent and alerted the joint operations center which has the power to deploy the SAS.

Controversy arose over several questions: whether or not the trio was offered a chance to surrender before being shot, whether the SAS honestly believed that a car bomb had been planted that day by the PIRA team, and whether the Spanish surveillance operation actually lost the trio two days before they appeared on Gibraltar or were asked by the British not to follow them onto the Rock. These matters are still unresolved and have led to claims and counterclaims by the Spanish and British authorities.[55] A suspicion lingers that a "take no prisoners" policy was operating in Gibraltar in March 1988. At the very least, the case illustrated the problems of conducting joint binational anti-terrorist surveillance operations, of using troops in "policing" operations, of determining "rules of engagement" for such actions, and of dealing with the legal "grey areas" that ensue.

The somewhat mythical notion of an unarmed British police force was undermined during the period under study, largely, but by no means solely, in response to the terrorist problem. The period from 1970 to 1990 was notable for the development of permanently armed specialist police units equipped with greater firepower. Early in 1973, armed officers—marksmen who were part of the Special Patrol Group (SPG)—killed two of the three Pakistani terrorists who briefly seized the Indian High Commission. The following year The SB formed the permanently armed Diplomatic Protection Group (DPG) in order to provide static security at foreign missions and roving patrols in areas heavily populated with such facilities.[56] The SPG acts as a rapid-response unit insofar as terrorist and other major criminal incidents are concerned.

In the mid-1970s, the government decided that the time lapse between the start of an incident and the deployment of troops might lengthen sufficiently so as to require armed police intervention in a siege, rather than just the traditional role of containment. The Indian High Commission incident was an ad hoc demonstration of just such a requirement. The Metropolitan Police firearms training wing, D 11, was nominated to fill this role. In August 1975, the Home Office received a proposal for the formation of four five-man teams.[57] D 11 was involved in the Balcombe Street siege, in the Iranian embassy seizure, and most visibly at the siege of the Libyan People's Bureau in 1984. They can be deployed only on the authority of the deputy assistant commissioner (operations). The unit, now known as PT 17, was also in evidence during major terrorist trials, providing armed security at the site of court proceedings. In addition to these units in London, each local constabulary has its own armed response unit; depending on the threat level, these are sometimes deployed on anti-terrorist duties.

The weaponry allocated to these specialist police units is a quantum leap from the truncheon available to the ordinary constable. In 1984, a furor arose in the press when it was announced that SB guards at the London Economic Summit would be armed with submachine guns similar to the type used by the SAS. Scotland Yard explained that such weapons were necessary due to changes in the nature of the international terrorist threat. Informed sources noted that the government had approved acquisition of several submachine guns by London police as early as 1976 and the D 11 unit acquired two types the following year.[58]

These specialist units are the closest the UK has yet come to a para-military response to terrorism in Great Britain. There is no permanent, large-scale para-military "Third Force" as exists in many of the countries on the continent. The existent division of responsibility between the police and the army appeared to work satisfactorily in several cases. This and the level of threat Britain experienced provided no justification for any other arrangement.

Target-Hardening

The aim of target-hardening is to make a potential target so uninviting that the terrorist will be dissuaded from attacking. This is usually accomplished by raising the level of visible security and applies equally to people and installations. Much of the British expertise in this field derives from experience in Northern Ireland.

That conflict has produced some relatively unsophisticated, but effective, techniques, such as the application of anti-magnetic paint to the underside of automobiles to foil car bombers.[59]

Since the Brighton bombing of 1984, visible security around the prime minister and Royal Family has increased in a measurable manner. The prime minister now travels in an armored Daimler equipped with its own oxygen supply, fourteen carriages of the Royal Train have been armored to withstand attack by rockets and armor-piercing bullets, and aircraft of the Queen's Flight have been fitted with an infrared jammer to deflect heat-seeking missiles thought to be in the hands of the PIRA. An extensive security operation was mounted for the Conservative Party Conference at Brighton in October 1988. It included a Royal Navy minesweeper anchored off the coast, Special Boat Squadron patrols in light craft between the vessel and the beach, police helicopters, and armed police.[60] The police created a Royalty Protection Group, which provides security for the Royal Family, and the Special Branch's Personal Protection Squad, which performs the same function for other, especially vulnerable public figures such as the secretary of state for Northern Ireland. When members of the Royal Family or VIPs travel outside London, these specialist groups are augmented by armed SB officers from local area forces.

Equally at risk in the period under study were both British officials overseas and foreign diplomats in the UK. The DPG has served to increase the level of security at foreign missions in London. In Birmingham, the West Midlands force has maintained a permanent armed presence at the Indian mission since the kidnap/murder of an Indian diplomat there in 1984. Overseas the FCO initially contracted with a private security company, known as KMS Ltd., comprised largely of former SAS personnel, to provide bodyguards for British diplomatic posts and officials in especially dangerous cities such as Beirut. However, a combination of cost factors and other features caused a rethinking of this approach. By 1982, the Thatcher government had turned this task over to the Royal Military Police (RMP) because of the experience it had gained in Northern Ireland.[61] In September 1984, one of the British ambassador's RMP bodyguards shot dead the driver of a truck bomb at the US embassy annex in East Beirut. In 1986, there was an increased security clampdown at British missions following a top-level FCO review, which recommended, among other things, the possible relocation of some buildings to safer sights. A further strengthening of security measures for diplomats occurred in April 1989 after several posts in Europe received death threats in connection with the Rushdie affair.[62]

Following the spate of terrorist hijackings, the introduction of armed police at British airports was only the most visible sign of this progressive upgrading of security. After the Rome and Vienna airport massacres in December 1985, armed officers from D 11 were visibly deployed at Heathrow. They filled this role until they could train ordinary, firearms-qualified police to take over. Following the 1986 discovery of a bomb carrier by El Al personnel at Heathrow, after the individual had passed through a British Airports Authority (BAA) screening, officials increased from one-in-ten to one-in-three the number of random searches of passengers and their luggage. However, with the growth of sophistication in terrorist weaponry, both the technology and the personnel at British airports came in for criticism. In June 1986, after a BBC team passed a powerful, unprimed suitcase bomb through careful security checks, the aviation minister acknowledged that "the state of the art is not adequate to meet all threats."[63]

At the close of 1986, the Parliamentary Select Committee on Transport criticized the training of private security firm employees subcontracted by the BAA. In 1987, a senior SB officer was drafted into the Home Office to oversee a security crackdown at British airports and seaports and became the first national coordinator of ports' units. However, none of this was sufficient to prevent the disastrous Pan Am airliner bombing over Lockerbie, Scotland, in December 1988.[64] Here, again, as is so often the case in such situations, a rush of media attention after the fact pointed out holes in the security network at British airports. Yet, as was demonstrated by the PIRA mortar attacks on Heathrow in 1994, [65] protecting an installation as large as an airport is virtually impossible, short of turning it into an armed fortress.

Owing to the special concerns arising from the possibility of terrorist attacks against nuclear facilities or on the nuclear materials in transit, the UK Atomic Energy Authority was authorized to create its own police force. Although designated special constables, they do have powers of arrest. Furthermore, they are armed when "on duties relating to guarding special nuclear materials on sites or in transit."[66]

Finally, security measures have spread into everyday life in Great Britain. The increase is most noticeable in London. At the lowest level, this encompasses the searches of personal belongings and packages at public buildings. The security apparatus visitors are required to pass through at the houses of Parliament is more elaborate than that at most major international airports. At the highest level is the construction of purpose-built secure buildings, such as the Queen Elizabeth Conference Centre just across from the House of Commons. In 1993 much of the financial district was banned to vehicular traffic following a massive and costly PIRA car bomb.[67]

International Cooperative Measures

Apart from intelligence the most important tool in the fight against international terrorism has been cooperation among like-minded states, and the UK was a leader in this area. In international and regional forums as well as in its bilateral relations, the British government has made major contributions to the legal mechanisms arising therefrom and has demonstrated leadership in encouraging increased cooperation.

There were two international forums in which debate on international terrorism produced concrete results: the United Nations (UN) and its constituent organizations, and the western economic summit gatherings. The UN's International Civil Aviation Organization (ICAO) fashioned two conventions directed specifically against acts of international terrorism. The Convention for the Suppression of Unlawful Seizure of Aircraft (Hague Convention 1970) was ratified by the UK and became the Hijacking Act 1971. The Convention for the Suppression of Unlawful Acts Against the Safety of Civil Aviation (Montreal Convention 1971) became the UK's Protection of Aircraft Act 1973.[68] Both agreements were based on the principle of "extradite or prosecute," and while they were designed to ensure the trial of international hijackers and saboteurs, they retained the significant loophole of the political offense exception to extradition.

This principle was also central to three anti-terrorist agreements constructed by the UN itself. The problem of attacks on diplomats was addressed in the UN Convention on Internationally Protected Persons of 1973, which the UK accepted by means of its Internationally Protected Persons Act 1978. In 1979, the UN formulated the Convention Against the Taking of Hostages and in the following year introduced the Convention on the Physical Protection of Nuclear Materials. British implementing legislation became law for these two agreements in 1982–1983. In conjunction with the "extradite or prosecute" principle, these agreements expanded the extraterritorial jurisdiction of states party to them in order to enable those states to meet the obligations contained therein. For example, a Palestinian terrorist arrested in Italy in July 1985 was tried, convicted, and sentenced there in 1988 for planting the bomb discovered outside the Syrian embassy in London on 3 June 1985.[69] The UK, however, has not yet been in the situation of having to try a fugitive for an "international" crime committed elsewhere.

The annual economic summit (attended by the Group of Seven) increasingly became a forum for discussions and pronouncements about international terrorism. At the 1978 meeting in Bonn, the attending heads of state agreed to impose boycotts on air traffic to those states providing sanctuary to aircraft hijackers. At the Ottawa Economic Summit in 1981, the Bonn sanction was invoked against Afghanistan, a Hague Convention signatory, for its failure to extradite or prosecute the hijackers of a Pakistani airliner. Following the mandatory one-year grace period, the British government banned the Afghan airline, Ariana, from operating its service from Kabul to London in December 1982.[70]

The 1984 economic summit was held in London, and, in the wake of the Libyan People's Bureau shootings, the British government was insistent in its condemnation of terrorism. One analyst wrote in 1985, "The new European drive against terrorism can be seen as having been set in motion as the result of pressure mounted by the British Government at the summit meeting in London."[71]

In 1986, the British role was even more pronounced. Spurred by evidence of Libyan complicity in numerous acts of terrorism and support for the PIRA and by the US bombing raid in April, at the Tokyo Economic Summit Prime Minister Thatcher pressed for a blacklist of suspected Libyan terrorists and the closure of all Libyan diplomatic missions in Europe. The end result did not single out Libya, but rather encompassed a wide-ranging series of anti-terrorist measures. A six-point action plan, for which Mrs. Thatcher took credit, was appended to the summit's terrorism declaration. It included proposals on limiting the size of diplomatic missions suspected of aiding terrorists and on denying entry to any other summit countries for persons expelled or excluded from one member on suspicion of involvement in terrorism. Britain received a specific undertaking that the other six would not admit a person excluded under the PTA.[72] The British were also in the forefront of moves to isolate Syria diplomatically after revelations of complicity in the attempt to bomb El Al aircraft at Heathrow in April 1986.

The UK has also been involved in anti-terrorist cooperation within two major regional organizations. The larger is the twenty-one-member Council of Europe. At a meeting of the Council's ministers of justice in 1984, following the Libyan People's Bureau incident, the British home secretary proposed that members not accept as diplomats those expelled by others for involvement in terrorism. He also suggested that the membership approve arrangements for information exchange on the terrorist threat. The Home Office proposed a conference of nominated officials from the twenty-one who could provide such cooperation. These proposals were unanimously endorsed and recommended to the Council's Committee of Ministers.[73]

However, the most significant effort of the Council of Europe in the anti-terrorism field, the European Convention on the Suppression of Terrorism (ECST), occurred in the mid-1970s. The ECST, under article 1, provides that a wide range of the types of offenses committed by terrorists will not qualify for the political offense exception between members that ratify the agreement. This includes attacks on internationally protected persons, kidnapping and hostage-taking, offenses involving the use of bombs that endanger people, and offenses under the Hague and Montreal Conventions. But the prohibition is not all-encompassing because article 5, included at the instigation of the UK, permits signatories to refuse extradition for a listed offense if they have "substantial grounds" to believe that the request has been made in order to prosecute or punish someone on account of his or her race, religion, nationality, or political opinion. This apparent loophole is qualified by article 7, which obliges a state refusing extradition to submit the case for prosecution by its own judicial authorities. One commentator believes that the ECST goes beyond the "aut dedere aut judicare" principle in the ICAO and UN conventions to tilt the balance in favor of extradition, noting "primo dedere secundo judicare."[74]

The UK ratified the ECST in 1978 and incorporated its provisions into British law in the Suppression of Terrorism Act 1978 (STA). The STA modified the Extradition Act 1870, the Fugitive Offenders Act 1967, and the Backing of Warrants (Republic of Ireland) Act 1965 to remove the offenses listed in the ECST from the political offense exception and also expanded extraterritorial jurisdiction with respect to the listed offenses. The STA also has the potential for extending the ECST, as applied by the UK, beyond Europe. Under the terms of the act, the home secretary, subject to affirmative resolution by Parliament, may apply it to either a designated Commonwealth country under the Fugitive Offenders Act 1967 or a foreign state with which the UK has extradition relations.[75]

Initially, adoption of the ECST was not as widespread as was hoped. Several major European countries, including France, attached reservations to their signatures and then waited years before ratifying the agreement. Belgium and the Netherlands failed to ratify until 1985. Eire finally signed on 24 February 1986 as the result of the conclusion of the Anglo-Irish Agreement and ratified it in December 1987.[76]

Great Britain has been equally involved in anti-terrorist initiatives at the second regional-level forum: European Community (EC). In December 1975, at an EC meeting in Paris, the British government proposed annual meetings of the members justice and interior ministers in order to discuss the problems of coping with terrorism and other international crime. This became the TREVI Group, which has been characterized as "a forum where police chiefs, ministers and senior officials from EC countries could meet regularly to discuss intelligence and police matters."[77] It operates at the level of occasional ministerial meetings, which became more regular in the mid-1980s, and at the practical level of police/security service contacts and working groups. The TREVI Group coordination office in the UK is the European Liaison Section of the Special Branch.[78]

In 1977, the EC's Council of Ministers detailed the justice ministers to draft an anti-terrorism treaty. This was formalized at a meeting of justice ministers in Luxembourg on 10 October 1978, and the resultant treaty was signed in Dublin in December 1979. The Dublin Agreement was an attempt to bring all members of the EC within the bounds of the ECST, which eight had signed, but only three had ratified. To become law, the Dublin Agreement had to be ratified by all nine members of the EC and was to cease operation when all members were party to the ECST. However, France refused to ratify, and it never became operational. The EC has made progress of a practical nature in other areas. In meetings at The Hague in April 1986, it was agreed that counter-terrorist cooperation should be extended beyond the now twelve EC members to countries such as the US. While much of the anti-terrorist activity in the EC has revolved around the TREVI Group, the foreign ministers of the member states also held increasingly regular meetings on terrorism in the 1980s. In 1984, on a British initiative, they agreed to draw up a blacklist to bar suspected terrorists from member states. In January 1986, the foreign ministers established a new political-cooperation working group on terrorism, which had close links to the TREVI Group. At that same meeting, it was agreed not to export arms or military equipment to state supporters of terrorism, and the foreign ministers applied that sanction against Libya in April and Syria in November.[79]

On 1 July 1986, the UK assumed the EC presidency for a six-month term and made anti-terrorism cooperation a key element in its leadership. In September, the TREVI Group held an emergency meeting at the ministerial level in the wake of the bombings in Paris. The group agreed that all European police forces would share a new, secure communications system to assist in tracking known terrorists and to aid in the selective intelligence targeting of specific, especially dangerous terrorists and in regular, updated threat assessments. A British Home Office official led the group responsible for putting the system into operation. In October, the justice ministers proposed a study on the means of achieving a common EC immigration policy with the aim of preventing terrorists and other international criminals from moving freely across EC boundaries. Finally, in December, at a London meeting chaired by Home Secretary Douglas Hurd, the TREVI Group agreed on the first comprehensive analysis of terrorist organizations and operations in Europe. It was then sent on to the foreign ministers to assist in the formation of a concerted political strategy against terrorism.[80] That Britain's EC presidency was so productive could be attributed to the combination of British determination and increased terrorism in Europe.

In 1987, the TREVI Group broadened its intelligence/communications network to collect data on terrorist-connected arms and explosives thefts and discoveries and approved practical measures to exclude non-EC nationals suspected of terrorism from member states. The TREVI network was expanded to include law enforcement ministers from the US, Canada and Austria. Also in 1987, the UK hosted a TREVI conference of directors of forensic and scientific laboratories to discuss the detection of arms and explosives at airports. Suggestions that TREVI set up a permanent secretariat have been opposed by the British, who object to the creation of a further level of "Euro-bureaucracy." The informal nature of the current apparatus appears to work relatively well and infringes on no state's notions of national sovereignty. It also precludes the problems that could plague attempts to create a formal arrangement because the Treaty of Rome, which set up the EC, is silent on the topic of terrorism and any formal EC institution must act within the terms of the treaty.[81]

The British government also attacked the problem of international terrorism at the bilateral level. Its initiatives have ranged from ministerial meetings between the home secretary and his European counterparts (especially from Italy, France, and West Germany) to the British-Soviet agreement to undertake a dialogue on anti-terrorism measures in 1986. Some of these bilateral contacts have had concrete results, as in the case of the British-Italian working group established in 1984 for liaison in counter-terrorism work.[82]

Often such bilateral contacts focus on one particular issue or problem. Courtesy of the Libyan government, the PIRA has large stockpiles of the Czech plastic explosive Semtex, whose most valuable characteristic is that it is odorless, thus making it difficult to trace. The British requested that the Czechs "fingerprint" the explosive by including a taggant detectable by scanners, and, in 1989, British and Czech specialists met to discuss the matter. After the collapse of the Communist regime in Czechoslovakia in the fall of 1989, the new government stopped shipments of Semtex.[83]

The majority of such contacts were on the level of the individual police forces involved. In January 1988, Belgian police uncovered an automobile with a Dutch license that contained a large quantity of Semtex plastic explosive, detonators, and a radio remote-control device. They informed the British Anti-Terrorist Squad, which identified it as bearing the hallmarks of the PIRA. Following the May 1988 shootings of British servicemen in Holland, officers from SO-13 and the SB Irish Desk flew to Holland to assist in the hunt for the killers. In June 1989, the Dutch police arrested a Swiss national suspected of laundering drug money to finance European operations of the PIRA, including the attacks in Holland during the previous year. In July 1991, however, a Dutch court freed suspected PIRA members, previously convicted for the murder of two Australians in 1990, on the grounds that there was insufficient proof that they had taken part in PIRA activities.[84]

There has been excellent cooperation for well over a decade between British and American authorities in combatting Irish Republican arms smuggling. This included the use of a US reconnaissance satellite to track an arms smuggling vessel as it crossed the Atlantic to Ireland, where it was intercepted. However, in 1984, there were reports that British officials were withholding intelligence information in this area from their American counterparts because of a senior US Customs Service official's apparent Irish Republican sympathies. The person in question, who formerly supervised all gun smuggling investigations in New York, had testified on behalf of someone charged with such activities for the Provisionals and had also disclosed the name of a British intelligence officer in open court. The individual was fired in November 1984, but appealed to a civil service tribunal, which ordered his reinstatement.[85]

Probably the most important area of anti-terrorist bilateral cooperation has been that which has led to the conclusion of new extradition treaties. Agreements concluded with the United States, Italy, and India in the 1980s dealt with specific problems and illustrate the importance of such agreements to the UK.

The British authorities were frustrated in several cases beginning in the late 1970s, when US courts refused to extradite PIRA terrorists on the grounds that they had committed political offenses. Both the Thatcher and the Reagan administrations agreed on the necessity of preventing this loophole from being exploited by Irish Republican terrorists. There were several attempts to narrowly define the political offense in bills placed before Congress in the early 1980s. Opposition to these bills among American politicians and interest groups centered around the fear that removing the political offense in general would subject political dissidents, and not just terrorists, to being returned to their country of origin when the US had extradition relations with it. This fear was circumvented vis-à-vis the UK when in 1985 the two governments agreed on a supplemental extradition treaty that removed the political offense exception from a list of crimes of violence. In July 1986, it was passed by the necessary two-thirds majority of the US Senate and was signed into law by President Reagan. The UK designated the US under the STA in November 1986, which then enabled it to ratify the treaty.[86] It has since been applied successfully.

With the escalation of Sikh separatist violence in 1984 and a sizeable Sikh population of over 200,000 in the UK, it was inevitable that extradition would occupy a major place in Anglo-Indian relations in the mid-1980s. The Indian government wanted removal of the humanitarian safeguard from extradition relations between the two countries as well as an increased list of extraditable offenses. Negotiations began in 1986 and continued into 1987, but ultimately failed to produce an agreement completely acceptable to both parties.

While in the US-UK treaty negotiations it was the British who were seeking the return of fugitives, the situation was reversed with regard to Italy. In 1981, British police arrested nine Italians linked to the neo-fascist terrorist group the Armed Revolutionary Nuclei. Italy requested the extradition of seven of the group on various charges relating to acts of violence in the 1970s. In January-February 1982, the chief magistrate discharged the entire group on the grounds that the Italian authorities had failed to establish a prima facie case against them. A report at the time alleged that British police believed another twenty-three fugitive Italian terrorists may have been sheltering in the UK,[87] giving rise to a concern that Britain was becoming a sanctuary for such individuals.

Nevertheless, the Italians successfully gained the return of two other neo-fascist terrorists in 1984 and 1986, while another went before the British courts in the spring of 1989. However, the original seven who escaped extradition in the early 1980s remained a sore point in Anglo-Italian relations. In 1984, senior Italian ministers asked the British home secretary to deport them, and Prime Minister Bettino Craxi made a personal appeal to Prime Minister Thatcher at the 1985 economic summit. Successive home secretaries have replied that the Italians could not be deported due to the requirements of EC freedom of movement laws, but have invited the Italians to reapply for extradition. In reply to a query from the Labour Party's home affairs spokesman, the Italian ambassador wrote: "the offence committed is not likely to correspond to English law and is not covered by the extradition treaty between the two countries . . . there is no point in renewing proceedings unless we could be assured that a new request would be successful."[88]

The home secretary himself admitted that in 1985 there were "deficiencies" in current Anglo-Italian extradition arrangements and noted that the two nations were working on an updated agreement. In March 1986, a new treaty was signed that would make it easier for the UK to extradite to Italy those convicted in absentia. The treaty was not to come into force until three months after ratification. In the British case, ratification was predicated on changes to the Extradition Act 1870 that came into effect with the Criminal Justice Act 1988, which, in turn, was replaced by the Extradition Act 1989.[89]

The major change in British extradition law contained in the new legislation was the selective removal of the prima facie requirement. After much study, in February 1985, the Home Office released a Green Paper on Extradition, which clearly and concisely laid out cases for both the retention and the scrapping of the requirement and invited comments on which option best suited British interests.

Then in March 1986, the government released a White Paper on Criminal Justice, which revealed plans for extradition law reforms, including removal of the prima facie requirement with respect to non-Commonwealth states. It said that the requirement, "does not offer a necessary safeguard for the person sought by the requesting state; it does, however, present a formidable impediment to entirely proper and legitimate extradition requests."[90]

These proposals ran into widespread, stiff opposition from the NCCL, the Law Society, and the Criminal Bar Association, as well as the House of Lords. A compromise solution was worked out whereby the prima facie requirement would only be removed with regard to those individual states concerning which an Order in Council had been made; this allowed the bill to pass.

CONCLUSIONS

The balancing act, whereby liberal democracies ensure their security through an effective response program while trying to provide as much freedom as possible, has been relatively easy in the British case. Except for Irish Republican violence, international terrorism in Great Britain was not directed against the British government and institutions. Indeed, some informed observers and officials have characterized the international terrorism threat in Great Britain as being no more than an irritant.[91]

It is difficult to measure the effectiveness of the British response to international terrorism. The threat from Irish and non-Irish international terrorism remains. Yet neither fundamentally threatens the stability of the state, that is, the (nearly) normal functioning of government and of social and commercial institutions. So the characterization of these threats as irritants, however costly and tragic, seems appropriate. What is less clear is the extent to which these threats have been contained by effective countermeasures or by the political and logistical limits of the groups themselves.

The British response to international terrorism can be characterized as a policy of deterrence and containment. The PTA's powers of exclusion and arrest acted as deterrents. And when deterrence failed and international terrorism occurred, the response mechanism attempted to contain the incident and ensure that the perpetrators were apprehended. Taking into account the level of threat in Great Britain, relative to the situation in many other countries plagued by the problem of international terrorism, the British met this challenge effectively. In short, they demonstrated the fallacy of the proposition that Great Britain is or was a "soft option" target for terrorists.

But at what price? Largely because of the "Irish dimension," the response to this irritant, while restrained relative to some states, changed the face of British society—and its democratic character—to a marked, if unquantifiable, degree. At the lowest level, it imposed restrictions (such as searches and security procedures) on the ordinary business of living that affects every Briton in some small way.

Terrorism also helped hasten the development of a partially armed police service in Great Britain, although this development owes as much to armed crime of the ordinary variety. In general, the public accepted these changes. In fact, after especially brutal incidents, there were indications that the British public desired stronger measures. This is clear in the support for the return of capital punishment for terrorist crimes. And in February 1986, following the Rome and Vienna airport massacres, an opinion poll found that 47 percent of Britons questioned felt the government was not doing enough to protect them.[92]

Less visible, but more significant in terms of the democratic character of the state, were the powers exercised under the PTA and the restrictions imposed on media coverage of terrorism. The former are fundamentally undemocratic; even if applied selectively, the PTA powers make Britain a subtly less-free society. Likewise, government efforts to limit the media with respect to their coverage of terrorism amounted to censorship, which is incompatible with democracy. Yet, in every other respect, Britain remains a viable democracy, so it is difficult to determine whether these powers have irreversibly damaged the state's democratic fabric and credentials. Indeed, questions in this regard may not be answerable. Perhaps the best that can be hoped is that such extraordinary powers will be applied as infrequently and as narrowly as possible, bringing the least harm to the least number of people. In the meantime, the last word is left to former Prime Minister Thatcher, herself a target of international terrorism: "None of us can be neutral as between the terrorist and the law-abiding citizen. None of us can be neutral toward the police and army whose job it is to uphold our liberty and security . . . we are not spectators in the battle of terrorism versus the law. Give those their chance and they will destroy democracy itself."[93]

NOTES

1. Based on the author's calculations from reports in the print media: 127 in the UK, 119 overseas. The UK total is higher than that estimated by the Research Institute for Studies in Conflict and Terrorism/University of St. Andrew's data archive (January 1993), which shows only seventy incidents from 1972 to 1992.

2. Ariel Merari, "The Future of Palestinian Terrorism," in Walter Laqueur, ed., *The Terrorism Reader* (New York: New American Library, 1987), p. 308.

3. See Helena Cobban, *The Palestinian Liberation Organization: People, Power and Politics* (Cambridge: Cambridge University Press, 1984), pp. 54–55; Moshe Shemesh, *The Palestinian Entity 1959–1974: Arab Politics and the PLO* (London: Frank Cass, 1988), pp. 151, 350 n.108; and Jillian Becker, *The PLO* (London: Weidenfeld and Nicolson, 1984), p. 107.

4. UK, Foreign and Commonwealth Office (FCO), *Abu Nidhal Group and State Terrorism* (London: FCO, December 1986), p. 2.

5. In February 1985, Home Secretary Leon Brittan stated that "the police . . . have so far been unable to find any firm evidence that [Iraqi] embassy officials are involved." *Hansard Parliamentary Debates*, vol. 72 (8 February 1985), col. 708. See also Samir Al-

Khalil, *Republic of Fear: The Inside Story of Saddam's Iraq* (New York: Pantheon Books, 1989), pp. 13–14; and Andrew Rathmell, "Iraqi Intelligence and Security Services," *International Defense Review* 5 (1991), pp. 394-95.

6. Amnesty International, International Secretariat, *Libya: Further Attacks on Exiled Political Opponents* (London: Amnesty International, 15 July 1987); Andrew Selth, *Against Every Human Law: The Terrorist Threat to Diplomacy* (Rushcutter's Bay, Australia: Pergamon, 1988), pp. 41, 63.

7. *Winnipeg Free Press*, 7 July 1989; *Times* (London), 23 May 1990 and 26 May 1990.

8. *Manchester Guardian*, 23 January 1981.

9. Quoted in *Now!*, 9 May 1980, pp. 39-40.

10. *Hansard*, vol. 105 (18 November 1986), col. 141.

11. FCO, *Abu Nidhal Group*, p. 3.

12. Quoted in *Manchester Guardian*, 6 March 1980.

13. Quoted in Desmond Hamill, *Pig in the Middle: The Army in Northern Ireland 1969–1985* (London: Methuen London, 1986), p. 246.

14. Quoted in Ibid.

15. UK Foreign and Commonwealth Office, *The IRA and Northern Ireland* (London: FCO, 1976), pp. 72–73, see also David Charters et al., *Trends in Low-intensity Conflict*, Operational Research and Analysis Establishment Extra-mural Paper no. 16 (Ottawa: Department of National Defence, 1981), part 5, p. 22; *Sunday Times*, 23 December 1979, and *Times*, 8 December 1981.

16. Quoted in Yossi Melman, *The Master Terrorist: The True Story of Abu Nidal* (New York: Avon Books, 1987), p. 85.

17. Quoted in Dennis Pluchinsky, "Middle Eastern Terrorist Activity in Western Europe: A Diagnosis and Prognosis," *Conflict Quarterly* 6, no. 3 (Summer 1986), p. 25, n.17; FCO, *Abu Nidal Group*, p. 7.

18. G. Davidson Smith, *Combating Terrorism* (London: Routledge, 1990), pp. 122–23, 125–29, 184–86.

19. Ibid., pp. 136–37; Christopher Andrew, "Whitehall, Washington and the Intelligence Services," *International Affairs* 53 (May 1977), p. 390; Michael Mates, *The Secret Services: Is There a Case for Greater Openness?* Occasional Paper No. 41 (London: Institute for European Defence and Strategic Studies, 1989), pp. 8, 17–18.

20. Anthony Sampson, *The Changing Anatomy of Britain* (London: Hodder and Stoughton, 1982), pp. 40–55.

21. Paul Wilkinson, "British Policy on Terrorism: An Assessment," in Juliet Lodge, ed., *The Threat of Terrorism* (Boulder, Colo.: Westview Press, 1988), p. 50.

22. Catherine Scorer, Sarah Spencer, and Patricia Hewitt, *The New Prevention of Terrorism Act: The Case for Repeal* (London: National Council for Civil Liberties, 1985), p. 13.

23. Ibid., pp. 13–14, 58; Lord Shackleton, *Review of the Operation of the Prevention of Terrorism (Temporary Provisions) Acts 1974 and 1976*, Cmd. 7324 (1978), p. 10; Brian Rose-Smith, "Police Powers and Terrorism Legislation," in Peter Hain, ed., *Policing the Police*, vol. 1 (London: John Calder, 1979), p. 123.

24. See section 4(3)(a) and (b) of the PTA (1976).

25. Cmd. 7324 (1978), p. 41; Reviews of the act by Lord Jellicoe, Cmd. 8803 (1983), and Viscount Colville, Cmd. 264 (1987); see also citations in *Hansard*, vol. 38 (7 March 1983), cols. 566, 594.

26. Quoted in Cmd. 264 (1987), par. 5.2.5; Scorer, Spencer, and Hewitt, *The New Prevention of Terrorism Act*, p. 47, and Rose-Smith, "Police Powers," pp. 138–42, 152–55; see also Clive Walker, *The Prevention of Terrorism in British Law* (Manchester: Manchester University Press, 1986).

27. *Manchester Guardian*, 24 May 1983.

28. The investigation feature, produced by Granada TV in the UK, was rebroadcast on the Canadian Broadcasting Corporation program, "The Journal," on 24 July 1990. See also Michael Ignatieff, "Scapegoats for Our Hatred of the IRA," *The Observer* (London), 17 March 1991.

29. Cmd. 8803 (1983), p. 9.

30. Quoted in Scorer, Spencer and Hewitt, *The New Prevention of Terrorism Act*, p. 53; *Hansard*, vol. 52 (25 January 1984), col. 1012.

31. Home Office Circular no. 26/1984, par. 91, quoted in Clive Walker, "Prevention of Terrorism (Temporary Provisions) Act 1984," *Modern Law Review* 47, no. 6 (November 1984), p. 706; *New York Times*, 17 February 1991.

32. Cmd. 264 (1987), par. 14.2 and recommendation 65.

33. Quoted in José Luis Amaral Nunes, and Lawrence J. Smith, *Interim Report of the Sub-committee on Terrorism* (Brussels: North Atlantic Assembly, 1987), p. 9; see also W. B. Jaehnig, "Terrorism in Britain: The Limits of Free Expression," in Abraham H. Miller, ed., *Terrorism, the Media, and the Law* (Dobbs Ferry, N.Y.: Transnational Publishers, 1982), p. 110.

34. Walker, "Prevention of Terrorism (Temporary Provisions) Act," p. 704.

35. *Hansard*, vol. 38 (7 March 1983), col. 568.

36. Dr. Richard L. Clutterbuck, "Kidnapping," *Army Quarterly and Defence Journal* 104, no. 5 (October 1974), p. 529; *The Observer*, 15 May 1983.

37. One source estimated that Control Risks had 75 percent of the British market in K&R insurance policies. *The Middle East*, July 1982, p. 27. See also *New Statesman*, 20 July 1979, pp. 78–79; *Sunday Times*, 1 December 1985; and *Hansard*, vol. 92, (19 February 1986), col. 432.

38. *Winnipeg Free Press*, 11, 12 and 14 August 1988.

39. Dr. Richard L. Clutterbuck, "Government Policy on Negotiation with Terrorists," in Richard Clutterbuck, ed., *The Future of Political Violence, Destabilization, Disorder and Terrorism* (London: Royal United Services Institute and Macmillan Press, 1986), p. 69.

40. Davidson Smith, *Combating Terrorism*, pp. 250–51.

41. *The Observer*, 16 March 1985. See also *Times*, 13 January 1988 and 9 May 1992.

42. Figures derived from a Home Office Memorandum submitted to the Home Affairs Committee in January 1985, cited in Peter Gill, *Policing Politics: Security Intelligence and the Liberal Democratic State* (London: Frank Cass, 1994), p. 228. This figure actually represents a decline from the mid-1970's, when the total was about 1,600: see, Statement by Home Secretary, *Hansard*, vol. 950 (24 May 1978), cols 1718-19.

43. Deputy Commissioner James Starritt, *Report on the Actions of Police Officers Concerned with the Case of Kenneth Joseph Lennon* (April 1974), as cited in Rose-Smith, "Police Powers," p. 147.

44. *Times*, 26 March 1989.

45. Quoted in Rose-Smith, "Police Powers," p. 118.

46. Quoted in *The Observer*, 28 October 1984; see also *Sunday Times*, 10 March 1985.

47. *Sunday Times*, 26 August 1990; *Times*, 5 March 1991; *Daily Telegraph* (London), 22 April 1992 and 4 May 1992.

48. *Daily Telegraph*, 23 October 1984, quoted in Davidson Smith, *Combating Terrorism*, p. 197.

49. Davidson Smith, *Combating Terrorism*, pp. 128, 197; see also, Gill, *Policing Politics*, pp. 140-43

50. See David A. Charters, "From Palestine to Northern Ireland: British Adaptation to Low-Intensity Operations," in David A. Charters and Maurice Tugwell, eds., *Armies in Low Intensity Conflicts: A Comparative Analysis* (London: Brassey's, 1989), pp. 169–249.

51. See UK Ministry of Defence, Defence Council, *Land Operations*, vol. III, *Counter-revolutionary Operations* (London: MoD, 29 August 1969), pt. 1, p. 5. Crown copyright material cited with permission of Her Majesty's Stationery Office.

52. *Times*, 9 May 1978. The Royal Marines, Royal Air Force, and Royal Navy were involved in these twice-yearly exercises. See also Alexander Morrison, "North Sea Oil: The Role of the Police," *Police Studies* 2, no. 1 (Spring 1979), p. 29; and *Manchester Guardian*, 11 June 1980.

53. *Manchester Guardian*, 29 June 1981; Tony Geraghty, *Who Dares Wins: The Story of the Special Air Service 1950–1980* (London: Arms and Armour Press, 1980), p. 169.

54. Centre for Conflict Studies, *Special Operations: Military Lessons from Six Selected Case Studies* (Fort Bragg, N.C.: Joint Special Operations Command, US Department of Defense, November 1982), pp. 234–53; see also Robert W. Gould and Michael J. Waldren, *London's Armed Police, 1829 to the Present* (London: Arms and Armour Press, 1986), p. 180; and John Strawson, *A History of the S.A.S. Regiment* (London: Secker and Warburg, 1984), pp. 222–24.

55. *Sunday Times*, 9 September 1988, 4 December 1988, 2 April 1989, and 9 April 1989; *The Observer*, 21 May 1989; *New Statesman*, 13 May 1988, pp. 10–11; *New Statesman*, 17 June 1988, p. 11. See also Ian Jack, "Gibraltar," *Granta*, no. 25 (Autumn 1988), pp. 13–86 for ? critique of the inquiries into the shootings.

56. Rupert Allason, *The Branch: A History of the Metropolitan Police Special Branch 1883–1983* (London: Secker and Warburg, 1983), p. 158.

57. Gould and Waldren, *London's Armed Police*, p. 157.

58. *Times*, 3 April 1984; Gould and Waldren, *London's Armed Police*, pp. 192.

59. *Times*, 7 March 1989.

60. *The Observer*, 23 October 1988; *Times*, 10 October 1988, 11 October 1988, and 27 February 1989; *Armed Forces* 7, no. 7 (July 1988), p. 299.

61. *New Statesman*, 28 June 1978, pp. 112–13, 4 August 1978, p. 139, and 4 July 1981, p. 3; *Illustrated London News*, 7 August 1987, p. 27. See also Geraghty, *Who Dares Wins*, pp. 209–10, 214–18.

62. *Times*, 22 May 1986, and 29 April 1989. See also Tony Geraghty, *The Bullet Catchers: Bodyguards and the World of Close Protection* (London Grafton Books, 1988), p. 237.

63. Quoted in *The Observer*, 29 June 1986.

64. The bomb was transferred from a connector flight to Pan Am Flight 103 in Frankfurt, Germany, and was not detected during the stopover at Heathrow. Steven Emerson and Brian Duffy, *The Fall of Pan Am 103* (New York: G.P. Putnam's, 1990), pp. 69–70, 159–61, 166–67, 183–90.

65. *Globe and Mail* (Toronto), 14 March 1994.

66. *State Research Bulletin*, no. 24 (June-July 1981), p. 141.

67. The large truck bomb on 24 April 1993 damaged several major banking buildings: *Globe and Mail*, 26 April 1993. The barricades were installed about a month later.

68. Hijacking Act 1971, c. 70, *Law Reports 1971*, vol. 2, pp. 327–30, and Protection of Aircraft Act 1973, c. 47, *Law Reports 1973*, vol. 2, pp. 1335–62. In 1982, these two acts were repealed and their provisions consolidated in the Aviation Security Act 1982, c. 36, *Law Reports 1982*, vol. 1, pp. 809–53.

69. Taking Hostages Act 1982, c. 28, *Law Reports 1982*, vol. 1, pp. 615–17, and Nuclear Material (Offences) Act 1983, c. 18, *Law Reports 1983*, vol. 1, pp. 320–26; *Department of State Bulletin* (February 1989), p. 65.

70. *International Legal Materials*, vol. 20 (1981), p. 956; *Manchester Guardian*, 2 December 1982.

71. Ian Greig, "Hitting Back at Terrorism," *Defence, Communications and Security Review*, no. 85/3 (1985), p. 57.

72. *Sunday Times*, 27 April 1986; *Times*, 7 May 1986. For the full text of the declaration and six-point plan, see *International Legal Materials*, vol. 25 (1986), p. 1005; *Hansard*, vol. 97 (12 May 1986), col. 307.

73. *Times*, 1 June 1984 and *Hansard*, vol. 61, (6 June 1984), col. 169.

74. Frank Brenchley, *Diplomatic Immunities and State-Sponsored Terrorism*, no. 164 (London: Institute for the Study of Conflict, 1986), p. 12.

75. *Suppression of Terrorism Act 1978*, c. 26, *Statutes in Force* (1978), pt. 48.

76. *Hansard*, vol. 92 (27 February 1986), col. 1053, vol. 100 (24 June 1986), col. 147; Chris Bowlby, *International Responses to Terrorism* (London: House of Commons Library, 1987), p. 12.

77. Quoted in Bruce George, *Working Group on Terrorism Final Report* (Brussels: North Atlantic Assembly, 1989), p. 43; see also *Hansard*, vol. 971 (11 December 1972), cols. 8-9.

78. Christopher Dobson and Ronald Payne, *Terror, The West Fights Back* (London: Macmillan Press, 1982), p. 27.

79. *Hansard*, vol. 91 (5 February 1986), col. 269, and vol. 96 (30 April 1986), col. 422; *Times*, 1 September 1984 and 4 February 1985.

80. *Times*, 26 September 1986, 27 September 1986 and 10 December 1986; *Hansard*, vol. 102 (21 October 1986), col. 800. See also Lodge, *The Threat of Terrorism*, p. 252.

81. Nunes and Smith, *Interim Report of the Sub-committee on Terrorism*, p. 10; Joanne Foakes, "The European Community and Terrorism: Legal Aspects," *Topical Law* 5 (1983), p. 19.

82. *Times*, 25 September 1986 and 12 November 1986; Greig, "Hitting Back," p. 58; *Hansard*, vol. 27 (15 July 1982), col. 449.

83. *Times*, 26 August 1988, 11 January and 12 January 1989, and 24 April 1989. In March 1990, Czechoslovakia confirmed that it had sold 2,000 tons of Semtex to Libya. *Toronto Star*, 23 March 1990.

84. *Sunday Times*, 8 May 1988; *Times*, 3 May 1988; *The Observer*, 18 June 1989.

85. *Sunday Times*, 2 September 1984, 20 January 1985, and 5 May 1985; *Manchester Guardian Weekly*, 23 December 1984.

86. *Hansard*, vol. 50 (8 December 1983), col. 458, and vol. 81, 24 June 1985, cols. 285–86. The finalized form of the treaty is in *United States—United Kingdom Exchange of Notes Amending the Supplementary Treaty of June 22, 1985*, Cmd. 9915 (1986). A commentary by the US State Department's legal advisor is found in Abraham Sofaer, "The Political Offence Exception and Terrorism," *Department of State Bulletin* (December 1985), pp. 58–62. See also *Hansard*, vol. 106 (26 November 1986), cols. 367–68.

87. *Searchlight*, no. 81 (March 1982), p. 3.

88. Quoted in *Searchlight*, no. 126 (December 1985); p. 3.

89. *Hansard*, vol. 83 (25 July 1985), col. 665; *Manchester Guardian*, 13 March 1986. Five of the seven Italians sought by Italy were convicted in absentia in March 1985. Criminal Justice Act 1988, c. 33, *Statutes in Force* (1988).

90. *Criminal Justice*, Cmd. 9658 (1986), par. 50.

91. Dr. Richard L. Clutterbuck, interview by author, Exeter, England, 3 March 1988; Superintendent David W. B. Webb, interview by author, Exeter, England, 10 March 1988.

92. *Times*, 11 March 1986. A total of 1,945 Britons were polled.

93. Quoted in *Times*, 26 October 1988.

3

Democratic Responses to International Terrorism in Germany

Stephen M. Sobieck

INTRODUCTION

Historians of terrorism may come to regard 1992 as a year of dramatic, even fundamental, change in Germany's twenty-year struggle with domestic and international terrorism. On the positive side, in April, the Red Army Faction (RAF) issued a communiqué that conceded defeat and pleaded for the release of jailed comrades—a concession that would allow the RAF an "honorable" surrender.[1] While this probably did not represent the end of domestic German leftist terrorism,[2] it was nonetheless a significant event.

However, this welcome change was offset, even overshadowed, by a negative development: a dramatic upsurge in right-wing terrorism, directed largely at foreigners residing in Germany, especially *gastarbeiter* (guest workers) and refugees. Nearly 1,900 attacks were registered in the first eleven months of 1992, more than four times the number recorded in 1990, the year Germany reunified. The attacks resulted in sixteen deaths, more than a fivefold increase over the previous year.[3] In response, hundreds of thousands of Germans demonstrated on several occasions to protest the violence and to show their displeasure with the German government's handling of the issue. The government, they believed, had been slow to address the problem, and its proposal to limit immigration was seen as a concession to the terrorists.[4]

This was not the first time that Germany had been singled out for criticism of its counter-terrorism efforts. Twenty years earlier, the Palestinian terrorist attack at the 1972 Munich Olympics, which left eleven Israeli athletes dead, revealed the shortcomings of West Germany's security apparatus at that time. Intelligence efforts to safeguard the Games were insufficient, an inadequately trained paramilitary unit carried out an ill-conceived rescue plan, and no single political figure had full responsibility in order to take charge of the crisis situation.[5] In subsequent years, West Germany adopted a variety of measures to correct these deficiencies. Stringent security was placed around vulnerable targets, such as airports, embassies, and government buildings; intelligence-gathering methods on foreigners were enhanced. West Germany created an elite anti-terrorist unit and adopted a tougher counter-terrorism policy, which enjoyed broad political and public support.

However, as the 1988 bombing of Pan Am Flight 103 demonstrated, countermeasures are not always foolproof and need to be continually upgraded to match the evolving nature of international terrorism. The bomb was placed aboard a Pan Am flight at Frankfurt and then was transferred to Flight 103 in London. In the wake of the bombing, West Germany was accused of botching an undercover operation that could have prevented the disaster, of cutting secret deals with terrorists (allowing them to operate in Germany so long as they did not target German citizens or property), and of not cooperating with British and American investigators. The relevance of the criticisms is now moot, since the US government in November 1991 delivered indictments against two Libyan officials charged with carrying out the bombing.[6]

In spite of these incidents, Germany has earned a reputation as a staunch opponent of international terrorism. Ironically, however, the improvement of West German security procedures provoked sharp criticism because the state acquired greater power, raising the possibility of abuse of civil liberties. However one interprets the severity of West German anti-terrorist measures, they were similar to those enacted by other major Western European countries.[7] In fact, West Germany's efforts against international terrorism had much in common with those of its European counterparts. Whereas in the early 1970s it tended to bow to terrorist demands, West Germany became a hard-line, anti-terrorist state and a prime mover for regional and international cooperation against international terrorism.

NATURE OF THE TERRORIST THREAT

West Germany displayed three conditions that were conducive to international terrorism: a greater degree of vulnerability due to the openness inherent in democratic states, a wide array of potential targets for various types of terrorist groups, and established networks of sympathizers. The Federal Republic experienced three types of political terrorism: indigenous, international, and foreign-state-directed. The differing objectives, targets, and tactics and the varying patterns of activity of these three types of terrorism posed different challenges to the Federal Republic.

Indigenous West German terrorists posed a far greater threat to West German businessmen and politicians than did foreign extremists. The international dimension arose from the contacts German terrorists maintained with foreign terrorist groups, the operations they committed outside of West Germany, and their efforts to seek refuge in other countries. From its inception, the RAF considered itself in solidarity with the Popular Front for the Liberation of Palestine (PFLP) because both groups favored a worldwide Marxist revolution. The PFLP was prepared to train foreigners in terrorist tactics, and it is alleged that as early as 1969, eighteen West Germans were present in PFLP camps in Jordan and Lebanon. From June to August 1970, the central figures of the RAF received rudimentary training in guerrilla tactics in these camps. The Germans and their Palestinian instructors, however, disagreed on the proper training methods for an urban guerrilla, and the Germans were eventually asked to leave.[8]

Nonetheless, the PFLP continued to maintain ties with the various West German terrorist groups. Hans-Joachim Klein, a former member of the June 2nd Movement, who renounced terrorism in 1976 and was in hiding until his capture in 1981, described the extensive connections between the Germans and the PFLP: "It is always said that the RAF, June 2, and the RZs [Revolutionary Cells] are totally independent. That is utterly untrue. Without Haddad, nothing works."[9] Wadi Haddad was the military director of the Palestinian terrorism network in Western Europe in the early 1970s. He controlled the people working for the Venezuelan international terrorist "Carlos" and was also responsible for running the training camps in Lebanon, Iraq, and South Yemen. Klein also talked about meetings with "Carlos" in Frankfurt and Paris, during which detailed plans were discussed for the attack on the oil ministers of the Organization of Petroleum Exporting Countries (OPEC) in Vienna. Operational support by Germans was virtually guaranteed by the $3,000 a month Haddad pumped into the Revolutionary Cells (RZs) along with assorted weapons. Ever fearful of being cut off from the monthly flow of money, the RZs proposed killing Simon Weisenthal, the head of the Jewish Documentation Center in Vienna, in order to further ingratiate themselves with the PFLP.[10]

These joint operations or attacks by a domestic terrorist group outside its own country compounded the threat because the problem spread to countries that initially were unprepared for violent activity by a group that normally operated only on its own territory. The RAF was particularly active in neutral countries such as Sweden, Austria, and Switzerland. In April 1975, members of the June 2nd Movement seized the West German embassy in Stockholm, killed two German diplomats, and then attempted to flee the besieged building by setting off diversionary explosives. Two years later Swedish police uncovered another June 2nd plot to kidnap the former Swedish minister of immigration. Most RAF operations in Austria involved bank robberies; however, on 9 November 1977, the June 2nd Movement kidnapped Walter Michael Palmers, a wealthy Austrian businessman. The RAF also committed bank robberies in Switzerland, but the true value of Switzerland to the terrorists has been its common frontier with West Germany through which weapons were smuggled.[11] Related to "supra-indigenous" terrorist activity was the German terrorists' unremitting campaign against the US military presence in West Germany, a favorite target because it represented (for the ideologically driven terrorists) the paramount symbol of imperialism. A two-week wave of bombings primarily against American targets preceded the capture of the leaders of the RAF in June 1972. In 1979, the RAF just missed killing General Alexander Haig, NATO's supreme allied commander, with a remote-controlled bomb in Belgium.

In September 1981, outside of Heidelberg, General Frederick J. Kroesen, the US Army's European commander, survived a direct hit on his armor-plated car by an anti-tank grenade fired by an RAF terrorist.[12] The attack on Kroesen was part of a widespread effort by German terrorists to disrupt the planned deployment of Pershing II missiles in Germany, commencing in December 1983. The drive escalated in 1982 when sixty-three terrorist attacks were recorded against American personnel and installations in West Germany. Terrorists increasingly shifted their emphasis away from property damage and toward people, as bombs were placed in cars and housing projects with the intention of harming American servicemen and their families.

In 1985, the RAF attempted to create a "Euroterrorist" front by collaborating with other European terrorist groups, notably *Action directe* (AD) of France and the Fighting Communist Cells (CCC) of Belgium. In letters sent in January to newspapers in France and Germany, The AD and the RAF announced the official formation of a "political-military front in Western Europe."[13] Their common goals were to destabilize NATO, wreck Europe's defense industry, and stir up anti-American sentiment. Within ten days of the announcement, Brigadier General René Audran, director of arms sales in the French Ministry of Defense, was shot and killed at his home. A week later, Ernst Zimmerman, a West German businessman whose company makes turbines for the North Atlantic Treaty Organization's (NATO's) Tornado jets, was also killed by terrorists at his home in Bonn. After each murder, the RAF and the AD claimed joint responsibility. Six alleged members of the RAF were captured with plans for the destruction of a NATO fuel pipeline in Belgium that was eventually bombed by the CCC.

A Portuguese terrorist group known as *Forcas Populares 25 de Abril* (FP-25) carried out a "solidarity attack" during an RAF hunger strike in January when it bombed eighteen Mercedes-Benz cars belonging mostly to West German military personnel at a German air force training base in southern Portugal. However, after the attack on the Rhine-Main Air Base in Frankfurt on 8 August 1985 (claimed jointly by the AD and the RAF), there was no further evidence of organizational and logistic cooperation between the two groups.[14]

Until reunification of Germany in 1990, indigenous left-wing terrorist groups remained the most dangerous terrorists in West Germany, even though their contacts with foreign groups had diminished. Despite the numerous arrests and convictions of several "generations" of its members, the RAF continually demonstrated the capacity to recruit new members and carry out spectacular attacks. The unification of Germany led to the apprehension of a number of RAF members in former East Germany, but the group remained active until 1992.

West German neo-Nazis also forged international connections, particularly with Palestinians, which predate those of the RAF. An obscure right-wing organization called *Bund Heimattreuer Jugend* (Association of Young People Loyal to the Homeland) created a *Hilfskorp Arabien* (Arabic Reserve Corps) after the Six-day War in 1967 in order to promote the cause of Palestinians against Israel. Attempts to establish contact with Al-Fatah were unsuccessful.

Three years later, Udo Albrecht founded the *Freikorps Adolf Hitler* (Adolph Hitler Free Corps). In 1970, Albrecht and twelve members of his organization fought alongside Palestinians in the Jordanian Civil War. An emigré from East Germany, Albrecht was a common criminal and a soldier of fortune, who spent more than half his lifetime since arriving in the West in jail. His connection with the Palestinian Liberation Organization (PLO) was first discovered in 1975 when he was arrested in Zurich, Switzerland, with an identification card of *Al-Fatah*. In 1976, four Germans hired by Albrecht as mercenaries for the PLO deserted in Lebanon to the Christian Falange. They told the press that the PLO understood the Germans were right-wing extremists, but they were trained anyway to fight the Israelis.[15]

It was Albrecht who suggested to Manfred Roeder, head of the *Deutsche Aktionsgruppen* (German Action Group), that he also approach the Palestinians. Between 1976 and 1978, Roeder went to Lebanon and met with Abu Jihad, Yasir Arafat's trusted advisor. Abu Jihad, who had become disenchanted with the neo-Nazis, refused to cooperate with Roeder. Roeder returned to West Germany to begin a campaign for the expulsion of foreigners and to stir up xenophobic feelings in the German public. He was eventually sentenced in July 1982 to thirteen years for his role in seven bombings of foreigner workers' hostels throughout West Germany, including a lethal incendiary attack that killed two Vietnamese refugees in Hamburg.[16]

By this time, neo-Nazi activities in West Germany began to increase markedly. In 1978, the first neo-Nazi raids and holdups occurred to secure weapons, ammunition, and money. The government acknowledged that neo-Nazi groups were becoming more militant, as Interior Minister Werner Maihofer noted that "for the first time right-wing extremist activities have gone into the terrorist area."[17] The *Wehrsportgruppe Hoffmann* (Hoffmann Military Sports Group), a band well known for its para-military exercises and contempt for the constitutional state, was banned by the Federal Constitutional Court in January 1980. Its leader, Karl-Heinz Hoffmann, also traveled to Beirut, seeking the support of Abu Iyad, a former PLO deputy.

While twenty members of the Military Sports Group were being trained by PLO officials in terrorist activities, it was reported that Hoffmann tried to found a new organization, under his leadership, of various neo-Nazi groups who had gone underground in Lebanon. In addition, German security authorities found that *Wehrsport* activists were selling old *Bundeswehr* (German Armed Forces) stock to Palestinian groups. Hoffmann was arrested in 1981 at the Frankfurt airport when he tried to leave the country. He was charged with ordering the murders of Shlomo Levin, a Jewish publisher who had written an article in an Italian magazine exposing the activities of Hoffmann's Sports Group, and his girlfriend. Although Hoffmann was acquitted for lack of sufficient evidence, he was sentenced to ten years for illegal possession of weapons and explosives.[18]

From 1968 to 1980, the Palestinians were the most active international terrorists in Western Europe; the Federal Republic was the site of their most significant terrorist attacks.[19] However, only the major Palestinian groups had the resources to maintain a sustained campaign in Western Europe.

In February 1970, the PFLP committed its first act of terrorism in West Germany. Three young Arabs bombed and machine-gunned Israeli passengers in the Munich transit lounge, killing one and wounding eleven, after their attempt to hijack an El Al airliner was aborted. The PFLP adopted airplane hijacking as its chief weapon, becoming the foremost practitioner of the activity. For example, as part of the deal to end the multiple hijacking incident in Jordan in September 1970, the three terrorists from the Munich shootout were released; and in February 1972, the PFLP forced the West German government to pay a $5 million ransom for a hijacked Lufthansa jet.[20]

The Black September Organization (BSO) was created out of the intelligence arm of *Al-Fatah*, Yasser Arafat's wing of the PLO. The BSO's modus operandi was to take "direct action" against Israeli and Jordanian targets by means of assassinations, hijackings, and other spectacular attacks. In February 1972, the BSO murdered five Jordanians living in West Germany whom it suspected of spying for Israel. A Hamburg factory was bombed in the same month because it manufactured electronic components for sale in Israel.[21]

The BSO attack at the Munich Olympic Games followed the guidelines of Faud Shemali, the Lebanese Christian who masterminded some of the group's earlier operations before he died in August 1972. His will advised the terrorists to concentrate on attacks against Israelis held in high esteem by the Israelis themselves, such as scholars, scientists, and athletes. The BSO attack at the Olympics resulted in the deaths of eleven Israeli athletes, five of the eight terrorists, and one German police officer. Most of the deaths occurred during the poorly planned and conducted German attempt to rescue the hostages.[22] The terrorist offensive by the BSO resulted in an Israeli-Palestinian covert mini-war of secret assassinations throughout Europe in which three Palestinians in West Germany vanished under mysterious circumstances. Black September tried to duplicate its Munich attack nearly two years later at the World Cup soccer matches, but the five Palestinians involved were arrested before they could act.[23]

The various terrorist groups emanating from the Croatian emigré population were the next largest source of international terrorist activity in West Germany. There always has been a persistent minority of Croats who never accepted the creation of Yugoslavia. Until recently, repressive measures inside Yugoslavia had prevented any political expression of Croatian separatism. However, Belgrade had allowed Croatian workers to migrate to northern Europe, particularly West Germany. By the mid-1970s, Sweden and West Germany had the largest number of Croats in Western Europe living outside of Yugoslavia. Between 1960 and 1976, the number of Yugoslav workers employed in the Federal Republic had swelled from less than 10,000 to a peak of 640,000. Most of these guest workers were Croats. Likewise, between 1962 and 1977, 67 percent of Croatian terrorist activity occurred in Sweden and Germany. The Croats carried out attacks on Yugoslav institutions abroad and assassinated government officials. In the early 1970s, there was a series of attacks on the Yugoslav military mission, trade mission, and consulates in West Germany.

Of the twenty-one major terrorist acts committed by foreign extremist groups in West Germany in 1976, Croatian groups were responsible for twelve. The more significant acts included the assassination of Vice-Consul Edvin Zdovc in Frankfurt and the attempted murder of a consular official in Dusseldorf. In conjunction with a crackdown on German terrorists, the Federal Republic took steps to neutralize the escalating Croatian violence. As a result of intensified police action, there was a considerable drop in Croatian terrorist activity in West Germany after 1977.[24] But the current civil war in Yugoslavia could rekindle Croatian terrorism in Germany.

The Kurdish Communist Party (PKK) is a separatist movement, which adopted terrorist tactics in the 1980s to support its campaign for independence from Turkey. Some of the more violent PKK members issued death sentences in kangaroo courts against compatriots whom they alleged were traitors to the movement. The PKK was suspected in the murders of alleged traitor Zulfi Gok near Frankfurt and Ramazan Adigunzel, a Kurdish teacher in Hanover. In 1987, sixteen members of the PKK were arrested in police raids and charged with murder and setting up a terrorist organization. They went on trial in 1989 in a highly fortified court in Dusseldorf reminiscent of the tight-security trials for the RAF in the late 1970s. The PKK general secretary, Abdullah Ocalan, was reported to have threatened to kidnap and kill a West German judge or public prosecutor if the men held in custody were not released. In January 1988, Siegfried Wielsputz, a consular affairs attaché to the West German embassy in Paris, was shot to death. Although an anti-German leaflet signed by the Kurdish National Liberation Front (an organ of the PKK) was found on his body, the PKK denied any responsibility, claiming that "no Kurd organization has ever attacked a Western diplomat."[25] Police investigators have since sought another motive for the crime.

The Provisional Irish Republican Army (PIRA) began attacking British targets in West Germany in the summer of 1978 when it detonated bombs at eight bases. Since 1988, PIRA members have intensified their campaign, committing numerous attacks, which have killed eight people and injured over fifty others. The PIRA resurgence was part of an aggressive campaign to target the British military overseas, and the British Army of the Rhine (BAOR) is the largest concentration of the British Army outside of Great Britain. BAOR units also train there in preparation for operations in Ulster against the PIRA. PIRA guerrillas were based in the Netherlands in order to have a freer range of movement and escape West German attention. West German agents confiscated a small PIRA arms cache near the Dutch border in early 1989; however, they also discovered a unit of the British Special Air Service Regiment (SAS) operating on West German territory, which has been suggested as a possible reason for the uncooperative attitude of West Germany in the Pan Am Flight 103 investigation. British soldiers and their families living among the civilian population remain PIRA targets, as random, sporadic attacks continued in the 1990s.[26]

Foreign state–directed and foreign state–sponsored terrorism placed West Germany in direct confrontations with Iran, Libya, Syria, and Yugoslavia, which were among those states that utilized terrorism to carry out political objectives. But since states directing terrorism usually go to great lengths to cover their tracks, hard evidence is usually scant. Consequently, West German security officials continually disagreed as to which states provided support to international terrorists and how intensely. For example, Gerhard Boeden, head of the Federal Criminal Office (the *Bundeskriminalamt* or BKA), stated in February 1982 that East bloc intelligence services were supporting left-wing and right-wing extremists in West Germany. The next day the Bonn government issued a denial, stating that there was no evidence to support Boeden's assertions.[27] Events in 1990 proved Boeden correct. More will be said of this later.

Libya employed both forms of state-sanctioned terrorism, although West Germany experienced fewer terrorist attacks from this source than did other Western European countries. Libya embarked in 1980 on a highly publicized campaign of intimidation and assassination against its political exiles, killing ten in one year. Former Libyan embassy official Omran el-Mehdawi was assassinated on 10 May 1980, in Bonn. A hiatus ensued, but a failed coup d'état attempt in May 1984 against Colonel Mummar Qaddafi prompted the Libyan leader to resume the liquidation of opponents living abroad. Gebril el-Denali, an ardent Libyan exile, was shot and killed (two Germans were also wounded) in Bonn by Fatahi el-Tarhouni, a fellow countryman, who confessed to police afterward that his motives were political. The German ambassador to Libya was recalled, but West Germany did not consider the incident severe enough to break diplomatic relations. In 1983, West Germany tried and deported two Libyans who had held and tortured two Libyan student dissidents at the People's Bureau in Bonn in November 1982. The deportees were traded for eight West Germans who had been arrested in Libya on charges of spying for the US.[28]

Yugoslavia used its security service, *Uprava Drzavne Bezbednosti* (UDBA), to wage a campaign of intimidation against Croatian and Serbian political dissidents residing in West Germany. Emigré circles have claimed that more than twenty prominent figures were murdered during the 1970s by agents of the UDBA. Some of these deaths were attributable to the rivalries between the various emigré groups, but one 7.65-mm pistol was used in seventeen cases. In April 1980, Jozo Molos, a Serbian nationalist, became the last notable emigré to be murdered, and he, too, was shot by a 7.65-mm gun. In July 1983, the BKA arrested Josip Majerski, a guest worker employed as a waiter, who allegedly was an agent of the UDBA and had vast knowledge about the operations of Yugoslavia's secret police in West Germany.[29] West Germany lodged diplomatic protests to Yugoslavia about these killings. These efforts appear to have been effective, as the murders ceased.

Iran, a practitioner of both state-directed and state-sponsored terrorism, viewed West Germany as an important center for counterrevolution when Iranian dissidents relocated there after being expelled from France in 1986. Teheran believed that its exiled opponents were responsible for directing a terrorist campaign of assassinations and bombings in Iran itself. In the following months, several Iranian dissidents in West Germany were murdered, including President Hashemi Rafsanjani's own personal pilot, who defected the previous summer. When Frankfurt police closed the Iranian booth at the 1986 Frankfurt Book Fair after anti-government Iranian students clashed with other Iranians running the exhibit, West Germany narrowly avoided having its embassy in Teheran taken over by fundamentalist Iranian students. A crowd of several hundred radicals, chanting "Vengeance for Frankfurt," attempted to storm the main gate of the embassy, using axes, saws, and other tools. However, good relations with Germany were important to Iran, since it was the latter's only major source of Western technology and credit. This gave Germany some leverage with Teheran; it apparently informed the Islamic regime that it would not tolerate Iranian-sponsored attacks on Americans in Germany, and there were none. Nevertheless, relations became chilled over the Salman Rushdie affair in 1989. Germany closed ranks with its European Community (EC) partners, withdrew its ambassador, and suspended all high-level exchanges.[30]

Syria's involvement in terrorism during the 1980s in West Germany severely strained relations between the two countries. In 1980, West Germany froze all development aid to Syria when it discovered that terrorists sent to the Federal Republic had attacked opponents of President Hafez Assad. Development aid resumed in 1985, but relations deteriorated again when Ahmed Nafawi Hasi was convicted in November 1986 and sentenced to fourteen years in prison for the March 1986 bombing of a building in West Berlin housing the German-Arab Friendship Society (the bomb injured nine people). Hasi admitted during his trial that he picked up the bomb from a Syrian agent in East Berlin.

Bonn stopped short of cutting diplomatic relations with Syria, but it did recall its ambassador from Damascus and expelled five Syrian diplomats in West Germany. West German police initially believed that Syria, rather than Libya, was responsible for the bomb explosion at the *La Belle* disco in West Berlin that killed 3 people and injured over 230 and that triggered the American bombing raid on Libya in 1986. But evidence since collected from former *Stasi* (secret police) files in East Germany indicates that the East German government knew of Libyan involvement.[31] In February 1987, West Germany moved to restore ties with Syria, a decision that probably facilitated the release of a West German hostage in Lebanon in September of that year. Relations between the two countries became less friendly after the bombing of Pan Am Flight 103 because the group initially suspected—the PFLP–General Command—had been allowed to train and reside in Syria for many years. Thereafter, West Germany put greater pressure on Syria to stop its support of terrorism.

THE RESPONSE

Political Setting

West Germany was a federation in which the *Bund* (national government) shared power equally with ten *Länder* (states). (It expanded upon reunification in 1990.) The federal system was adopted to preclude the recurrence of a Nazi-style strong central government. According to the West German Constitution, the states have almost exclusive authority in local government, which includes the police. Civil and criminal law, however, is an area where the *Bund* and the *Länder* share concurrent jurisdiction. There was intense rivalry between the two levels of government in setting anti-terrorism policy, and, as is the case in most Western democracies, de facto power shifted toward the central government in order to handle a complex problem that is both national and international in scope.

The Basic Law, the West German Constitution, doubles as the source of fundamental human rights and as the foundation of the political system. When the West German Constitution was drafted, it recognized the essential role of political parties in the governing process. Article 21 of the Basic Law requires that political parties "conform to democratic principles," and if they "seek to impair or abolish the free democratic basic order or to endanger the Federal Republic of Germany," they will be ruled unconstitutional. Thus, if the Federal Constitutional Court rules that a political party or organization is subversive, it can be banned.[32] While article 21 has contributed to the remarkable political stability of the Federal Republic, it has also become an effective anti-terrorist weapon.

The constitutional sanction to outlaw violent political organizations allows the West German judicial system to play an important role in eliminating international terrorism. The West German judiciary is a network of local, regional, and federal courts, with the Federal Constitutional Court at the apex of the system. West Germany is a civil law country; therefore, a person accused of a crime may be incarcerated for an indefinite period of time if the magistrate believes that the accused may interfere with the pretrial investigation by the state's prosecuting attorney. Thus, hard-core members of the RAF were detained for three years before their trial began. Mohammed Ali Hamadei, a Lebanese Shiite arrested in West Germany and accused of playing a role in hijacking an American airliner, was held for sixteen months before his trial started.

West German citizens have always considered domestic terrorists more threatening than international ones. The *New York Times* conducted a poll on European attitudes toward international terrorism in February 1986—two months after the attacks on the Rome and Vienna airports and nearly two months before the American raid on Libya. By 41 to 35 percent, West Germans still thought domestic terrorists were more of a threat.[33] The West German perception that the state is threatened by terrorism had declined only slightly over the previous decade. The Allensbach Institute, a private polling organization, routinely monitors West German public opinion on the threat of terrorism. From November 1977 to November 1986, the number of people who thought that the state was extremely threatened dropped from 34 to 24 percent, but those who felt that the state was only slightly threatened rose from 8 to 11 percent. Nearly two-thirds, 64 percent of those polled in 1986, felt that the state was moderately threatened, as opposed to 57 percent in 1977.[34] These results demonstrate the long-lasting impact of terrorism because 1977 was the worst year for terrorism in West Germany and there had been no spectacular incidents since the Octoberfest bombing in October 1980.

West Germans have totally rejected terrorists and consistently demanded strong government action. At a time when the German public opposed the death penalty by more than two to one, it was nearly evenly divided (41 percent for and 42 percent against) on the question of the death penalty for terrorists who commit murder. Moreover, in August 1986, a majority of West Germans (56 percent) still thought stronger anti-terrorist laws were necessary, although this figure was down from a high of 71 percent (polled in February 1978) in the aftermath of the kidnapping of Hanns-Martin Schleyer, President of the West German Federation of Industries by the RAF. When two West Germans were kidnapped by Shiites in January 1987 in Beirut in retaliation for the arrest of Mohammed Ali Hamadei in Frankfurt, West German opinion opposed a swap of German hostages for an alleged terrorist by a margin 46 to 29 percent.[35] This support for such a fundamental anti-terrorist policy demonstrates how much West German attitudes had changed over time because, as the "Negotiation Policies" section explains below, this was not always the case.

Anti-terrorist Legislation

Initial anti-terrorist legislation derived from a reaction to the domestic extraparliamentary movement in the late 1960s. The Bundestag incorporated amendments into the Basic Law that introduced the constitutional concepts of a "state of tension" and "state of defense" provisions to handle emergency situations.[36] While these amendments empowered the Federal Republic to manage an emergency situation, the government has never invoked these extraordinary powers. The real effects of these amendments have been, first, the gradual shifting of power away from the *Länd* governments and toward the central government and, second, the conflict between the two levels that occurred due to this process.

The provisions of substantive criminal law governing the violent crimes of murder, bodily harm, robbery, crimes with explosives, and threats and acts of extortion were considered adequate for the punishment of any terrorist acts of violence.[37] Minor changes were introduced to cover the crimes which endanger the safety of the general public, such as the poisoning of water supplies and the toppling of power pylons. Penalties for crimes favored by terrorists were stiffened. On 16 December 1971, sections 239a and 239b were inserted into the German

Criminal Code; these raised the minimum penalties for extortionate kidnapping and hostage-taking.

The most effective legal action has been the insertion of new provisions into the Criminal Code that outlaw subversive groups with anti-democratic objectives. Articles 9 and 21 of the Basic Law were designed to prevent political extremism, particularly the revival of Nazism, and were utilized in the 1950s to ban a neo-Nazi organization and a nascent Communist party. In 1968, the Federal Constitutional Court first applied article 21 against a foreign group when it banned an extremist Croatian exile group (the Croatian Revolutionary Brotherhood). Likewise, a month after the Munich Olympics massacre, two Palestinian organizations with a total membership of nearly 1,800 were banned. Sections 129 and 129a were amended on 22 April 1976, making it illegal to form a "terrorist organization," with penalties for people who participate in, recruit for, or aid such associations. In addition, persons identified as leaders of these associations could be jailed for ten years.[38]

In an effort to dismantle a secret support network of sympathizers for domestic terrorists, Federal Chancellor Willy Brandt adopted a resolution, which the heads of *Länd* governments recommended, that attempted to delineate specific criteria for the evaluation of civil service applicants. The resolution, known as the *Berufsverbot*, which was adopted on 28 January 1972, enacted no new legislation, but rather created a set of guidelines. It required applicants for civil service employment to acknowledge as binding the principles of freedom and constitutional government they are pledged to uphold. Membership in an organization pursuing anti-constitutional aims and the failure to demonstrate support of constitutional principles of freedom could cast doubt on a candidate's willingness to defend these fundamental principles and fitness to hold a public-sector job.[39]

Throughout 1977, the Bundestag moved closer to the point of enacting more stringent anti-terrorist laws. The assassination of Chief Federal Prosecutor Siegfried Buback in April prompted the debate, and the outcome of the Schleyer kidnapping and Lufthansa hijacking affair in October led to the decision that preventive measures were needed to preempt terrorist acts. The new legislation, which was passed on 16 February 1978, amended five articles of the Criminal Code pertaining to search warrants, police checkpoints, the apprehension of suspects, and the conduct of defense attorneys. The police were now authorized to search whole apartment buildings for suspected terrorists, whereas previously searches were limited to specific apartments. Police, possessing sufficient cause to believe that a roadblock is necessary, could establish checkpoints in order to conduct identity checks.[40]

Revisions to criminal procedure law were also enacted in response to domestic terrorists who were abusing the proceedings during courtroom trials. The adopted measures speeded up trials, restricted the lawyer-client relationship so as to ensure proper conduct by the defense counsel, and provided for the complete isolation of prisoners by banning all contact with them when it was suspected that they were masterminding terrorist attacks. The *Kontaktsperregesetz* (the Contact Ban Law) was declared permissible if terrorists posed an imminent "present danger to life, limb, or freedom." Accordingly, a *Länd* government or the federal minister of justice could order that "every association of prisoners with one another and with the outside world, inclusive of written and spoken communication with the defense counsel," be severed.[41] The request for a contact ban had to be accompanied by a judicial decree within two weeks; otherwise, it expired.

Until 1989, German criminal procedure law did not allow for either plea bargaining or a crown witness. Prosecutors in West Germany were required by statute to try the accused for all criminal offenses. Even after observing the success that the Italians had with the Cossiga Law in the early 1980s, when the Red Brigades were severely weakened by informants seeking leniency, the government in Bonn and members of the *Bundestag* rejected any idea of instituting a crown-witness system. By 1989, however, opinion had changed, and a law was passed to permit *Aussteiger* (repentant terrorists) to receive reduced sentences or to be released from custody in return for information and cooperation.[42] In addition, sections 239a and 239b provide for sentence reduction if a terrorist holding hostages agrees to release the captives and drop the ransom demands. Similar considerations apply to attacks on aviation under section 316C of the German Criminal Code and to other comparable crimes involving the safety of innocent civilians.

Negotiation Policies

West Germany made a dramatic turnaround in its policy of negotiating with terrorists. From 1975, it was firmly in the rank of states that profess the no-negotiation, no-concession approach. Previously, in an attempt to make a break with its Nazi past, West Germany emphasized the strong sanctity of human life and rights, which meant avoiding bloodshed at all costs. Initially, therefore, the West German policy was to resolve any hostage situation without any loss of life, conceding almost entirely to terrorist demands. The German response to the multiple hijackings by Palestinian terrorists in September 1970 was the quick release of terrorists imprisoned after their grenade attack against Israeli citizens at the Munich airport earlier that year. After the PFLP hijacked a Lufthansa jet in February 1972, the German government paid $5 million in ransom without the slightest hesitation.

When the BSO seized the Israeli athletes at the Munich Olympics, Bonn reluctantly made the choice to attempt a rescue operation because Israel refused to negotiate and West Germany had no Arab or Palestinian prisoners with which to trade. Less than two months after the Olympics massacre, West Germany freed the surviving terrorists from the Munich operation when a Lufthansa jet was hijacked from Beirut to Cyprus. Bonn officials had never made any secret of their expectation that terrorists sooner or later would succeed in hijacking a Lufthansa jet, and they also left no doubt that West Germany would exchange the three Arabs for the plane and its passengers.[43] By this time, however, the policy of obsequiousness was becoming untenable in the face of the growing threat of international terrorism and the increasing foreign criticism of Germany's policy. There was an urgent need to reassess its counter-terrorism strategy.

The conversion of West Germany to the no deals position occurred when a domestic German terrorist group seized hostages in two separate instances in the early part of 1975. On the eve of the elections in West Berlin, the June 2nd Movement kidnapped Peter Lorenz, the Christian Democratic candidate for mayor, and demanded the release of six imprisoned comrades. The Bonn government released the prisoners (each of whom was also given DM 20,000) and flew them to South Yemen. The press castigated the government for its decision and called the action humiliating to the West German state.[44] The government had even lost control of the national television network as the terrorists compelled it to cancel the regular viewing schedule and to broadcast both the departure of the imprisoned terrorists and the kidnappers' prepared statements.

Emboldened by Bonn's feeble response and pliant behavior, the Holger Meins Commando then attacked the West German embassy in Stockholm, threatening to kill twelve hostages and blow up the embassy if their demands were not met. This time the demands and stakes had risen dramatically. The terrorists were seeking the release of twenty-six people held in German jails, including the hard-core members of the Baader-Meinhof gang, and they held twelve hostages (all government employees), instead of just one. But this time the German government rejected the terrorists' ultimatum and refused to meet their demands. Apparently with no alternative plan or tactics, the terrorists tried to escape following a diversionary explosion, which blew an enormous hole in the embassy roof. The building, however, was ringed with Swedish police, and the terrorists were easily apprehended.[45]

In a speech before the Bundestag the next day, Chancellor Helmut Schmidt characterized the Stockholm attack as an "unimaginable test of will for our entire security and for the state." He understood that the policy of continually acceding to terrorist demands would have a deleterious effect on the state: "Then all the authority of the constitutional state will crumble, and then we cannot guarantee protection for anyone any more."[46] In a reversal from the Lorenz kidnapping, the public perception of the Schmidt government was that it had acted forcefully and decisively on matters concerning terrorism.

Although the West German government has since maintained its tough policy of not acceding to terrorist demands, it does not entirely preclude negotiations. During the Schleyer kidnapping, the crisis committee used Denis Payot, a left-wing Swiss lawyer, as an intermediary or, in the terms of a government spokesman, "a human mailbox" in the government's contacts with the terrorists. Despite this public display of flexibility, a report released by the government revealed that there was a unanimous decision by the crisis committee one day after the kidnapping to reject any demands involving the exchange of imprisoned terrorists for Schleyer.[47]

In the 1980s, the government demonstrated greater flexibility in applying the no-concessions policy to the abductors of German citizens in Lebanon. In January

1987, Mohammed Ali Hamadei, a Lebanese Shiite Muslim accused of the 1985 hijacking of a TWA jet and the on board murder of a US Navy diver, Robert Stethem, was arrested at the Frankfurt airport for smuggling explosives into the country. In retaliation, his brother, Ali Abbas Hamadei, and fellow Shiite terrorists then kidnapped two West German businessmen, Alfred Schmidt and Rudolf Cordes, in Lebanon. Ali Abbas Hamadei, who has joint Lebanese–West German citizenship, was arrested himself two weeks after his brother and charged with the kidnappings. Besides the obvious reason of holding German nationals as hostages to swap for Mohammed Ali Hamadei, the Shiites were also attempting to block his extradition to the United States.

The timing of these events was unfortunate, as Iran and West Germany were trying to normalize relations. Despite its no-concessions policy, West Germany engaged in talks with Iran in May to resolve the hostage problem. When West Germany refused to extradite Mohammed Ali Hamadei to the United States in June 1987 and opted to try him in West Germany, Alfred Schmidt was released three months later. An aide to Chancellor Helmut Kohl did admit that threats to kill the hostages were influential in the decision not to extradite.[48] This placed the Bonn government in an awkward position with its allies—France, Great Britain, and the United States—which had no diplomatic relations with Teheran and had hostages held in Lebanon by pro-Iranian terrorists.

Ali Abbas Hamadei went to trial in January 1988 and was sentenced to thirteen years for smuggling explosives into West Germany and participating in the kidnapping of the two West German citizens. His conviction was based on the evidence furnished by BKA telephone intercepts. Hamadei had telephoned West Germany from Beirut four days after his brother's arrest and described in detail the abduction of Cordes. Nearly one year later, a West German court convicted Mohammed Ali Hamadei of killing Stethem and gave him a life sentence, the harshest sentence that West German law provides.[49] Rudolf Cordes was released by his abductors in September 1988, midway through Mohammed Hamadei's trial, following intercession by Iran.[50] American prosecutors were disappointed that Hamadei was not extradited to the United States, but West Germany more than fulfilled its international obligations, given that neither the airliner nor the terrorist nor the murder victim was West German, and that the incident had not occurred within the Federal Republic's territorial jurisdiction. It was, in fact, both a test and a measure of West Germany's commitment to international cooperation against terrorism, a subject that will be examined later in this chapter.

Security and Intelligence

Law enforcement is a responsibility of the *Länd*, but it is shared between institutions at both the Federal Republic and the *Länd* levels with overlapping jurisdictions. The Basic Law clearly gives the *Länder* responsibility for the police, but the principle of cooperative federalism applies—as article 73, section 10 of the Basic Law specifies—"in matters of criminal police and of protection of the constitution, establishment of a Federal Criminal Office, as well as international control of crime."[51] The attack on the Munich Olympics exposed the weakness of this structure with its lack of coordination, command and control, and communication. While the Schmidt government in Bonn was trying to resolve the crisis on the international level, the Munich police department was responsible for the hostage rescue attempt, for which it proved inadequately trained. Three months prior to the Munich attack, the Conference of Ministers of the Interior addressed this very issue; they recognized the need for better cooperation between state and federal levels of law enforcement and recommended further collaboration among members of the European Community.[52] The need to develop better coordination between the two levels of government was an ongoing issue in the Federal Republic. The measures that have been adopted have had a more "centralizing" effect, rather than a "coordinating" one, as increased funding and political mandates enhanced the position of the federal institutions, expanding greatly their roles in the security apparatus.

The Office for the Protection of the Constitution (*Bundesamt fur Verfassungsschutz*—BfV) is one agency within the federal Interior Ministry that extended its scope and influence as a result of counter-terrorism efforts. When the BfV was established, its function was to monitor any internal groups that demonstrated a propensity for extremist views and to thwart infiltration by foreign spies from Communist countries. As terrorism in West Germany became more prevalent, the BfV was formally authorized to set up a new section (Section VI), its sole purpose being to conduct surveillance of foreigners and to counteract external militants suspected of plotting violence. The organization has nationwide investigatory powers and authority to supervise government responses to all terrorist attacks. By law, the BfV must publish an annual book-length report, the *Protection of the Constitution Report* (*Verfassungschutzbericht*), which discloses information on all types of extremist organizations: their membership, publications, and activities. The distinguishing characteristic of the BfV is that it has no police powers—it may not arrest, search, confiscate, or otherwise prosecute citizens.[53] In addition, each *Länd* has the right to have its own BfV. Consequently, there has been a great amount of overlap and competition between the federal and the state levels in the domain of intelligence gathering.

The BKA is charged with the responsibility for federal law enforcement. It investigates terrorism, white-collar crime, and organized crime, and it does have the power to arrest suspects. Thus, the BfV has been dubbed the organization that "knows everything," while the BKA has been characterized as the agency that "does everything." The BKA, however, does not possess the overarching jurisdiction of the American FBI, as its functions are also duplicated by the *Länder,* with their own police forces investigating the same types of crimes.

After the Lorenz kidnapping and the Stockholm embassy attack in 1975, the federal government and the *Länder* assigned the BKA two new duties: the central direction of all anti-terrorist operations and the central evaluation of all intelligence.

This authorization created two new departments within the BKA: the Suppression of Terrorism (*Terrorismus* or TE) and the Special Branch (*Staatsschutz* or ST). The TE is responsible for investigating politically motivated crimes and apprehending those terrorists being sought under arrest warrants in order to bring them to trial. The new office was initially assigned 180 officials, funded with a $3 million budget, and situated near Bonn, providing direct access for national decision-makers. The TE staff was later expanded to 300.[54] The ST was created with the intention of being a complement to the BfV's new Section VII, established in 1974 to gather information on domestic terrorists who resort to violence. The ST was placed in charge of collating information and entering it in the massive central computer, which the BKA was authorized to incorporate into its operations in 1973. The BKA is renowned for this computer at its headquarters in Wiesbaden. When terrorism began to escalate in the 1970s, the BKA was ill-prepared, as staff members had to pore over several million photographs and fingerprints individually and nearly 3 million documents were filed by a card-index system. Horst Herold, the former chief of police in Nuremberg, is credited with introducing electronic data-processing equipment to the BKA. Herold's staff systematically recorded all aspects related to acts of terrorism—perpetrators, venues, dates, methods, escape routes, car registrations, residences; this allowed them to recognize basic patterns of activities. The data in these computerized files were separated in 1975 into two large files: PIOS (persons, institutions, objects, and things) and BEFA (*Beobachtende Fahndung* or observations and search). In the mid-1980s, PIOS listed more than 135,000 people, 5,500 institutions, and 115,000 objects and things, such as lost passports, guns, and cars; BEFA contained more than 6,000 persons who in some way had a connection to known terrorists, keeping track of travel routes, border crossings, time schedules, and meetings and contacts of sympathizers of the RAF.[55]

The BKA has shared this data bank with foreign law enforcement agencies. When Aldo Moro was kidnapped by the Red Brigades in March 1978 in Italy, a special team of computer experts from the BKA was sent to Rome to help in the Italian search. In addition, the West German government has invited other countries to input data on terrorists whom they are investigating, which could be the first step toward the integration of Western European police agencies. State-of-the-art data processing coupled with high-technology forensics has made the BKA a world leader in scientific research on terrorism.

Detractors of the centralized computer of the BKA charge that technical systems are beneficial only if there is true cooperation by all levels of government. A tip on Schleyer's whereabouts was "lost" for several days due to a jurisdictional dispute between state and city officials. In addition, police officers in the *Länder* complained that their computers were not compatible with those in Wiesbaden. It is claimed that conventional police methods are often neglected in favor of ritualistically following prepared computer programs set up for data processing.[56]

The chief criticism about electronic data processing is that the use of computers by police—and by other agencies of government—allows for the misuse of personal data, and thus the violation of human rights. Despite the popular demand to eradicate terrorism, German citizens are apprehensive about the total domination and manipulation of individuals by an all-powerful, omniscient state. Serious disputes arose in the Bundestag when hearings were held on the introduction of a new plastic identity card, which would store vital information about an individual and would be accessible to police departments. There was even widespread resistance to conducting the census in West Germany, complicating policies, such as social-welfare benefits, that are implemented on the basis of demographic statistics. One report on the Baader-Meinhof gang in 1974 revealed that the BKA and the BfV wrongly named a number of persons in connection with offenses they had not committed.

When Gerhard Baum became the minister of the interior in 1978, he ordered an inquiry into the BKA's central computing system. It was discovered that the BKA had accumulated a total of thirty-seven data banks, containing 4.7 million names, 3,100 organizations, 2.1 million fingerprints, and 1.9 million photographs of people. Indigenous left-wing terrorist groups attempted to exploit discontent over these systems by targeting computer centers of American multi-national companies and West German government data-processing centers.[57]

Para-military Measures

The Federal Border Police (the *Bundesgrenzschutz*, or BGS) evolved from manning obscure posts at the frontier to being a front-line agency responsible for anti-terrorism countermeasures. The BGS was created in 1951 to patrol the border areas, especially with East Germany. Following the passage of two laws in 1968 and 1972, however, it obtained additional internal security functions and is now used specifically for some anti-terrorist duties. Hans-Dietrich Genscher, then interior minister under Chancellor Willy Brandt, was responsible for the metamorphosis of the BGS. The BGS began to protect West German embassies when Count Karl Von Spreti, the German ambassador to Guatemala, was murdered in 1970. In 1971, as the threat of hijacking grew, the BGS was assigned the duty of guarding airports. In addition to patrolling airports in highly discernible uniforms and visibly carrying machine guns, other border guards were disguised as Lufthansa employees, frisking passengers and examining luggage.[58]

The elite anti-terrorist commando unit, GSG-9 (*Grenzschutzgruppen* 9), draws its personnel from the BGS. In an emergency meeting less than ten days after the Munich Olympics attack, the *Länd* interior ministers unanimously authorized the creation of a special federal police unit to combat international terrorism. GSG-9, however, was designed primarily as a deterrent. When it was first unveiled a year after Munich, Genscher said, "People need to know this unit exists. We hope that it will never be necessary to put the unit into action."[59] On 15 February 1974, the Conference of Ministers of the Interior specified the duties of GSG-9 more precisely:

The GSG-9 is to be used in the carrying out of police missions of special significance. They may above all be employed in cases when the situation necessitates a single operation, whether openly or in secret, bringing to bear immediate force against violent criminals. This is especially the case when larger, organized groups of terrorists become active.[60]

The initial eight-month training period (later reduced to three months) consisted of tactical operations training, weapons and target practice, legal instruction, martial arts and close combat training, and seminars in psychology. In addition to the basic training, there is continuous training for assaults and rescues for any conceivable situation and regular study of terrorist activities and methods.[61]

The first operational use of GSG-9 did not occur until October 1977. Four Palestinians hijacked a Lufthansa jet after its takeoff from Majorca, Spain, in order to put additional pressure on the Bonn government during the Schleyer kidnapping affair by demanding the release of eleven imprisoned RAF members. After a four-day odyssey through the Middle East during which several countries, including Iraq, Lebanon, and Syria, refused the jet permission to land, it finally touched down in Mogadishu, Somalia. After securing the permission of the Somalian government, two GSG-9 commando units stormed the plane at the Mogadishu airport in a well-executed, thirty-minute assault, safely rescuing all ninety passengers and killing three of the four hijackers.[62]

The rescue at Mogadishu represented the culmination of a rigorous training program. Colonel Ulrich Wegener, GSG-9's founder and first commander, had asked Lufthansa to create mock-ups of all types of aircraft used commercially; GSG-9 trained on the mock-ups. Special grenades (developed by the British Army's SAS), which emit a bright light, but no shrapnel, were used in order to stun and confuse the terrorists. The flawless execution of the operation at Mogadishu demonstrated not only the effectiveness of a military option, but also its deterrent value; no West German aircraft has been hijacked since by international terrorists.

Despite its international reputation as a superior anti-terrorist unit, GSG-9 has rarely been utilized for operations inside the Federal Republic. Since the *Länd* interior ministers are responsible for policing their own territories, the *Länd* must make a formal request to the federal government before GSG-9 can be deployed within German territory. The *Länder* have resisted using GSG-9 because of the federal-state rivalry; in fact, the states have created their own anti-terrorist units (although they are not as formidable as GSG-9). GSG-9 participated in the apprehension of Brigitte Mohnhaupt, Adelheid Schulz, and Christian Klar, the RAF's main leaders, in November 1982; this marked the first time that the unit was involved in a major operation on German territory, a full ten years after its creation.[63]

Target-Hardening

Preventive security measures increased significantly following the outbreak of terrorism in the Federal Republic. Public figures were classified in categories according to their susceptibility to attack. Politicians were divided into three danger groups according to their rank and duty. According to Police Regulation 100, for group 1 there is a constant escort and property protection. Group 2 calls for escort in special situations and at special times. Group 3 calls for patrols and sporadic protection.[64] Numerous public buildings, such as airports, courts, and consulates which were prone to attack, were under constant guard by police and security officials. For example, in Bad Godesberg, the Bonn suburb where embassies were located and many diplomats resided, the neighborhoods were "swept" by the police at irregular, but frequent, intervals; police cars and armored vehicles were on constant patrol. Bodyguards to protect prominent individuals cost the Bonn government DM 160 million in 1979.[65] Personal protection cost the *Länder* DM 100 million for the same year, and the combined costs to both levels of government exceeded DM 300 million for 1980.

Terrorist attacks on vulnerable targets usually induce the tightening of security by authorities. Airline hijackings are among the most spectacular terrorist incidents, and, accordingly, airport security is the most visible commitment of a government to target-hardening. In the aftermath of the Mogadishu rescue, extra security precautions were taken in and around German airports. Helicopters patrolled at low altitudes, and armored cars lined the runways. Landing patterns were varied, and airplanes were advised to extinguish the interior cabin lights during the landing approaches.[66] The German government also asked twelve countries where it considered security precautions inadequate to permit Bonn to set up its own security checks at airports. When Algeria, one of the twelve, refused, Lufthansa quickly canceled all its flights there.

The Frankfurt airport, Europe's busiest, is equipped with the latest technological devices, ranging from X-ray machines to a simulation chamber, which duplicates the pressure of an aircraft so as to detonate pressure-sensitive bombs. In the mid-1980s, *Flughafen AG* (the airport operating company), the state of Hesse, and the central government spent about DM 100 million annually for airport security. A major portion of these funds was spent on personnel, as 1,500 to 2,000 persons are employed on security duty every day. Individual airlines that are likely terrorist targets, such as the Israeli airline, El Al, undertake additional security precautions; El Al thoroughly searches all luggage. Yet, as the 1988 Pan Am bombing demonstrated, even the best security is not flawless.[67]

International Collaboration on Legal and Security Measures

West Germany has always had a policy of strengthening international agreements and striving with its allies for greater cooperation on security measures. It ratified all the major international treaties—the Tokyo, Hague, and Montreal Conventions—concerned with aircraft hijacking. It was the principle of *aut dedere aut punire* found in both the Hague and the Montreal Conventions that obliged West Germany either to extradite Mohammed Ali Hamadei to the United States or prosecute him in West Germany. West Germany was also a party to the Convention on the

Prevention and Punishment of Crimes Against Internationally Protected Persons, including Diplomatic Agents (the New York Convention, 1979) and the International Convention Against the Taking of Hostages (the West Germany Convention, 1979). As the name implies, the West German government was the prime mover to frame the latter convention and get it passed at the United Nations (UN). These treaties, however, deal only with very specific areas on which most states can agree—the hijacking of aircraft, the protection of diplomatic personnel, and the taking of hostages. The task of actually defining terrorism proved to be intractable in international forums such as the UN, and until consensus in this area is achieved, the only effective international legal regime against terrorism will be derived from regional and bilateral agreements. An equally exasperating problem of international terrorism was the political exception clause found in most extradition treaties. The European Convention on the Suppression of Terrorism (ECST) represented an attempt on a regional basis (by the countries in the Council of Europe) to facilitate the process of bringing fugitive terrorists to justice. Europe had all the conditions that are necessary for an effective treaty against international terrorism: common institutions, a long tradition of extradition, and a greater degree of political consensus than other regions. West Germany, at the heart of central Europe and with a disproportionate number of wanted terrorists residing outside its borders, had the most to gain from such a treaty.

West Germany and the United Kingdom quickly ratified the convention, but its impact was still considered negligible by the mid-1980s. Not enough states had ratified the convention to make it binding, and those that did had registered reservations under article 13, which permits a state to define for itself what constitutes a political crime and thus to refuse extradition. Italy was notable in this regard. It may be no coincidence that France's decision to ratify the ECST in 1986 came only after German and French terrorists conducted a joint offensive against the European democracies. As Western Europe strives for a greater integration after 1992, closer cooperation against international terrorism may occur.[68]

In addition to the multilateral treaties, West Germany has pursued bilateral agreements in response to indigenous terrorists fleeing the country. Between 1972 and 1977, heightened pressure by West German police forced domestic terrorists to seek refuge outside of Germany. This intensified effort by the internal security forces was complemented by increased cooperation from its foreign counterparts. The Dutch proved the most eager to aid the West Germans in police investigations. They did not wish to be perceived as a safe haven for fleeing terrorists. Moreover, when Dutch police captured RAF terrorist Knut Folkerts in a gun battle that killed an officer, the Dutch were genuinely shocked at the violence. The extradition of Folkerts was appealed up through the Dutch court system, and the High Court of the Netherlands made no legal objections to the extradition of Folkerts and two other terrorists sought by West Germany. The Swedish police returned to West Germany within a day the four surviving German terrorists who had seized the German embassy in Stockholm. Two years later, Swedish police thwarted

Operation Leo, a plan to kidnap the former Swedish minister of the interior, when they arrested fourteen terrorists from various countries, two of them being West Germans.[69]

While the capture of German terrorists throughout Europe has prompted the Bonn government to request their return to West Germany, decisions on extradition were made on a case-by-case basis, with political considerations being paramount. Between 1977 and 1982, twenty-five German terrorists were arrested abroad. Four of the most wanted German terrorists were arrested in Yugoslavia in May 1978, but Belgrade demanded the return of eight Croatian exiles from West Germany as part of the deal to extradite the captured Germans. Notwithstanding the Federal Constitutional Court's decision, which ruled only in favor of the extradition of Stephan Bilandzic, the man Belgrade wanted the most, the Bonn government had made it clear even before the court's ruling that it would not extradite Bilandzic. In short, Bonn was unwilling to equate Croatian political dissidents (some of whom had committed no crimes) with German terrorists. Yugoslavia eventually released the Germans, citing insufficient evidence provided by West Germany.[70]

By contrast, in 1976, Rolf Pohle, a convicted terrorist who had been released during the Lorenz kidnapping episode, was arrested in Greece. An Athens court ruled in August that Pohle could not be extradited because his 1974 sentence in Munich had been for a political offense. Greece's Supreme Court reversed the lower court's decision, rejecting the reasoning that Pohle's actions were those of a genuine revolutionary, and permitted his extradition.[71] West Germany's considerable economic strength and influence in the European Economic Community may have affected the decision of the Greek Supreme Court because at that time Greece was seeking West Germany's support for admission into the Common Market.

In April 1978, a special West German *Spezialeinsatzkommandos* team of the BKA was allowed to participate in the arrest of four more German terrorists in Bulgaria, who were immediately returned to West Germany.[72] At the time, the Soviet bloc—including Bulgaria—was suspected of involvement in international terrorism; thus, the unprecedented Bulgarian action was viewed as an effort to dispel these allegations and "clean up" the Soviet bloc's image. However, the real "sea change" in counter-terrorism relations with the East bloc did not come until 1990, with the collapse of the East German Communist regime. Following the abolition of the *Stasi* (secret police) in December 1989, captured files and tips from former *Stasi* agents revealed that East Germany's security service had provided "aid and comfort" to fugitive members of the RAF. As East and West Germany moved toward unification, the police forces of the two states began cooperating in anti-terrorist investigations. This led to a series of joint raids in East Berlin and other East German cities in June 1990, which netted ten RAF members. Two, Susanne Albrecht and Inge Viett, had been sought by the West Germans for more than ten years in connection with major terrorist incidents in West Germany, including the murders of Jürgen Ponto and Hanns Martin Schleyer. Another,

Henning Beer, who apparently had spent eight years in East Germany, was wanted in connection with the bombing assassination of West German banker Alfred Herrhausen in November 1989 and several other terrorist incidents in the Federal Republic.

At least one German terrorist expert, however, doubts that the *Stasi* would have been permitted to support such politically risky operations. Nevertheless, protecting the RAF terrorists was apparently the responsibility of the *Stasi's* so-called anti-terrorist Division XXII and could not have been undertaken without the knowledge and approval of *Stasi* chief Erich Mielke and former East German Communist party chief Erich Honecker. While the arrests clearly were a major blow against the RAF, West German security officials cautioned against predicting the imminent demise of the RAF. However, the remaining active members of the movement retained only a limited capacity for violence, and the reunification of Germany— along with other changes—seems to have hastened the RAF's demise.[73]

West Germany and France improved their cooperation against international terrorism in the 1980s after a decade of turmoil and mistrust. France frustrated West Germany in the 1970s by refusing to extradite fugitive terrorists, lacking forcefulness in pursuing and condemning international terrorism, and smugly criticizing the shortcomings of other states for terrorism occurring in their countries. Two weeks before President Valery Giscard d'Estaing was to introduce the ECST to the European Parliament, the French government quickly expelled Abu Daoud, the mastermind behind the 1972 Olympics attack, before West Germany could file the formal extradition papers. The extradition request was dismissed on a bogus technicality; French Prime Minister Raymond Barre cited "hesitation" on West Germany's part in filing the proper extradition papers, even though the West German government had twenty days to comply and Daoud was held for only four days.[74]

West German security officials were dissatisfied with the lackadaisical effort by the French police when tips indicated that Schleyer might have been held in France. The growing German anger over the Schleyer affair led to the French extradition of Klaus Croissant, a left-wing lawyer and member of the RAF inner circle, who fled West Germany in 1976 and had been residing in France. Anti-German sentiment had been building in France, where West German anti-terrorist laws were viewed as repressive, and some openly questioned the German commitment to democracy.

In the immediate aftermath of the Schleyer kidnapping, Chancellor Schmidt appeared on French television, disputing charges by some segments of the French media about a revival of fascism, the danger to civil liberties, and possible police excesses in West Germany. French attitudes began to change only in the mid-1980s, due to the increased terrorism in France, the pressure exerted by other governments, the assassination of René Audran, and the concern expressed by the general population. Shortly after Audran was killed, France and West Germany created a special joint anti-terrorist working group and set up a hotline between the two countries to allow rapid transmission of information. West German Interior Minister Friedrich Zimmerman and French Interior Minister Charles Pasqua signed a formal agreement in April 1987, providing for the two countries to exchange terrorist experts and allowing joint border operations in special circumstances.[75]

CONCLUSIONS

The incidence of both domestic revolutionary and international terrorism in West Germany showed a marked decline, commencing in the early 1980s and continuing into the 1990s. There were exceptions, however: the resurgence of neo-Nazi/racist political violence following reunification and a modest increase in international incidents toward the end of the decade, related both to Germany's continued anti-terrorist efforts and to foreign issues indirectly related to Germany, such as PIRA attacks on British troops based in the Federal Republic.[76] Generally speaking, however, pragmatic West German foreign policy, the influence of events unrelated to terrorism, and effective security measures combined to reduce and to contain terrorism (both domestic and international) at manageable levels.

However, no state responds to a terrorist campaign without changing its institutions, and hence society itself, even if only slightly. As noted earlier, some inside and outside Germany had criticized its anti-terrorist measures for being excessively repressive: "the most comprehensive system of police surveillance and anti-terrorist legislation in Western Europe."[77] However, only in exceptional cases did German legal restrictions exceed those of other liberal democracies. By approving the *Berufsverbot*, the West German government became the target of heavy domestic and international criticism. *Die Zeit* wrote that "A free democracy cannot exclude entire groups of citizens from service of the state simply according to categories determined by the government."[78] The Bertrand Russell Peace Foundation set up a tribunal in 1977 to investigate allegations that human rights in West Germany were being endangered by anti-terrorist measures. In particular, the tribunal wanted to determine whether German citizens were being denied the right to exercise their professions on account of their political views. Yet many countries, including the United States, have similar provisions for employment in government.[79]

The *Berufsverbot* investigation process, however, had weakened many young Germans' confidence in the constitutional state. One poll of students showed that in a decade there had been a doubling of the number of those who thought the constitution was being used in an increasingly reactionary and authoritarian way. Despite a low number of rejections (320), 454,585 applicants for civil service had been screened within a twelve-month period during 1974–1975. In November 1978, Interior Minister Gerhard Baum, whose ministry was responsible for conducting loyalty investigations, considered it a "very troubling situation" and called for a change in the decree. "The climate in our country has degenerated through the discussion of the decree. Young people's mistrust about the state has grown and there is real skepticism among them that this is the freest state in German history."[80] In January 1979, the government called the background checks of all federal job applicants "a wrong answer" for dealing with extremism, and it announced that such routine investigations would be abandoned. Investigations by national security officials now must be based on "tangible indications that a candidate does not fulfill requirements of public service."[81]

The most "repressive" anti-terrorist legislation was passed by the *Bundestag* in the first half of 1978. The passing vote (245–244) reflected the strong opposition to the legislation. The initial package was rejected by the *Bundesrat*, the upper house, declaring the measures too weak. Another vote was taken in April in which the *Bundestag* approved the same legislation, overcoming demands by conservative Christian Democratic Union members for greater restrictions. Specific procedures for the check of identity were designed to protect the rights of citizens. The deprivation of liberty may not exceed twelve hours, and individuals have the right to contact a friend or relative about their situation. All documentation used to establish the identity of non-suspects, including fingerprints and photographs, must be destroyed. In order to conduct building searches, the "strong suspicions" of the police must be approved by the courts. And the police may not confiscate any evidence that is unrelated to terrorist offenses.

Other countries place limited restrictions on access to prisoners. The German *Kontaktsperregestz*, however, is the most severe and unprecedented. Despite its severity, the European Court ruled that it was a legal and appropriate response to terrorism. It ruled that extraordinary security measures used against Andreas Baader, Gudrun Ensslin, and Jan-Carl Raspe "in no way characterized inhuman or degrading treatment," considering the dangerous nature of the inmates and the terrorist threat to West German society.[82] During its only implementation, confederates of the imprisoned terrorists were still able to hijack a Lufthansa jet, calling into question its utility as an anti-terrorist measure. The *Kontaktsperregesetz* has not been used since.

The Horchel Report, a parliamentary investigation into the Schleyer affair, also revealed that the BGS were used to conduct illegal frontier searches of automobiles. Following the ministerial inquiry into the BKA's centralized computer files, new guidelines were issued on the criteria for the collection and storage of data about citizens. However, public skepticism of centralized data banks generated by the government remained widespread.[83]

The criticism that West Germany overreacted to the terrorist threat and enacted repressive legislation is greatly exaggerated. Since 1978, the Bundestag has passed no new anti-terrorist legislation. The *Berufsverbot* was substantially revised to correct the potential for discrimination based on political beliefs. The *Bundestag* enacted legislation that created parliamentary oversight by the Internal Affairs Committee, requiring the intelligence agencies to disclose any information about their activities that the committee demands. Whenever West Germany has been brought before the European Court for Human Rights for its anti-terrorist laws, the court has always ruled that the West German legislation (including its surveillance law) does not violate the European Convention on Human Rights.

West Germany's contributions to democratic responses to international terrorism are several. While West Germany adopted restrictive anti-terrorist measures, the state has adhered to democratic principles by publicly debating the issues, properly enacting legislation, and scrupulously complying with the law. It was sensitive to charges of repression and took steps to correct injustices and institute reform. The federal government has also taken a multilateral approach on the international level as it has attempted to forge cooperative relationships with other states that oppose international terrorism. West Germany created an elite para-military unit as a necessary component of an offensive anti-terrorist strategy, but equally valued its deterrent effect. When the use of force was necessary, it was used sparingly. As Germany entered the 1990s, a united nation after forty-five years, it was well equipped both to counter international terrorism and to protect its democratic institutions. Only the hesitant response to neo-Nazi anti-foreigner terrorism in 1992 raised doubts about Germany's commitment to protection of universal human rights.

NOTES

1. The text of the communiqué (translated) is reproduced in Bruce A. Scharlau and Donald Philips, "Not the End of German Left-wing Terrorism," *Terrorism and Political Violence* 4, no. 3 (Autumn 1992), pp. 110–15; see also *The European*, 23–26 April 1992.

2. Scharlau and Philips, "Not the End," p. 109.

3. *Liberation* (Paris), 4 December 1992.

4. *Le Monde* (Paris), 10 November 1992; *Globe and Mail* (Toronto), 24 November 1992.

5. David T. Schiller, "The Police Response to Terrorism: A Critical Overview," in Paul Wilkinson and Alasdair M. Stewart, eds., *Contemporary Research on Terrorism* (Aberdeen, UK: Aberdeen University Press, 1987), p. 537.

6. Steven Emerson and Brian Duffy, *The Fall of Pan Am 103* (New York: G. P. Putnam's Sons, 1990). On the Libyan indictments, see US Department of State, *Dispatch* 2, no. 46 (18 November 1991), pp. 854–58.

7. *Der Spiegel*, 5 December 1977, reporting on a comparative study conducted by the Max Planck Institute of Foreign and International Criminal Law. The countries included in the survey were France, Sweden, and the United Kingdom.

8. Claire Sterling, *The Terror Network: The Secret War of International Terrorism* (New York: Holt, Rinehart, and Winston, 1981), p. 122; Jillian Becker, *Hitler's Children: The Story of the Baader-Meinhof Terrorist Gang* (Philadelphia: J. B. Lippincott Company, 1977), p. 180.

9. Quoted in Sterling, *The Terror Network*, p. 140.

10. *Der Spiegel*, 7 August 1978 and 10 December 1979.

11. Dennis Pluchinsky, "Political Terrorism in Western Europe: Some Themes and Variations," in Yonah Alexander and Kenneth A. Myers, eds., *Terrorism in Europe* (New York: St. Martin's Press, 1982), p. 48; David T. Schiller, "The European Experience," in

Brian M. Jenkins, ed., *Terrorism and Personal Protection* (Boston: Butterworth Publishers 1985), p. 57; *Neue Zuercher Zeitung*, 6 October 1977.

12. *New York Times*, 16 September 1981.

13. RAF and Action Directe, *Für die Einheit der Revolutionare in West Europa* (Communiqué, January 1985).

14. Ibid.; *U.S. News & World Report*, 25 February 1985; *New Republic*, 1 April 1985; Gerd Langguth, "Euroterrorism: Fact or Fiction?" *Terrorism, Violence, and Insurgency* 7, no. 3 (1987), pp. 8-12; *Verfassungschutzbericht 1986* (Bonn: Federal Ministry of the Interior, 1987), p. 23.

15. Hans Josef Horchem, "Terrorism in Germany: 1985," in Wilkinson and Stewart, *Contemporary Research on Terrorism*, p. 155.

16. Bruce Hoffman, *Right-wing Terrorism in West Germany*, no. P-7270 (Santa Monica, Calif.: Rand Corp., 1986), p. 18; *Stuttgarter Zeitung*, 29 June 1982.

17. Quoted in *New York Times*, 1 May 1978; Peter H. Merkl, "Rollerball or Neo-Nazi Violence?" in Peter H. Merkl, ed., *Political Violence and Terror: Motifs and Motivations* (Berkeley: University of California Press, 1986), p. 236.

18. *Der Taggesspiegel*, 26 June 1981; Bruce Hoffman, *Right-wing Terrorism in Europe Since 1980*, P-7029 (Santa Monica, Calif.: Rand Corp., 1984), p. 6; *Kolner Stadt-Anzeiger*, 12 September 1984 and 25 June 1986.

19. Pluchinsky, "Political Terrorism," p. 53.

20. *New York Times*, 30 September 1970 and 26 February 1972.

21. *New York Times*, 18 September 1972; *Time*, 18 September 1972.

22. Ovid Demaris, *Brothers in Blood: The International Terrorist Network* (New York: Charles Scribner's Sons, 1977), p. 179. For a journalistic account of the incident, see Serge Groussard, *The Blood of Israel: The Massacre of the Israeli Athletes, the Olympics, 1972* (New York: William Morrow, 1975). Police planning, hostage negotiations, and rescue efforts are described in abbreviated form in *After Action Report of Terrorist Activities, 20th Olympic Games, Munich, West Germany, September 1972*, written by Dr. Manfred Schreiber, president of police, Munich (1972).

23. *Washington Post*, 12 March 1973; *New York Times*, 14 June 1974.

24. Stephen Clissold, "Croat Separatism: Nationalism, Dissidence and Terrorism," *Conflict Studies*, no. 103 (January 1979), p. 8; Pluchinsky, "Political Terrorism," p. 60; *Verfassungschutzbericht 1977* (Bonn: Federal Ministry of the Interior, 1978), p. 153; *New York Times*, 8 February 1976.

25. Quoted in *Allgemeine Zeitung*, 8 August 1988; *New York Times*, 5 January 1988.

26. Emerson and Duffy, *The Fall of Pan Am 103*, p. 218. See also Patrick Bishop and Eamonn Mallie, *The Provisional IRA* (London: Heinemann, 1987), p. 245.

27. *Der Tagesspiegel*, 20 February 1982.

28. *Frankfurter Rundschau*, 12 April 1985; *Globe and Mail*, 9 November 1985.

29. Clissold, "Croat Separatism," p. 14. The total number of murders that leaders of emigré organizations charge the Yugoslav secret service with is fairly accurate. In interviews with officials at the Verfassungschutz in Cologne, I was told that the number of Yugoslav emigrants killed by the UDBA during the 1960s and 1970s is around "two dozen." See also *Die Welt*, 25 February 1980; *Die Zeit*, 18 April 1980; *Der Spiegel*, 29 August 1983.

30. *Washington Times*, 9 October 1986 and 21 July 1987. See also Sean K. Anderson, "Iranian State Sponsored Terrorism," *Conflict Quarterly* 11, no. 4 (Fall 1991), pp. 19–34. The German warning to Iran is based on the author's private information.

31. Brian L. Davis, in *Qaddafi, Terrorism, and the Origins of the U.S. Attack on Libya* (New York: Praeger, 1990), pp. 116–18 argues that it is possible that both Syria and Libya were involved in the disco bombing. In January 1988, police arrested a West German woman in connection with the bombing. She was suspected of having planted the bomb on orders from Ahmed Hasi who, as noted in the text, was linked to Syria. *Washington Post*, 12 January 1988; *Boston Globe*, 12 July 1990.

32. Lewis J. Endinger, *West German Politics* (New York: Columbia University Press, 1986), p. 9.

33. *New York Times*, 9 March 1986. The countries included in the poll were Italy, France, Great Britain, West Germany, and the United States.

34. Allensbach Archiv, IfD-Umfragen 3049, 3053, 4076, 4081/I.

35. Ibid., IfD-Umfrage 4076; IfD-Umfragen, 3053, 3054, 4076; IfD-Umfrage 4087/I.

36. Miklkos Radvanyi, *Anti-terrorist Legislation in the Federal Republic of Germany* (Washington, D.C.: Library of Congress, 1979), pp. 36, 39, 128.

37. Erich Corves, "Terrorism and Criminal Justice Operations in the Federal Republic of Germany," in Ronald D. Crelinsten, Danielle Laberge-Altmejd, and Denis Szabo, eds., *Terrorism and Criminal Justice: An International Perspective* (Lexington, Mass.: Lexington Books, 1978), p. 94.

38. *New York Times*, 5 October 1972; US Congress, Senate Committee on the Judiciary, *West Germany's Political Response to Terrorism: Hearings Before the Subcommittee on Criminal Laws and Procedures*, 95th Cong., 2d sess., 26 April 1978 (Washington, D.C.: Government Printing Office, 1978), p. 8; Radvanyi, *Anti-terrorist Legislation*, p. 74.

39. *Die Zeit*, 24 February 1978; Radvanyi, *Anti-terrorist Legislation*, p. 62.

40. Testimony of Major John D. Elliott, in US Congress, *West Germany's Political Response to Terrorism*, p. 10.

41. Radvanyi, *Anti-terrorist Legislation,* p. 82.

42. *Christian Science Monitor*, 10 November 1986; Hans Josef Horchem, "The Decline of the Red Army Faction," *Terrorism and Political Violence* 3, no. 2 (Summer 1991), pp. 64, 73; *La Tribune d'Allemagne*, 16 June 1991.

43. *Washington Post*, 11 November 1972.

44. *Die Zeit*, 14 March 1975.

45. Becker, *Hitler's Children*, pp. 315–22.

46. Quoted in *Der Spiegel*, 28 April 1975.

47. *German Tribune*, 13 November 1977.

48. For details of Hamadei's arrest and his brother's role in the kidnappings, see *New York Times*, 16 January 1987; and *Die Zeit*, 23 January 1987; it was also confirmed in conversation with Klaus Gruenwald of the *Verfassungschutz*. It is alleged that Siemens AG, Schmidt's employer, and other private interests paid $2 million for Schmidt's release. *Washington Post*, 6 January 1988; *Baltimore Sun*, 27 January 1988.

49. *Stuttgarter Zeitung*, 20 April 1988; *Globe and Mail*, 18 May 1989.

50. It is believed that the Iranians tricked the captors by agreeing to hold Rudolf Cordes and then handed him over to the West Germans. *Los Angeles Times*, 14 September 1988 and 5 June 1989.

51. Quoted in Geoffrey Pridham, "Terrorism and the State in West Germany During the 1970s: A Threat to Stability or a Case of Political Over-reaction?" in Juliet Lodge, ed., *Terrorism: A Challenge to the State* (New York: St. Martin's Press, 1981), p. 49.

52. US Congress, *West Germany's Political Response to Terrorism*, p. 9:

53. *New York Times*, 11 March 1973; see also Sebastian Cobler, *Law, Order and Politics in West Germany*, trans. Francis McDonash (Harmondsworth, UK: Penguin, 1978), p. 55; and Guenter Lewy, "Does America Need a Verfassungschutzbericht?" *Orbis* (Fall 1987), p. 286.

54. *New York Times*, 8 May 1975; Christopher Dobson and Ronald Payne, *The Terrorists: Their Weapons, Leaders, and Tactics* (New York: Facts on File, 1982), p. 140.

55. *German Tribune*, 10 April 1975; David T. Schiller, "The Police Response to Terrorism," pp. 541–42.

56. *German Tribune*, 26 March 1978. The Horchel Report, an examination by an independent investigative agency assigned to analyze the Schleyer kidnapping affair, was particularly harsh on this point. The report prompted the resignation of Werner Maihofer, minister of the interior, in June 1978; Schiller, "The Police Response to Terrorism," p. 542.

57. *Frankfurter Allgemeine*, 4 April 1974; Schiller, "The Police Response to Terrorism," p. 541; *Suddeutsche Zeitung*, 6 February 1986; *Die Zeit*, 13 April 1974; *New York Times*, 10 May 1987; *Dusseldorf Handelsbatt*, 8 November 1983.

58. *German Tribune*, 12 April 1973.

59. Quoted in *German Tribune*, 18 October 1973.

60. Quoted in Rolf Tophoven, *GSG 9: German Response to Terrorism* (Koblenz: Bernard & Gaefe Verlag, 1984), p. 11.

61. Robert Harnishmacher, "The Federal Border Guard Group 9 Special: The German Response to Terrorism," *Royal Canadian Mounted Police Gazette* 49, no. 2 (1987), pp. 1–5. In 1987, the unit was 200 strong, divided into headquarters, communications, and three combat subunits, plus supporting services.

62. A detailed official account of the terrorist incident and the successful rescue operation is provided in *DOKUMENTATION zu den Ereignissen und Entscheidungen im Zusammenhang mit Entfuhrung von Hanns Martin Schleyer und der Lufthansa-Maschine "Landshut"* (Bonn: Presse-und Informationsamt der Bundesregierung, 2 November 1977).

63. *German Tribune*, 28 November 1982.

64. *Der Spiegel*, 19 May 1981.

65. John Newhouse, "The Diplomatic Round: A Freemasonry of Terrorism," *New Yorker*, 8 July 1985, p. 59; *German Tribune*, 27 January 1980.

66. *New York Times*, 16 November 1977.

67. *German Tribune*, 6 June 1986; Emerson and Duffy, *The Fall of Pan Am 103*, pp. 159–61, 166–67, 184–89. Questions still surround the placement of the bomb aboard Flight 103 at Frankfurt. See *Time*, 27 April 1992, pp. 23–24, 26.

68. Richard B. Lillich, *Transnational Terrorism: Conventions and Commentary* (Charlottesville, Vir.: Michie Co., 1982), p. 120. On the counter–terrorism implications, see Juliet Lodge, "Terrorism and the European Community: Towards 1992," *Terrorism and Political Violence* 1, no. 1 (January 1989), pp. 28–47; and K. G. Robertson, *1992: The Security Implications*, Occasional Paper no. 43 (London: Institute for European Defence and Strategic Studies, 1989), pp. 20, 22, 27–35.

69. *German Tribune*, 2 October 1977; *New York Times*, 9 May 1978; Jacob Sundberg, "Operation Leo: Description and Analysis of a European Terrorist Operation," in Brian M. Jenkins, ed., *Terrorism and Beyond: An International Conference on Terrorism and Low-Level Conflict* (Santa Monica, Calif.: Rand Corp., December 1982), pp. 174–202.

70. Pluchinsky, "Political Terrorism," p. 52; *Chicago Tribune*, 18 August 1978.

71. *Deutsche Presse-Agentur* (Hamburg), 20 August 1976; *Washington Post*, 4 October 1976.

72. Christopher Dobson and Ronald Payne, *Counterattack: The West's Battle Against the Terrorists* (New York: Facts on File, 1982), p. 101.

73. *Der Spiegel*, 13 August 1990, pp. 56–7. See also *Economist*, 23 June 1990; *Newsweek*, 2 July 1990; *Time*, 13 August 1990; *Montreal Gazette*, 14 June 1990; *Globe and Mail*, 8, 16 June 1990; Horchem, "Decline of the Red Army Faction," pp. 61–63; Scharlau and Philips, "Not the End," pp. 107–16.

74. *Washington Post*, 1 January 1977; *Los Angeles Times*, 15 January 1977.

75. *Suddeutsche Zeitung*, 29 May 1976; *New York Times*, 11 November 1977; *Washington Post*, 6 February 1985; *Stuttgarter Zeitung*, 8 April 1987.

76. *German Tribune*, 15 November 1987. See also, José Luis Nunes and Lawrence J. Smith, Co-Rapporteurs, *Sub-Committee on Terrorism Final Report*, (Brussels, Belgium: North Atlantic Assembly, January 1989), p. 10, Table 5; Office of the Ambassador-at-Large for Counter-terrorism, *Patterns of Global Terrorism: 1988* (Washington, D.C.: US Department of State, March 1989), pp. 34–35; and Edward F. Mickolus, Todd Sandler, and Jean M. Murdock, *International Terrorism in the 1980s: A Chronology of Events*, 2 vols. (Ames: Iowa State University Press, 1989), [covering period 1980–1987].

77. Quoted in *Guardian*, 22 February 1980, cited in David Freestone, "Legal Responses to Terrorism: Towards European Cooperation?" in Lodge, ed., *Terrorism: A Challenge to the State*, p. 215.

78. Quoted in *New York Times*, 11 August 1975.

79. Grant Wardlaw, *Political Terrorism: Theory, Tactics, and Counter-measures*, 2d ed. (Cambridge: Cambridge University Press, 1989), p. 122.

80. Quoted in *New York Times*, 14 March 1976; see also 19 January 1979 and 7 November 1978.

81. Quoted in *New York Times*, 19 January 1979.

82. *Times* (London), 20 July 1978.

83. *Suddeutsche Zeitung*, 11 February 1986.

4

Italy and International Terrorism

Robert H. Evans

INTRODUCTION

The casual observer of the Italian political scene in 1992 could be forgiven for being unaware that only a few years earlier, terrorism was a major issue in Italian politics. After all, in 1992, criminal violence by the Mafia was the dominant security problem.[1] Moreover, in 1989, more than 400 people charged with involvement in Red Brigades terrorism had been acquitted; the judges stated that the leftist group had never posed a serious threat to Italian democracy.[2] Yet there remains an undercurrent of fear that terrorism could return.[3]

Lying at the root of such fear is lingering suspicion that the indigenous terrorism of "the leaden years" (the late 1970s) was manipulated by sinister forces, some of which were foreign.[4] The Italian media contine to report revelations and allegations of international "connections" to terrorist incidents that occurred more than a decade ago.[5] This chapter will show that, even if occasionally overstated, these suspicions were not merely the product of fevered imaginations. International terrorism was a legitimate security concern for Italy throughout the 1970s and 1980s. Indeed, for Italy's political leaders, "terrorism of one form or another" had become "a normal aspect of the political process" by the late 1980s.[6] While domestic terrorism has been defeated, international terrorism has been far more difficult to control, given the endemic conflict in the Mediterranean region. Italy's geographic position, its system of global alliances and regional bilateral agreements, and its economic interests and patterns of trade all put Italy in the center of an area of tension and violence, which occasionally spilled over onto Italian soil.

The terrorist threat to Italy is the subject of the first part of this chapter. The chapter will then describe the political context in which responses were developed and, finally, the special measures undertaken to cope with the problem.

THE NATURE OF THE TERRORIST THREAT

Italy has been at the center of terrorist attacks in Western Europe, subject to over 14,500 violent incidents, 419 deaths, and some 1,400 injuries since 1969.[7] Forty-four percent of these occurred between 1978 and 1980, "the leaden years," and most of these terrorist actions were domestic in origin. They focused on Italian nationals, leaving among the victims statesman Aldo Moro and eighty-five people massacred by a bomb at the railway station in Bologna in 1980. Nowhere else in continental Europe did the attack on the state reach such proportions, and nowhere else did the state appear to offer so mild a deterrence to terrorist attacks. The intensity and seriousness of the domestic terrorist menace were not acknowledged quickly enough, and unfortunate delays occurred before the government organized a successful response. These delays imposed a heavy cost in life and in material destruction. The attempts to destabilize the country through a *strategia della tensione*[8] failed nevertheless, fundamental civil liberties were maintained, and, when jolted, the system devised effective legal responses to indigenous terrorism. By the mid-1980s, domestic terrorism was close to complete defeat. "Without their traditional leaders, . . . [the Red Brigades] can rely on only a few dozen diehards committed to a hopeless ideology," stated Interior Minister Antonio Gava, in his address to the Italian Senate on 26 April 1988. He went on to note that in the past the terrorist groups "comprised hundreds and hundreds of full-time members, thousands of supporters and many sinister individuals, 'evil masters' and instigators of criminal activity" who now had been "defeated, dismantled, and dispersed primarily on the political plane rather than the military plane."[9] Gava's comments concerned leftist terrorism specifically, but were equally applicable to the neo-fascists. Their ability to carry out spectacular bomb massacres notwithstanding, the para-military extreme right was a spent force by the middle of the decade.[10]

The first episodes of international terrorism in post-war Italy occurred in 1946, when some 250,000 German-speaking South Tyrolese sought to be reattached to Austria. Agreements between the two states in 1947 and in 1969, followed by the implementation of a regional statute providing near total autonomy to the German-speaking population and making it the "most spoilt minority group in the world," reduced tensions to a considerable extent. Nevertheless, with the support of extreme-rightist Austrian groups, alto-altesini terrorists continued into the 1980s to bomb Italian targets and then seek refuge in Austria, Switzerland, and Germany. Violence escalated considerably during the 1988 electoral campaign. It led, however, to the establishment of close links between the Italian police and their Austrian and German counterparts.[11]

By virtue of its location, Italy has also been a focus for political terrorism spilling over from the Middle East, and the first incident of this type also took place in 1946. On 31 October the *Irgun Zvai Leumi*, a Jewish Zionist insurgent group involved in a campaign to force Britain out of the Palestine Mandate, set off a bomb at the British embassy in Rome, causing extensive damage. In June 1947, the Stern Gang, another Jewish terrorist group, mailed a series of letter bombs from Italy to Britain.[12]

Middle Eastern terrorism returned to Italy in the 1970s, principally in the form of actions by substate groups such as the Palestinians, Armenians, and, later, Shiites. The picture was complicated by rivalries between such groups or factions within them and by the involvement of state agents from countries such as Libya and of the transnational criminal underworld, trafficking in drugs and guns. Groups that claimed to represent the Palestinian people, notably the Palestine Liberation Organization (PLO) and its many warring factions, were responsible for at least two separate periods of terrorist activity in Italy, separated by a lengthy truce. In the early 1970s, Palestinian terrorism in Italy culminated with an attack on a Pan Am plane at the Rome airport on 17 December 1973. A Palestinian commando group calling itself The Front Against the Conference on the Palestinian Question carried out the particularly murderous assault with phosphorous bombs, which killed thirty-four passengers, mostly Americans.[13]

A serious recrudescence of Middle Eastern terrorism affected Italy in the 1980s. The busiest year, 1985, saw twenty international incidents, including attacks on the offices of Jordanian Airlines and the Jordanian embassy, the hijacking of TWA Flight 847 in June, the bombing of the Café de Paris and the British Airways offices in September, the hijacking of the Italian cruise ship *Achille Lauro* in October, the foiled attempt against the US embassy in November, and a second massacre at the Rome airport (27 December), where seventeen people were killed by an Abu Nidal faction suicide squad.[14]

With the exception of the period 1979–1981, the Armenians were not especially active in Italy. They were dependent on fellow citizens long established in Rome who were kept under close surveillance by the Italian security services, which had been able to penetrate their groups.[15] The activity of Shiite terrorists, to whom one murder in 1984 is attributed, was also quite limited due to the security services' careful monitoring of Iranian diplomats and citizens. There is also some evidence that until the mid-1980s, the Italian security services maintained close relations with Shiite leaders in Beirut. However, Lebanese Shiites carried out the hijacking of TWA Flight 847 enroute from Rome to Athens.[16]

Prior to 1983, Muammar Qaddafi's secret police killed several Libyan refugees in Rome, while in 1984 and 1985 the Libyan ambassador and the press attaché were assassinated by Libyan opposition groups and two Libyan refugees were gunned down, probably by agents of the Libyan regime. In 1983, there was an unsuccessful attempt on the life of the Jordanian ambassador, and a Syrian Boeing 727 was firebombed before takeoff from the Rome airport. It has also been reported that a network of Shia Muslim politico-religious fanatics (organized in Rome by Ayatollah Hadi Khosraw-Shahi) was responsible for the assassination of PLO representative Ismail Darwish on 14 December 1984.[17] As to the assassination attempt on Pope John Paul II by the Turk Mehmet Ali Agca in 1981, evidence of the so-called Bulgarian connection was insufficient to gain a conviction. However, suspicion lingers and the final verdict remains open.[18]

International terrorist activities, usually centered in Rome, mainly involved attacks on foreigners by foreigners, whose political agendas had little or nothing to do with Italy. However, their occurrence in a country already plagued by internal violence enhanced the destabilizing effects of domestic terrorism, and, of course, Italian citizens were sometimes the unintended casualties of these "foreign wars." Yet it is equally important to note that domestic Italian terrorism also had various international dimensions.

On 16 March 1978, Aldo Moro, leader of the Christian Democratic party and former prime minister, was abducted from his car, and his five bodyguards were assassinated. He was held captive for fifty-four days and then killed. The military-like precision of the operation and the fact that Moro's kidnapping occurred on the day that the Italian Communist Party (PCI) was to be brought into the governing coalition, as a result of Moro's political handiwork, led many Italians to believe that only foreigners could have pulled it off. Very quickly, American, German, Czech, Russian, and Japanese connections were sought, but in vain.[19] However, the inquiry conducted by the Joint Parliamentary Commission of the Senate and the Chamber of Deputies made abundantly clear the internationalization of Italian terrorism. That the Red Brigades (BR) maintained links with other European terrorist organizations, notably the German Red Army Faction, was well known. France, a refuge for some 300 Italian terrorists, served as a safe haven and a center for communications between the various groups through the Hyperion Institute language school, and this was occasion for serious tensions between the two states.[20]

While Moro was still a prisoner, spokesmen for the Palestinian movement informed the Italian minister of the interior that members of the movement "would seek information from any militant belonging to the organization who could have had contacts with the Red Brigades or with other groups that could know about the Moro operation";[21] Yasser Arafat appealed for his release. Informal contacts also took place between a BR representative (Mario Moretti) and the PLO in Paris, through the Hyperion Institute. But the Red Brigades dealt above all with minority and dissident groups of the PLO, notably with George Habash of the Popular Front for the Liberation of Palestine (PFLP). Impressed by their efficiency, Habash provided them with money and weapons to attack Israeli and North Atlantic Treaty Organization (NATO) targets. Jealous of and fearful for their autonomy, once they had obtained weapons, which flowed abundantly in 1979, the BR quickly reneged on their promises. By January 1981, most contacts appeared to have been discontinued.[22]

The threat of PCI entry into government made the BR (sometimes mistakenly considered an offshoot of the PCI) a prime target for infiltration by foreign intelligence services. During the Moro inquiry, it became clear that the Israeli Mossad had sought to penetrate the Red Brigades. In 1973, as proof of good faith, the Israeli services informed the BR that Marco Pisetta, considered a traitor to the

Brigades' cause and on the run, was living in Freiburg. He left Germany before a BR hit squad could reach him. Weapons and money were also offered in 1974. Israel appeared to pursue two objectives: First, the destabilization of Italy would make it more difficult for the PCI to enter government, where it would support a pro-Arab policy; and, second, an increasingly unstable Italy would make Israel appear more important in American eyes and lead to increased political, economic, and military support. The Moro commission notes

we should not forget that the Israeli motivation of their initiatives is confirmed by the position of the Israeli government, which, specifically in 1974, when President Leone and Prime Minister Moro are on official visit to Washington, has Prime Minister Rabin outline the risks the western system is exposed to by the political unreliability of Italy.[23]

The commission also mentioned the case of Richard Stark, an American operative who sought to penetrate the BR under the disguise of a Palestinian. Several members of *Prima Linea*, a rival leftist terrorist group, referred to a connection with the KGB via "the milanese Armando" (Maurizio Folini, a member of the *Comitati Rivoluzionari*), while all militants in the BR have denied ever maintaining any such contacts. Documentation is available on the relationship between *Autonomia* (a radical group linked to BR) and the Czech secret services, which provided monetary support via the Skoda automobile company representative in Italy. The Bulgarian secret services approached the BR following the kidnapping of US General James Dozier in 1981, and offered military and financial support in exchange of information.[24]

While acknowledging the internationalization of Italian terrorism, the commission clearly underlined that it was foremost a national phenomenon, which held foreign intelligence services at arm's length, but greatly benefited from Palestinian arms supplies, especially in 1978 and 1979. The commission also noted that since the crisis of the BR in 1983, and in "coincidence with a deterioration of the international situation, [Italian terrorists] could become open to troublesome foreign influences."[25] It became common knowledge that Italian terrorists could be hired as hitmen, and that Middle Eastern terrorist groups and the Mafia utilized their services.[26] The reverse may also have been true. In December 1991, Italian police arrested a Palestinian member of the Abu Nidal group in connection with the 1988 assassination of Senator Roberto Ruffilli. Responsibility for the killing had been claimed by the *Partito Communista Combattente* (Fighting Communist Party), and a number of Italians had been arrested for the crime.[27]

The Byzantine ramifications of international terrorism were highlighted in what has been called the Italian "Irangate." Initially, the illegal sale of mines to Iran, via Spain and Syria, was solely a scandal involving a prominent Italian arms manufacturer. The affair became more complicated in September 1987 when the Finance Police intercepted a freighter carrying weapons and narcotics. Documents left by the alleged middleman established a connection between the mines sale and the shipment of weapons and drugs. The prosecutor's office claimed to have evidence that the arms were being brought to Italy for Arab terrorists associated with the Abu Nidal group. Up to seven boats were involved in shipping the illegal mines from Italy to Syria and in bringing the weapons to the terrorists and the drugs to the Mafia. The drug money, recycled in dollars, covered part of the costs of the illegal arms shipments.[28]

Much of the abundant writing by Italian terrorists has been devoted to attacks on the bourgeois capitalist state and has taken on an internationalist flavor aimed at the multinational companies dominated by American interests. Italy was accused of conducting an imperialist and warmongering foreign policy contrary to its true interests, and its people were urged by the terrorist groups to abandon membership in NATO.[29] According to the government, in the early 1980s, leftist terrorist groups made a concerted effort to mobilize Italian pacifist groups in order "to increase the anti-western orientation of the contestation, to provoke incidents with the forces of order, to instrumentalize . . . convinced and good faith pacifists and transform this group into a culture for terrorist activity."[30] It was the weakness of the indigenous terrorist groups that led them to an internationalist reorientation to shore up their declining strength. "The concept of internationalizing the armed struggle is a common factor, on which all the factions that contain remnants of terrorism have aligned, albeit with slightly different orientations, and including those which so far had given scarce attention to such objectives."[31]

Thus, Italian terrorism became Euroterrorism. Its first manifestation in Italy was the kidnapping of US and NATO General James Dozier in Verona in December 1981. Subsequent actions included the assassination in Rome in February 1984 of Leamon Hunt, the American director of the peace-keeping Multinational Force and Observers in the Sinai, and the killing in March 1987 of General Licio Giorgieri by the Red Brigades, who (mistakenly) believed that he was responsible for Italian participation in the American "Star Wars" program.[32] Like their European counterparts, the Italian security services concluded that while a common leftist ideological matrix provided the inspiration for the Euroterrorist assassins, there were no systematic links among the Red Brigades, the Red Army Faction, and *Action directe*. Rather, connections and collaboration were casual, based on individuals who were acquainted with each other and who had as their major aim the provision of safe houses, travel documents, and weapons. Similar links—of mutual convenience and revolutionary solidarity—with the Abu Nidal faction may explain the latter's involvement in the Ruffilli assassination.[33]

The nature of the problems that provided the engine for international terrorist activities was totally different from the social, political, and economic factors that drove domestic terrorism. So containing international terrorism was not only a military, a police, or a judicial task; it was also political. Thus, one finds that the Italian response to international terrorism was rooted in international politics and foreign policy.

THE RESPONSE

Political Setting and Policy-Making

Italian responses to the terrorist threat, whose international dimensions were important for the foreign policy of the country, but not critical for the physical safety of its citizens, were determined by a series of complex and interacting factors. Of primary importance were the stable/unstable equilibria of the political coalitions that determined the survival or demise of Italian governments (which have numbered about fifty since World War II). In turn, these have produced foreign and military policies that were seldom unified and were occasionally incoherent. Furthermore, the historical divisions of the police forces implied multiple sources of enforcement and conflicts of jurisdiction, while the Italian security services were reorganized several times during the period when Italy was most severely affected by international terrorism. The politicization of the judiciary and the fact that the people were accustomed to internal terrorist activities must also be taken into account.

There is some truth to the perception that the Italian political system consists of unstable and weak coalitions, manipulated by a gerontocratic political class and multiple parties striving to gain the upper hand in frequently changing governments. Italy's coalition governments seldom have been characterized by effective decision-making; Italy is the country of *leggine* (collections of individual laws), rather than of all-encompassing legislation. But Italy is also the country where the often-divided party of relative majority, the Christian Democrats (DC), pulls together when its fundamental interests are threatened, and where parties sometimes considered to be polar opposites, such as the PCI and the DC, can join forces together as in the *compromesso storico* (historic compromise), to face a serious crisis such as terrorism.[34]

Compromise, in fact, permeates Italian political culture, which emphasizes the containment, transformation, and diffusion of conflict situations and the need to reach negotiated solutions. This has affected the way the country's leaders dealt with terrorism, national and international, as well as the way the people perceived the problem. The undeniable effectiveness of the legislation that underpinned the defeat of indigenous terrorism was based less on the increase in the severity of sanctions than on the reduction of those sanctions for terrorists willing to collaborate, "to compromise" with the state that sought to reintegrate them, "to coopt" them back into society. Likewise, international terrorists were not cast as absolute villains, however despicable their acts, but rather as members of groups with which some agreement or compromise must be possible, and from which all parties involved should derive some benefit.

The Italian people do not give high priority to matters of foreign policy, and their politicians are free to follow divergent policies. In a broader context, Italy has three main foreign policy lines and interests: European (European Community or EC), Atlantic (NATO), and Mediterranean. Over the last two decades, Italy has come to play a more significant and important role in the first two as the country's economic situation has improved, increasing Italy's commitment to them and leading it to switch from a low profile in the Mediterranean to an activist policy in that area. This is clear in terms of the Arab-Israeli conflict and international terrorism. In fact, the *classe politica* has at least two Mediterranean policies: The small Republican and Liberal parties align closely with the United States, while the Christian Democrats, Socialists, and Communists consider Washington brash and imprudent in its dealings in the area. These differences create tensions and difficulties in problem solving. However, at a minimum, on matters involving international terrorism, all the Italian parties emphasize the need to search for peaceful political solutions, rather than military ones—solutions that are based on compromise and negotiation, rather than on force, and that ultimately favor Italian foreign policy in the Mediterranean region.

The general framework of Italy's response to international terrorism was outlined by Prime Minister Arnaldo Forlani in a debate held in the Chamber of Deputies on 3 February 1981, and this position is widely accepted in Italy today:

The World reality of these years indicates how terrorism in many situations has dimensions and aspects that are function[s] and dependant[s] of international conflicts and that it has become an element of interference in the affairs of many states in a general context that has all the connotations of a true and real surrogate war . . . . Terrorism and surrogate warfare will be the strategic problem of the next ten years because conventional and nuclear wars are too expensive and too dangerous to wage. In substance, terrorism has revealed itself through a series of circumstances as a new element of the relationship among states . . . . [And we must not] overlook the fact that our country is centered in a precise context of alliances and can be a critical point on the international checkerboard, and a possible point of pressure considering the fragility of its internal social and political equilibrium, and its economic, cultural and geographical importance that lead it to play a key strategic role in the Mediterranean.[35]

Italy quite naturally has always had an active Mediterranean foreign policy, with an economic and cultural focus since 1945,[36] concentrating in the 1970s and 1980s primarily on Yugoslavia, Libya, Tunisia, Egypt, Iran, and the Horn of Africa. But since the 1960s, the fundamental characteristics of Italy's Mediterranean foreign policy, as a consequence of the internal political debates and divisions in the DC, have been the lack of coordination and the action and reaction of different power centers: economic (Fiat, ENI, Oto-Melara), political (Christian Democrats, Republicans, Socialists, and Communists), and personal (Fanfani, Moro, Andreotti, Craxi).[37] This has led to what may be viewed as an inconsistent foreign policy (for example, Italy developed extensive commercial links with Libya *following* the 1970 expulsion from Libya of several thousand Italians) or, as an extremely pragmatic one.

Italy quickly accepted the pro-revolutionary and pro-Arab orientation of her oil industry, which in 1985 obtained 61.2 percent of its petroleum imports from the Middle East, with one-half coming from Libya, Egypt, and Algeria. Fifty percent of all EC exports to Libya in the mid-1980s were Italian, several thousand Italians worked there, credits extended to the country exceeded 100 billion lire, and Italy received between one-fifth and one-sixth of its petroleum from that country. Of Italy's foreign trade, 14 to 15 percent was with the Middle East (compared to only 9 percent with the United States). Economic circumstances dictated that Italy espouse a pro-Arab policy, and this has been a consistent line of Italian diplomacy. But the different nuances are well illustrated in what may be termed the "Moro" and the "Andreotti-Craxi" lines.

Moro's policy remained pro-Arab. It was somewhat neutral toward the PLO until Italy became affected by the rivalries within that body, between the aggressively militarist wing led by Abu Nidal and the slightly more conciliatory one headed by Yasser Arafat. Moro's policy then tilted toward Arafat for reasons that will become clear later. Italy's policy of the 1970s was reactive and motivated by a search for economic peace and accommodation with international terrorists. In contrast, its Mediterranean policy of the 1980s was an activist one, at times independent, at others cast in an EC framework. Terrorism at home was defeated, and three years of permanence for Bettino Craxi in the prime minister's office gave the country the confidence it had lacked for so long. Thus, Italy joined all the peace-keeping operations in the Mediterranean area and (somewhat reluctantly) dispatched a flotilla to the Persian Gulf during the latter stages of the Iran-Iraq war. Thus, Italy conducted a "diplomacy of attention, encouragement and good will in the narrow furrow of the Community tradition."[38]

The explosion of terrorism in 1985 quickly revealed that while Craxi and his foreign minister were in agreement on the need to find a solution to the Arab-Israeli conflict, the policies they proposed to reach that goal were quite different. Craxi, the Socialist, supported the national aspirations of the Palestinians, which he viewed as a legitimate goal. He believed that Italy should be directly involved in the process, seeking alliances with the moderate states (such as Tunisia, Egypt, and Jordan) and with the PLO, pursuing a line independent of the United States if necessary, and attempting to defuse the hostility that existed before 1989 between the Eastern and Western blocs. This would assert Italy's importance as an intermediate power. Giulio Andreotti, by contrast, was a practitioner of *realpolitik*; he believed that only the Arab states in the region could provide the solution to the Palestinian question. For him, it was essential not to divide the Arabs, so he supported all, including Arafat, Assad, Mubarak, and Qaddafi, which meant that he supported none in particular.[39] The reactions of both men to international terrorist incidents and to the Libyan-American confrontation differed considerably.

Membership in NATO and the very close links maintained with the United States represented an additional complicating factor in the difficulties Italy faced when confronted by international terrorism. This became evident during the *Achille Lauro* crisis, the US bombing of Tripoli in April 1986, and the attempted Libyan missile attack on the Italian island of Lampedusa, launched in response to the US raid. First, there was a fundamental disagreement between Italian and

American interpretations of international terrorism, which helps explain the difficulties that developed between the two partners. For the United States, international terrorism was a global phenomenon whose boundaries were fluid and whose manifestations affected the United States directly or indirectly. The Italians perceived matters differently; from their perspective, Shiite terrorism affected the US directly in an immediate way, although its geographic limitations made it less international, while Palestinian terrorism, which had strong international relevance and visibility, only considered the United States an indirect target. But, curiously, the United States had covertly and openly bargained with the Shiites and had intervened militarily against Palestinian terrorist supporters such as Libya. This is exactly the opposite of what the Italians expected,[40] so a degree of confusion and misunderstanding was inevitable.

Second, the political consequences of international terrorism for Italian-American relations were very significant, as the *Achille Lauro* and the Libyan crises demonstrated. The seizure of an Italian cruise ship off the coast of Egypt by a Palestine Liberation Front (PLF) terrorist squad in October 1985, the holding of its passengers as hostages, and the assassination of an elderly and handicapped US citizen comprised one of the most dramatic international terrorist acts committed against Italy. A quick release of the passengers was sought, and both Egypt and the PLO were involved in the negotiations, which led to the surrender of the terrorists in Alexandria in exchange for an Egyptian agreement of safe conduct out of the country. Italy used its privileged relationship with Egypt and with Arafat, who conducted the negotiations in person (and received public thanks from Craxi). The agreement, which sought to downplay the whole matter, was probably based on a rather hypocritical Italian refusal to admit the death of Leon Klinghoffer until the terrorists were in Egyptian hands.

The plane that flew them out of Egypt, with Abu al-Abbas (the organizer of the operation) traveling on an Iraqi diplomatic passport, was forced down by US interceptors onto the Italian base at Sigonella. Fifty Italian Carabinieri approached the aircraft and were quickly surrounded by an equal number of the US Delta Force, which in turn found itself hemmed between two groups of Italian forces. A standoff ensued until, in a series of telephone calls between Craxi and President Ronald Reagan, it was agreed that Italy would exercise jurisdiction over the passengers of the Egyptian plane. Abu al-Abbas was released, allegedly on the basis of lack of incriminating evidence (a decision reversed too late), and the four terrorists were tried and convicted later in Genoa.[41]

The incident caused the gravest crisis in Italian-American relations in the post-war period. Upon seizure of the vessel, a clear contrast developed between Italian policy—which called for negotiation—and the US desire to intervene militarily, although the ship was under exclusive Italian jurisdiction.[42] Further tension developed when US military forces threatened their ally's Carabinieri on their own soil; it was increased when the Italians released Abu Abbas after rejecting evidence provided by the FBI.[43]

Craxi, discussing the episode in the Italian Parliament, expressed his "surprise and bitterness for the non-recognition by a friendly government of all that the Italian government had done" and while he hoped that a climate of friendship would be reestablished, it would have to be in the context of the full "respect of the dignity and national sovereignty of the respective countries."[44] Only a "Dear Bettino" letter from President Reagan finally defused the crisis.[45] By that time, Craxi had already resigned as prime minister, but continued to head a caretaker coalition government. For the first time in the history of the republic a government had fallen over a foreign policy crisis. The Republican party challenged Craxi on the lack of collegiality he had shown in making decisions, while the true disagreement rested on the divergence between Craxi's independent Mediterranean policy and Republican Minister of Defense Giovanni Spadolini's desire to see Italy follow a policy closer to that of the United States.

The same issue reemerged during the escalating crisis between the US and Libya in the spring of 1986. In an address to the Italian Parliament on 25 March, Craxi declared, "We don't want war on our doorstep," and on 15 April he stated in the Italian Senate that "Far from defeating terrorism, as we have advised on several occasions, such military actions risk increasing further explosions of fanaticism, extremism, and criminal and suicidal action."[46] Italy deplored the US attack on Libya as destabilizing and dangerous, and the Craxi government refused to acknowledge its effectiveness as a deterrent to Libyan terrorism. Furthermore, while Craxi stated on 4 June that Italian-American cooperation against international terrorism should set an example for others, he withdrew the Loran base of Sellia Marina on Lampedusa Island (the target of a Libyan reprisal missile attack) from under the control of the US Coast Guard and put into discussion the extension of NATO policy on the southern Mediterranean.

On 12 June, in a speech at the World Affairs Council in Philadelphia, Andreotti, the minister of foreign affairs, outlined the Italian position very clearly to the Americans: "It is an error to contrast your strong America,—strong in her principles that we all admire—to a Machiavellian and unreliable Europe. We must prevent international terrorism from provoking a separation, a decoupling between the United States and Europe, in other terms that it may succeed where the Soviet Union failed when it deployed its SS20."[47]

Finally, the repercussions of terrorist activity and military reprisals on Italian–American commercial relations were also striking. In 1986, American tourism to Italy declined by 80 percent, forcing the Italian Tourist Office to launch a $5 million campaign to bring Americans back. On 15 May 1986, the US Department of Defense suspended an $8 million contract with Fiat-Allis for the production of 178 earth-moving machines for the Marine Corps, pending further clarification of Libya's financial interest in Fiat.[48] These reactions, natural in the case of tourists and petty in the other case, indicated that international terrorism had serious, but not drastic, consequences for the *economic* dimension of American-Italian relations. Nevertheless, both Craxi and Andreotti made it perfectly clear to US Undersecretary of State Michael Armacost on 4 June 1986, that Italy's position in the Libyan affair would remain limited to diplomatic sanctions agreed on by the EC, and that the need to maintain petroleum imports would prevent Italy from engaging in any kind of embargo.

This was not a rejection of international cooperation against terrorism, but rather a reaffirmation of Italy's preferred approach to the problem, which emphasized diplomacy and compromise. Italy firmly condemned all terrorist activity, though "expressing comprehension for the causes of Middle Eastern terrorism." Craxi stated that "No system of prevention or repression of terrorism can give us the peaceful and free life to which we aspire, unless terrorism can be fought through political and diplomatic means, where it is born, in the wars, the sufferings, the injustice, the atrocities which take place daily in the Mediterranean." He went on to add that

If the Palestinian national question exists, if it has a foundation, if the Palestinians have a right to national revindication, the actions of the PLO must be measured by a certain yardstick which is the yardstick of history. I blame the PLO for its armed struggle, not because I believe it is not within its rights, but because I am convinced its armed struggle will lead to no solution.[49]

Nevertheless, in spite of these differences over Middle East policy in general, and the response to terrorism in particular, American-Italian relations were on a sound footing throughout the 1990–1991 Gulf crisis and War. The Andreotti government, with solid public support, cooperated fully with the US-led Coalition. Italy supported all resolutions against Iraq in the United Nations, committed air and naval forces to operations in the theater, and provided other forces for support and defensive measures in the eastern Mediterranean.[50]

Tensions also occurred with Israel. Craxi was severe in condemning the 1985 Israeli attack on PLO headquarters in Tunis, which then Foreign Minister Andreotti would later compare to the 1944 German massacre of Italians in Rome.[51] Israeli criticisms were equally cutting following the *Achille Lauro* incident, when the hijackers were seeking the release of terrorists from Israeli prisons. The Italian position remained that "an examination of the context shows that armed struggle and terrorism . . . will not resolve the Palestinian question. But [we] do not question the legitimacy of the use of force which is different." Israel considered this as an "ideological justification of PLO terrorism."[52] Tension was again visible following Khalil Al-Wazir's assassination in Tunis in March 1988 and the Israeli handling of the *Intifada* (The Palestinian uprising), which led to a worrisome increase of anti-semitism in Catholic publications, including some emanating from sources close to the Vatican and to the DC.[53] But this has not altered Italian conviction about the fundamental correctness of its Mediterranean policy, in relation to Italian national interests. Those interests, more than anything else, dictated Italy's approach to containing international terrorism. Along with the other complicating factors that influence Italian politics, they influenced the application of legal and security measures to deal with the problem.

Anti-terrorist Legal Measures and the Judiciary

A substantial part of the legislation dealing with national terrorism was also applicable to international terrorists. But, in responding to domestic terrorism, the republican state depended initially on the outdated, partially revised civil code of the fascist period, which was not well adapted to the new circumstances. Moreover, legal procedure dictated that justice proceed at a pace incompatible with the load it had to confront.[54] A third, and more important, factor was the guarantee of fundamental rights in the Italian constitution. It explicitly invokes the need for judicial intervention before the police can seek to limit those rights. This made the task of the police more difficult, although more democratic. The Constitutional Court, established in 1956, also emphasized that the maintenance of public order had to be fully compatible with the maintenance and preservation of fundamental rights.

The Italian penal code, in articles 271 and 273, makes unlawful "associations intent on destroying or undermining the national sentiment" and "unauthorized international associations." Article 285 imposes a life sentence on "whoever attacking the security of the State, commits an action which leads to devastation, pillage or slaughter," and article 306 prohibits armed bands. Outside of a state of war, national terrorist organizations are dealt with in articles 270 and 270bis, which address "Subversive associations with a program of violence" and "Terrorist or subversive associations."[55] A judge could extend these national anti-terrorist laws to international terrorism.

Between 1974 and 1987, Italy passed a series of laws that centered on increasing police powers (Law No. 152, 22 May 1975, known as *Legge Reale*), doubling the severity of sanctions (Law No. 15, 6 February 1980), and rewarding terrorists willing to cooperate with police (Law No. 304, 29 May 1982; Law No. 34, 18 February 1987).[56] These laws provided the police with the means to detain, stop, and search individuals, Italian or foreign, who were thought to associate with extremist groups or the Mafia. In case of suspicion or available circumstantial evidence of participation in attacks utilizing military weapons or explosives, suspects could be detained and isolated for a time sufficient to pursue proper inquiries, subject to immediately informing the public prosecutor, who was required to question the suspect within forty-eight hours and either release or detain him/her. In exceptional circumstances, such as those that prevailed during the Moro kidnapping, police could search individuals and their vehicles, without a warrant, to ascertain if they were in possession of weapons. Wiretapping was facilitated. In executing an arrest warrant against anybody involved in suspected terrorist activity, upon authorization of the public prosecutor (obtained even by telephone),

officers of the judiciary police may proceed to search premises, including entire buildings, and blocks of buildings, where they have reason to believe that the person, or things that could be subject to seizure or indices that could be destroyed, may be located. In case of necessity or utmost urgency the officers of the judiciary police may also proceed without authorization of the competent magistrate, subject to informing the public prosecutor as soon as possible. [57]

In short, the police gained the means to arrest and detain suspected terrorists, and judges witnessed a doubling of the severity of the sentences they were required to impose. From the perspective of the Italian left, this meant that judicial discretion was increased at the expense of individual rights, defendants were less free, penal justice was in the hands of the police, and lawyers were absent at critical junctures. In other words, Italy was moving closer to becoming a police state. However, the applicability of the most extreme measures was limited in time (six months to one year). Moreover, in a referendum held 11 June 1978, 76.5 percent of the Italian people supported the *Legge Reale*, the basis of all new anti-terrorist legislation.[58] With this, the state had the means, and the popular support, to dismantle most of the domestic terrorist network.

It was, however, neither the increase in the severity of sanctions nor the increase in police powers that led to the end of terrorist violence in Italy; Italian legislators decided that magnanimity would produce better results against the terrorists. As early as 1980, Law 15 (known as the Cossiga Law) permitted the courts to reduce sentences significantly for those terrorists willing to cooperate with the police. The law produced immediate results. Beginning with Patrizio Peci, captured shortly after the law came into effect, Red Brigades members came forward and provided information to the authorities in exchange for prospects of reduced punishment. The government then enacted legislation that systematically encouraged cooperation from repentant terrorists. Law 304, Measures in Defense of the Constitutional Order (1982), established a reduction of sentence equivalent to at least one-third of the time for those terrorists who would dissociate themselves from their companions. For those who helped the police and the judiciary obtain decisive evidence leading to the identification or capture of terrorists with whom the *pentiti* had consorted in the crimes they had confessed, life sentences were reduced to ten to twelve years, and other prison sentences were halved, and not to exceed ten years. In cases of exceptional information, sentences could be further reduced by one-third, bringing a life sentence down to seven to nine years' time.

In February 1987, the minister of justice offered terrorists a slightly less generous "final" law (No. 34), a message of pacification entitled Measures in Favor of Those Who Dissociate Themselves From Terrorism. It was cast in the spirit of Law 304, which had depenalized serious crimes by granting conditional liberty to terrorists who had served half of their sentences; the 1987 law proposed conditional liberty only for terrorists who had less than ten years to serve.[59] By enacting these laws, the legislators sought to break a cycle of violence, to coopt jailed terrorists and eventually return them to society. It was a political gambit that appears to have succeeded. The domestic terrorist groups never fully recovered from the waves of arrests that followed the *pentiti's* confessions.

For international terrorists the situation was different. Since international terrorism was dealt with as a political/foreign policy issue related to events over which Italy had little control, policy and responses were flexible. On the one hand, raison d'état did lead to the release or the non-arrest and deportation of some terrorists, as in the case of Abu al-Abbas. On the other, if the magistrates chose to interpret in a restrictive way their discretion in applying the law, the Italian judiciary could be among the most severe in dealing with foreign terrorists arrested in Italy. So while the commando who attacked the Rome airport in 1973 was flown to Kuwait, the survivor of the 1985 massacre was given thirty years, the most severe sentence possible short of a life sentence (which was imposed on his leaders, including Abu Nidal, who were judged in absentia).[60]

In November 1984, a group of terrorists belonging to the Islamic Jihad was arrested while planning an attack on the US embassy in Rome. One was picked up at the Zurich airport carrying detonators and explosives; seven were stopped in Rome. The Swiss sentenced their prisoner (who pleaded that he intended to commit a political act) to eighteen months in jail, suspended the sentence, and sent him off to Beirut. In exchange, the Swiss chargé d'affaires who had been kidnapped in Beirut was freed.[61] By contrast, the Italians released two of the accused for lack of proof, but imposed sentences of fifteen years on three of the Lebanese co-conspirators.

The situation of the *Achille Lauro* hijackers was somewhat unique because Italy had negotiated with Egypt and agreed that they would receive safe conduct upon release of all the passengers. Taken into custody by Italy, after having been forced by US aircraft to land there, and the death of an American at their hands being known and undeniable, they were judged and condemned to sentences varying from thirty years for the killer to seven to eleven years for his accomplices. Many in the United States considered their punishment mild, but the president of the Assizes Court noted that the accusation that they were an armed band (article 306) had not been sustained because the PLF was not acting against the Italian state: "[The] essential objective of the PLF is to liberate Palestine, utilizing terrorism when necessary, not to damage the Italian state."[62] While Italy's security forces recognize the political imperatives that underlie the republic's approach to international terrorism, they have expressed frustration when inconsistent sentences were handed down. Such inconsistency can be attributed to the nature of the judiciary.

The Italian judiciary is characterized by contradiction: its independence *and* its politicization. It is divided between those on the right, who endorse a restrictive view of the judicial role, and the majority on the left, who are willing to grant the courts a political function. These divisions also apply to the magistrates dealing with international terrorism. Thus, Ferdinando Imposimato, *Giudice istruttore* in the Tribunal of Rome, whose views are quite representative of the left and center, asserted that a judge, short of espousing a repressive view of the law and reacting to the effects but not to the cause of terrorism, cannot impose a sentence without taking into consideration the political context in which the events have occurred:

Furthermore, one cannot ignore that very often magistrates, during trials against exponents of international terrorism have been subject to solicitation in favor of the detainees by members of the government. Magistrates are usually asked to grant provisional liberty or domiciliary arrest, and internal and international reasons are given to justify this intervention. The relations between Italy and third countries that seek the release of the terrorists are invoked . . . . I must say I have never considered these interventions as uncalled for interference in my work or as symptoms of sympathy towards the terrorists, but rather as proper political initiatives taken in the interest of the country.[63]

Imposimato stressed that within judicial discretion (which in Italy is limited and explains the harsh sentences given to international terrorists), the judge should be fully sympathetic to a request coming from a government representative. In short, justice must take into account national interest. This view is not unique to Imposimato. For a large portion of the Italian judiciary, international terrorism is not considered a phenomenon to be dealt with by repressive measures. "Our judiciary policy of great firmness is not the best to contrast [sic] the phenomenon of international terrorism. It is evident that the arrest and the condemnation to severe sanctions has no deterrent power, and on the contrary produces ever more severe and indiscriminate reprisals against our country."[64]

In rejecting violence, but offering understanding for those who have erred, Italians accepted extensive legislation that in fact decriminalized terrorist acts and offered rewards for dissociation from terrorist groups. However, the people also expressed very little sympathy for granting amnesty to terrorists, national or international. Italians became supporters of the state in order to break the cycle of violence, whose origins extended beyond their national frontiers.[65]

Negotiations with Terrorists and Sponsors

As was stated at the beginning of this chapter, changing role of the terrorist and his or her possible acquisition of legitimacy complicate the analysis of the relationship between the state and terrorist groups. In the Italian case, this is clear in its relationships with the PLO and with Libya. The Italian official public position, under which the government refuses to negotiate with terrorists, particularly if they hold hostages, is similar to that of the United States. But Italy maintains special relations with the PLO and its leader, Yasser Arafat, who has visited Rome on several occasions and has met several Italian prime ministers. Because of his key position in the leadership of the Palestinian movement Arafat is a favored interlocutor. For example, it is alleged that the attack that resulted in the firebombing of the Pan Am plane at the Rome airport in December 1973 represented an effort by Abu Nidal to torpedo any agreement on the Palestinian question. Following this incident, Moro and his military advisor held informal negotiations in Cairo with both Arafat and Nidal, leading to an understanding that Italian targets would be spared and violence avoided in exchange for unhindered transit through Italian territory. Following Moro's death, and through the late 1970s, this arrangement remained in an off-and-on status, for periods of up to two months, depending on the relationships between the Italian security services and the PLO.[66] Since then, Arafat has served as the link between the Italian government and Middle Eastern terrorist groups.

The case of Qaddafi is more ambiguous due to his erratic behavior. For many years, he threatened Italy with war and demanded war damages for Italian action during World War II, but the Italians were careful not to provoke a break. This was made clear when the Libyan news agency declared the 1985 raid on the Rome airport a "daring operation undertaken by the sons of the martyrs of Palestine from the Sabra and Chatila camps."[67] A note published in reply by the office of the Italian prime minister indignantly stated, "Whoever has defined the attack on Fiumicino airport which was a barbaric slaughter as an act of heroism lifted the veils on a fanatic and blood thirsty face."[68] But the minister of foreign affairs more laconically expressed "stupor and disappointment" about Qaddafi's statement.[69]

As noted earlier, it is Italy's view that it must maintain relationships with all parties involved in the Israeli-Arab conflict, reconcile those relationships if possible, and maintain Italy's interests as necessary. This can mean indirect negotiations with terrorists, as may be required. The position is unofficial, unacknowledged, and in stark contrast to Italy's very active role in multilateral and bilateral cooperative enterprises aimed at defeating terrorism, which are discussed later.

Security and Intelligence

The Italian police forces comprise some 200,000 people, divided into three different corps, each with its different structures, rules, mores, and traditions of independence. These are the Corps of Public Safety, which comes under the minister of the interior; the *Carabinieri*, which are part of the armed forces and take orders from the minister of defense; and the Finance Police, which are subject to the minister of finance. In 1981, all three forces were demilitarized, grouped under the heading of *Polizia di Stato*, and placed under the coordinating direction of the Ministry of the Interior. However, this has eliminated neither the separate intelligence services of each corps, whose jurisdictions may include the control of international terrorism, nor the intercorps rivalries.[70]

The secret services have a checkered history in republican Italy. They were under the control of the Ministry of Defense until 1977, when they were reorganized in response to a series of scandals centering on the existence of confidential dossiers on the parliamentary and economic elites, involvement in neo-fascist terrorism, and the preparation of at least two military coups in 1964 and 1970. The reorganization of the services (Law 801, 24 October 1977), now known as the Service for Information and Security (SIS), tied them directly to the office of the prime minister (who can explicitly invoke a state secret clause). An interministerial committee for information and security (chaired by the prime minister and including the ministers of foreign affairs, interior, grace and justice, defense, industry, and finance) "plays a consulting and orientation role on the general direction and fundamental objectives to be followed in the framework of a policy of information and safety." It "assists the PM in elaborating a general policy of information and safety, and in the strategic determination of objectives to assign to the Services."

The services are divided into two branches—the Service for Information and Democratic Security (SISDE), which deals with internal affairs, and the Service for Information and Military Security (SISMI), which is in charge of external security—coordinated by the Executive Committee for the Services of Information and Security (CESIS). The CESIS is meant to ensure that the interministerial committee's directives are properly executed. In short, it is a controlling body; it also plays a functional role, collating the information gathered by the two branches, whose "spheres of action are contiguous and consequently the information produced by one must be completed by that of the other." The government explicitly stated this was not to be understood as a third branch or a "super service," though it has permanent personnel. The definition of the specific tasks of the two services in relation to each other and to the police forces presented serious political, functional, and administrative problems, and the delineation of the various areas of jurisdiction with respect to the interpenetration of military and political/institutional security has not been fully resolved.[71]

The crux of the matter is political, and in the 1980s, the services—while not ineffective—did not make a strong contribution to the struggle against international terrorism, as there was less coordination than was desirable and more territorial rivalries than were officially acknowledged. Furthermore, the "Secret of State" provision allowed the prime minister to pursue a foreign policy that avoided the scrutiny of the Parliamentary Control Committee of the Activities of the Secret Services. In 1981, political suspicions about the secret services were confirmed when, in the wake of the P2 scandal, it became known that the heads of both branches of the secret services and of the CESIS were members of P2. The services labored under the heavy shadow of continued association with right-wing subversion and terrorism, suffered from morale problems, and by the end of the decade had not rebuilt to a point where they could be considered fully effective against international terrorism.[72]

It is, of course, difficult to obtain information on the Italians' counter-terrorism intelligence methods. Both the secret services (SISMI and SISDE) and the Ministry of the Interior are naturally reluctant to discuss specific countermeasures they adopt, while the Parliamentary Commission to which the prime minister reports on matters of state security also remains vague and general in most of its reports. Several traits emerge nevertheless. In contrast to operations ten or fifteen years ago, increased importance is being given to long-term, ongoing research. As one person put it: "To truly understand terrorist motives you have to live several years in the areas where the groups are born."[73] The various services made a considerable investment in computerized data processing, specialized libraries, and training courses that deal with terrorism. The data banks were supposed to be accessible to the different police bodies, but this did not occur because interservice jealousies were not eliminated and each service sought to protect its own sources. In fact, the different services may have acquired more information through international collaboration than through sharing among themselves.

Overt surveillance, collection, and protection methods overlapped in a highly visible manner, particularly in Rome. Large numbers of police were assigned to surveillance of Middle Eastern diplomatic personnel and of students from the region. In Rome, the number of undercover and out-of-uniform agents appeared to be extremely high, as neighborhoods of the capital considered critical were carefully guarded on a twenty-four-hour basis. Mobile surveillance units and radio-linked patrols reportedly exceeded 1,000.

All of those interviewed leave considerable room for *fortuna* in the intelligence battle against international terrorism. They acknowledge that however effective their system of prevention may be, "there will always be a hole the terrorist can discover." The Italians maintain an extensive intelligence network abroad (especially in the Middle East), to which the late Prime Minister Moro attributed much importance—so much, in fact, that at one point during his ordeal, he expressed the hope that the head of Italian intelligence in Lebanon could negotiate his release. The network is said to have been effective, although it is not clear if its operatives were able to infiltrate terrorist groups. But, as noted earlier, their role in arranging a "truce" with the Palestinians has probably been just as important.

Security Forces

Legal and judicial frustrations notwithstanding, the efficiency of the Italian police has increased since 1975. Its effectiveness in dealing with national terrorism (greatly facilitated by the *Pentiti* laws) provided it with a considerable boost in morale and fostered an atmosphere where police personnel were more alert and confident that they could contribute to limiting international terrorist activities. The major Italian police operation against international terrorism was the rescue of General Dozier and the arrest of his kidnappers in Padua in 1982. The operation was spectacular and exclusively Italian, though American counter-terrorism intelligence personnel contributed to the investigation.[74] Some attribute the success to luck, others to methodical police work, and in a sense those are two essential ingredients in the fight against international terrorists. Since the Dozier kidnapping, the Italian police have been quite successful in controlling international terrorists in Rome. They arrested the attackers of Jordanian Airlines and of the Café de Paris in 1985 in less than an hour after the events and quickly identified the group that bombed the USO Club in Naples in April 1988: the Japanese Red Army (JRA).[75] Yet these incidents illustrate both the strengths and the weaknesses of Italian police action against international terrorists; in 1985, the attackers were students and/or residents in Rome, who were subject to regular surveillance; the "professional" JRA terrorists of 1988 evaded capture.

In this regard, one should distinguish between the *Carabinieri* and the other *Polizia di Stato*. The former are present in all Italian cities and most villages and are carefully attuned to notice the presence of foreigners. The latter operate against more specific local targets. But the task of both is complicated by the several million people from abroad who visit Italy every year. Specialized rapid-intervention forces (colloquially known as *le teste di cuoio*, "the leather-heads") can also be called on for tasks such as hostage rescue operations, the Dozier incident being a case in point.[76]

International terrorism has had a substantial impact on the military, not only in terms of its target-hardening tasks, but more so in the way in which the armed forces conceive of their task in the case of limited conflicts. This became apparent following US intervention in Libya and the Libyan reprisal missile attack on Lampedusa. The head of the general staff for southern Europe, General Lucio Innecco, was quick to declare that "if terrorism were to wage a series of actions— a massive reaction would become necessary against what we consider terrorist sanctuaries."[77] Italian military journals analyzed scenarios of terrorist actions, and the three armed services seized on the opportunity to request increases in their budgets and to modify their doctrines to provide new tasks for their forces. Defense spending continued to increase through the end of the decade. During the Gulf War, about 96 percent of the Italian army was mobilized to protect some 1,500 potential targets from possible terrorist attack.[78]

Target-Hardening

On 26 April 1988, Interior Minister Antonio Gava acknowledged that "almost 3,000 agents are employed in protecting 569 individuals—151 politicians, 279 magistrates, and 139 prominent economic and social figures . . . . There are also many others provided on 'justifiable request.'"[79] While these measures were put in place in response to domestic terrorism, they also served to prevent international incidents. For example, access to all ministries and some public offices calls for presentation and surrender of an identity document and for elaborate passage through metal detectors and armored doors under the watchful eye of heavily armed guards.

Embassies in Rome have become more like armed compounds than formal representative offices. Here Italian and national security measures combine. Italian police and the Secret Services provide outside surveillance. In many cases, private Italian guards secure the main gates and the walls of each embassy, with national guards protecting the interior of the buildings. The American embassy has various hydraulically operated gates and metal obstacles, and the metal railings are backed by green steel plates. All cars entering embassy grounds must submit to thorough internal and external inspections.

Railroads and airports are also subject to constant and careful scrutiny. The stations are entrusted to the *Polizia Ferroviaria* (Railroad Police) and the municipal police. Airport security is the task of the army, which provides armed patrols on the perimeter and carefully trained and heavily armed guards on the inside. Several international airlines utilize their own security personnel. Airport security involves considerable use of profiling; individuals of Middle Eastern appearance are systematically questioned and their luggage carefully examined. Beyond standard X-ray procedures, luggage in the major airports is run through compression chambers to test for explosives. As noted above, the army provided forces for target-hardening on a large scale during the Gulf War.

International Cooperation

There is a natural tendency among states "to avoid dealing with terrorism outside their borders . . . [especially] out of a desire to evade the difficult political problems sustained by a terrorist campaign."[80] The European states have sought, nevertheless, legal agreements on terrorism and especially on extradition. The Council of Europe has served as an important forum, condemning in May 1973 "acts of terrorism . . . whatever their cause," and inviting member governments "to reach a common definition of 'political infraction' so that such a 'political' justification could not be invoked each time a terrorist act endangers innocent lives."[81] On 17 January 1977, the European Convention for the Suppression of Terrorism (ECST) was signed. But it took Italy over eight years to ratify it, with reservations, in November 1985.[82]

But the convention has been a failure. Articles 5 to 13 allow states to introduce reservations (as Italy did), whereby each state is the sole judge of what it considers to be a political crime subject to extradition. Furthermore, the convention is not a treaty and creates no obligation on the state with regard to extradition. This became bitterly clear when Italy sought extradition from France of 120 individuals considered terrorists by Italy and granted asylum by France.[83] France did not ratify the ECST until 1986.

On 10 March 1988, in response to the *Achille Lauro* hijacking, and at Italian initiative, the International Maritime Organization convened in Rome and approved a convention against acts of terrorism on the high seas. It requires the signatories to hand down "adequate sentences" against those who commit crimes against navigation and to urgently develop international cooperation on practical and effective measures to prevent acts against the security of maritime navigation.[84]

Italy also sought to utilize its chairmanship of the Council of the EC to convince her partners of the need to act as a community and to provide some form of intermediation between the parties of the Arab-Israeli conflict. In preparation for assuming the presidency of the EC during the first part of 1985, Italy engaged in intense bilateral negotiations with most of the Arab states, the PLO, and the EC member states. Italy tried to move the EC Council beyond the statement of the December 1984 Dublin summit (which encouraged PLO involvement in the peace process), but at the end of its six-month presidency, no progress was evident. Following the attack on the Rome airport and the US imposition of economic sanctions against Libya, the EC on 27 January 1986, approved an embargo on weapons "to countries clearly implicated in supporting terrorism." On 14 April 1986, at a special meeting called by Italy and Spain, agreement was reached on limiting the numbers of Libyan diplomats in the member countries. But following the US bombing of Tripoli on 14–15 April, the European foreign ministers declared "that all must be done to avoid further military action," and Italy deplored the US operation. Nonetheless, diplomatic expulsion, restrictions, and other sanctions were continued or enhanced.[85]

On 6 May 1986, the heads of state gathered at the Tokyo summit condemned terrorism once again, but observers noted that "what is necessary is not a continuous gush of vibrant resolutions condemning terrorism, but rather the adoption of concrete measures."[86] Italy has been willing to undertake major initiatives in that area. The first was to bring together in 1977 the EC ministers of the interior and justice in what became known as the TREVI Group. It has held yearly meetings that foster more cooperation on technical matters between national police forces, and in April 1986, the ministers agreed to hold regular meetings. In September 1986, Italy proposed that diplomatic pouches be submitted to metal detectors, and the ministers of the interior unanimously agreed not to negotiate with terrorist states. In parallel to the TREVI Group, the so-called Geneva Group brings together the heads of the intelligence services, while the foreign ministers also analyze the problems of terrorism in regular meetings. "The groups analyze the phenomenon, and one group completes the others with optimum results. There are no reticences, we communicate well with each other," declared a highly placed Italian civil servant. A computerized system that tracks terrorists is now available to the European police forces and to Interpol, which also has entered data on terrorists into its files.[87] However, national files constitute the basic data bank, and many an Italian terrorist is not recognized as such by other nations.

The greatest success and collaboration have come among executives of the national police services, who now meet regularly. Many of the first connections were made at FBI-organized seminars, held at the FBI's Academy in Quantico, Virginia. The Police Working Group on Terrorism has been established to provide a forum for cooperation between European police forces. It has opened lines of communication that bypass the difficulties of official bureaucratic and political channels.[88]

At the bilateral level, Italy has entered into several agreements that relate to international terrorism. For instance, talks were held in February and December 1985 and in March 1986 between the Italian and British ministers of the interior, who revised a 1973 agreement, on extradition to include political crimes. Some twenty Italian neo-fascist terrorists who had sought refuge in Great Britain were subject to the agreement, though only one was immediately extradited to Italy. Italy signed a protocol with Egypt on 13 June 1985, which requires that the two parties appoint representatives of their security services who will maintain continuous contact, that they hold periodic meetings at political levels at least every six months and regular technical meetings between their respective police forces. Agreement was also reached to coordinate defense and security measures in ports and airports.[89]

Italy has signed several extradition treaties with the United States, which emphasize that criminal matters such as narcotics do not include crime that could be construed as political.[90] However, on 2 October 1984, Italy and the United States established a Commission Against Crime and Drugs, co-chaired by the US attorney general and the Italian interior minister. This commission served as a basis for regular exchange visits between Americans and their Italian counterparts at the highest levels (e.g. director of the FBI, head of the State Department's anti-terrorism operations, head of the Senate Judiciary Committee). The commission itself has met regularly twice a year. "Informed sources" all emphasize the excellent level of cooperation, mutual respect, and protection that exists among forces in the field. The successful prosecution in the US of JRA terrorist Yu Kukimura in February 1989 on charges of transporting bombs can be attributed in part to collaborative work done in Rome by American and Italian agents, who investigated links between Kukimura and the JRA members who bombed the USO Club in Naples in April 1988.[91]

On 1 January 1993, the Single Market came into effect throughout the EC under the terms of the Single European Act (1987). The principal aim of the Single Market was to permit the free movement of goods and services between EC member states. However, its provisions for the free movement of people, without border checks, have raised a host of internal security concerns (the control of terrorism being a case in point), which have not yet been fully resolved. Consequently, in November 1990, Italy signed the parallel Schengen Agreement, intended to compensate for the Single Market's more relaxed internal European borders by enhancing inter-European police cooperation and imposing stricter frontier controls at external points of entry to the signatory area. However, since not all the countries party to the Single Market had signed the Schengen Agreement, border controls between EC members did not disappear altogether in January 1993.[92]

CONCLUSIONS

The example of highly successful international collaboration provided by the Kukimura case may have been exceptional. On questions that are viewed as political and connected to foreign policy, such as Middle East terrorism, official Italian cooperation is often less forthcoming. Nonetheless, Italian leaders recognize that it is not in the country's interest to be seen as passive in the face of a problem it shares with many of its allies. This undoubtedly is why Italy has taken the lead in a number of international anti-terrorist initiatives, such as the founding of the TREVI group. Generally speaking, however, Italy sought to defuse international terrorism problems through foreign policy choices and interpreted terrorist events on its soil as actions against third parties, rather than against itself. In this way, Italy tried to "square the circle" of its Mediterranean interests and its European Community obligations. And this approach has not been without success.

Through careful police work Italy has been able to anticipate and prevent a number of international terrorist acts. It has also been willing to bring to justice terrorists who have been arrested. The Italian government is also fully cognizant of the fact that sanctions alone do not deter international terrorists. In its struggle against domestic terrorism, the state avoided creating an atmosphere that the country was at war. The powers of the police were extended, but fundamental liberties were maintained. Greater police powers of investigation were offset by providing legal opportunities for terrorists to recant, to reduce their penalties through cooperation, and thus eventually to reenter society. The guiding philosophy was that "You cannot militarize the country" because "in the long run cases of serious emergency become tiring in a democracy."[93]

This is not to suggest that there were no problems. These were manifest in a certain inertia in the Italian political system, in the politicization of the judiciary, in the division of the police forces, and in the dubious loyalties of the secret services. Thus, it is a testament to the underlying strength of Italian democracy that it did not succumb to the combined pressures of these problems and political terrorism. In this respect, Italy has set a remarkable example for other struggling democracies.

In spite of the fact that Italy was the site or jurisdiction of numerous international terrorist actions, including several involving horrendous murder, the Italian response to these events was usually cautious, but ultimately effective. Moreover, the response did not affect adversely Italian democracy or the liberties of its citizens. Out of experience with domestic terrorism, the governments of the day did not overreact, recognizing that international terrorism was only a minor threat to the state. By treating international terrorism principally as a foreign policy issue, Italian authorities effectively isolated it from those aspects of national policy where it might have interfered with democratic processes. If this approach occasionally complicated Italy's foreign interests, and irritated its allies, those problems could be overcome by diplomacy and compromise. Italy is likely to continue to treat international terrorism as a political problem which must be solved or contained by foreign policy means and for which police action is a necessary palliative and military intervention an unwelcome solution.

NOTES

1. See, for example, reports of Mafia attacks on the judiciary in *La Stampa*, 13 March 1992 and 13 June 1992; *International Herald Tribune*, 20 July 1992; *Le Nouvel Observateur*, no. 1446 (23–29 July 1992).

2. *Globe and Mail* (Toronto), 14 December 1989.

3. *Corriere della Sera*, 21 November 1992.

4. Francesco Sidoti, "Terrorism Supporters in the West: The Italian Case," in Noemi

Gal-Or, ed., *Tolerating Terrorism in the West: An International Survey* (London: Routledge, 1991), pp. 105–42. A more pointed, but persuasively argued, case for domestic and international manipulation of Italian terrorism can be found in Philip Willan, *Puppet Masters: The Political Use of Terrorism in Italy* (London: Constable, 1991).

5. See, for example, allegations of a Libyan connection to the 1980 Bologna bombing in *Corriere della Sera*, 21 July 1991.

6. Joseph La Palombara, "The Reality of Italian Politics," in *Italian Journal*, no 1 (1988), p. 16.

7. Sidoti, "Terrorism Supporters," p. 108, Table 5.1, citing the Interior Ministry; *Corriere della Sera*, 25 January 1988.

8. Since the "Strategy of Tension" was usually associated with the subversive activities and violence of the extreme right in Italy, Italian politicians initially tended to interpret the Red Brigades' actions as part of that strategy—a conspiracy of the right masquerading as the left. See David Moss, *The Politics of Left-wing Violence in Italy 1969–85* (New York: St. Martin's Press, 1989), p. 133; Robert C. Meade, Jr., *Red Brigades: The Story of Italian Terrorism* (New York: St. Martin's Press, 1990), pp. 36, 47–48, 53, 74, 156; and Leonard Weinberg and William Lee Eubank, *The Rise and Fall of Italian Terrorism* (Boulder, Colo.: Westview Press, 1987), pp. 9–10, 31–52.

9. US, Foreign Broadcast Information Service, Western Europe (FBIS-WEU) 88-086 (4 May 1988), p. 2.

10. Weinberg and Eubank, *The Rise and Fall*, pp. 48–49.

11. *La Repubblica*, 22 October 1987; Senato della Repubblica, X Legislatura, *Relazione sulla politica informativa e della sicurezza*, doc. XLVII, no. 1 (23 November 1986–22 May 1987), pp. 24–25; FBIS-WEU-88-097 (19 May 1988), p. 6; *Corriere della Sera*, 22 August 1988; Sidoti, *The Rise and Fall*, pp. 125–26.

12. David A. Charters, *The British Army and Jewish Insurgency in Palestine, 1945–47* (London: Macmillan, 1989), pp. 64–65, 75–76.

13. The incident is described in considerable detail in Edgar O'Ballance, *Language of Violence: The Blood Politics of Terrorism* (Novato, Calif.: Presidio Press, 1979), pp. 201–203.

14. On the *Achille Lauro* incident, see Antonio Cassese, *Terrorism, Politics and Law: The Achille Lauro Affair* (Princeton, N.J.: Princeton University Press, 1989), pp. 23–43. On the Rome airport massacre of December 1985 (which was carried out simultaneously with a similar operation in Vienna), see Edward F. Mickolus, Todd Sandler, and Jean M. Murdock, *International Terrorism in the 1980s: A Chronology of Events*, vol. 2 (Ames: Iowa State University Press, 1989), pp. 325–28.

15. Camera dei Deputati, VIII Legislatura, *Relazione sulla politica informativa e della sicurezza* doc. LI, no. 3 (22 November 1979–22 May 1980), p. 11, and doc. LI, no. 4 (22 May 1980-22 November 1980), p. 6.

16. US Congress, Senate Subcommittee on Security and Terrorism, *Terrorism in Italy: An Update Report 1983–1985*, 99th Cong., 1st sess. (Washington, D.C.: US Government Printing Office, 1985), p. 30; *Washington Post*, 14 October 1987.

17. US Congress, *Terrorism in Italy*, pp. 28–30. See also "Chronology of Libyan Support for Terrorism 1980–85," in US Department of State, *Libya Under Qadhafi: a Pattern of Aggression* (Washington, D.C.: Department of State, January 1986), pp. 7–11.

18. The circumstantial case is articulated clearly in Paul Henze, *The Plot to Kill the Pope* (New York: Scribners, 1983). Former KGB officer Victor Shemyov, who defected to the

U.S. in 1980, was serving in Warsaw in 1979. He claims that then KGB head Yuri Andropov sent a cable to the KGB *Rezident* in Warsaw, asking him to obtain all possible information on how "to get physically close to the Pope," a phrase that all concerned understood to mean that the Pope was to be assassinated. See *International Herald Tribune*, 3–4 March 1990.

19. On the suspicions of foreign involvement, see Alison Jamieson, *The Heart Attacked: Terrorism and Conflict in the Italian State* (London: Marion Boyars Publishers, 1989), p. 127; Meade, *Red Brigades*, pp. 137–38; Weinberg and Eubank, *The Rise and Fall*, pp. 7–8; Richard Drake, *The Revolutionary Mystique and Terrorism in Contemporary Italy* (Bloomington: Indiana University Press, 1989), p. 75; and David A. Charters, "Red Herring: FM 30-31B and the Murder of Aldo Moro," in David A. Charters and Maurice Tugwell, eds., *Deception Operations: Studies in the East-West Context* (London: Brassey's, 1990), pp. 197–209.

20. Senato della Repubblica, Camera dei Deputati, VIII Legislatura, *Relazione della commissione parlamentare d'inchiesta sulla strage di via Fani sul sequestro e l'assassinio di Aldo Moro e sul terrorismo in Italia*, doc. XXIII, no. 5, vols 1 and 2 (1983) [hereafter cited as *Relazione*]. See vol. 1, pp. 129–30, 135–37.

21. Ibid., p. 128.

22. Ibid., pp. 131–35; vol. 2, pp. 379–82. On pages 371 through 396, a top secret study of the secret services entitled "Implicazioni internazionali del terrorismo" is declassified and reproduced. See also Meade, *Red Brigades,* p. 224.

23. *Relazione*, vol. 1, pp. 141–44. See also *New York Times*, 27 September 1974, p. 1.

24. *Relazione*, vol. 1, pp. 144–46; US Congress, *Terrorism in Italy*, p. 23; Meade, *Red Brigades*, p. 221.

25. *Relazione*, vol. 1, p. 151.

26. Presidenza del Consiglio dei Ministri, *Relazione sulla politica informativa e della sicurezza*, (23 November 1983–22 May 1984), p. 31 (mimeographed, no date).

27. *Il Popolo*, 18 December 1991; Jamieson, *The Heart Attacked*, pp. 217–18. The Palestinian, Thamer Birawi, was also charged with participation in some earlier Abu Nidal attacks in Rome.

28. *Washington Post*, 8 September 1987, pp. 13, 16. For Mafia involvement in narcoterrorism, see part 2 of Corrado Stajano, ed., *Mafia, l'atto d'accusa dei giudici di Palermo*, (Rome: Editori Riuniti, 1986), pp. 103–218.

29. For an example, see Sylvere Lotringer, ed., *Italy: Autonomia, Post-Political Politico*, Semeiotext(e), vol. 3 no. 3, 1980. For an analysis, see Sabino S. Acquaviva, *Guerriglia e guerra rivoluzionaria in Italia* (Milan: Rizzoli, 1979); Giorgio Bocca, *Il terrorismo italiano, 1970–1978* (Milan: Rizzoli, 1978); Giorgio Galli, *Storia del partito armato* (Milan: Rizzoli, 1986); Camera dei Deputati, VII Legislatura, *Atti Parlamentari*, p. 23241.

30. Presidenza del Consiglio dei Ministri, *Relazione,* p. 37.

31. Senato della Repubblica, *Relazione*, doc. XLVIII, no. 1, p. 7.

32. Details of the Dozier kidnapping and rescue and of the Red Brigades' explanations of the reasons for the operation may be found in Drake, *The Revolutionary Mystique*, pp. 143–46. On the Hunt assassination, see Mickolus, Sandler, and Murdock, *International Terrorism*, vol. 2, pp. 16–17. The Giorgieri killing is discussed in Jamieson, *The Heart Attacked*, pp. 215–16.

33. Meade, *Red Brigades*, p. 238; Jamieson, *The Heart Attacked*, pp. 210–11, 216–17; Mickolus, Sandler and Murdock, *International Terrorism*, vol. 2, pp. 564–65.

34. See Frederic Spotts and Theodor Wieser, *Italy, A Difficult Democracy* (Cambridge: Cambridge University Press, 1986); and Joseph La Palombara, *Democracy Italian Style*

(New Haven, Conn.: Yale University Press, 1987).

35. Camera dei Deputati, VII Legislatura, *Atti Parlamentari*, pp. 23239–23241.

36. Giuseppe Mammarela, *Italy After Fascism* (Montreal: Mario Casalini, 1964), p. 302.

37. Stefano Silvestri, "Italy Between the Mediterranean and Europe," in A. Cottrell and J. Theberge, eds., *The Western Mediterranean, Its Political, Economic and Strategic Importance* (New York: Praeger, 1974), pp. 108–109.

38. Istituti Affari Internazionali, *L'Italia nella politica internazionale, Anno tredicesimo: 1984–1985*, p. 58 [hereafter cited as IAI, XIII].

39. Ibid., p. 59; Istituti Affari Internazionali, *L'Italia nella politica internazionale, Anno quattordicesimo: 1985–1986*, pp. 52–55 [hereafter cited as IAI, XIV].

40. IAI, XIV, p. 48; L. Paul Bremer III, "Terrorism: Myths and Reality," *Current Policy*, No. 1047 (Washington, D.C.: US Department of State, 4 February 1988), pp. 1-4.

41. Cassese, *Terrorism, Politics and Law*, pp. 24–43, 103–104.

42. The Italians were also prepared to storm the ship and deployed troops and helicopters in preparation for an assault. Ibid., pp. 27, 83. See reports on these preparations in FBIS-WEU-85-195 (8 October 1985), pp. 1–7. Reports on US preparations are in *Washington Post*, 9 October 1985.

43. Cassese, *Terrorism, Politics and Law*, pp. 86–89, 92–102. Egidio Sterpa, deputy secretary general of the Italian Liberal party said in 1986 that the Italians might have held and tried Abu Abbas, but for the visible US pressure on the Italian government and the US violation of Italian sovereignty by deploying troops at the Sigonella base. *Washington Times*, 17 July 1986.

44. Carlo de Risio, *L'odissea segreta dell' Achille Lauro* (Rome, 1985), pp. 77–91, carries the complete text of Craxi's statement, and outlines the position of the various parties. See also Silvano Labriola, "La questione costituzionale del caso dell' Achille Lauro," *Rivista di diritto internazionale privato e processuale* 22, no. 2 (1986).

45. IAI, XIV, p. 343.

46. Ibid., p. 351.

47. Ibid., p. 355.

48. Ibid., p. 353. In the 1970s, Libya had extended a loan to Fiat and thus gained a seat on the board of directors; it has since been rescinded.

49. Ibid., p. 331.

50. Bruce Watson et al., *Military Lessons of the Gulf War* (Novato, Calif.: Presidio Press, 1991), pp. 20, 23–24, 63, 65, 123–24, 128.

51. FBIS-WEU-85-196 (9 October 1985), p. 2.

52. IAI, XIV, p. 398.

53. *New York Times*, 24 May 1988.

54. Robert H. Evans, "Terrorism and Subversion of the State: Italian Legal Responses," *Terrorism and Political Violence* 1, no. 3 (July 1989), p. 335.

55. See Vincenzo Manzani, *Trattato di diritto penale italiano*, 5th ed., vol. 4 (Milan: UTET, 1985), pp. 383ff.

56. Evans, "Terrorism and Subversion," pp. 338, 340–42. Reale was the interior minister at the time.

57. Article 224 of the Penal Code.

58. Evans, "Terrorism and Subversion," p. 339.

59. Ibid., pp. 341–43; see also Moss, *The Politics of Left-wing Violence*, pp. 146, 193–96, 199, 221–22. The courts, of course, were not obliged to provide reduced sentences, and

in some cases did not do so. And the law has been criticized for being too lenient on convicted murderers. Its effects on the Red Brigades and other groups are described in Jamieson, *The Heart Attacked*, pp. 179–80, 197, 210; and Meade, *Red Brigades*, pp. 194–95, 216, 232–41.

60. *Globe and Mail,* 13 February 1988, p. A9. Granting reduced sentences to captured international terrorists who collaborate with authorities has been discussed in the parliament, but not passed into law.

61. John Newhouse, "The Diplomatic Round. A Freemasonry of Terrorism," *New Yorker*, 8 July 1985, p. 52.

62. IAI, XIV, p. 611.

63. Ferdinando Imposimato, "Il terrorismo ieri e oggi," *Avel* (June 1986), p. 10.

64. Ibid., p. 22.

65. Lenient sentences for the *pentiti* notwithstanding, Italian public opinion in the 1980s favored more severe penalties and stronger police powers. Christopher Hewitt, "Terrorism and Public Opinion: a Five Country Comparison," *Terrorism and Political Violence* 2, no. 2 (Summer 1990), p. 163.

66. *Globe and Mail*, 20 May 1985; *Washington Post*, 16 October 1985; *La Repubblica*, 28 November 1986.

67. Quoted in *Globe and Mail*, 30 December 1985.

68. IAI, XIV, p. 406.

69. Ibid., p. 53.

70. "Italy," in John Andrade, *World Police and Parliamentary Forces* (London: Macmillan, 1985), pp. 101–105 still draws a distinction between the *polizia di stato* and the other two forces.

71. See Meade, *Red Brigades*, pp. 35–37, 57, 197, 226–31; Moss, *The Politics of Left-wing Violence*, pp. 128–29; Camera dei Deputati, VII Legislatura, *Relazione sulla politica informativa e della sicurezza e sui risultati ottenuti*, doc. LI, no. 1 (22 November 1977-22 May 1978), pp. 4–6. See also Moss, *The Politics of Left-wing Violence*, pp. 176–78 with emphasis on its impact on the Moro investigation.

72. P2 (Propaganda Due) was a highly secret "Masonic" lodge, consisting of more than 900 members of government, business, finance, the military, and the secret services. While its objectives have never been clearly stated, its leader—influential rightist Licio Gelli—and its association with other shady characters and corrupt activities suggested a sinister, subversive purpose. The verdict remains open. See Drake, *The Revolutionary Mystique*, p. 140; Meade, *Red Brigades*, pp. 226–31; Sidoti, "Terrorism Supporters," pp. 111–12, 114–16.

73. Much of what follows was gained in five interviews conducted in Rome in October 1987 with senior officials of the government.

74. Drake, *The Revolutionary Mystique*, p. 146, and Meade, *Red Brigades*, p. 206 both refer, in slightly differing detail, to police exploitation of informant intelligence as the key to resolving the Dozier case. The identity of the leader of the kidnap team, Antonio Savasta, was known within days of the abduction. *Globe and Mail*, 22 December 1981. The involvement of American anti-terrorist specialists in the investigation is mentioned in *Baltimore Sun*, 21 December 1981; *New York Times*, 29 January 1982. Steven Emerson, *Secret Warriors* (New York: Putnam's, 1988), pp. 58–69, provides more detail, based on interviews, which implies that *several* American anti-terrorist teams were involved in the Dozier search.

75. The USO Club bombers included Fusako Shigenobu, the leader of the JRA, and Junzo Okudaira, a JRA member. *Washington Post*, 15–16 April 1988; FBIS-WEU-88-078, (22 April 1988), p. 13.

76. The rescue team's formal title is the *Nucleo Operativo Centrale di Sicurezza* (NOCS)—Central Operative Security Nucleus. It is a special police commando team modeled on the German *Grenzschutzgruppen 9* (GSG-9) and the British Army's Special Air Service Regiment (SAS). After the Dozier rescue, however, four NOCS members were suspended, tried, and convicted of using excessive force against the captured terrorists. The convictions were overturned on appeal. This was one of the very few documented cases of police brutality in Italy. See "Leatherhead Heroes," *Newsweek*, 8 February 1982; *Globe and Mail*, 16 July 1983; Drake, *The Revolutionary Mystique*, pp. 146, 197 n.35; and Moss, *The Politics of Left-wing Violence*, pp. 174–75.

77. IAI, XIV, p. 172.

78. Ibid., pp. 172–81. See also *The Military Balance* (London: International Institute for Strategic Studies, 1986–1989); and Watson et al., *Military Lessons*, p.24 (based on testimony of the Italian chiefs of staff to the Parliamentary Defense Committee, March 1991).

79. FBIS-WEU-88-086 (4 May 1988), p. 2.

80. R. M. Govea, "The European Response to Terrorism," in Leon Hurwitz, ed., *The Harmonization of European Public Policy* (Westport, Conn.: Greenwood Press, 1983), p. 97.

81. Counseil de l'Europe, *Rapport explicatif sur la Convention europeenne pour la repression du terrorisme. Recommendation 703 Relative au Terrorisme International*, Discussion Par l'Assemblée, 15–16 May 1973, 2d and 4th meetings, doc. 3285, *rapport de la commission des questions politiques.*

82. Maria Riccarda Marchetti, *Instituzioni europee e lotta al terrorismo* (Padua: CEDAM, 1986), p. 155. See "The European Convention on the Suppression of Terrorism," reprinted in Noemi Gal-Or, *International Cooperation to Suppress Terrorism* (New York: St. Martin's Press, 1985), pp. 370–71, app. 1.

83. IAI, XIII, p. 477.

84. Cassese, *Terrorism, Politics, and Law*, p. 144.

85. IAI, XIII, p. 60; IAI XIV, p. 237; *New York Times*, 15 April 1986; UK Foreign and Commonwealth Office, *International Terrorism: The European Response* (London: FCO, June 1986); Geoffrey M. Levitt, *Democracies Against Terror: The Western Response to State-supported Terrorism*, Washington Papers, no. 134 (New York: Praeger; Washington, D.C.: Center for Strategic and International Studies, 1988), pp. 79–80.

86. Marchetti, *Instituzione europee*, p. 115.

87. James Adams, "How Europe Got Tough on Terrorism," *Washington Post*, 14 February 1988, pp. C1 and C2. See also Juliet Lodge, ed., *The Threat of Terrorism* (Boulder, Colo.: Westview Press, 1988), p. 252; and José Luis Nunes and Lawrence J. Smith, co-rapporteurs, *Sub-committee on Terrorism: Final Report*, North Atlantic Assembly Papers (Brussels: North Atlantic Assembly, January 1989), p. 28. Author's interview, name withheld upon request.

88. Keith Hellawell, "Terrorism and the Police," in Brenda Almond, ed., *Terrorism in the New Europe* (Hull, UK: Social Values Research Center, University of Hull, 1992), p. 22.

89. IAI, XIII, p. 478; IAI XIV, pp. 379, 395.

90. See Paolo Mengozzi, "A View from Italy on Judicial Cooperation Between Italy and the United States," *New York University Journal of International Law and Politics* 18, no. 3 (Spring 1986), pp. 813–31.

91. *New York Times*, 17 April 1988; *Washington Times*, 18 April 1988; *Globe and Mail*, 22 April 1988; *Washington Post*, 8 February 1989.

92. For a discussion of the Schengen agreement and the contentious security issues, see Juliet Lodge, "Internal Security and Judicial Cooperation Beyond Maastricht," *Terrorism and Political Violence* 4, no. 3 (Autumn 1992), pp. 1–29; Richard Clutterbuck, *Terrorism, Drugs and Crime in Europe After 1992* (London: Routledge, 1990), pp. 125–26, 188; and K. G. Robertson, *1992—The Security Implications*, Occasional Paper no. 43 (London: Institute for European Defence and Strategic Studies, 1989).

93. Interview with Italian government official, 1987.

5

France and International Terrorism: Problem and Response

Michael M. Harrison

INTRODUCTION

On 17 July 1980 five persons acting under the group name The Guards of Islam tried, but failed, to assassinate Shahpour Bakhtiar, the former prime minister of Iran, in a suburb of Paris. They killed two persons and wounded three others in the botched attack. The whole group was captured, tried, and convicted. Four were sentenced to life imprisonment; one received a twenty-year sentence. Although the Islamic revolutionary government of Iran was suspected of involvement in the attack, the French government accepted Iran's denial. Ten years later, all five were granted presidential pardons, and were flown to Iran. Bakhtiar was assassinated by suspected pro-regime agents in Paris in August 1991.

The stiff sentences handed the perpetrators of the 1980 attack contrast neatly with France's uncritical acceptance of Iran's claim of innocence in 1980 and with its willingness to "forgive and forget" a decade later, in spite of considerable evidence of official Iranian sponsorship of international terrorism throughout the 1980s.[2] Indeed, the French actions in the case embody the seemingly ambivalent, even contradictory, French approach to the problem of international terrorism. On the one hand, the French authorities have at certain times vigorously suppressed groups suspected of involvement in terrorism. At other times, French policy apparently favored a laissez-faire, hands-off approach, which gave some terrorists a degree of freedom to act without fear of reprisal by France itself.

If the ambivalence is genuine, and not merely a matter of perception, it might be explained, at least in part, by French political culture. Political terrorism, in a wide variety of forms, has been part of modern French politics since the revolution. At different times, French institutions and citizens have been perpetrators of, collaborators in, and victims of state terrorism, both domestic and foreign-instigated. France has also been the target of terrorism by anti-state groups. Some of these have used France as a sanctuary, a safe haven in which to regroup and to prepare for operations elsewhere. Terrorism has originated from the left, from the right, and from anarchists of uncertain persuasion; from domestic groups and foreigners; from national and international issues. It has been directed against both French and foreign targets, in France and abroad. On more than one occasion, it has had a significant impact on French society and politics.

First, the experience of French revolutionary terror in the eighteenth century legitimized the notion that revolutionaries were entitled to use these means to create the "new order," the new society.[3] This notion complicated France's efforts to deal with modern terrorists—domestic and foreign—who proclaimed for themselves a mantle of revolutionary legitimacy.

Second, during the Nazi occupation, 1940–1944, France experienced a second reign of terror, also in the name of creating a new order. These events left deep scars on French society, not least because many French citizens, inside and outside the Nazi-sanctioned Vichy government, connived and collaborated in the Nazi terror-ism.[4] The experience poisoned and divided French political culture in the post-war period; conspiracy, violence, terror, and counter-terror continued to influence French foreign and domestic affairs even into the 1980s.

The 1970s saw the emergence of several domestic terrorist groups, most of which still influence the French political scene in one way or another. In pursuit of vaguely defined "liberation" from French rule in Brittany, the Breton Liberation Front/Breton Revolutionary Army (FLB-ARB) set off some 300 bombs between 1966 and 1979. Economic development and promotion of Breton culture took the impetus out of the drive for independence, but incidents continued in the 1980s on a limited scale.[5]

Political terrorism by Corsican nationalists has been a more prolonged and serious problem. Separatist sentiment and clandestine violence were more deeply entrenched on the culturally distinct island of Corsica than in Brittany. Terrorist incidents in support of the nationalist cause occurred as early as 1954, but increased significantly with the formation of the Corsican National Liberation Front (FLNC) in 1976. The FLNC terrorism campaign escalated the violence on the island (and, with some frequency, in mainland France) to levels that exceeded the worst days of the Algerian war; between 1976 and 1987, there were some 4,500 incidents. The FLNC was responsible for most of these. A truce agreed to in 1988 split the movement. In 1991, terrorism resumed on a major scale and continued through 1992. FLNC targets have included French government officials, police, govern-ment buildings, and the Corsican tourist industry.[6]

The Basque region of France has its own violent nationalist group, the *Iparretarak* ("those from the North"). It was created in 1973, then went into decline, and revived again in 1982 with the murder of some French state police. From then to 1985, it carried out more than sixty attacks on public buildings and was still active in 1992.[7] By far the most serious counter-terrorism problem, however, came from the *Euzakadi ta Askatasuna* (ETA), the violent Spanish Basque separatist movement, which used France as a sanctuary for carrying out activities in Spain. This is discussed later in the chapter.

INTERNATIONAL TERRORISM AND FRANCE

In the post-war period, it was the Algerian War, 1954-1962, that provided France with its first experience with significant *international* anti-state terrorism. Although the nationalist National Liberation Front (FLN) conducted a largely guerrilla-style war in the rural areas of Algeria, it also extended its terrorist campaign to France itself.[8] But the most serious terrorist threat to the French state came not from the FLN, but from the use of officially sanctioned counter-terror against the Algerian nationalist FLN. This state terrorism corrupted and politicized the army, which, along with French Algerians (*pieds noirs*), ultimately became a threat to France itself.

The threat manifested itself in the *Organization armée secret* (OAS), which was comprised of disaffected soldiers and *pied noirs* civilians and administrators who felt betrayed by the decision to grant Algeria's independence. Beginning in 1961, it continued into the mid-1960s, operating both within France and from sanctuaries abroad. The OAS reserved a special enmity for President Charles de Gaulle and made numerous attempts to assassinate him.[9] The OAS campaign in France involved political terrorism on a large scale and—for a time at least—enjoyed the support of a substantial portion of the French population. The OAS was the most widely supported, organized, and sustained right-wing terrorist movement in post-war Europe. Once Algeria became independent, however, the OAS's cause was irrelevant; its support evaporated, its activities petered out, and the few remaining members were captured and prosecuted or forced into exile.

The foregoing illustrates the extent to which political terrorism was part of French political life, long before the events of the 1980s. So when international terrorism began to affect France again in the 1970s, the nation, its leaders, and its security authorities were not confronting an entirely new phenomenon. Yet there were differences in the nature of the threat. Consequently, different responses were called for and were tried, with mixed success. But there were some continuities in French practice as well.

In the case of at least one group, international terrorism in France had indigenous origins. *Action directe* (AD), whose name refers to an anarchist concept,[10] was formed in 1979 in an apparent attempt to create "a French version of the Red Brigades and the Red Army Faction."[11] It is believed to have evolved out of remnants of two French radical groups of the 1970s, the neo-anarchist *Groupe d'action révolutionnaire internationaliste* (GARI) and a Maoist group, *Noyaux armées pours l'autonomité populaire*. The founder and leader was Jean-Marc Rouillan, who had learned his skills in action with anti-Franco groups in Spain and had originally founded the GARI group. His co-leader and long-time companion was Nathalie Menignon.

Commencing operations in 1979, the group was nearly wiped out by a police crackdown in March 1980, in which thirty AD activists were arrested; nineteen were charged with criminal offenses. The following month the remaining elements of the group held up a Paris bank and then embarked on a series of attacks on corporate and government computer offices. Rouillan and Menignon were arrested in September 1980, along with several other members, leaving the police to conclude that AD was broken. But, in May 1981, the new Mitterand government proclaimed an amnesty and released Rouillan and fifteen others (Menignon was freed several months later).[12]

Once at liberty, the group resumed its campaign of bombings against "capitalist" targets, but shifted from buildings and offices to assassinations and mass-casualty bombings. It was at this time that AD's terrorism became truly international, as American and Israeli targets inside France were selected for attack. Following the bombing of an Israeli company's offices in August 1982, the French government banned the group (AD was also suspected of having collaborated with a Palestinian group in a bloody shooting attack on a Jewish restaurant in Paris a few days earlier). About twenty group members were taken in for questioning in connection with the attack.[13]

More arrests followed, but the group continued its activities. By 1983, AD was thought to have split into at least two factions, one domestic (and less violent) and the other an "international" wing. Rouillan and Menignon gravitated to the latter, which was believed to have contacts with a number of other European and Middle Eastern terrorist groups. That these links were more than rhetorical became clear on 15 January 1985, when AD, the West German Red Army Faction (RAF) and the Belgian Communist Combatant Cells (CCC) announced the formation of a coordinated joint struggle against North Atlantic Treaty Organization (NATO) and other Western (particularly American) military and industrial targets. The announcement was preceded and followed by a series of attacks on military bases and installations, military-industrial facilities, and individuals associated with them. AD's first target in this category was French General René Audran. Responsible for French arms sales, he was assassinated on 25 January, only ten days after the united front was announced.[14]

The groups apparently operated independently; it was their targeting strategies that were coordinated. The only attack claimed jointly by the RAF and AD was the bombing of Rhein-Main Air Base, near Frankfurt, West Germany, in August 1985. But evidence of genuine cooperation had emerged even before that incident. All three groups had used explosives stolen from the same source near Brussels in June 1984. At about that time, intelligence sources said later, representatives of all of the established European terrorists groups (except the Provisional Irish Republican Army) had met in Lisbon to arrange cooperation. In late 1985, Belgian police found the fingerprints of Rouillan and Menignon in a hideout used by the suspected leader of the CCC. However, AD concentrated most of its "international" attacks on targets in France: Interpol, the Organization for Economic Cooperation and Development (OECD), the NATO oil pipeline agency, and businesses with links to South Africa.[15]

On 21 February 1987, Rouillan, Menignon, and two other leading figures in AD were arrested near Orleans, France. They were charged with a variety of crimes, including several murders, and were convicted and sentenced in June 1988. AD had always been a small organization, numbering perhaps no more than twenty full-time members, with a few dozen supporters. Consequently, when the entire leadership was captured and jailed, the group collapsed. It has been inactive since that time.[16]

The conflicts in the Middle East have been the source of many terrorist incidents involving France. Most were related to the Israeli-Palestinian conflict, but terrorism emanating from Iran, Lebanon, and the Armenian issue also contributed to a rising incidence of violence. This could be attributed to several factors. First, France has long offered safe haven to political dissidents exiled from their homelands; Paris became a focal point for Palestinians who were prepared to use French sanctuary to plan and carry out operations against Israeli targets or against rival Arab factions. They were aided in this by a second factor: the large community of Arab and Muslim expatriates (numbering some 2.5 million in the mid-1980s) who were living and working in France. Sympathetic to the Palestinian cause and (from the late 1970s) to religious fundamentalism and marginalized by high unemployment and French racism, they provided fertile ground for recruiting new members and for initiating clandestine activity. Third, a number of Middle Eastern countries were prepared to violate France's sanctuary status, using their own agents or surrogates to carry out operations against each other. Finally, various French governments, for a variety of raisons d'état, were willing to "look the other way," so long as the activities of these foreigners did not put French citizens at great risk.[17] The result was that at different times French territory became a surrogate battleground for Middle Eastern belligerents; inevitably, French citizens became the unintended victims.

France experienced relatively low levels of Middle Eastern terrorism in the 1970s. In 1973, several incidents occurred that suggested a covert war between the Black September Organization (BSO), the Palestinian group responsible for the 1972 Munich Olympics massacre, and Israeli agents determined to avenge the Munich murders. In June 1973, Mohammed Boudia, alleged BSO European organizer, was killed in Paris by a bomb planted in his car. (In fact, Boudia probably was not a BSO member, but rather the European representative for a rival group, the Popular Front for the Liberation of Palestine or PFLP). In September 1973, five Palestinians seized thirteen hostages at the Saudi Arabian embassy in Paris in an effort to force Jordan to release Abu Daoud, the leader of BSO. The extortion failed; the terrorists had to settle for being flown out of France with four hostages who were later released.[18]

Operations by the PFLP dominated the 1974–1976 period. The principal figure in many of these was Ilich Ramirez Sanchez, a Venezuelan leftist revolutionary who worked for the PFLP and who later came to be known as "Carlos." Based as a "sleeper" agent in Paris and London, he took over PFLP operations in Europe after the murder of Boudia; indeed, several of the operations in which he is believed to have taken part were claimed by the Mohammed Boudia Commando. The most infamous of these was a grenade attack on the Jewish-owned Le Drugstore café complex in Paris in September 1974. Two people died, and thirty four were wounded in the explosion, which was launched in support of another operation: a hostage siege at the French embassy in The Hague, where Japanese Red Army (JRA) terrorists were trying to force the French government to release one of their members. This operation succeeded; the jailed terrorist was released, and he and his colleagues were flown to the Middle East with hostages and a large cash ransom.[19]

In January 1975, PFLP teams under Carlos's direction, armed with RPG-7 rocket launchers, tried and failed twice to attack Israeli airliners at Orly Airport. The second incident degenerated into a hostage-taking, which ended with the terrorists being flown to the Middle East. Then, in June, Carlos narrowly escaped capture; in doing so, he killed two French security agents who had come to question him, along with a formerly trusted colleague who had been "turned" by the French. Carlos then fled France, but continued his operations elsewhere. In June 1976, along with Wadi Haddad, he is thought to have masterminded the hijacking of an Air France airliner to Entebbe, Uganda. The aim of the operation was to force Israel, France, and other countries to release jailed terrorists. The leaders of the hijack team were Wilfred Böse and Brigitte Kohlmann, West German leftist terrorists working for and with the PFLP. Both were killed when Israeli commandos rescued the hostages at Entebbe.[20]

The next Palestinian group to make its presence felt in France was *Fatah*—The Revolutionary Council, also known as the Abu Nidal Organization, after the nom de guerre of its leader. Resolutely opposed to the slightly more moderate stance of the PLO under Yasser Arafat's leadership, the Abu Nidal faction was emerging as the most violent of the PLO factions. Since splitting with Arafat in 1973, Abu Nidal had turned against his former comrades, whom he regarded as traitors to the Palestinian cause. They, in turn, had sentenced him to death in absentia. The blood feud spilled over into France in 1977–1978, when two PLO representatives in Paris were assassinated (Abu Nidal might have been responsible for only one of these). His group was suspected in the assassination of the deputy director of the PLO's Paris office in July 1982 and the ambassador of the United Arab Emirates in February 1984.

The bloodiest attack linked to the Abu Nidal Organization was that on Goldenberg's Restaurant in Paris in August 1982. Two men threw a grenade and fired machine guns at people in and near the restaurant; six people died, and twenty two were wounded. As noted earlier, AD was also suspected of complicity in this attack, and there is some evidence to suggest that the two groups were collaborating. Police detention of AD members after the restaurant attack appeared to disrupt Abu Nidal's infrastructure in France temporarily.[21] In any case, most of Abu Nidal's subsequent operations occurred outside France against non-French targets.

Between 1979 and 1984, Armenian terrorists carried out seventeen attacks in France; five of these occurred in 1981. They attempted to assassinate a number of Turkish diplomats and succeeded in a few cases. In other incidents, they bombed Turkish businesses and other targets at random. The most serious incident was the bombing of the Turkish Airlines counter at Orly Airport on 15 July 1983. Seven people were killed and sixty two wounded in the attack, claimed by the Armenian Secret Army for the Liberation of Armenia (ASALA).[22]

But it was spillover from the civil war in Lebanon that caused the worst and most politically complex series of international terrorist incidents. The complicating factors included the Iranian revolution and the spread of fundamentalist Islamic political violence in Lebanon and elsewhere, factional fighting between Christians and Moslems in Lebanon, Syrian intervention in Lebanon, France's relations with the Lebanese Christian community and French participation in the multinational force in Beirut, and French support (particularly arms sales) for Iraq in its war with Iran.[23] The result was a series of incidents spanning the decade 1979–1989 in which foreigners were attacked in France and French targets were attacked at home and abroad. In short, France became a surrogate battlefield of the Lebanese civil war.

There were forty three incidents relating to these issues between 1979 and 1989; three-quarters of them occurred in the five-year period from 1982–1986, with the largest number (twelve incidents) coming during the last year. Most of the attacks outside France occurred in Beirut and were claimed by or attributed to the terrorist network known as Islamic Jihad, the nom de guerre of the fundamentalist pro-Iranian Shia faction *Hizb'Allah* (Party of God). Islamic Jihad claimed responsibility for the truck bomb that killed fifty six French troops of the multinational force in October 1983 and for the kidnapping of nine French citizens in 1985–1986. A group allied with Islamic Jihad also set off a car bomb at the French embassy in Kuwait in December 1983, but caused only minor damage. The French ambassador was assassinated in Beirut in 1981, and the French military attaché and two embassy guards were killed there in separate incidents in 1986. In September 1989, a French airliner was downed by a bomb over Niger in west Africa, with a loss of 171 people. The incident, which has since been attributed to Libya, may have been linked to France's involvement in the civil war in Chad (in which it supported the government against Libyan-backed insurgents).[24]

The foregoing attacks caused large loss of life (more than 230 French lives) and complicated France's Middle East policy-making. But for sheer terror, they did not match the series of incidents that occurred in Paris in 1986. The ten attacks claimed by the Committee of Solidarity with Arab and Middle East Political Prisoners (CSPPA) killed less than a dozen people, but wounded more than 220. Most of the attacks and casualties occurred in a ten-day period in September 1986; the bombs were set off at times and places apparently intended to cause many casualties. The wave of bombings was the product of a convoluted international conspiracy involving Lebanese, Tunisians, and Moroccans, possibly with the support of the Iranian government, and certainly at the instigation of *Hizb'Allah*. The CSPPA carried out the bombings in an attempt to force the French government to release three jailed terrorists: Anis Naccache, who was convicted for the attempt to assassinate Bakhtiar (mentioned at the outset of this chapter); Varadjian Garbidjan, jailed for his involvement in the ASALA attack on Orly Airport in July 1983; and Georges Ibrahim Abdallah, thought to be the leader of the Lebanese Armed Revolutionary Faction (LARF).

Between 1981 and 1984, the LARF, a Maronite Marxist group modeled loosely on the European leftist terrorist groups, carried out a series of attacks against American and Israeli targets in France, including the assassination of one diplomat from each country. In addition, the LARF claimed responsibility for the kidnapping of a French diplomat in Beirut and for the assassination in Rome in 1984 of the American director-general of the Multinational Force and Observers (the Sinai peace-keeping force). The LARF, like many Lebanese political factions, was family-based, but also had extensive international links, with Syria, the PFLP, the Italian Red Brigades, and AD. Abdallah was arrested in October 1984. During his trial in 1986, the CSPPA set off bombs in Paris and demanded his release; the September bombing wave followed his conviction for possession of arms, explosives, and false documents and for criminal association. Since there appeared to be a direct relationship between Abdallah's trial and the CSPPA bombings, French authorities initially concluded that the CSPPA was merely Abdallah's LARF "family" operating under a different name.[25]

The *Direction de la surveillance du territoire* (DST), the French security service, had doubts about this theory, however. Eyewitness accounts placed two members of Abdallah's family (suspected of planting one of the September bombs) in northern Lebanon the following day, casting doubts on their presence in Paris on the day of the bombing. The DST, in any case, suspected an Iranian connection to the CSPPA. The arrest of Mohammed Ali Hamadei, a *Hizb'Allah* member, in Germany in 1987 led the DST to Fouad Ben Ali Saleh, the real leader of the CSPPA. Further information from an informer exposed much of the rest of the network. Ali Saleh, a Tunisian convert to Shi'ism, had created a multinational team of bomb-makers, bombers, and couriers, eighteen in all, directed by *Hizb'Allah* from Beirut. The eight Lebanese members, who escaped to Lebanon, were thought to be members of *Hizb'Allah*. The DST also suspected that the CSPPA had more direct links to Iran, and their suspicions in this regard fell on Wahid Gordji, an interpreter at the Iranian embassy in Paris. In July 1987, Gordji took refuge in the embassy to avoid questioning in the case. French police blocked access to the embassy for more than four months (Iran did the same to the French embassy in Teheran). When the standoff was resolved, following the release of French hostages in Lebanon, Gordji was allowed to leave France after perfunctory questioning by a French judge. With his departure, the evidentiary trail linking Iran to the CSPPA apparently went cold.

The link between the LARF and the CSPPA seems to have been equally tenuous. French prosecutors concluded that the bombings were intended to persuade France to stop selling arms to Iraq (or to punish it for doing so). But if so, that demand was never stated explicitly in communiqués related to the bombings. It may be that the focus on Abdallah and the two others was a deliberate effort by the CSPPA to mislead French authorities about the reasons for and the instigators of the attacks; if that was the case, they succeeded for more than a year.[26]

Like West Germany and Italy, France in the late 1970s experienced an upsurge of racist and neo-fascist terrorism. The targets of these attacks were immigrant communities, particularly North African, and Jewish or Israeli people or premises.

The worst year was 1980, in which there were more than 120 incidents of violence attributed to neo-fascist groups. The major incident in that year was the bombing of a synagogue in Paris in October; four people were killed and twenty wounded in that attack. Racially motivated attacks and other incidents (such as the desecration of Jewish cemeteries) continued through the 1980s, but the various chronologies of international terrorism do not record any other major incidents of neo-fascist terrorism in France or against French targets elsewhere.

On the basis of existing data, several observations can be made. First, most of the incidents were probably perpetrated by indigenous French racist or neo-fascist groups and individuals. Although similar groups exist in Italy and West Germany, they do not appear to have developed the extensive collaborative network and joint operations that characterized Palestinian, Shiite, and European leftist groups in that period. Second, it is possible that some incidents attributed to neo-fascist groups, such as the synagogue bombing, were in fact carried out by others who had their own motives to attack the same targets—Palestinians, for example.[27] So while neo-fascist terrorism was—and remains—a threat in Europe, at least with respect to France it is difficult to assess its significance in the context of international terrorism.

The foregoing suggests several conclusions about the French experience of political terrorism. First, the only terrorist campaigns since 1945 that were sustained in significant intensity were those of the FLNC, a domestic irredentist movement, and the OAS, which had both domestic and external connections. Therefore, it seems fair to suggest that domestic terrorism has posed a much greater threat to France than has international terrorism.

That said, it would be a mistake to minimize the importance of international terrorism. Its principal effects were two: first, it caused death and injury to many French citizens and foreigners in France. That, in itself, made it a problem requiring attention and response, if only out of humanitarian decency. Second, and no less important, it complicated French foreign policy-making, particularly with respect to the Middle East. Over time, as more foreign targets were attacked in France, it became harder for France to justify its tradition of asylum for political dissidents. Gradually, France succumbed to pressure from its European neighbors and the United States to restrict the practice of sanctuary and to put action behind its words of support for the suppression of international terrorism. How it went about doing so is the focus of the remainder of this chapter.

COUNTERING TERRORISM

Policy and Legislative Measures

French counter-terrorism policy during the period under study appears to have been guided by several contradictory influences: first, the French government has wanted to preserve the French tradition of political asylum for foreign activists. Second, and closely related to the first, a degree of legitimacy has been accorded to the notion that revolutionaries were entitled to use violence to create the "new order" and hence were to be permitted some freedom of action. Third, there was a determination to pursue French foreign policy interests, particularly in the Middle East, in a manner designed to minimize the political risks of such policies. Finally, the French government intended to uphold its obligations to protect French citizens at home and abroad and to fulfill commitments to France's allies in the counter-terrorism effort, at least to the minimum degree that would keep disputes with allies manageable.[28] Not surprisingly, the result has been a patchwork of policies and actions that were inconsistent and contradictory in both fact and appearance. That is not to say, however, that within the context of French policy they were not without some logic.

It is important to bear in mind as well that there has been a certain commonality of response between the socialist and the conservative governments. Both have veered from "soft" to "hard-line" policies on terrorism; both have made deals with terrorist groups or their sponsors; and because of the inherent political divisions within the French political system—which, for example, pairs a socialist president with a conservative prime minister—French governments have experienced internal disputes over the handling of counter-terrorism policy. Such disputes have become public, and there have been some political casualties.

In a comparative study of national policies for dealing with aircraft hijackings, Peter St. John asserts that the French pattern of response was shaped by the hostage-taking carried out by the JRA at the French embassy in The Hague in September 1974. The Dutch were prepared to storm the building, but the French government forestalled the assault by agreeing to release the jailed Japanese terrorist. He and the hostage-takers were flown to the Middle East, with a large ransom in hand. This, St. John says, quoting several authorities, established a pattern that was difficult to reverse because it provided future terrorists with a basis by which to judge the government's will to resist.[29] When the Air France jet was hijacked to Entebbe in June 1976, the French government did little to resolve the incident, which was terminated by the Israeli raid. Indeed, the French inadvertently may have made the hijacking possible; shortly before, they had arrested Carlos's associate Wilfred Böse and deported him quickly to Germany. Although Böse was wanted by the West German Federal Border Police, he was released and became the leader of the hijacking team.[30]

The most egregious incident of this type occurred in January 1977. Following the assassination of the PLO representative in Paris, the French government permitted the PLO to send a two-man delegation to the funeral. One of the two was Abu Daoud, the reputed mastermind of the 1972 Munich massacre (traveling under another name). Alerted by Israeli or US intelligence, the DST arrested him. West Germany and Israel immediately commenced extradition proceedings. This set off a diplomatic crisis and revealed divisions within the French government. There were allegations that the DST had acted without notifying the Interior Ministry; it was also alleged that Interior Minister Michel Poniatowski, known to be pro-Israeli and to favor a hard line against terrorism, had approved the arrest, in spite of the problems it could create for the French government.

The problems arose from the fact that it probably was not in France's interest at that time to reverse the policy of accommodating international terrorists, particularly those associated with the Middle East. President Valery Giscard d'Estaing was carefully cultivating improved relations with the Arab world and was promoting not insignificant French exports (especially arms) to the region. In fact, he was due to visit Saudi Arabia the following week, so the seizure of Abu Daoud could not have come at a worse time. The result was that the government supported Daoud's claim before the French court that he was a political representative and thus protected from arrest, the West German extradition application was rejected on technical grounds, and Abu Daoud was flown to Algeria with all expenses paid by France.[31] In protest, Israel recalled its ambassador.

However, Poniatowski was not always so summarily overruled. The previous year, he had taken a firm stand in forcing the surrender of Croatian hijackers at De Gaulle Airport.[32] Moreover, in the first half of the 1970s, French law had been amended to incorporate new offenses and new penalties for violent group action, hijacking, and hostage-taking.[33] Yet a degree of ambivalence remained. With the other members of the European Community, France took part in drafting the European Convention on the Suppression of Terrorism (ECST), which was signed in 1977. But for the next decade it refused to ratify the convention. Edward Moxon-Browne has suggested several reasons for this: the relatively low incidence of terrorism in France at the time the convention was drafted; a sense that existing French laws were adequate to deal with terrorism; and, probably most important, considerable opposition within France to the provisions for extradition of those who were suspected of offenses, but whose motives were political, which appeared to violate France's tradition of asylum. So France did not ratify the convention until 1986 and, upon signing, also invoked the political exception clause.[34] The practical effects of this will be discussed later.

The dichotomy in French counter-terrorism policy was neatly encapsulated in President Giscard d'Estaing's 1980 statement after the attempted assassination of Shahpour Bakhtiar. "France must and will remain a land of the asylum,"[35] he told his cabinet and then went on to add, "France will not allow its soil to become a base for foreigners seeking to organize violent actions here."[36] French policy tilted temporarily in favor of greater tolerance for political extremism following the election of President François Mitterand and his socialist government in 1981. The government declared an amnesty, which freed a large number of convicted terrorists, including the leaders of AD, who quickly returned to violent activity. In August 1981, the government abolished the State Security Court, which had been created in 1963 to deal with violent political crimes. In September, the National Assembly voted to end use of the death penalty. Finally, the government passed resolutions confirming the asylum policy and France's refusal to extradite to other European countries those suspected of politically motivated crimes.[37]

Although popular at the time they were passed, these measures lost their appeal as AD and various Middle Eastern groups escalated the violence in Paris in 1982. At the end of April, President Mitterand summoned the leaders of the security forces for a "council of war" on terrorism; two days later, the government announced a counteroffensive against terrorism. Thus, the pendulum was already swinging back in favor of a more concerted effort when the attack on Goldenberg's Restaurant occurred in August, but it took that attack to produce concrete measures. Mitterand created the new position of secretary of state for public security and appointed Joseph Franceschi to the post. He also instituted a number of other measures: the appointment of a permanent advisory council on terrorism to keep a "watching brief" on the problem, a ban on the sale of certain weapons and a crackdown on arms smuggling, stricter border controls and increased surveillance of foreign diplomats suspected of illegal activities, and the establishment of a central computerized data bank on terrorists and extremist sympathizers (to replace the file system destroyed by the government the previous year as part of its liberalization policy).

The most startling turnabout came in November when the cabinet decided to restrict the right of asylum. Existing legislation on asylum was left intact, but the government warned that those who committed "unacceptable" acts of violence risked extradition by order of the courts; the "political exception" could no longer be invoked.[38] Even so, it was some time before France acted on this change.

In October 1984, following a change of government the previous year, the new interior minister, Pierre Joxe, created a new counter-terrorism coordinating body. The *Unité de coordination de la lutte anti-terroriste* (UCLAT) was established within the National Police; it was headed by a senior police officer and reported directly to the director general of the national force. UCLAT was staffed by senior police officers and civil servants and included representatives of the armed forces and the Gendarmerie Nationale. The duties of UCLAT and its director included maintaining liaisons with relevant government departments and preparing the meetings of the Inter-ministerial Anti-Terrorist Liaison Committee (CILAT). The CILAT met weekly under the chairmanship of the ministerial delegate for security, with representation from the prime minister's office and the departments of justice, foreign affairs, defense, budget and interior.[39]

In March 1986, a conservative government under Prime Minister Jacques Chirac replaced the socialists, although François Mitterand remained the president. Clearly prompted by the increased activity of AD and the CSPPA, the Chirac government indicated early in its term that it would pursue a more aggressive policy against terrorism. Initially, police powers were reinforced, the most controversial measure being an extension of the period the police could hold someone for questioning. The new government's attitude was summarized by Jacques Godfrain, the member of the assembly who had drafted the program: "Our approach will be to suppress the terrorists without talking to them," he said. "We will make it clear that we will stop the suppression of terrorists only when they have stopped their terrorist action."[40] The Chirac government also imposed mandatory sentences of twenty to twenty five years (for life sentences) and upgraded the secretary of state's position to a full minister of security. Robert Paindraud, the former director general of the National Police, was appointed to the post.[41]

These measures had no immediate impact on terrorism, which continued into the summer and then escalated in September. At that time, the assembly passed a special anti-terrorist law, sometimes referred to as the *loi Pasqua* for Charles Pasqua, Chirac's interior minister, who guided the legislation through the Chamber of Deputies. The law was promulgated initially for a six-month period. It was a complicated document, which was intended to deal with a range of criminal activities, including terrorism. In that regard, its principal features included, first, an attempt to define terrorism by citing various acts that might fit under the definition, such as threats of assassination and the taking of hostages. Specifically, the law defined terrorist acts as those "having as an aim to gravely trouble public order by intimidation or terror."[42]

The law also formalized the earlier decision to extend the period of holding suspects to four days and tightened up existing powers of the police to verify the identities of foreigners in France. With a few exceptions, nationals from countries outside the European Community would have to acquire visas to enter France and to demonstrate their financial "means of existence" before doing so. It simplified the process of expulsion of foreigners by making such expulsions possible through administrative measures (at the direction of the interior minister), rather than through the judicial process. Moreover, foreigners could be expelled by a looser judgment of the threat they posed: that of a simple "menace to public order," rather than a "*grave* menace to public order."[43] The law reinstated a special court to hear terrorism cases only and also provided for victim compensation. At the same time, the government called out some 1,000 troops to assist the customs, airport, and border police in patrolling the more remote and porous sections of the French frontiers, along the Pyrenees and the Alps.[44]

To underscore these measures, Chirac took an uncompromising stance in an interview several days after the law was passed.

I would like everyone to know without a doubt . . . when we catch a terrorist red-handed, he will speak. And those who manipulate him . . . must know without a doubt that they will be the object of Draconian reprisals, that we will be without mercy, no matter what the consequences may be; our resolve to demand high payment, in capital and interest, from those who are known to have manipulated terrorists, is a resolve which knows no reservations or weakness, whoever those people may be, whether they be French or—more probably—foreign.[45]

The following day, the government announced that it was offering a reward of one million francs for information on those suspected of responsibility for the wave of CSPPA bombings.[46] The government's tough stand on terrorism was popular; both Chirac and Mitterand benefited from increased support in public opinion polls. That support was soon threatened, however, when the newspaper *Le Canard*

Enchaîné reported that the government had attempted, earlier in the year, to negotiate a deal with Abdallah's terrorist supporters. Chirac was forced to deny that any deal was contemplated and to restate his unswerving commitment to fighting terrorism resolutely.[47] Informed observers expressed skepticism at such categorical denials, however, and reports of "behind the scenes deals" continued through the months that followed. More will be said of these later.

Of greater significance is the fact that the government proceeded in February 1987 with the second trial of Georges Abdallah, this time for the murder of American and Israeli diplomats, in spite of the threats of terrorism, which were supposed to dissuade France from pursuing a prosecution. Of course, the government may have felt that it had little choice but to proceed, if only to counter the accusations that it had made a deal to free Abdallah in return for a terrorist truce. Moreover, it was under some pressure from the United States, which was a co-respondent in the case against Abdallah for the murder of diplomat Charles Ray. The courts secured a conviction, Abdallah was awarded a life sentence, and the sky did not fall; there was no repeat of the bombing offensive of 1986. Shortly after the trial was completed, the DST broke up the CSPPA network discussed earlier in the chapter.

Since that time, there have been no international terrorism campaigns in France on the same scale as those of 1986. Accordingly, in spite of a change of government (to socialists again) in 1988, there was no significant change of policy.

Negotiations with Terrorists and Sponsors

The official position of the French government has always been that—as a matter of policy and principle—it does not negotiate *directly* with terrorists and does not make concessions to them.[48] The evidence from several cases discussed earlier suggests that the norm was the exact opposite of the official position: that negotiations with international terrorists played a major role in French counter-terrorism policy. Even a cursory review of the incidents indicates a pattern of actions distinctly at variance with official policy.

* In 1981, the head of the French secret service negotiated a deal with the head of the Syrian secret service, under which Abu Nidal was supposed to refrain from further attacks in France. When that failed to stop Abu Nidal's operations there, Joseph Franceschi, the secretary of state for public security, had a secret meeting with Abu Iyad, the second in command in *Al-Fatah*, with a view to gaining *Al-Fatah's* cooperation against Abu Nidal.[49]

* Reports surfaced in October 1983 that, with the knowledge of President Mitterand's advisor on anti-terrorist measures, a French police officer had been dealing with AD and the FLNC.[50]

* In January 1986, the French government held indirect talks in Damascus with intermediaries for pro-Iranian groups holding French hostages in Lebanon. The

terrorists' main demand was the release of Anis Naccache (who was serving a life sentence for the attempted assassination of Bakhtiar). The deal ultimately failed when the French refused to release him. In the meantime, however, they declined to arrest a suspect in the 1985 TWA hijacking, possibly because this might have disrupted these hostage negotiations.[51]

- French negotiations with Iran on matters of debt repayment and release of hostages in Iran continued through the bombings of 1986. French officials declined to link the hostage issue to the debt repayment nor to the bombings in Paris and the rumors of the possible release of Abdallah. Those rumors were given additional credence by the fact that Archbishop Hilarion Capucci, who claimed that he was on a "mission" and that "negotiations" were under way, met with Public Security Minister Paindraud both before and after his meeting with Abdallah. By the end of October 1986, the French media were reporting that, with the help of Syria and Algeria, the French government had reached a deal to end the bombing offensive. While denying that any "deal" had been reached with "terrorists" per se, the government confirmed the basic accuracy of the media reports.[52]

- In July 1987, when Wahid Gordji took refuge in the Iranian embassy to avoid questioning in the CSPPA investigation, the French government initially stood firm. Chirac stated that it was "out of the question" that Gordji could leave France without being interrogated about the CSPPA bombings. Five months later, however, that is exactly what happened. Gordji appeared before a French magistrate on 30 November, but only as a witness, not a suspect, and it was apparently understood that he would face no charges (in any case, the evidence linking him to the case was inconclusive). He was quickly taken to a waiting aircraft and flown to Karachi, where he was exchanged for the French diplomat who had been besieged in his embassy in Teheran in retaliation for the French blockade of the Iranian embassy in Paris. More important, two French hostages were released in Lebanon, upon payment of a ransom (denied by the French government). France and Iran resumed diplomatic relations, which had been broken when the embassy sieges began.[53]

- In May 1988, the government confirmed that a "bargain" had been arranged that facilitated the release and return home of three French hostages in Lebanon. Although French authorities denied that a ransom was paid, they declined to discuss specific details of the deal. Other sources inside the government stated that France paid the kidnappers US $1.8 million and agreed to sell weapons to Iran and to repay part of a $1 billion loan outstanding since the reign of the Shah.[54]

These "deals" were almost always controversial, and several, such as the Abu Daoud and Gordji affairs, as well as indirect contacts with Iraq, leading to the release of French hostages during the 1990 Gulf crisis, drew considerable criticism at home and abroad.[55] The government's standard response was either to deny that any deals had been made or, if that position were untenable in the face of public knowledge, to dismiss criticism and insist that it was not dealing directly with terrorists, and that in any case the deals were in France's best interests.[56]

How can this blatantly duplicitous policy be explained? It cannot be simply the result of a collapse of will, since France has demonstrated its willingness to act firmly in other situations involving the use of force—by or against France. Nor can it be attributed to the "weakness" of one political party; both Gaullists and Socialists have made deals, so the policy transcends simple party politics. The answer, if there is one, probably lies in the nature of the terrorist threat itself and in the context of French foreign policy. In all but one of the cases noted above, the "arrangements" related to terrorism originating in the Middle East. This fact is important in two respects: first, none of the Middle Eastern terrorist campaigns in France—however horrific their results—threatened in any fundamental way the stability of the French state. The violence was a costly, deadly nuisance, but was not aimed at subverting the French government. So it could be argued that making deals with such groups was almost harmless from the perspective of domestic politics. They did not impede or undermine the ability of the authorities to govern effectively.

Second, the Middle Eastern context is important because it places any "deals" in this regard firmly in the province of French foreign policy. Since 1967, that policy has been increasingly and consistently pro-Arab and has generated considerable commercial benefits for France, particularly, but not exclusively, in the realm of arms sales. However, the Iran-Iraq War and the Lebanese civil war, with their attendant surrogate wars between rival factions, were complicating factors for French foreign policy, since these events tended to force France to choose sides in situations where the French would have preferred to pursue a neutral path, maintaining good relations with all parties concerned. As the Iran-Iraq War continued, French policy increasingly favored Iraq, if only to ensure that it was not defeated; France made a number of significant arms sales to Iraq, notably sales of advanced combat aircraft. In Lebanon, the French participated in the multinational peace-keeping force, which was meant to be a neutral presence, but which came to be seen by the pro-Iranian Shia as favoring the Lebanese Christians. Consequently, the Shiite extremists targeted the French along with the Americans in October 1983.[57]

The Iran-Iraq War and the Lebanese civil war clearly complicated French foreign policy in the region in a manner that threatened the continuity and productivity of that policy. France's relations with Iran and Syria had deteriorated during these events. It seems reasonable to conclude, therefore, that there was a direct connection between France's desire to normalize its Middle East policy and its willingness to enter into arrangements with Iran and Syria that would be of mutual benefit. Chirac said as much in defending the hostage release deal in May 1988.[58]

The foregoing suggests that to comprehend the French penchant for "dealing their way" out of international terrorism, one cannot focus solely on the counter-terrorism implications. The problem was handled—and must be seen— in the wider arena of foreign policy. In that arena, a "long view," a "Gaullist vision," of French national interest predominated, regardless of the complexion of the government and the politics of the immediate moment. Still, such a policy bears scrutiny in order to question whether any of the deals that were entered into actually furthered those long-term interests and, if so, whether the price was acceptable. For there was a price paid in French blood, even as deals were pursued; there were no guarantees from attack. Furthermore, there was also a cost incurred in terms of relations and cooperation with some of France's principal western allies.

Security and Intelligence

There are three security/intelligence services in France that handle anti-terrorist activities, each in a different way, and until recently, none was very effective. The *Direction générale de la sécurité extérieure* (DGSE) comes under the Ministry of Defense. Responsible for foreign intelligence collection and analysis and for counterintelligence, it is in theory limited to foreign operations, but in reality it sometimes becomes involved in domestic activities. It was reorganized in 1981-1982 by the Mitterand government, which was dissatisfied with its performance with respect to the Middle East, including its ability to warn about terrorism. The service, which employs some 2,000 people, was divided into several departments: research; intelligence, which handles human sources; analysis; planning, prospects, and evaluations, which is supposed to provide warnings; and the "action division," whose tasks include SIGINT and cryptanalysis, the monitoring for quality and reliability of the intelligence department's sources, and other "special services." It was the action division, notorious for its penchant for skullduggery and para-military activities, that carried out the attack on the *Rainbow Warrior*. This led to yet another "purge," but the DGSE continued to live with an image of near incompetence.

Its critics have suggested that the problems can be attributed largely to the fact that the mostly civilian staff is directed by military officers who serve only temporarily in the organization and whose outlook and skills are not oriented to intelligence. Others have pointed out that the DGSE has also been overcommitted, understaffed, and underfunded.[59] If the provision of warning about terrorist attack is a fair criterion for judging the quality of DGSE's work, then the bombings of French targets in Beirut in 1983 and Paris in 1986 would appear to validate the criticisms of the service. The latter series occurred in spite of the fact that the DGSE had an agent in direct contact with Georges Ibrahim Abdallah—his lawyer. However, as noted earlier, Abdallah's group probably was not responsible for the September bombings,[60] so the DGSE agent was not in a position to provide the necessary warning.

Furthermore, counter-terrorist intelligence on French territory is really the responsibility of the DST, which is part of the Ministry of the Interior. Also reorganized in 1982, its staff of 1,600 became more effective and had some success penetrating Syrian and Libyan networks operating in France. Perhaps the most significant success was its breaking of the CSPPA network in 1987. These successes might be attributed in part to the DST's wide mandate, which includes both criminal investigation work and the collection of intelligence that could be used to counter the actions of foreign states. When the two tasks are combined, the DST is able to pursue all intelligence leads relevant to prosecution. But this broad approach also entails some problems.

First, the police have complained that the DST demonstrated a tendency to "go it alone," to exploit its own sources and contacts without consulting the other French services. One study quotes a report by French senators, which observes that "when the DST needs information, either on foreign terrorism, or about support given to terrorists outside our frontiers, it is more willing to seek it from certain foreign services than from colleagues in the DGSE."[61]

Second, such a broad mandate inevitably permitted the DST to stray into the realms of politics and diplomacy, thereby entangling it in controversy. These cases included the Abu Daoud incident in 1977 and negotiations with Middle East terrorist groups and their sponsors, such as Syria, in the 1980s. The DST has also had its share of failures: in June 1975, Carlos murdered two DST agents who had come to question him unarmed, so ignorant were they of his real identity. In 1983 the DST was unable to prevent the bombing of the Turkish Airlines ticket counter at Orly Airport, in spite of a seven-month investigation, which included tailing the leader of ASALA during his visit to Paris and thereby identifying most of that terrorist network.[62] The DST's successes depended, in some cases, on the simple good fortune that is often the key to intelligence and criminal investigation. When the West German police arrested Mohammed Ali Hamadei in 1987, he was carrying an address book containing the phone number of Ali Saleh (the leader of the CSPPA), which the Germans passed on to the DST. But it was a "walk-in" informer that clinched the case against him. This case at least demonstrates the value of the DST's international contacts, and the Abdallah case itself clearly indicates that the DST's combined intelligence collection and criminal investigation skills did assist the police in arresting many people suspected of involvement in international terrorism.[63]

The third security/intelligence service involved in countering terrorism is the *Direction centrale de renseignments généraux* (RG), which is a major directorate of the National Police. Its three subdirectorates collect information on a wide range of subjects, including organized crime and the domestic political, social, and economic situation. The RG also maintains a computer-based data retrieval system on known and suspected terrorists and their sympathizers. While the RG is responsible for the system, all of the security forces have quick access to the data.[64] But, as suggested earlier, the security forces do not always cooperate readily; the National Police frequently complained that the DST does not consult the RG in anti-terrorist investigations. The UCLAT coordinating body was created in order to overcome some of these problems, but clearly was unable to eliminate them completely. At the international level, even where relations were good, exchanges of intelligence were hampered by different national attitudes toward privacy of information, the desire to protect sources of intelligence, and incompatible data-sharing technology.[65] In 1986, the French government warned that it would "reassert the role of the secret services"[66] and try to "terrorize the terrorists."[67] If this was done, it is not apparent from the evidence. Either the results were negligible, or the successes have been carefully concealed.

Military and Para-military Measures

When confronted by political terrorism in the 1970s, the French government concluded that its existing para-military forces—the *Compagnies républicaines de sécurité* (CRS) and the *Gendarmerie nationale*—were not suitable for the sophisticated siege-breaking/hostage-rescue task. So, in 1974, France decided to create a new specialized unit within the Gendarmerie to respond to hijackings and other terrorist siege situations. This unit was designated the *Groupe d'intervention de gendarmerie nationale* (GIGN). The fifty four-man GIGN has carried out many operations, including, it is alleged, assisting the Saudi Arabian security forces in recapturing the Grand Mosque at Mecca, which had been seized by Muslim extremists in 1980.

Although the GIGN was held in high regard for its technical competence, the French decided to create a second anti-terrorist unit in 1985. Designated RAID, (for *Unité de recherche, d'assistance, d'intervention et de dissuasion*) (Search, Assistance, Intervention, and Deterrence Unit), it operates under the direction of the head of the National Police. The RAID is designed for several missions: long-term surveillance, immediate or preplanned intervention (such as to end a hijacking or hostage-taking), and VIP escort and protection. Like their counterparts in the British Special Air Service (SAS) regiment and the German *Grenzschutzgruppen 9* (GSG-9), the RAID members are carefully selected and well trained; only seventy seven were accepted out of 1,000 applicants. There are, however, insufficient data available to assess RAID's operational performance.[68]

Published sources do not indicate why the French government concluded it was necessary to create a new force in 1985. But it is possible that the government had come to regard the GIGN as a political liability. In 1983, the French press revealed that Captain Paul Barril, former acting head of the GIGN, had been involved in "negotiations" with the leaders of AD and the FLNC, apparently with the knowledge and approval of President Mitterand's advisor on counter-terrorism. Barril's contacts were at first denied, then confirmed. It appeared that he had created a "special cell," independent of the GIGN, but making use of it as necessary. In addition to making contact with illegal groups, the special team was also implicated in "unofficial" phone taps and the mishandling of evidence. A year earlier, the GIGN itself and Captain Barril had been at the center of another controversy, arising from their arrest of three Irish nationals suspected of involvement in terrorism in Europe. While the arrests were made "quietly and without violence," the GIGN made a number of errors in procedure. Consequently, the court ruled that the three had to be released, and what had been touted as a major breakthrough against terrorism collapsed in ignominy.[69]

Generally speaking, since the Algerian War the armed forces have not been used for counter-terrorism operations. The few exceptions arose in circumstances where military means could be applied in a conventional manner outside France. In 1978, French paratroopers dropped into action to rescue a large number of European hostages seized by rebels at Kolwezi, Zaire. In November 1983, French carrier-launched jets carried out attacks on the suspected headquarters of Shiite terrorists in Lebanon in retaliation for the bombing of the French contingent of the multinational peace-keeping force in Beirut the previous month.[70]

Target-Hardening

In fact, most of the work undertaken by the security forces was of a much more mundane nature and consisted largely of target-hardening. In order to make it harder for terrorists to strike at high-risk targets, French police and Gendarmerie periodically tightened security around government buildings, foreign embassies, and public facilities, such as train stations. They increased identity checks and examinations of hand baggage in stores, theaters, and restaurants and searched diplomatic bags for weapons and explosives. After the 1986 bombing wave, the armed forces were called out to patrol France's land borders, which are marked by more than 1,000 crossing points. During the second trial of Georges Ibrahim Abdallah in 1987, court security was bolstered by extra Gendarmerie, helicopter surveillance, and twenty four-hour bodyguards for the seven judges hearing the case. Such stringent security was not an idle consideration; the trial of three AD members collapsed in December 1986 when jurors refused to serve after being threatened with vengeance by one of the defendants, Régis Schleicher.[71]

While hardly futile, there were obvious limits to the effectiveness of target-hardening. Like most Western countries, France has too many points of entry—land, sea, and air—and too few resources to catch every terrorist infiltrator. Furthermore, in quiet periods, security naturally was reduced; this was a common tendency among democratic states and was not a phenomenon peculiar to France. Increased target-hardening measures usually *followed* a series of attacks. Thus, they probably had more value as a psychological reassurance to the public than as a deterrent, since the attacks had already occurred. Whether such measures actually deterred further attacks is not known; confirmations could only really come from the terrorists themselves.

International Cooperation

The central issues affecting French cooperation with other states against international terrorism were the closely related questions of asylum and extradition. Since 1927, the "right" of asylum for political refugees has been enshrined in French law. It was, and is, regarded as a sacred trust. Clearly an honorable policy that favors the protection of human rights, its very open-ended nature left it vulnerable to abuse. It could be—and was—exploited by extremist groups and individuals who used France as a base for preparing for violent actions elsewhere, protected from retribution by the shield of France's asylum law. It was also abused by successive French governments who, in the interests of higher policy (as in the Middle East) or in order to express their opposition to a particular government (such as Spain's Franco regime), were prepared to "look the other way." Requests for extradition were denied, and so long as French lives were not endangered, foreign terrorists were allowed to go about their deadly business.

As discussed earlier, there was a significant Palestinian presence in France, and in spite of their occasionally bloody attacks, they were handled with "kid gloves," much to the anger and frustration of their victims, principally the Israelis. The Italian government believed that France provided sanctuary for several hundred members of the Red Brigades (BR) and related groups, who were suspected of violent crimes in Italy. Some, like BR founder Mario Moretti, came and went, using France as a base for smuggling arms and Paris as a venue for making contact with other European terrorist groups. While French authorities were prepared to make occasional arrests of Italian terrorists, they rejected Italian requests for their extradition. In doing so, the French either cited the law on asylum or invoked the political exception clause of the ECST.[72] Although there was no doubting the BR's role in Italian terrorism, and the Italian police were able to amass considerable evidence against specific individuals, the French remained unmoved. Until the lives of French citizens were seriously jeopardized, the French view appeared to be that the principle of asylum could not be tampered with. To make exceptions to this rule for one state would undermine the entire arrangement, thereby putting at risk genuine political refugees of conscience.

The change in the French position on this issue came slowly. When it did come, however, it was significant in that it was applied effectively against France's most serious and politically complex sanctuary problem—that of the ETA, the Spanish Basque separatist movement. The French government, which was opposed to the authoritarian rule of Spain's General Franco, did nothing to restrict the ETA's actions on French territory, as long as Franco remained in power and the ETA did not attempt to mobilize French Basques. That policy began to change after two events in 1973. First, the French Basque separatist movement *Iparretarak* emerged that year. Second, the ETA assassinated the Spanish prime minister in December 1973; the perpetrators fled across the border to France, where they held a press conference in order to claim responsibility for the killing. That event marked the beginning of the shift in French policy. The assassins were arrested in January 1974, and later that year the ETA was declared a prohibited organization, along with Breton and Corsican separatist movements. But until Franco died in November 1975, France did little more to restrict the ETA's activities in France.[73]

In 1976, with significant political change under way in Spain, French authorities began to place greater restrictions on Spanish Basques in France. Although they were not extradited and the ETA's headquarters and training facilities were not broken up, refugee status and residency and work permits became harder to obtain. Suspected ETA leaders were subjected to increased surveillance, harassment, searches without warrant, and other forms of intimidation. Some were taken into preventive detention in remote locations, and as early as January 1977, seven Basques were sent back to Spain. But France steadfastly refused to extradite any known members of the ETA, even though by the late 1970s Spain was well advanced in the transition to democratic rule.[74]

As noted earlier, however, by the early 1980s, the Basque terrorist problem had become a French as well as a Spanish one. To complicate matters, since the late 1970s, Spanish anti-Basque terrorists, possibly with official support, had carried out attacks and assassinations inside France.[75] These developments sent an unmistakable message to the French: playing host to terrorists is not a risk-free option; it is dangerous and costly, and two can play the game. Even so, it was not until 1984 that the French government commenced extradition of ETA suspects to Spain.

Cooperative efforts in this regard had got off to a bad start in June-August 1981. In June, a French court ruled in favor of extraditing Tomas Linaza, wanted in Spain for involvement in the murder of six civil guards in 1980. This was the first time a French court had so ruled, but the final decision on extradition—which was considered a political, not a legal, matter—was left to the government. On government instruction, Linaza was released. Shortly thereafter, Gaston Defferre, then interior minister in the new socialist government, publicly ruled out extradition of any of the twelve ETA members being held in French jails; indeed, his remarks, comparing the ETA to the French resistance, deeply offended the Spanish government, which was committed to democracy and had granted "autonomy" to the Basque region. The Spanish prime minister called off a planned meeting with Defferre, and a meeting of justice ministers in August produced only an agreement to continue cooperation against ETA terrorism.[76]

In November 1982, when the government announced that it had decided to review its asylum and extradition policies, the view expressed was that France could not continue on its present course, which clearly was having negative domestic and foreign consequences. The criterion for extradition would be whether the violence used in a particular incident was so excessive that it could not be justified by the political end for which it was carried out.[77] Of course, that criterion was very elastic, open to subjective judgment. Not surprisingly, there were no immediate extraditions. The turnabout of French policy was not complete until the summer of 1984. By that time, there was concern that Spain's socialist government, whose credentials were impeccably democratic by any standard the French cared to use, was genuinely threatened by the cycle of terrorism and counter-terrorism in the Basque region, and that France would be at least partly to blame if the democratic regime were destabilized. Moreover, by this time, the Spanish government's policy of permitting exiled or jailed ETA members to rejoin normal society on the conditions of renouncing violence and pursuing their cause through legitimate channels clearly had demonstrated some success.

A policy of reconciliation rather than retribution, aimed specifically at ETA members and supporters living in France, it was an initiative the French government could hardly ignore. So, in June 1984, Spain and France signed an agreement on anti-terrorist cooperation. The change in French attitudes was symbolized by the words of Gaston Defferre at the signing: he declared, "A terrorist is not a political refugee."[78] In August, French courts ruled against the asylum claims of seven ETA members. In September, four were deported to Africa, and three were extradited to Spain. Other ETA extraditions, arrests, and many expulsions followed. The French decision was significant for its wider anti-terrorist implications. Once the principle of asylum was breached with respect to the Basques, no group or individual could assume that its sanctuary in France was secure. And while there has not been a flood of extraditions, since 1986 the French have been much more vigorous in pursuing and prosecuting foreign terrorists on French territory. In November 1986, France announced that it would ratify the ECST.[79] They have also expanded their cooperation with other European countries.

France has been active in a number of international organizations whose mandates included the promotion of increased interstate cooperation against international terrorism. These include the "Summit Seven," the Council of Europe, and various European Community (EC) endeavors, such as the Club of Berne (meetings of the EC intelligence chiefs) and the TREVI Group of interior/justice ministers and police chiefs. In May 1987, France hosted a joint Summit Seven/EC meeting of interior and justice ministers, which was hailed as a breakthrough. French Interior Minister Pasqua claimed that the conference demonstrated "a willingness to take all the measures necessary" to improve international cooperation against terrorism.[80] Yet it is clear that France prefers the bilateral approach, wherein it is not subject to high-visibility "ganging up" and pressure by a number of governments.

In February 1986, France resisted a proposal that joint efforts to respond to terrorism be placed on the agenda of the forthcoming Summit Seven meeting in Tokyo. Clearly concerned that France's diplomatic interests and negotiating techniques could be hampered by a high-profile show of solidarity, French officials emphasized that they were hostile to any initiative "that would create the impression" that the Summit Seven were acting "as an executive body."[81] But when the summit was held in May, shortly after the US confrontation with and bombing of Libya (on April 15), France was overruled; the summit issued a strong condemnation of terrorism, which urged a wide range of cooperative efforts, although it stopped short of making them mandatory.[82]

Likewise, later that year, France (along with Greece) prevented a unified EC effort to isolate Syria diplomatically as punishment for its involvement in the attempted bombing of an El Al airliner in April. As a result, only limited sanctions were applied to Syria. Citing France's historical interest in the region, particularly in trying to promote peace in Lebanon, Prime Minister Chirac stated that France's relations with Syria "could only ever be upset if it was stunningly clear that Syria had committed aggression against France."[83] Chirac had earlier lent credence to the rumor that the El Al bombing attempt was, in fact, an Israeli provocation to discredit Syria. As noted earlier, in the wake of the September bombings, France had been negotiating with Syria to secure its cooperation in ending the offensive. Syria rewarded France for its refusal to support strong sanctions (France did agree to block two arms deals) by facilitating the release of two French hostages held in Lebanon. According to the Syrian foreign minister, "The French government position has certainly helped in gaining the release of the hostages."[84]

At the bilateral level, France and West Germany have cooperated in joint security efforts to suppress terrorism emanating from and directed against both countries.[85] A more cooperative relationship with the United States did not develop until the latter half of 1986. In April, the French government denied the US the right to overfly France in carrying out the air raid against Libya in response to the *La Belle* discotheque bombing. France claimed to fear that such an attack would only incite Qaddafi further and complicate French efforts to secure the release of hostages in Lebanon. Privately, in a meeting with the US envoy, Ambassador Vernon Walters, President Mitterand hinted that France might actually consider stronger joint military action to *topple* Qaddafi. However, in his study of the crisis, Brian L. Davis suggests this might have been merely a pose, advanced by Mitterand "in full knowledge that Washington would not consider an invasion of Libya politically viable."[86] After the air raid, the French foreign minister criticized the American action, but also warned Libya not to consider a reprisal against southern Europe. In spite of damage caused to the French embassy in Tripoli, French public opinion strongly supported *both* the air raid *and* France's denial of overflight rights.[87]

If France's lack of support soured relations, it did so only temporarily. At the end of June, France sent a delegation to Washington for talks with the State Department's Office for Counter-terrorism. In the autumn, following the CSPPA bombings, Robert Paindraud—France's counter-terrorism coordinator—announced that the two countries had agreed to an accelerated program of anti-terrorist cooperation, including improved intelligence exchanges and contact between law enforcement officials. The 1989 State Department report on terrorism praised France for its positive contributions to the international campaign against terrorism.[88] Indeed, it may be fair to suggest that it was at the level of bilateral cooperation between police and security services of different states that France felt it was most free to act. While this sort of activity was not glamorous and attracted much less attention than high-profile summits, that might have been part of its appeal. Cooperation with other states could proceed discreetly, without necessarily compromising France's wider and more visible national interests. In this respect, it was little different from France's practice of using "back channels" to "negotiate" with terrorists and their sponsors.

CONCLUSIONS

In the first part of this chapter, the survey of terrorism in France concluded that international terrorism was a less significant threat to France than its domestic counterpart, particularly that of the FLNC, whose campaign was prolonged, sustained, and directed at removing a part of French territory from French control. But it also noted that if international terrorism did not, in and of itself, undermine the foundations of the state, it did pose a major threat to the lives of those living in France. It also complicated French foreign policy-making. These observations raise fundamental questions: was the French response to international terrorism effective? Was it appropriate and proportionate to the actual level of threat? Or was there an unnecessary erosion of democratic values and practices?

Turning first to the issue of effectiveness, this is, in fact, one of the hardest factors to measure. The French case is instructive in this regard. The relatively low level of Middle Eastern terrorism in France in the early to mid-1970s could be attributed to several non-deterrence factors: French foreign policy, which at that time favored the Arab cause in the struggle with Israel, and the French policy of sanctuary, which allowed Palestinian groups a certain freedom of action on French territory (it was to their advantage not to draw too much attention to themselves by carrying out many operations in France). Similarly, operations by the ASALA in France ended not because French countermeasures were effective, but because internal dissension disrupted the group—a factor over which the French had no influence.

What, then, if anything, can be said about the effectiveness of the French approach to countering international terrorism? To the extent that it can be measured at all, clearly it had a mixed record of success. On the positive side, the courts—both regular and special—functioned properly; those convicted of serious terrorism-related crimes received lengthy sentences, which at least kept them from committing further acts of violence. Several terrorist campaigns, such as that of the LARF, were terminated in this way. Extradition of ETA suspects to Spain helped to make that problem more manageable for both countries, even if it did not eliminate ETA terrorism altogether. International cooperation paid off in the CSPPA case; information from the West Germans allowed the French to capture an entire terrorist network.

On balance, however, the French approach weighs heavily on the negative side. The asylum policy and the refusal to ratify the ECST offered no disincentives to terrorists. There was no deterrent to operating in France, and every major Middle Eastern group—such as the PFLP and the Abu Nidal Organization and some state terrorists—operated in France at one time or another. Indeed, it can be credibly argued that the combination of the asylum policy and the refusal to extradite actually prolonged the French experience of terrorism and cost French and foreign lives. Likewise, Mitterand's amnesty freed the leaders of AD, who returned to terrorism without hesitation; their activities plagued France for six more years. Secret negotiations and "under the table" deals freed some hostages, but did not prevent others from being taken; in fact, this may have encouraged more kidnapping. In the Wahid Gordji case, it probably prevented the police and the courts from making a final determination regarding Iran's degree of responsibility for the CSPPA bombings.[89] In any case, deals and negotiations brought, at best, only a temporary respite from terrorist attacks.

The DST's successes notwithstanding, the performance of the security/intelligence services was less than impressive. Nor is it clear that France has overcome its counter-terrorism policy and intelligence coordination problems. Finally, above the level of agency-to-agency contacts (which were productive), French counter-terrorism policies did not favor international cooperation until the end of 1986. In fact, the reverse may be true: the asylum policy, the refusal to extradite, and negotiations with terrorist groups and their sponsors, such as Syria, may have actually worked against multinational efforts to curb international terrorism. In this sense, the counter-terrorism policies—pursued with the aim of furthering (or at least not interfering with) France's narrowly defined, even self-serving, "national interests" in the Middle East—probably worked against France's wider interests by angering its European neighbors and global allies. If so, then the French approach was counterproductive in the most important sense.

But if French policies were less than wholly effective and even at times detrimental to the national interest, were they appropriate and proportionate in relation to the threat, and did they protect French democracy and human rights? The evidence suggests that no one could accuse the French of overreacting. They have placed few limits on fundamental freedoms and have acquiesced to limits only gradually and with considerable reluctance. The prolonged adherence to the principle of asylum, the refusal to ratify the ECST, the refusal to extradite, the use of amnesties, and the abolition (temporarily) of the special court for political violence offenses represented efforts to preserve France's commitment to political rights and freedoms. There is no equivalent in France of Britain's Prevention of Terrorism Act; the regime of French law dealing with political violence was extended narrowly, and even the *loi Pasqua*, which provides for administrative measures that *are* harsh by French standards, falls far short of the special British powers in this area. Moreover, there is no persuasive evidence that it has been rigorously enforced. The French courts have proven to be sticklers for detail and have thrown out otherwise clear-cut cases when they suspected that the police had not followed proper criminal investigation or arrest procedures.

This is not to suggest that no one's rights have been violated in the execution of counter-terrorism policy and countermeasures. Some felt, not without some justification, that such measures were applied disproportionately against visible minorities, particularly immigrant groups and individuals from North Africa and the Middle East. Worse still, official identification of such groups as being suspected of complicity in terrorism had the effect of singling them out for attacks by racists. Other areas of concern with respect to civil liberties included the wide mandate and investigative powers of the DST, which appeared to provide carte blanche for politically influenced investigations and intrusive surveillance of legitimate dissidents and other innocent persons; the expansion of identity checks to include financial means of support; the extension of police powers to detain and question suspects; the creation of a special non-jury court to hear terrorism cases; and increasingly subjective and arbitrary criteria for the expulsion of persons suspected of posing a threat to public order.

The most significant regression from France's liberal tradition was the retreat from unquestioned and open-ended asylum for all who claimed political refugee status.[90] Yet this was surrendered under protest, and only after it was clear that France could no longer justify asylum for ETA members on moral and political grounds, and that terrorists were undeniably abusing the privilege at the cost of the lives of French citizens and those foreigners whom the French had a responsibility to protect, such as diplomats.

This leads to one final question: did France achieve proper balance between effectiveness and protection of democratic principles, practices, and freedoms? The answer is no; the French in the 1980s experienced democracy and freedom, but not security, and the cost was lives lost or irreparably harmed. Freedom was purchased at the expense of security, and the human cost was very high. There is an ironic lesson in this, the importance of which ought not to be lost on other countries. It is that the pursuit or preservation of liberties and human rights unfettered by security may lead ultimately to the loss or erosion of the very rights and liberties the democracy was supposed to protect. In short, the preservation of human rights *presupposes* a degree of security. Without it, a most fundamental human right—the right to life without fear and threat of arbitrary violence—can be lost, even in a liberal democracy.

NOTES

1. Edward F. Mickolus, Todd Sandler, and Jean M. Murdock, *International Terrorism in the 1980s: A Chronology of Events*, vol. 1 (Ames: Iowa State University Press, 1989), pp. 65-66. See also "The Hit Men Strike Again," *Newsweek*, 4 August 1980; and *The Globe and Mail* (Toronto), 28 July 1990.

2. See, for example, Bruce Hoffman, *Recent Trends and Future Prospects of Iranian Sponsored International Terrorism*, no. R-3783-USDP (Santa Monica, Calif.: Rand Corp., March 1990), pp. 2-34.

3. Norman Hampson, "From Regeneration to Terror: The Ideology of the French Revolution," in Noel O'Sullivan, ed., *Terrorism, Ideology and Revolution: The Origins of Modern Political Violence* (Boulder, Colo.: Westview Press, 1986), pp. 65-66.

4. Nora Levin, *The Holocaust: The Destruction of European Jewry* (New York: Schocken Books, 1973), pp. 402-3, 427-58; see also Bertram M. Gordon, *Collaborationism in France During the Second World War* (Ithaca, N.Y.: Cornell University Press, 1980).

5. Edward Moxon-Browne, *Terrorism in France*, Conflict Studies no. 144 (London: Institute for the Study of Conflict [hereafter cited as ISC], 1983), pp. 8-10; Peter Janke, *Guerrilla and Terrorist Organizations: A World Directory and Bibliography* (Brighton, England: Harvester Press, 1983), pp. 28-30. In 1987, a court building in Rennes was attacked. *Le Figaro*, 8 July 1987.

6. On the origins of the Corsican conflict and of FLNC, see Robert Ramsay, *The Corsican Time Bomb* (Manchester, England: Manchester University Press, 1983). On FLNC's terrorist campaign, see Moxon-Browne, pp. 10-16; Peter Savigear, *Corsica: Regional Autonomy or Violence*, Conflict Studies no. 149 (London: ISC, 1983); Guy Arnold et al., *Revolutionary and Dissident Movements: An International Guide*, 3d ed., (Detroit: Gale

Research/Longman, 1991), pp. 98-100; US Department of State, *Patterns of Global Terrorism: 1989* (Washington, D.C.: Department of State, April 1990), p. 27. See also *The European*, 11-14 June 1992; François Caviglioli, "Corse le temps des cagoules," *Le Nouvel Observateur*, no. 1452 (3-9 September 1992), pp. 40-43; *Nice-Matin*, 5 December 1992.

7. Philippe Madelin, *La Galaxie Terroriste* (Paris: Plon, 1986), pp. 211-15; *Le Figaro*, 8 July 1987; Arnold et al., p. 96; *Le Parisien*, 11 May 1992.

8. Alistair Horne, *A Savage War of Peace: Algeria, 1954-1962* (New York: Viking, 1977), pp. 236-37, 317-19.

9. Ibid., pp. 183-207, 416, 492-95, 500-504; Paul Henissart, *Wolves in the City: The Death of French Algeria* (New York: Simon and Schuster, 1970), pp. 195-201, 244-58, 270-72, 288-91, 476-77.

10. The anarchist concept of direct action refers to the practice of taking action directly against the perceived source of oppression (e.g., government, business, the police). See Nicholas Walter, "Anarchist Action," in George Woodcock, ed., *The Anarchist Reader* (Glasgow: Fontana/Collins, 1977; repr. 1983), pp. 168-69

11. "Direct Action, Action Directe (AD)," *TVI Profile* 8, no. 2 (1988), p. 1. On AD's ideology, see Michael Dartnell, "France's *Action Directe:* Terrorists in Search of a Revolution," *Terrorism and Political Violence* 2, no. 4 (Winter 1990), pp. 457-88.

12. Arnold et al., p. 95; US Defense Intelligence Agency, *Terrorist Group Profiles* (Washington, D.C.: US Government Printing Office, December 1988), pp. 42-3; Roland Jacquard, *La Longe Traque d'Action Directe* (Paris: Albin Michel, 1987); "A War on French Computers," *Newsweek*, 28 April 1980, p. 56.

13. Arnold et al., p. 95; Mickolus, Sandler, and Murdock, vol. 1, pp. 307-8.

14. Dartnell, pp. 459, 461, 469-75, 477-79; Edwy Plenel, "The Anatomy of a French Terrorist Sect," *Le Monde,* 15-16 May 1986, reprinted in *Manchester Guardian Weekly*, 1 June 1986; RAF and *Action Directe, Pour L'Unite des Revolutionnaires en Europe de l'Ouest* [Communiqué], 15 January 1985); *Washington Post*, 29 January 1985; Jacques Isnard, "Action Directe Joins Terrorist International," *Le Monde*, 27-28 January 1985, reprinted in *Manchester Guardian Weekly*, 3 February 1985; Arnold et al., pp. 95-96. A later report suggested that *Action Directe* and the RAF carried out the assassination at Iranian instigation, under the (mistaken) belief that Audran had blocked arms sales to Iran. On this, see *Newsweek*, 9 March 1987.

15. *Washington Post*, 29 January 1985, and 6 September 1985; James Adams, "Terrorism Incorporated," *Sunday Times* (London), 3 February 1985; *New York Times*, 10 August 1985; Laurent Greilsamer, "Action Directe Renews Its Bloody Campaign," *Le Monde*, 30 November 1986; Mickolus, Sandler, and Murdock, vol. 2, pp. 255-56; Arnold et al., p. 96.

16. *The Economist*, 28 February 1987, p. 45; US Defense Intelligence Agency, *Terrorist Group Profiles*, p. 43.

17. Edward Moxon-Browne, "Terrorism in France," in Juliet Lodge, ed., *The Threat of Terrorism* (Boulder, Colo.: Westview Press, 1988), pp. 213-16.

18. Ovid Demaris, *Brothers in Blood: The International Terrorist Network* (New York: Scribners, 1977), p. 32; Brian M. Jenkins and Janera Johnson, *International Terrorism: A Chronology, 1968-1974*, no. R-1597-DOS/ARPA (Santa Monica, Calif.: Rand Corp., March 1975), p. 48.

19. Colin Smith, *Carlos: Portrait of a Terrorist* (New York: Holt, Rinehart and Winston, 1976), pp. 9-11, 123, 125, 139-42, 170-81.

20. Ibid., pp. 184-90, 199-211, 293-96; Demaris, pp. 203-7. Both Smith and Demaris incorrectly identified the German woman terrorist as Gabrielle Kroecher-Tiedemann.

Kroecher-Tiedemann was arrested in Switzerland in 1977 and sentenced to fifteen years in prison in 1978 for the attempted murder of two border guards.

21. U.K. Foreign and Commonwealth Office, "Abu Nidal Group and State Terrorism," *Background Brief* (London: Foreign and Commonwealth Office, December 1986). See also Yossi Melman, *The Master Terrorist: The True Story of Abu Nidal* (New York: Adams Books, 1986), pp. 119-21; Mickolus, Sandler, and Murdock, vol. 1, p. 307; *The Globe and Mail*, 11 August 1982.

22. Anat Kurz and Ariel Merari, *ASALA: Irrational Terror or Political Tool* (Boulder, Colo.: Westview Press, 1985), pp. 23-29 and p. 78, app. 4; Michael M. Gunter, *"Pursuing the Just Cause of Their People": A Study of Contemporary Armenian Terrorism* (Westport, Conn.: Greenwood Press, 1986), pp. 44-45, 68-69; Mickolus, Sandler, and Murdock, vol. 1, pp. 417-18.

23. David Gilmour, *Lebanon: The Fractured Country* (Oxford: Martin Robertson, 1983), pp. 25-27, 60-62, 76-78; Augustus Richard Norton, *Amal and the Shia: Struggle for the Soul of Lebanon* (Austin: University of Texas Press, 1987), pp. 105, 172-73; Ralph King, *The Iran-Iraq War: The Political Implications*, Adelphi Papers no. 219 (London: International Institute for Strategic Studies, Spring 1987), pp. 55-56.

24. Robin Wright, *Sacred Rage: The Wrath of Militant Islam* (New York: Simon and Schuster, 1985), pp. 72, 112; US Defense Intelligence Agency, *Terrorist Group Profiles*, pp. 15-18; US Department of State, *Patterns of Global Terrorism: 1989*, p. 41. On the airliner bombing, see "Libyan Sponsored Terrorism Exclusive Evidence," *Political Warfare* (Special Issue) no. 19 (November 1991).

25. *The Globe and Mail*, 19 September 1986; Georges Marion and Edwy Plenel, "Portrait of a Terrorist Family," *Le Monde*, 10 September 1986, reprinted in *Manchester Guardian Weekly*, 21 September 1986; "The Bombs of September," *Newsweek*, 29 September 1986, pp. 30-34; Laurent Greilsamer, "Anatomy of a Middle Eastern Terrorist Network," *Le Monde*, 30 January 1990, reprinted in *Manchester Guardian Weekly*, 11 February 1990.

26. Greilsamer, "Anatomy"; and Laurent Greilsamer, "Fouad Saleh—The Militant Who Declared War on France" 30 January 1990; "The Name of the Rose," *The Economist*, 3 February 1990; *Washington Post*, 8 July 1987; *The Globe and Mail*, 1 December 1987.

27. Mickolus, Sandler and Murdock, vol. 1, pp. 89-90; Moxon-Browne, *Terrorism in France*, pp. 20-22; Arnold et al., pp. 92, 94; Bruce Hoffman, *Right-wing Terrorism in Europe*, no. N-1856-AF (Santa Monica, Calif.: Rand Corp., March 1982), pp. 8-10, 12-13.

28. Moxon-Browne, *Terrorism in France*, pp. 25-6.

29. Peter St. John, "Counter-terrorism Policy-making: The Case of Aircraft Hijacking, 1968-1988," in David A. Charters, ed., *Democratic Responses to International Terrorism* (Dobbs Ferry, N.Y.: Transnational Publishers, 1991), p. 96.

30. Smith, *Carlos*, pp. 114, 202-3, 211, 294-5.

31. *International Herald Tribune*, 12 January 1977; "The Prisoner Who Was Too Hot to Handle," *Time*, 24 January 1977, pp. 6-9.

32. J. Bowyer Bell, *A Time of Terror: How Democratic Societies Respond to Revolutionary Violence* (New York: Basic Books, 1978), pp. 23-29.

33. Jacques Léauté, "Terrorist Incidents and Legislation in France," in Ronald D. Crelinsten et al., eds., *Terrorism and Criminal Justice* (Lexington, Mass.: Lexington Books, 1978), p. 69.

34. Noemi Gal-Or, *International Cooperation to Suppress Terrorism* (New York: St. Martin's Press, 1985), pp. 298-300, 325-28; Moxon-Browne, "Terrorism in France," pp.

214, 216, 227-28; Juliet Lodge, "Terrorism and Europe: Some General Considerations," in Juliet Lodge, ed., *The Threat of Terrorism* (Boulder, Colo.: Westview Press, 1988), pp. 19-20, 23.

35. Quoted in *The Guardian* (London), 24 July 1980.

36. *The Gazette* (Montreal), 24 July 1980.

37. Moxon-Browne, *Terrorism in France*, pp. 25-26.

38. Moxon-Browne, "Terrorism in France," in Lodge, p. 226; *The Globe and Mail* (Toronto), 24 April 1982; *The Economist*, 1 May 1982 and, 21 August 1982; Philippe Boucher, "Mitterand's Measured Action," *Le Monde*, 19 August 1982, reprinted in *Manchester Guardian Weekly*, 29 August 1982; Bertrand Le Gendré, "France Rethinks its Policy on the Right of Asylum," *Le Monde*, 12 November 1982, reprinted in *Manchester Guardian Weekly*, 28 November 1982.

39. Ivan Barbot et al., "Combatting Terrorism in France: New Bearings," *International Criminal Police Review*, no. 410 (January-February 1988), p. 12.

40. Quoted in *New York Times*, 11 April 1986.

41. *The Globe and Mail*, 24 April 1986.

42. Jacques Robert, "Terrorisme, idéologie sécuritaire et libertés publiques," *Revue de Droit Public et de la Science Politque en France et à l'étranger*, no. 6 (December 1986), pp. 1651-66.

43. Ibid.

44. Ibid.; "Chirac on Champs-Elysees Explosion, Terrorism," Luxembourg Domestic Service, LD 142227, Foreign Broadcast Information Service (FBIS), 14 September 1986.

45. "Chirac on Champs-Elysees Explosion."

46. Edwy Plenel, "France Offers Big Reward in Bid to Catch Terrorists," *Le Monde*, 21-22 September 1986, reprinted in *Manchester Guardian Weekly*, 28 September 1986.

47. *Washington Times*, 22 September 1986; *New York Times*, 24 September 1986; *Washington Post*, 26 September 1986.

48. See, for example, Anis Nacrour, "The Diplomatic Approach to Terrorism: the French Response" (Paper presented at the annual conference of the International Studies Association, April 1987), p. 6.

49. "Countering Terrorism: Operation Long-Spoon," *Le Monde*, 14 April 1983, reprinted in *Manchester Guardian Weekly*, 24 April 1983; *Washington Post*, 26 September 1986.

50. *The Globe and Mail*, 8 October 1983. The government's view was explained in "All the President's Men," *Le Monde*, 13-14 March 1985, reprinted in *Manchester Guardian Weekly*, 21 April 1985.

51. *New York Times*, 14 March 1986 and 11 April 1986. Naccache was one of those whose release was demanded by the CSPPA.

52. Jacques Amalric and Bernard Brigouleix, "France Walks a Tightrope over the Hostage Issue," *Le Monde*, 9 September 1986, reprinted in *Manchester Guardian Weekly*, 21 September 1986;

53. *Washington Post*, 8 July 1987; *The Globe and Mail*, 18 July 1987, 30 November 1987, and 1 December 1987; "A Deal, a Bribe, or a Neat Solution?" *The Economist*, 5 December 1987, p. 54; Paul Webster, "Another Double Cross by Chirac," *Manchester Guardian Weekly,* 6 December 1987.

54. *Washington Post*, 6 May 1988; *The Globe and Mail*, 6-7 May 1988.

55. On the Daoud case, see *International Herald Tribune*, 12 January 1977; "The Prisoner Who Was Too Hot to Handle." On Gordji, see *The Guardian* , 1 December 1987; *Los*

Angeles Times, 3 December 1987; Webster, "Another Double Cross"; and Paul Webster, "The Price That Paris Has Paid," *Manchester Guardian Weekly*, 6 December 1987. On France's "unofficial" diplomacy with Iraq, see Lawrence Freedman and Efraim Karsh, *The Gulf Conflict 1990-1991: Diplomacy and War in the New World Order* (Princeton, N.J.: Princeton University Press, 1993), pp. 157-59; 170-72.

56. "The Prisoner Who Was Too Hot to Handle"; *The Globe and Mail*, 8 October 1983; Edwy Plenel, "Special Missions of the Elysee Cell," *Le Monde*, 30 September 1983, reprinted in *Manchester Guardian Weekly*, 16 October 1983; Amalric and Brigouleix, "France Walks a Tightrope"; *Washington Post*, 25-26 September 1986; *The Globe and Mail*, 31 October 1986; André Fontaine, "A Question of Credibility," in *Manchester Guardian Weekly*, 9 November 1986; Kenneth R. Timmerman, "Chirac's Hostage Dilemma," *The Nation*, pp. 600-603; *The Globe and Mail*, 30 November 1987 and 1 December 1987; Jacques Amalric, "Gordji Walks Free," *Le Monde*, 1 December 1987, reprinted in *Manchester Guardian Weekly*, 6 December 1987; *Washington Post*, 6 May 1988; *The Globe and Mail*, 6 May 1988.

57. Stanley Hoffman, "Mitterand's Foreign Policy, or Gaullism by Any Other Name," in George Ross et al., eds., *The Mitterand Experiment: Continuity and Change in Modern France* (Cambridge, England: Polity Press, 1987), pp. 294, 296-98; Dominique Moisi, "French Foreign Policy: The Challenge of Adaptation," *Foreign Affairs* 67, no. 1 (Fall 1988), pp. 158-60; King, *The Iran-Iraq War*, pp. 55-56; John Mackinlay, *The Peacekeepers: An Assessment of Peacekeeping Operations at the Arab-Israel Interface* (London: Urwin Hyman, 1989), pp. 78-86, 90-93, 98.

58. Jacques Amalric, "French Chickens Coming Home to Roost," *Le Monde*, 29 July 1987, reprinted in *Manchester Guardian Weekly*, 9 August 1987; Webster, "Another Double Cross"; *Washington Post*, 6 May 1988.

59. Jacques Isnard, "France's Counter Intelligence Service: Mission Impossible," *Le Monde*, 19 April 1981, reprinted in *Manchester Guardian Weekly*, 10 May 1981; Jacques Isnard, "Secret Service Reshuffle Not a Political Purge," *Le Monde*, 27 January 1982, reprinted in *Manchester Guardian Weekly*, 7 February 1982; Paul Webster, "Action Division Out of Control," *Manchester Guardian Weekly*, 25 August 1985; "On His Socialists' Secret Service," *The Economist*, 27 November 1982, pp. 43-44; *Washington Post*, 22 January 1986; Edwy Plenel, "Police et Terrorisme," *Esprit* 11 (November 1986), pp. 8-9 and notes.

60. Laurent Gally, *The Black Agent: Traitor to an Unjust Cause*, trans. Victoria Reiter (London: Andre Deutsch, 1988), pp. 122-46, 157-67. Jean Paul Mazurier, the lawyer and DGSE agent, also had doubts about the alleged involvement of Abdallah's group in the September bombings. See also Jacques Isnard, "French Intelligence Handicapped in War on FARL," *Le Monde*, 16 September 1986, reprinted in *Manchester Guardian Weekly*, 28 September 1986.

61. Quoted in Christopher Dobson and Ronald Payne, *The Never Ending War: Terrorism in the 80s* (New York: Facts on File, 1987), p. 156; Plenel, "Police et Terrorisme," pp. 8-9; Georges Marion and Edwy Plenel, "Christians and Muslims in Unholy Terrorist Alliance," *Le Monde*, 26-27 April 1987, reprinted in *Manchester Guardian Weekly*, 3 May 1987.

62. "An Armenian Roundup," *Newsweek*, 1 August 1983, p. 39.

63. Georges Marion and Edwy Plenel, "Islamic Bombing Campaign Foiled by DST Swoop," *Le Monde*, 28 March 1987, reprinted in *Manchester Guardian Weekly*, 5 April 1987; "Name of the Rose," *The Economist*; Greilsamer, "Anatomy"; Greilsamer, "Fouad Saleh"; Gally, pp. 49-52. Mazurier was already working for the DGSE against Abdallah at the time the terrorist was arrested, but it was DST surveillance that drove him into police custody. At that time, the DST may not have been aware of the DGSE's interest in Abdallah.

64. John Andrade, *World Police and Paramilitary Forces* (New York: Stockton Press/ Macmillan, 1985), p. 68. The estimated number of entries in the computer system is 30,000-100,000.

65. *Washington Post*, 6 February 1985 and 26 September 1986; *Financial Times* (London), 26 September 1986.

66. Quoted in *New York Times*, 11 April 1986.

67. Quoted in Henrik Bering-Jensen, "Off the Antiterrorism Fence, but Not Sure How Far to Go," *Insight*, 27 October 1986, p. 28.

68. Christopher Dobson and Ronald Payne, *Counter-attack: The West's Battle Against the Terrorists* (New York: Facts on File, 1982), pp. 123-26; Barbot et al., pp. 12-13.

69. *The Globe and Mail*, 8 October 1983; Plenel, "Special Missions"; "All the President's Men," in *Manchester Guardian Weekly*, 21 April 1985; Dobson and Payne, *The Never Ending War*, pp. 155-57. Nor did the GIGN distinguish itself in an assault to rescue hostages in New Caledonia; all twenty three hostages were rescued, but the nineteen hostage-takers and two French officers were killed in the assault. See reports in *Manchester Guardian Weekly*, 22 and 29 May 1988 and 12 and 19 June 1988.

70. Centre for Conflict Studies, *Special Operations: Military Lessons from Six Selected Case Studies* (Fort Bragg, N.C.: Joint Special Operations Command, US Department of Defense, November 1982), pp. 125-71; *The Globe and Mail*, 18 November 1983.

71. *The Globe and Mail*, 24 April 1982, 2 January 1984, 22 March 1986, 16 September 1986, and 23 February 1987; Boucher, "Mitterand's Measured Action," in *Manchester Guardian Weekly*, 29 August 1982; "Chirac on Champs-Elysees Explosion"; *Washington Times*, 31 October 1986; "Nine Men Good and Through," *The Economist*, 13 December 1986. Schleicher was eventually convicted (in June 1987) in the same special court used for Abdallah's second trial.

72. See Chapter 4 of this volume on Italy. See also Robert C. Meade, Jr., *Red Brigades: The Story of Italian Terrorism* (New York: St. Martin's Press, 1990), pp. 221, 223-24; Le Gendré, "France Rethinks Its Policy."

73. Robert P. Clark, *The Basque Insurgents: ETA, 1952-1980* (Madison: University of Wisconsin Press, 1984), pp. 215-16.

74. Ibid., pp. 216-18.

75. Arnold et al., p. 308; Control Risks Information Service, *France*, (London: Control Risks Information Service, December 1980); Jean-Marc Theolleyre, "Basques Murdered in France: Who Pays the Piper?" *Le Monde*, 31 January 1981 and 1 February 1981, reprinted in *Manchester Guardian Weekly*, 1 March 1981; Philippe Boggio, "Terror and Counter-terror Haunt French Basques," *Le Monde*, 29 February 1984, reprinted in *Manchester Guardian Weekly*, 11 March 1984.

76. *New York Times*, 8 June 1981; "A Poor Start," *The Economist*, 20 June 1981; *Times* (London), 5 August 1981.

77. Le Gendré, "France Rethinks Its Policy."

78. Quoted in "France and ETA," *Le Monde*, 8 August 1984, reprinted in *Manchester Guardian Weekly*, 19 August 1984; see also, "Bolting ETA's Bolthole," *The Economist*, 18 August 1984; Jane Walker, "Why Mitterand Joined Madrid's Fight," *Manchester Guardian Weekly*, 7 October 1984; and Benny Pollack and Graham Hunter, "Dictatorship, Democracy and Terrorism in Spain," in Lodge, ed., *The Threat of Terrorism*, pp. 135-37.

79. Bertrand Le Gendré, "Extraditing the Wanted Basques," *Le Monde*, 30 August 1984, reprinted in *Manchester Guardian Weekly*, 9 September 1984; "One-Way Ticket," *The*

Economist 29 September 1984, pp. 44-46; *The Globe and Mail*, 5 November 1986; Arnold et al., pp. 313-14.

80. Quoted in José Luis Nunes and Lawrence J. Smith, co-rapporteurs, *Sub-committee on Terrorism: Final Report*, North Atlantic Assembly Papers (Brussels: North Atlantic Assembly, January 1989), p. 28; "A French Turnabout on Terrorism," *Newsweek*, 8 June 1987. France convened a further meeting in 1989 to discuss language for the Group of Seven Summit communiqué on terrorism. US, Department of State, *Patterns of International Terrorism: 1989*, p. 27.

81. Quoted in *New York Times*, 4 February 1986.

82. "Summit Statement on Terrorism" (5 May 1986), *Department of State Bulletin* 86, no. 2112 (July 1986), p. 5.

83. Quoted in *The Globe and Mail*, 1 December 1986. See also, *The Globe and Mail*, 11 November 1986; "No Firm Stand," *Time*, 17 November 1986, p. 48.

84. Quoted in "No Firm Stand."

85. *Washington Post*, 6 February 1985.

86. Brian L. Davis, *Qadaffi, Terrorism, and the Origins of the U.S. Attack on Libya* (New York: Praeger, 1990), p. 126.

87. Ibid., p. 153.

88. *Washington Post*, 13 June 1986 and 17 October 1986; US Department of State, *Patterns of International Terrorism 1989*, p. 27.

89. Nevertheless, Fouad Saleh and eight others were convicted for their role in the bombings.

90. "Immigrés: Une Politique d'exclusion," *Actes* 59 (Spring 1987), pp. 31-45; "Libertés/ le nouvel ordre libéral," *Justice* 114 (March 1987), pp. 4-45; J. Morange, "Le Nouveau régime des controles d'identité," *Revue Française de Droit Administratif* 3 (January-February 1987), pp. 85-88. See also, *The Globe and Mail*, 9 March 1985 and 24 September 1986; Bering-Jensen, "Off the Antiterrorism Fence." For example, in the fall of 1986, a group of refugees from Mali were expelled. While the government expelled them in an apparent demonstration of France's determination to crack down on terrorism, it did not offer any evidence that those expelled were actually involved in terrorism.

6

Countering Terrorism in Israel

Noemi Gal-Or

INTRODUCTION

Israel is almost not hurt by Palestinian terrorism. After 20 years of rule over a Palestinian population counting nearly 1.5 million people, on the background of a policy of establishing steadfast facts in [the] direction of integration and annexation, if this is all the harm caused to Israel and if this is the total volume of losses—it [Israel's counter-terrorism policy] is a tremendous success.[1]

In light of Israel's current and recent problems, this 1987 statement by former Israeli Chief of Intelligence Shlomo Gazit makes some dubious assertions. Thus, it provides a fitting overture to this chapter, the purpose of which is to analyze Israeli responses to international terrorism.

THE NATURE OF THE TERRORIST THREAT

In the period since 1968, Israel was challenged mainly, though not exclusively, by Palestinian terrorism. Palestinian and Arab terrorism was often labeled "international" terrorism and certainly manifested some of its characteristics. In fact, this problem predates the establishment of the state of Israel. It has influenced Israeli politics, politicians, and society, albeit gradually. Living with terrorism imposes costs on all sides involved, and Israeli society—like other societies plagued by terrorism—has not escaped this fact.

The terrorist groups involved in anti-Israeli activity comprised a wide cross-section: Palestinians, non-Palestinian Arabs, Europeans, Third World nationalities, and Jewish-Israeli terrorists. This variety and socio-political heterogeneity reflect well the significant and diverse nature of the terrorist challenge to Israel, which appeared to encompass every form of terrorism: from nationalist groups struggling for national self-determination to Third World revolutionaries, nationalist right-ists, anarchist revolutionaries, and psychopathic, state-sponsored, and nationalist-religious-messianic terrorist groups. Moreover, the duration of this sort of warfare increased as newly established groups joined or replaced the old ones, be it only momentarily or as independent new trends.

Since much has been written about Palestinian terrorism, a brief survey of the dominant groups engaged in terrorism against Israel will suffice. *Al-Fatah*, headed by Yasser Arafat, is the largest component of the overall Palestinian Liberation Organization (PLO). Other organizations—some of them PLO members, some dissidents—include *Fatah*—The Revolutionary Council, headed by Abu Nidal; the Popular Front for the Liberation of Palestine (PFLP), headed by George Habash; the Democratic Front for the Liberation of Palestine (DFLP), led by Nayef Hawatmeh; the PFLP–General Command (PFLP–GC), with its commander Ahmed Jibril; the Palestine Liberation Front (PLF), headed by Abu al-Abbas; and lately the Islamic Jihad for the Liberation of Palestine (IJLP) and the Islamic Resistance Movement (*Hamas*). Among non-Palestinian Arabs who have engaged in anti-Israeli terrorism, one may count the Nasserite group, the Arab Sinai Organization (ASO); the pro-Qaddafi Arm of Arab Revolution (AAR); and the Arab Liberation Front (ALF), which is an Iraqi-sponsored organization. More recently, the Islamic Shiite groups became dominant, in some respects even rivals of the PLO. These are mainly the *Amal* and the *Hizb'Allah* organizations, which operate in Lebanon under various cover names, such as the Islamic Jihad and the Revolutionary Justice Organization. They are believed to be linked to the government of Iran. But there are also Palestinian groups whose activities fall under the narrower category of state-sponsored terrorism. These include Al-Saiqa, belonging to the Syrian Ba'ath party, and the Abu-Moussa Flank of the Fatah, also sustained by Syria.[2]

Among the European terrorist organizations that have operated against Israel or against Jews (who are perceived by Israel to be among its legitimate interests) are the German Red Army Faction (RAF), *Wehrsportgruppe Hoffmann*, the French *Action directe* (AD), and the Japanese Red Army. The notorious representative of Third World terrorism, Ilich Ramirez Sanchez, known as "Carlos," was also said to be involved with Palestinian terrorism. Successful containment of Palestinian terrorism would almost automatically entail the end of terrorism against Israel by European and Third World groups motivated by revolutionary ideologies and by their identification with the Palestinian cause. Practical considerations, such as logistics or even financial dependence on the Palestinians also drove such groups toward anti-Israeli, or at least anti-Jewish, positions.[3] Loss of that cooperation, among other factors, has already had a significant negative impact on the opera-tional capabilities of some of these groups, who are now hard-pressed in their own countries or sanctuaries.

The main motivation of anti-Israeli terrorists, the Palestinian issue, is nourished by the deprivation of their rights as individuals and as a people and by the fact that they have been prevented from achieving national self-determination. This motivation is stated explicitly in the Palestinian National Covenant of 17 July 1968.[4] Under the covenant's terms, national self-liberation is expressed both as a Palestinian right and as a duty for the greater Arab nation. A "liberated" Palestine would replace Israel and would restrict the right of citizenship to only those members of the Jewish population who inhabited Palestine prior to the establishment of Israel in 1948; the rest would be expatriated.[5] The extent to which the PLO remains committed to the terms of its covenant, however, has been called into question by the September 1993 Israeli-PLO agreement on Palestinian autonomy. A different nuance to the formulation of Palestinian motivation is present in the Covenant *Hamas*, which links the Palestinian national aspirations to Islamic fundamentalist endeavors.[6]

To achieve its goal, the Palestinian movement's 1968 covenant adopted armed struggle as its strategy of national liberation.[7] This included Maoist Vietnam-like guerrilla warfare and particularly emphasized terrorism as the spearhead. Eliezer Ben-Rafael writes that

This aspect of the Israeli-Palestinian conflict is congruent with the PLO's definition of the aim of the conflict, namely, the total destruction of the Zionist state. Such a definition, indeed, gives the conflict a basis that makes its solution quite unrealistic. ... The unrealistic definition of the conflict now prevents the movement from taking a realistic approach to the achievement of national goals within the limits of the possibilities. On the other hand, it perpetuates—on the behalf of the combat—that very situation of "profitability of violence." Herein lies a partial explanation of the reluctance of the PLO to translate its impressive assets into conceivable Israeli concessions.[8]

In addition to the PLO's objectives, Palestinian terrorism served as a low-cost weapon in the hands of Arab states, most of which until recently were in a state of war with Israel. Terrorism allowed them to wage a war of attrition that did not involve their own nationals and that had great psychological and political effects on Israel. Moreover, Palestinian terrorism was an instrument for Arab states to conduct internal Arab politics and to test their mutual power relations. The PLO and the Palestinian people thus served as a "game ball" for Arab interests.[9]

The terrorists' targets were representatives of the Israeli state: soldiers, ambassadors and embassies, citizens, and Jews identified as Israeli "branches" or "agents" around the world. That said, except for one case, no anti-Israeli terrorist agenda (even among non-Palestinian terrorists) included the assassination of Israeli politicians. However, Palestinian terrorism was often perceived as differing from other national liberation terrorism because "Palestinian terror has been not just political but also societal. What is involved here is not just an attempt to destroy a particular political elite or to remove individuals who belong to that elite. It is not even an attempt to destroy a political entity, but rather, to destroy an entire society. One might say that it seeks 'to terrorize a society out of being.'"[10] In fact, one of the *Al-Fatah* publications contains the following declaration:

The liberation action is not only the removal of an armed imperialist base, but more important—it is the destruction of a society. [Our] armed violence will be expressed in many ways in addition to the destruction of the military force of the Zionist occupying state, it will also be turned towards the destruction of the means of life of Zionist society in all their forms—industrial, agricultural and financial. The armed violence must seek to destroy the military, political, economic, financial and ideological institutions of the Zionist occupying state, so as to prevent all possibility of the growth of a new Zionist society. The aim of the Liberation war is not only to inflict a military defeat but also to destroy the Zionist character of the occupied land, whether it is human or social.[11]

The anti-Israeli terrorists employed different and varied tactics. These methods include kidnapping; aircraft and bus hijacking; hostage-taking; the planting of bombs in public places; raids into homes, schools, and hotels; stabbings; booby traps; letter bombs; murder by shooting; seaborne assaults; and the use of Katyusha rockets to attack civilian communities. Israel's government and society were thus faced with a highly heterogeneous array of terrorist methods and with the urgent necessity of finding the proper response to deter each of these tactics.

Anti-Israeli terrorism has experienced both peaks and valleys. Its level and patterns of activity clearly depended on the political setting and political dynamics on the one hand and on the specific measures undertaken to counter the terrorist activity on the other. The political setting influencing and affecting the developments concerning terrorism may be divided into two components: the internal/local politics occurring within the terrorist movements and the political situation in the Middle Eastern arena regarding Arab-Israeli relations, including its wider international dimensions. Of course, such divisions are artificial; in real life, events and developments on the macro level impact on and have resonance in the domestic micro level and vice versa. What follows is a brief examination of the major milestones of anti-Israeli terrorism.

The first Jewish settlers in Palestine suffered from mixed nationalist-criminal terrorist assaults as early as the turn of the century. These outbursts of violence continued intermittently up to the creation of the state of Israel in 1948. The Israeli defeat of conventional Arab armies in 1949 induced the Arab states to support the terrorist option in their conflict with Israel. During the 1950s, this meant terrorism from Syrian, Egyptian, and Jordanian territories by Palestinian commandos known as the Fedayeen. The Sinai operation of 1956 put a temporary end to this kind of state-sponsored terrorism. Subsequently, the Israeli army sealed up the southern frontiers. Military "operations" against the responsible governments, target-hardening by installing a wire fence all along the border and obscuring border routes, ambushes, and hot pursuit did the preventive job. Yet the waning enthusiasm of the Arab states to continue this part of the struggle created a vacuum that was only slowly filled by an independent Palestinian entity, which later revived the terrorist strategy.

The PLO was founded by Arab leaders in 1964. The first sabotage operation attributed to the PLO (in January 1965) was actually perpetrated by *Al-Fatah*, at that time still nominally independent of the PLO, which it regarded as a Nasserite rival. But Palestinian terrorism remained sporadic until after the Six-day War (in June 1967). Since then, it has been frequent and widespread, despite the turmoil caused by disputes inside and outside of the PLO. Its persistence reflected the strong conviction on the part of Palestinian leaders in the correctness of their choice of strategy.

The late 1960s were characterized by two kinds of strategies. First, the *Al-Fatah* tried to direct Palestinian dissent and opposition on the West Bank and in the Gaza Strip (territories now occupied by Israel) into a popular revolt. They quickly discovered, however, that conditions for such a revolt were not yet ripe. So, increasingly, Palestinian groups, with the PFLP taking the lead, chose a second approach: international terrorism. Indeed, the latter flourished the more the possibilities for terrorism from across the Israeli borders and from within the territories diminished. The 1970 confrontation with the Jordanian regime (an event known as Black September) was significant in this regard. It ended with the destruction of the Palestinian sanctuary—*Fatah*-Land—on Jordanian territory. International overseas terrorist activities intensified in the years thereafter (1971–1973), as the PLO attempted to arouse international public opinion and political support. The Palestinian struggle attracted the attention not just of world leaders, but also of radical extremist groups. From 1970 until the 1982 Lebanon War, the PLO provided extensive logistic support to European, Latin American, Japanese, Armenian, and other terrorist organizations. In exchange, the PLO received their help in building up its international infrastructure in Europe and in perpetrating attacks. The Japanese Red Army's assault at Lod Airport in 1972 and the RAF-PFLP cooperation in the Air France hijacking to Entebbe (1976) are only two examples of this quid pro quo.

During this time, the PLO gradually established a new and more useful base in Lebanon, until then the most peaceful neighboring enemy of Israel. Thus, Lebanon came to acquire the unwanted reputation as the center of international terrorism. Since the 1970s, the PLO's terrorist speciality has been Katyusha rocket bombardment of the northern Israeli settlements from across the Lebanese border. The 1982 expulsion of Arafat and the PLO from Lebanon resulted in a temporary, but significant, reduction of PLO terrorist capabilities and of the intensity of their attacks (except for a brief, but intensive, outburst in 1985), both against Israel and against Jewish and related targets in Europe. This reduced level of activity has not, however, put an end to small-scale violence against Israel. The PLO's campaign has been succeeded by Shiite and Iranian guerrilla warfare against Israeli military targets in Lebanon. In addition, there has been ad hoc, locally organized, and spontaneous "primitive" terrorism within Israel and the territories. This terrorism was directed primarily against Israelis, but also against tourists and Palestinian collaborators. This last category of targets is a noticeable feature of the *Intifada* (uprising),[12] which is not a terrorist campaign *per se*, but an insurrection.[13]

Describing the patterns and levels of terrorist activities against Israel is not, however, the whole story. This analysis concludes by highlighting some specific vital turning points in the linkage between the Arab-Israeli conflict and the development of the "Palestinian Problem," which directed the terrorist struggle into the paths it followed. The Palestinian strategy (up to the outbreak of the *Intifada* in 1987) has been described as follows:

Unlike general guerrilla theory, the Palestinian case does not demonstrate the use of terrorism as an early stage of guerrilla warfare, ... Rather, we witness terrorism here as a substitute for guerrilla warfare after the failure to organize a large-scale guerrilla uprising in the early stages of the struggle. . . . The failure of the Palestinians to gain even a minimal territorial base in Israel-held territory and their despair of bringing about an uprising of the Palestinian population against Israel have led them to use terrorism.[14]

The Arab summit's declaration of 1974, designating the PLO as the sole legitimate representative of the Palestinian people, gave added impetus to Palestinian terrorism. This was followed in November 1974 by the address to the United Nations (UN) General Assembly by the armed Yasser Arafat. Both events signified diplomatic success for the PLO, which also started to open diplomatically recognized "interest offices" in many countries. From the Palestinian perspective, these events showed that in certain circumstances terrorism succeeds. However, this development also forced the organization to reduce, to some extent, the use it made of terrorism, in particular international terrorism, in order to retain political respectability.

The spring of 1976 marked a renewed upsurge of terrorist activity, which continued until 1981. The trigger was the imposition of the Israeli value-added tax on the administered territories, the significance of which was to strengthen the economic interdependence between the Palestinian population there and Israel. Resentment was enhanced by Egyptian President Anwar Sadat's visit in Jerusalem (1977) and especially by the Camp David Agreement (1979), which represented a setback to Palestinian efforts toward total rejection of the Jewish state.[15] The consequence was a new wave of international terrorism launched against Israeli and Jewish targets. The establishment of the Council of National Guidance, led by militant Palestinian leaders, reflected the institutionalization of PLO dominance within the territories, in spite of internal Palestinian divisions, and also the endorsement of terrorist tactics.

In response to these events, the Israeli armed forces invaded southern Lebanon in 1978 with the intention of preventing further Palestinian terrorism from Lebanon. Only temporary success was achieved, however, and was followed by renewed artillery exchanges between Jewish settlements in the northern Galilee and Palestinian bases in the south of Lebanon. American mediation brought about a cease-fire agreement between Israel and the PLO, an organization that until then had not been recognized as a partner for politico-military negotiations.[16] On the propaganda level, however, according to the long-standing Israeli political viewpoint, the PLO remained stigmatized as no more than a terrorist organization.

The 1982 Lebanon War resulted in the destruction of the military infrastructure that the PLO had methodically built up and undermined its delicate and unstable political unity.[17] Its internal divisions, aggravated by Syrian manipulation, led to a civil war inside the movement.[18] Consequently, in order to reassert its credibility, the PLO once again turned to international terrorism. However, the opportunities for success at that time had been reduced because the European terrorist infrastructure had suffered some serious defeats. The new political setting thus required new tactics, and, at this point, the entry of Muslim non-Palestinians—in particular Lebanese Shiites—into the struggle became a valuable asset. Although they had their own political agendas, their aims included waging war against Israel and Zionism and furthering the Palestinian cause.[19] Shiite extremists introduced a new terrorist method—suicide bombings—which were used against the Americans in Beirut twice in 1983 and against the Israeli headquarters in Tyre the same year. The Lebanese Shiite groups also employed extortion by taking and holding hostages. At the end of the 1980s, this was still being used against West European states and the United States (and was not resolved until after the Gulf War in 1991).

What did the Palestinian movement gain from its terrorist campaign? First, the theory of the armed struggle strengthened and crystallized the Palestinian national movement. Indeed, terrorism has been a crucial component of the raison d'être of the organization. It fulfilled the important role of cohesion for a scattered organization; it supplied symbols for identification and reasons for joining it, as well as an outlet for frustration. The ever-growing bureaucracy and para-military complex of the PLO have their origins in the terrorist organization.[20] In short, terrorism was the lever used to mobilize the Palestinian people. Second, it introduced their issue onto the international scene. Palestinian terrorism profited from suitable political-economic conditions and proper timing: the Arab-Israeli conflict, the occupation of the territories, and Western vulnerability in matters of energy supply. Thus, by the mid-1970s, the PLO had succeeded in making the Palestinian question a permanent issue on the international agenda. Moreover, the PLO tried to manipulate terrorism (more or less successfully) so as to continue to profit from it on the micro-organizational level and to prepare the ground for extensive diplomatic activity. But although terrorism drew attention to the Palestinian cause, it also limited the possibilities of finding a solution to the conflict, at least to its Palestinian aspects, because Palestinian international terrorism offended major powers, such as the United States, whose influence was important.

Nevertheless, Arafat's reception at the UN General Assembly and the Arab League's recognition of the PLO as the only legitimate representative of the Palestinian people demonstrated the PLO's success in balancing diplomacy with terrorism. Likewise, in spite of the fact that the PLO threw its support behind Iraq's ill-fated occupation of Kuwait in 1990–1991, the Palestinians have been represented at the peace conferences convened since the 1991 Gulf war. Of greater significance is the fact that Israel negotiated with the Palestinians both at the conferences and in the secret bilateral talks which led to the September 1993 agreement on Palestinian self-government.[21] If the PLO's terrorism has yet to gain a state, its diplomacy has finally persuaded Israel to negotiate with—and thus implicitly to recognize—the PLO as a legitimate political entity. That is no small achievement, given the impact of Palestinian terrorism on Israeli society.

THE RESPONSE

The Political Setting of Anti-terrorist Policy

Israel has been in a state of war with most of its neighbors and until recently many Arab states refused to recognize its existence. In such a situation, terrorism aimed at eroding the security of the state, perpetrated with the assistance of enemy states, has double amplitude. The threat to Israel posed by terrorism could not be measured except in political terms. Since Israel has been faced with an enemy striving for its annihilation, the political costs of defeat would be extraordinary. In short, terrorism against Israel threatened the very existence of the state. However, terrorism was perceived not as the tactic that would defeat Israel by itself, but as one very important component in the anti-Israeli Palestinian struggle. Moreover, it affected the larger Arab-Israeli conflict, which in turn influenced Israel's internal and external position over the long term.

Unlike war with a major Arab power, Palestinian and international anti-Israeli terrorism could not by itself undermine the fundamental security of the Israeli state. But, in addition to human casualties, it has complicated political decision-making by occasionally forcing Israel to take unintended and undesirable political and military actions. Furthermore, incrementally, it has had a significant impact on the mutual perceptions of Jews and Arabs and on the chances for peaceful coexistence between Israel and both its Arab neighbors and its Arab citizens. Feelings of hostility on both sides, strengthening mutual fears and anxieties and enhancing the stigmatization of negative stereotypes, were the direct result of terrorism.[22] Terrorism engenders terrorism, especially the less sophisticated methods: The more "primitive" the attack is (a stabbing, for example), the more personal it is, and the greater is the hatred that ensues. In the 1980s, and again in the 1990s, Jewish counter-terrorism and vigilantism emerged in response to Palestinian terrorism.[23]

Moreover, hatred did not confine itself to individuals. It spilled over into public opinion and affected attitudes concerning crucial issues of political decision-making.[24] It influenced politicians and was used by them. Excessive Palestinian terrorism enabled Israeli politicians to explicitly stigmatize the PLO and the Palestinian national movement as being exclusively a murderous gang of terrorists. Such attitudes were commonplace in the governments of Menachem Begin and Yitshak Shamir. The impact of semantically using "PLO" either synonymously or indivisibly with "terrorist group" proved to be an effective diplomatic tool, which allowed the Israeli government to refuse to negotiate with the PLO because it was labeled a "terrorist" organization, when the real reason was Israeli unwillingness to reach an agreement that would trade territory for peace.

Terrorism had an impact on Israeli society and contributed to dissent among Israelis. It exerted influence on Israel's standing in the international arena, where it is permanently exposed to diverse pressures. The terrorist threat translated into costs and risks to be borne, some of which are only secondary, but nonetheless important. Among these have been the destabilizing effects of terrorism on tourism, an important source of income for the Israeli economy. Ironically, decisions to cancel travel and cultural and sporting events were based on the state of Palestinian terrorism abroad, rather than on the situation inside Israel itself.[25]

A much larger cost was the military one. Terrorism diverted attention and resources away from the central security concern of the state: maintaining the highest standard of operational preparedness for the next war. The military was forced to give up otherwise essential additional training and exercises. Israel's counter-terrorism efforts drew off additional resources from a national budget already deeply in a deficit situation. Decision-makers were forced to devote a major portion of their time to dealing with terrorist events and sometimes wasted much energy on the political consequences of such events.[26] Thus, Israel considers terrorism as an additional, albeit unique, front in its security framework.

All of this aggregated into a third cost category, which is the nature of Israeli society and its political regime.

Among the features that make Israel particularly vulnerable to terrorism, . . . are the following: the small size of the population . . .; the relatively long lines of communication within the occupied territories, as well as to the outside world because of the Arab land blockade; the importance of immigration and tourism; the great sensitivity to loss of life; the preoccupation with the threat of conventional warfare from the Arab states on its borders; many moral inhibitions against retaliation and counter-terrorism; the dependence on target audiences; and, finally, the tremendous asymmetry in resources in the Arab-Israel conflict. These disadvantages for Israel play a role in its counter-terror activities as well.[27]

The political setting in which Israeli responses to terrorism were developed reveals a picture different from what is typical of the Western countries analyzed in this volume. In contrast to Israel, they have reached political maturity and enjoy long-established sovereign statehood. Systems of law, civil rights, and political participation, as well as a tradition of institutionalized violence (the military and the police), have been developing for centuries and had matured prior to the present era.

By contrast, Israel has modest experience as a sovereign state—only forty-six years—and is poorly equipped politically and legally to face the challenge of illegal political violence. The Jewish population includes a high proportion (more than 40 percent) of immigrants, many of whom have grown up in non-democratic states.[28] Israel recognized and emphasized the urgent necessity of transforming diverse patterns of political behavior into democratic ones. From this perspective, Israeli society is, in fact, a mixed "developed-developing" society.

Although political culture lagged behind the Western democratic standards, defense and security skills developed quickly out of necessity. Two points are important here with respect to recent Israeli anti-terrorist policy: First, today's decision-makers were military and underground leaders in the past. In many respects, they are still captive of security concepts elaborated in earlier periods. These proved to be effective at their time, but are only partly valid today. Second, Israeli independence was achieved during two kinds of conflicts—an international one and a sub-national one—both of which involved terrorism in some form. The sub-national conflict also included internal struggles among Jewish rivals. Indeed, one of the first things done upon independence was the enactment of a law against terrorism, the first anti-terrorist step undertaken by the sovereign state of Israel.[29]

Israeli Anti-terrorism Policy

The popular impression transmitted by the media has been that in counter-terrorism matters, Israel is ahead of other countries, with a comprehensive conceptual framework that explains how to deal with the problem, clear in content and rich in methods and tactics. In fact, this impression was based on only a few successful and sometimes spectacular Israeli responses to terrorism, in particular in the field of international terrorism. While the journalists' image was not false, it nevertheless was incomplete. It was derived from experience with only one type of terrorism; it was limited in time, too, since it ignored earlier Israeli experience with terrorism. It was true, insofar as it illuminated and emphasized one major, longstanding principle guiding Israeli attitudes: the absolute negation of terrorism. Closely related to this was the second principle: a policy of non-negotiation with terrorists—no surrender to blackmail. As with any narrowly defined declaratory principle, this one has proven difficult to enforce absolutely. The third principle, the innovative development of the hostage rescue assault, was a technical/tactical one, the product of the subsequent evolution of terrorism.

These pillars of Israeli anti-terrorist response became its hallmark in the 1970s. However, they did not constitute an anti-terrorism policy: a planned and coordinated strategy comprising suitable political, military, and psychological tactics, clear and unambiguous on the one hand and innovative, flexible, and adaptable on the other. Indeed, according to Israeli terrorism expert Dr. Ariel Merari, no Israeli government has ever formulated an anti-terrorist strategy; furthermore, as late as 1985, there had been neither a government meeting to deal with the issue nor a respective military forum and initiative.[30] Instead, Israeli anti-terrorism preparedness developed incrementally over the years, according to the types of terrorist attacks that were occurring and requiring response; this ad hoc approach was the result of the lack of preparedness each time a new type of attack was introduced. With every new terrorist tactic, an ad hoc "fire extinction" policy was applied and experience gathered. When the new tactic became the norm, efforts were undertaken to improve anti-terrorist techniques on both the strategic and the operational levels.[31] Simultaneously, earlier methods were preserved and used, especially against cross-border terrorism. In summary, Israel used preventive anti-terrorism measures as a response, rather than as the outcome of premeditated decision and definition of standards of administration and behavior.

Israeli approaches to terrorism have been determined by the declared strategic objective of encircling terrorism on all fronts. This guiding principle expresses Israeli determination to prevent any outlet for terrorists, to outflank them everywhere and with respect to any sort of terrorist activity. However, the policy applied was not exhaustively researched and tested. In fact, the Israeli decision-making process depended mainly on the army's initiative and intervention; the Israel Defence Forces (IDF) took the lead in formulating and sending to the government proposals relevant to combatting terrorism. Yet, since the army was too often preoccupied with current security problems to respond to the terrorist challenge, it failed until recently to undertake an overall study of the subject. Thus, it was dominated by, and dragged the government into, a reactive mode. Seen from the narrow operational point of view, this approach has, in general, justified itself. It succeeded in keeping anti-Israeli terrorism at an endurable level and in diverting it out of the country. However, this would not have been possible had not the financial restraints been removed in order to enable the IDF to pursue the policy of sealing off the country on all possible terrorist fronts.[32]

Israeli policy did not, however, succeed in suppressing terrorism totally. Hanan Alon asserts that "Israel has demonstrated a huge reaction, in all categories, and by so doing has responded to a major element in the terrorists' calculations."[33] Sometimes the measures used caused the terrorists to change tactics. Doubts arose at home and abroad as to the operational effectiveness and the political wisdom of reprisals when such methods were discussed. Alon claims that while the reprisal policy of the 1950s was based on a strategic view that saw terrorism as part of the hostile relations with the enemy Arab states, the continuation of the reprisal strategy after 1967 was characterized by intuition rather than by objective analysis and strategic calculation. The same argument applies to the more recent reprisals, which have perfected the tactics of intensive aerial bombardments, commando raids, and artillery and naval attacks. These measures did not take into account the deep absorption of the terrorists within the local population, the irregular structure of the forces, their high mobility, and, finally, the fact that the Palestinians reign over an endless reservoir of recruits, which can hardly be exhausted, at least physically, if not morally.[34]

The danger inherent in a reprisal strategy policy arises from the fact that decision-makers too often forget that the terrorist struggle is not a one-shot, zero-sum game; it is continuous, and counter-terrorism policy must adapt itself to this fact. Therefore, the wisdom of the government's decision-makers must express itself in the choice not only of the measures applied, but also of the amount or frequency with which they are applied. Only the correct proportion of reprisals and a variety of tactics of reprisal will achieve the objectives of prevention and deterrence without raising the domestic and international political costs to unacceptable levels. Reprisals in Lebanon, Jordan, and elsewhere did not put an end to terrorism (though sometimes they temporarily reduced its level). In addition, reprisal policy frequently generated opposition within the country and anti-Israeli criticism from the members of the international community, thereby increasing domestic and international political costs.[35]

It is evident that Israeli national security doctrine did not take into consideration all of the components required to develop an overall strategy against terrorism. While acknowledging the relevance of the Palestinian national development to Israeli security, Israeli military strategists did not incorporate the implications of this factor into their military doctrine. The result was that IDF counter-terrorism thought failed to achieve a synthesis of military preparedness, which would link the terrorist threat, its relevant political components, and the appropriate response measures. Although terrorism was seen as a threat to the existence of the state, the *decisive* threatening actors were nevertheless believed to be only the Arab regular armies. Therefore, the IDF was inclined to think in strategic-territorial patterns, rather than in strategic-political terms. In other words, the strategists misinterpreted, even ignored, the human asset component of the Palestinians and thus were unable to understand the significance and sincerity of the armed struggle and its relevance to terrorism and anti-terrorism.[36]

In addition, Israeli strategists violated Israel's basic credo concerning terrorism. First, in 1979, they withdrew from the principle of non-negotiation with terrorists. The second principle the Israeli authorities violated was that of total negation of terrorism, a matter of absolute and overriding moral, rather than tactical, significance. It was "publicly" violated only as a result of the unraveling of the Jewish terrorist underground, which operated from 1980 to 1984 in the territories. There were rumors insinuating that this activity was passively tolerated by the authorities. The attitudes of the ministers, including then Prime Minister Yitshak Shamir, and the position taken by some Knesset members left no doubt that a breach had occurred in the consensual Israeli anti-terrorism wall.

Practically seen, this had immediate influence on the overall Israeli anti-terrorism immunity. Israeli efforts to distinguish between "good and justified" terrorism and "bad and guilty" terrorists probably strengthened bitterness on the Palestinian side and were interpreted as encouragement for terrorism on the Israeli side. Indeed, the exchange of prisoners with the PFLP–GC, which took place in 1985, could only have come about in the prevailing atmosphere of the growing moral and psychological confusion caused by the extending circle of terrorism. Moreover, the demands—by government minister Ariel Sharon—to link the May exchange with pardons, or even with collective amnesty, for all of the members of the Jewish Underground may have been influential as well. Of the twenty-seven convicted in 1984, twenty were released by September 1986.[37] Since that time, both Israeli authorities and society have been trying to "pick up the pieces" of this moral and legal dilemma. But there is no unanimity about the right way of putting them together again, or even of the need to do it at all.

The Legal Framework of Counter-terrorism Policy

Upon gaining independence, Israel did not create its own secular, liberal democratic legal system simply because as a new, inexperienced nation state, it lacked a long-established and fully developed democratic political culture. Instead, Israel adopted the existing British mandate's legal code, which included remnants of the Ottoman laws incorporated into the British mandate. Moreover, the first Israeli legal experts, trained within the British legal system, transmitted the common law approach to the Israeli legal system. Like the United Kingdom, Israel does not have a written constitution; there are, as partial substitutes, Basic Laws.

The first piece of "emergency" legislation was the Prevention of Terrorism Decree—1948. Adopted after the assassination of UN mediator Count Folke Bernadotte by Jewish terrorists, it was intended to eradicate domestic Jewish terrorism. The decree prohibited the existence of, membership in, and assistance to a terrorist organization, which it defined as an association of people using violence (which may be lethal or physically harmful) or threatening to use it. Members of a terrorist organization included anyone who participates in or promotes support for the organization and its activities or goals or who collects funds and materials for it.[38] The political component of the offense is not mentioned in the decree; terrorism has only a common criminal meaning. The law determined the penalties for the various offenses possible under these definitions, that is, for carrying out attacks, for holding membership, and for providing various kinds of assistance to the organization. This last item was not part of the original 1948 law, but was added in August 1986 as a result of growing concern among politicians opposed to negotiations with the PLO. It was adopted as part of a political compromise surrounding passage of a new law condemning and prohibiting racism.[39] The political and strategic considerations leading to it will be discussed later.

Prior to the 1986 addition, article 6 (known as the 1980 amendment) was adopted. It extended the power of the police to close down any place serving a terrorist organization. The supervisor general of the police may issue such a written order to be carried out by any police supervisor. There is no need for judicial approval, though any person may appeal to court within fifteen days. Among other amendments to the law, the most significant one states that the entire law is valid only under "emergency rule." However, that has been in effect in Israel since its declaration in Palestine in 1945. Indeed, the origins of institutionalized legal anti-terrorist policy can be found in the pre-independence mandatorial decrees and the penal code concerning the security of the state.[40]

During the first eighteen years of the state's existence, the Israelis also employed military rule and emergency decrees (for example, to issue curfews and to prohibit public protests) in order to prevent political violence in the densely populated Arab districts. These controls helped to reduce domestic terrorism to the minimum, but at the time Arab terrorism was mainly foreign-based anyway. To forestall the risk of treason by Jewish as well as Arab citizens, the Commission of the Prison Service introduced the status of "security prisoner." In contrast to the political offender, who enjoys the right of privileges, the security prisoner is a person threatening the safety or survival of the state and, therefore, is deprived of rights endowed to the common criminal, except for those permitted under the 1949 Geneva Conventions. Obviously, this category has been applied to Arab terrorists and guerrillas.[41]

The issue of capital punishment has been on the Israeli political agenda for many years, forgotten during peaceful times and then vehemently raised and debated in more turbulent periods. It was raised more often in the 1980s than ever before, due to the increased intensity of Palestinian terrorism and the rising incidence of terrorism by West Bank Palestinians and Israeli-Arabs. The security legislation contains only one article sanctioning capital punishment: Article 51 provides for death as the maximum penalty for an offender intentionally causing death or damaging IDF installations. Furthermore, it applies only in cases involving firearms or explosives.[42] The death penalty has been implemented only once, in the Adolf Eichmann war crimes case. Military courts are endowed with the prerogative of imposing the death sentence, but, until 1979, there was a directive prohibiting military attorneys from requiring the death sentence for terrorists. This directive was then canceled, but there has been only one case since in which it was requested, and a life term was imposed instead. Nevertheless, the existence of the provision has been raised unconvincingly by the French authorities when seeking an excuse to justify their refusal to extradite a terrorist to Israel.[43]

Apart from the direct legal and ideological pros and cons raised during the debates, there are also practical arguments against using capital punishment for the suppression of terrorism. It is argued that, first, such a change in policy would suggest a weakening of the state of Israel, that circumstances were driving it to drastic measures, alien to its basic belief and values and to its general policy. Second, applying this legal provision would transform criminal terrorists into Arab martyrs, thereby providing a useful propaganda device to mobilize the supportive population. Finally, it is thought to be counterproductive, since terrorists may thus be driven to murder or torture any kidnapped victim.[44]

Political terrorism originating in the occupied territories (the West Bank and the Gaza Strip) constitutes something of a "gray area" insofar as this chapter is concerned. Since these areas are not part of Israel proper, terrorism arising there is not purely domestic. Yet, since the areas are under Israeli control—by means of occupation—neither is it truly *international*, as this category applies to this volume. Technically, therefore, political violence and countermeasures there lie outside the scope of this chapter. Nevertheless, it can be argued with considerable force that like Britain's experience in Northern Ireland, events and policies related to the occupied territories have had a significant impact on Israel's political culture and on its democratic character, particularly in the way it responded to terrorism. Therefore, a brief exploration of the legal dimension is appropriate.

The Six-day War (1967) altered what had been a relatively static legal situation with regard to political violence. In the aftermath of the war, Israeli administration of the occupied territories involved complex legal obligations. Law enforcement required the simultaneous application of several legal systems: local (Jordanian) law, which applied in cases of common criminal offenses by the indigenous population; Israeli law, to which Israeli inhabitants of the territories were subject; and military regulations for security offenses which, in theory, applied to both peoples. But, in fact, Israeli offenders, such as the Jewish Underground terrorists, were usually tried in the Israeli courts. In effect, this created two unequal categories of terrorism and legal process, based on the nationality of the accused—hardly a model of democratic justice.[45]

The other dimension of counter-terrorism law in the territories that bears mentioning here is the Decree of Security Regulations. This is based on the British mandatory emergency powers still in force as part of Israeli law. Two aspects of the decree merit attention. First, following legislation that gave Israeli laws the force of extra-territorial jurisdiction, the regulations under the decree were extended to empower the military courts to try, under the security regulations, suspects who were charged with offenses that were committed *outside* the territories, but that harmed or could have harmed security or public order *within* the territories. This covered specific terrorist activities, such as rocket bombardment from Jordan or Lebanon, and the instigation of terrorism from abroad, and was also applied to non-violent activities, such as maintaining contact with organizations designated as hostile under the decree. Second, the decree empowered the security forces in the territories to apply a wide range of repressive countermeasures, including deportation, the demolition and sealing up of houses, administrative detention (without trial), house arrest, curfews, closed areas, and road blocks.[46]

While these regulations were applied only in the occupied territories, and not in Israel proper, they reveal much about the character of Israel's approach to counter-terrorism generally. As the following sections of the chapter demonstrate, the existence of repressive legal powers, which violated the spirit of Israel's democratic political culture, set the tone for other countermeasures, which may have eroded Israeli democracy even further.

Negotiation

Israel's policy of non-negotiation held firm for more than a decade. The first sign of retreat came from the Likud government in 1979. For the first time, Israel engaged in negotiations (with Ahmed Jibril's PFLF–GC), which led to the release of seventy-six terrorists (including perpetrators of the most atrocious terrorist assaults) in exchange for one Israeli soldier held captive by Jibril's forces. This was followed by a negotiation and exchange avalanche leading up to the biggest exchange deal ever done with terrorists. In May 1985, after a lengthy negotiation process with Jibril's organization that involved international mediation through the Red Cross, Israel freed 1,150 terrorists and guerrillas for three Israeli soldiers.

Not only did the exchange itself undermine the objective of deterring and fighting terrorism; also the terms of the agreement made Israel appear ridiculous.

Terrorists were allowed to choose whether to return to their homes within Israel and the territories or to go abroad. Moreover, Israel let itself be blackmailed into violating, by its own hand, its laws and the authority of its judicial system, thereby overriding basic legal procedures.[47] Furthermore, the return home of the terrorists freed in May laid the foundations for the *Intifada* in the territories.

Subsequent terrorist attacks, such as the hijacking of TWA Flight 847 barely a month later, were seen as having been encouraged by this agreement. During and immediately after the TWA hijacking, Israel released 331 Lebanese prisoners in an obvious exchange for the thirty-nine American passenger hostages—although the Israeli government denied that this constituted an exchange. Another 435 prisoners, whose release was demanded by the hijackers, were freed by September 1985. Clearly, this was a major blow to Israeli credibility in matters of fighting terrorism, as well as to the legitimacy of its demands and expectations from other states on the question of surrendering to terrorism.[48] The secret direct talks between Israel and the PLO in 1993 further undercut the no-negotiation policy, but the subsequent Israeli-PLO agreement may render it unnecessary.

Security and Intelligence

The intelligence community is responsible for the most important part of the anti-terrorist efforts: prevention. The intelligence services also provide indispensable support to any countermeasure undertaken. A PLO leaflet found in 1980 warned members as follows:

Our worst enemy is the Israeli intelligence. This intelligence has vast experience in warfare against organized cells. . . . This service has succeeded because of its means and its experience and has bypassed the defensive phase for the offensive phase. . . . It has bases in every village and neighbourhood . . . [and only] a strong local secret organization is powerful enough to challenge [it].[49]

The organization responsible for internal security is the General Security Service (*Shabak*). Directly subordinate to the prime minister, *Shabak* is an executive arm, which collaborates with all other executive branches responsible for the suppression of terrorism. Moreover, it assists the judicial system, either by providing information and evidence or by having its investigators serve as witnesses during terrorist trials. *Shabak* effectively reduces the level and number of terrorist attacks by uncovering terrorist organizations or plans, by providing the information required to apprehend terrorists and their resources (weapons, documents, finances, hiding places, etc.), and even by preventing the creation of terrorist cells.

Shabak is responsible for infiltrating the terrorist population base, "buying" collaborators, and persuading and deterring potential offenders from adhering to the terrorist agenda. In addition to collecting intelligence, it propagates disinformation among the terrorists and their supporting constituency in order to misdirect and ruin their plans and to weaken their motivation. In this way, *Shabak* achieves deterrence and prevention through psychological warfare. This sort of work, keeping close contact with terrorism's grass roots, generated strong views within *Shabak* about the most effective ways to suppress it, which were at odds with the legalist views held by the judicial system. *Shabak* claimed, for instance, that permitting appeals against the military courts' verdicts in the territories, as was done in the 1980s, would clog the legal channels and diminish the deterrent effect of the anti-terrorist measures. In short, abiding strictly by the law would prevent them from effectively countering terrorism. According to *Shabak* terrorism cannot be effectively repressed by means applied to counter common criminality; any weakness is quickly interpreted as an opportunity for further terrorism. Thus, within the political context of the administered territories, *Shabak's* assumption has been that there can be no "enlightened occupation," and, therefore, its counter-terrorism methods could not be "enlightened" either.[50]

Normally and understandably secret, some aspects of *Shabak's* investigation methods and working procedures were exposed to public scrutiny in the 1987 Landau Report. The Landau Committee came into being following the exposure of the killing of two captured terrorists and of *Shabak's* attempt to deceive the authorities concerning the affair. Development of the case was complicated because *Shabak* officers deliberately mislead the investigating bodies and attributed the guilt to a high military officer.[51]

The report disclosed that the *Shabak* was using force (including torture) to extract information and confessions from terrorist suspects. It also stated that for sixteen years *Shabak* investigators, with the compliance of the military attorneys, had provided false testimonies to discredit the accusations of suspects who claimed that confessions were achieved from them by illegal forceful means. The report stated that lying and deceiving the judges concerning the methods applied had become the norm in *Shabak*. Both the heads of *Shabak* and their partners (the military attorneys) were aware of it. The committee found that the political control over and accountability of *Shabak* were defective. The prime minister's direct responsibility for the security service, as well as the internal control organ of *Shabak*, was not sufficient to guarantee effective supervision and to prevent abuses.[52]

The Landau Report recommended the definition of a somewhat special status for *Shabak's* interrogations in anti-terrorist investigations. It legitimized, indeed nearly legalized, a range of tactics to be applied to suspects, including psychological pressure (such as "tricks" and deception) and, if necessary, a "modest degree of physical pressure." However, arbitrary violence and torture were explicitly prohibited.[53] Recently, however, a committee appointed to revise the Landau Report recommendations suggested that *Shabak* interrogators should be guaranteed immunity from prosecution in the event of prisoners dying during interrogation.[54]

Regarding the territories, the rest of the intelligence organs are of secondary importance. Collecting information abroad lies within the competence of the

Mossad (the Institute for Special Services) and the intelligence branch of the IDF. Army intelligence focuses on the collection and analysis of information on terrorism in terms of its links to the hostile states. It takes part, first, in interrogations of captured terrorists; second, when *Shabak* is overstretched and needs help; and, finally, when a terrorist case is closely connected with a hostile state. *Shabak*-gathered information completes the circle, which encompasses the internal and external spread of the Palestinian organizations and their activities.[55]

The police forces become involved when they receive information from *Shabak* or when an attack occurs. The police have designated three units to deal with terrorism; one is the Special Unit for Fighting Terrorism (JAMAM), created in 1975. Combining intelligence and commando capabilities, it can handle a hostage negotiation and assault. However, it is deployed less frequently than military, intelligence, or other security forces.[56] Another police organ is the Border Guard, which is a para-military organization similar to the German Bundesgrenzschutz. Its security/intelligence tasks include patrolling, control, and surveillance functions along the border; it is also used for countering terrorism within the country and the territories. A special body affiliated with the police is the Civil Guard, which was established shortly after 1967, with the specific mission of responding to the threat of terrorism. It consists of professional police commanding a volunteer civilian police force, comprised of community members. Residents of villages, suburbs, or town quarters volunteer for this patrolling body and commit themselves to regular guard duties in their neighborhoods. This releases the already overloaded police force from these duties and is more effective in the sense that the guards are best acquainted with their neighbors and know better than the police how to discern aliens and suspects. The Civil Guard is also empowered to search suspects and hand them over to the nearest police station as well as to search personal belongings (usually at the entrances to public buildings). The recruits come mainly from the pensioner population and briefly were also recruited from among high school students. However, it became apparent that this body had been only partially effective in preventing terrorism, and its function was gradually changed into civilian protection against common criminal activity.

Military and Para-military Measures

Within Israel proper, the army usually is not involved in internal security, except for hostage rescue assaults. It has been much more involved in the territories, where it is the governing authority. Since the outbreak of the *Intifada*, however, it has become difficult to distinguish between those efforts designed to prevent disturbances of public order in the territories and those directed at countering terrorism. This uncertainty exists because those involved in the uprising employ a wide range of violent methods including terrorism. The army's response to violence in the territories can be summarized briefly. It consists essentially of three tasks: The first, long-term prevention, is a "carrot and stick" approach, which is supposed to ameliorate the quality of life and thus approach, though minimally, what are thought to be the underlying causes of terrorism. This task combines what might be described as civic action techniques with the application (or elimination) of public order controls (such as roadblocks, censorship, and closure of the Palestinian universities).[57]

The second task is short-term prevention, undertaken in anticipation of or in the wake of terrorist incidents. This is achieved mainly through the application of the emergency regulations mentioned earlier. It includes curfews, roadblocks, and snap searches of vehicles, buildings, and people. There is also the punitive dimension: administrative detention, deportation, and the demolition or sealing up of houses suspected of harboring terrorists. These measures, essentially collective punishment, must be sanctioned by the military court. In 1991, the IDF acknowledged that it was using special undercover squads. Disguised as Palestinians, they shadow and arrest leaders of the *Intifada*.[58] As the recent controversy over the deportation of 400 fundamentalists from Gaza demonstrates, such collective punishments do not pacify the territories. And since Israeli settlers there have often seen such repressive measures as insufficient to deter further Palestinian attacks on them, the army has often been driven to apply more severe measures against the Palestinians than were justified. But this did not stop some of the settlers from engaging in vigilante justice; thus, the problem of the Jewish Underground terrorists developed in the early 1980s. This did nothing to improve the army's image among the Palestinians, since many of the army reservists who served in the territories were settlers who were suspected of carrying out "death squad" attacks that the army could not be permitted to do openly.[59]

The third component of counter-terrorism policy in the territories is the political dimension. The technical means of countering terrorism proved insufficient because Israel lacked any general, consistent, and coordinated political objective. Moreover, the government has been unable or unwilling to prevent the security forces from exceeding or abusing their authority; each failure in this regard has increased the hatred and frustration on both sides. This was clear to the instigators of violence on the Palestinian side too. After twenty years of occupation, they have gained enough experience to know how to manipulate and provoke the Israeli political culture in order to keep the armed struggle going and to justify it to the Palestinian population.

In 1986, Shimon Peres raised and recommended former Prime Minister David Ben-Gurion's policy of self-restraint, claiming that Jewish extremism would enhance Palestinian extremism and transform PLO and Palestinian (and Muslim) terrorism into sources of popular upheaval.[60] As the *Intifada* shows, he was correct. This suggests that Israeli counter-terrorism policy in the territories has been only partially successful politically. Technical anti-terrorism measures kept the level of terrorism in and from the territories to a minimum. In the absence of policy, however, they could not prevent a popular insurrection. The significance of this is that in spite of the fact that most of the spectacular terrorist assaults occurred abroad or were launched into Israel from across its borders, it is the effort to contain terrorism within the country and the occupied territories that has imposed the greater moral and ethical burden on Israeli society.

Israeli strategy to counter *international* terrorism has been reactive and was based on the principle of maximum force. The logic of this strategy was founded on three clear and unambiguous principles:

1. Israeli territory must be sealed up against terrorists;

2. Israel will hit back at the terrorists no matter where they are;

3. Neighboring and enemy states, including their civilian populations, that host, tolerate on their soil, and shelter anti-Israeli terrorists cannot evade responsibility and escape being drawn into this violent circle.[61]

In other words, Israeli strategy against external terrorism was based on two pillars: target-hardening (or passive defense) and attack and retribution (or active defense). These pillars were expected to fulfill preventive, deterrent, and punitive functions. The bodies responsible for carrying out this strategy were the armed forces and the intelligence services. Obviously, in case of a successful terrorist assault on Israeli soil, the internal defense elements already described joined the operations.

Dealing with active defense first, Israeli external anti-terrorism policy has always included a substantial offensive component. During the 1950s, the offensive capability complemented the passive defense strategy. Small commando units carried out attacks on villages across the frontiers that served as bases for Fedayeen infiltration.[62] The Sinai operation of 1956 was both a full-scale war and a counter-terrorism reprisal operation. This and the subsequent UN involvement in the Sinai Peninsula, and the Gaza Strip, reduced the Fedayeen infiltrations from Jordan and Egypt to a minimum until the formation of the new Palestinian movements nearly ten years later.

From that point on, the Israeli armed forces were forced to develop numerous changing and innovative tactics of an offensive nature for the anti-terrorist strategy. The new circumstances dictated new goals: to destroy the infrastructure, bases, and manpower of the terrorists, which had acquired the proportions of small states (the so-called *Fatah*-Land) in Jordan and, later, in Lebanon; to incessantly harass the terrorists into a state of fatigue; to shatter organizational cohesion and the terrorists' self-confidence; to deter the supportive population from cooperating and thus undermine the vital sanctuary areas; and to make it clear to the host countries that collaborating with, and even tolerating, terrorists involved high costs. This policy usually was applied in reaction to a terrorist assault (carried out either in Israel or abroad) and was called a "reprisal." Israel also applied preemptive offensive measures, unrelated to a specific terrorist attack. Alon groups the aims of the active defense into three categories: reducing terrorists' resources, reducing terrorists' propensity to strike, and reducing damage inflicted by terrorists. These goals were achieved by applying counterforce, impeding attempts to attack, and meting out punishment. The Lebanon invasion (1982) and the air raid on the PLO's headquarters in Tunis (1986) were examples of this offensive counter-terrorism strategy.[63]

The least sophisticated means applied was artillery fire. In reply to the Katyusha rocket bombardment of northern Israel from Lebanon, the IDF directed massive artillery fire against the locations from which the rockets were thought to have been launched. Such artillery duels occurred frequently until the IDF drove the Palestinians out of southern Lebanon in 1982.[64]

Commando raids were intended to harass or destroy the enemy by liquidating the terrorist leaders and thus disrupting the organization "in the center." Although risky, such operations were applied often during the 1970s. One example was Operation Spring of the Youth (Aviv Neurim), carried out in 1973, whereby a commando force landed by sea in Beirut and liquidated three leaders of the PLO in their homes.[65] Other kinds of commando operations included the "hot pursuit" of infiltrating or escaping terrorists and larger infantry and paratroop raids on terrorist bases, which occurred as early as the 1950s. These operations often resulted in high casualties to the IDF. One such action was Operation TOFET at Karameh in Jordan. The IDF launched the attack in response to the mining of the road to Eilat in March 1968, which caused injury to twenty-eight schoolchildren and the death of the guide and the accompanying physician. Although similar to larger operations in later years (for example, the Litani Operation—the invasion of southern Lebanon in March 1978), Operation TOFET failed militarily and politically, resulting in high casualties to the Israeli side.[66] Such full-scale military operations proved time and again that conventional warfare does not fulfill the requirements of anti-terrorist efforts.[67] The only alternative is to develop unconventional techniques and to think in innovative and unique patterns.

Based on the lessons of the Litani Operation, the solution chosen in the early 1980s was air and sea bombardment of Palestinian bases. Such massive reprisal activity was carried out intensively for about a year prior to the 1982 Lebanon War and has continued intermittently since. Until the 1993 agreement it was widely believed that, in the absence of a political solution, Palestinian terrorism and Israeli reprisal had become inevitable. Moreover, it has been suggested that the Israeli anti-terrorist response had become an end in itself. Therefore, it is essential to examine critically the central pillar of the strategy: The concept of reprisal.

The decision to use the air force to counter terrorism resulted from the need to choose one among almost equally difficult alternatives. On one hand, there were high economic, political, and military operational costs associated with using bombers to liquidate terrorists, particularly when attacks often resulted in destroying only tents or innocent civilians. On the other, as the Karameh incident showed, intensive infantry or commando operations involved a high price in Israeli casualties, which for political reasons had to be kept to a minimum.[68] In addition, the IDF believed that attacking from the air when the enemy is unable to respond in the same way would be annoying and disturbing to the daily routine of the terrorists and might cause panic.

This was supposed to inflict a war of attrition on the PLO. However, due to the high mobility of the terrorists, air raids often failed to achieve this purpose. Such PLO bases were usually situated in the midst of civilian settlements, so that air strikes hit the civilian population and entangled the Israeli government in a controversial propaganda/public opinion campaign. The Israeli government believed that the benefits of selective air raids outweighed the costs. However, while the security objectives of this strategy may have been satisfied in part, its negative effects tended to detract from Israel's wider political-strategic objectives. Consequently, the IDF changed the collective and retributive bombardments into selective targeting based on specific intelligence information. Attacks became motivated less by retributive and more by preventive considerations.

Nevertheless, this type of warfare could not be and was not intended to be strategically decisive. Reprisals in form of the Sinai Operation (1956) and the Lebanon War (1982) did more than form a premeditated anti-terrorist policy. They evolved into wider conflict situations, in which Israel became entangled. On the other hand, reprisals of a more modest scale did not put an end to the terrorist threat. Citizens residing in northern Israel learned from experience that Israeli military reprisals did not stop, but rather were followed by more, terrorist rocket attacks. The boomerang effect neutralized deterrence; reprisal became a double-edged sword. Indeed, the only sure result of reprisals applied without an overall security concept was that the civil population got caught in the cross fire.[69] Raymond Tanter and Lisa Kaufman claim that reprisals have only a weak effect on subsequent terrorism, and that Arab casualties caused by Israeli reprisals did not change this fact. In general, the authors claim:

Nevertheless, the study . . . concludes that reprisals do result in lower levels of subsequent violence. . . . Reprisals seem to be less effective when they are used to coerce Arab states to prevent infiltration of regular forces from their territories. The current work also uncovers a set of processes which suggest a weak effect of reprisals on terror (infiltration and sabotage); a stronger effect exists in the opposite direction: there is a greater effect of terror on reprisals than the reverse. *Arab terror appears to have a life of its own, relatively independent of Israeli reprisals.* In other words, Arab terrorism goes on irrespective of Israeli reprisals, although the level of terror does decline in certain cases apparently as a result of reprisals. Only in Egypt after the 1967 June War is there a relationship where reprisals seem to reduce the small amount of terror coming from Egypt in 1967–69. . . . higher Arab casualties may not result in lower level of terror; *Large-scale reprisals that kill many Arabs may be no more effective than smaller actions in reducing terror.*[70]

The operations of the 1970s, moreover demonstrated that even if reprisals are effective in challenging terrorism, they may be politically counterproductive. The Litani operation achieved only temporary relief from terrorism. While it widened the so-called security buffer strip, which did reduce terrorist assaults against Israel, it also introduced the UN force, which limited Israeli activity there, and did not stop Palestinian shelling of Galilean settlements.[71] Moreover, Israeli bombing in the vicinity of Beirut led Israel and the PLO to conclude a cease-fire agreement (through the mediation of US special envoy Philip Habib). Thus, instead of wearing down Palestinian resistance, Israel was dragged into a negotiation process and political recognition of its adversary. Likewise, the goals of the 1982 Lebanon War were not limited to countering terrorism. The war was intended to disrupt the depth and expansion of the PLO forces, which might have enabled them to extend their capabilities from using terrorism into conducting more sophisticated warfare. In this sense, then, the 1982 Lebanon War was actually not an attack on terrorism, but a preemptive strike against the growing *conventional* war potential of the PLO.[72]

As the foregoing shows, depending on geopolitical circumstances, when confronted with cross-border terrorism, Israel tended to use readily the armed forces and a coercive, military strategy. However, international terrorism occurring well beyond Israel's borders entangled not only enemy states, but friendly governments as well, in the anti-terrorist cycle. Moreover, these states sometimes found themselves forced to react against their will and interests.[73] Thus, the first important problem resulting from this situation was the prohibition against, or at least the limitation of, the use of force against terrorists on these friendly territories. These strictures notwithstanding, "sophisticated" Israeli transnational anti-terrorism efforts are believed to have included covert assassination operations, whose aims were the liquidation of terrorists and their leaders and the disruption of their overseas infrastructure. One infamous, outstanding failure in this context, which brought this activity to light, was the Lillehammer affair in which a completely innocent Palestinian was assassinated by mistake in Norway in 1974. Apart from this event, however, there is no reliable, first-hand, official confirmation of the activity attributed to Mossad abroad, such as the assassination of Kalil al Wazir (Abu Jihad), PLO chief of military operations, in 1988 and Salah Khalaf (Abu Iyad), deputy head of *Al-Fatah* and one-time chief of Black September, in January 1991 (both were killed in Tunis). In the absence of confirmation from credible sources, all accounts of such events should be treated with skepticism.[74]

On the other hand, the Entebbe rescue operation (Uganda, 1976) and the air strike on PLO headquarters in Tunis (1985) serve as unique and outstanding examples of both Israeli transnational anti-terrorism initiatives and the efficiency of its military and intelligence services. The spectacular Entebbe operation was a psychological turning point in Western efforts against international terrorism and provided a model for another operation of a similar nature, namely, the German rescue of the hijacked Lufthansa aircraft passengers and crew in Mogadishu, Somalia in 1977.[75]

Target-Hardening

The police, the IDF, and the Border Guard are all responsible for limiting the opportunities for terrorists to infiltrate Israel by land, sea, or air. Prevention is achieved by the border security system, which includes patrolling (by the Border Guard and by selected army units), installing electric wire fences all along the borders, "blurring" roads, sending out search patrols comprised of trackers, and mining certain routes.[76]

In the so-called security belt of southern Lebanon, terrorists and guerrillas were kept away from the Israeli border through the intensive Israeli military presence on Lebanese soil with the assistance of the South Lebanese Army (SLA) (an Israeli-assisted Lebanese Christian para-military organization). This activity was intended, first, to prevent infiltration into Israeli territory.[77] There have been numerous cases of Israeli or SLA patrols engaging in close combat with terrorists trying to cross the border on their way to commit a hostage-taking or other form of attack. Second, frequent military operations were designed to prevent the establishment of a terrorist infrastructure and reliable bases within the population. Finally, security belt operations were supposed to prevent and reduce opportunities for shelling Israeli territory with Katyusha rockets, and thus to reduce the cost incurred by providing attack-proof shelters for inhabitants of Israeli border settlements. However, a permanent Israeli presence in a neighboring state and in cooperation with a foreign army was impossible in other states from whose territory terrorism was launched. So until the peace treaty with Egypt secured that border, target-hardening was restricted to activity on the Israeli side of the frontier.

A very important component of target-hardening involved preventing infiltration along the coastline by terrorists who intended either to carry out attacks or to deliver weapons into Israel. This prevention task was the Israeli navy's responsibility and involved two types of operations. First, it engaged in defensive activity. It defined a maritime buffer zone extending as far as Cyprus. Operations in the zone consisted of maritime patrols, assisted by aerial escort and surveillance along the Israeli coastline. This was complemented by the work of the intelligence services, who operated from navy patrol vessels. Israeli intelligence monitored all maritime activity in the area, including shipping patterns and routes. If suspicions arose, the suspected vessel was identified, intercepted, and stopped. Its crew and passengers might be held for interrogation, and any terrorists would be arrested by the Israeli authorities.[78] The navy also patrolled the Lebanese coast and the Red Sea, but did not blockade the ports of southern Lebanon. The navy tried to ensure that any clash with terrorists would occur as far out to sea as possible. For this mission, the Israeli navy deployed fast patrol boats, including small missile boats. The navy began to apply its sealing-off strategy at current levels in 1979 as a result of terrorist success in launching several spectacular operations inside Israel after having infiltrated by sea. The Israeli navy's second mission involved offensive operations in conjunction with land and air forces. These involved launching and supporting commando operations across the border, into Lebanon in particular.

The main task of the police was to ensure target-hardening inside Israel. This has been carried out over a long period of time by means of roadblocks and searches for suspects or wanted vehicles. The police were also involved in the protection of VIPs, public or secret meetings, demonstrations, processions, and similar activities as part of their routine duty in securing public order. Target-hardening techniques included educating the public to the need for vigilance in order to identify suspicious persons or unattended packages left behind in bus stations (a popular target for terrorist bombs), within buses, and on sidewalks. This internalized alertness became a kind of second nature which, until the recent attacks by *Hamas*,[79] had proved effective in preventing terrorist assaults from causing damage and casualties.

To cope with terrorism outside Israel and the region, preventive security measures were developed and constantly improved, in line with innovations in terrorist tactics. They included stationing security agents on board El Al (Israeli airline) aircraft and in all official Israeli offices abroad, installing electronic detection devices in Israeli offices abroad and in the Israeli airports, and using bodyguards to accompany Israeli official delegations participating in international events abroad.[80]

International Cooperation

Over the years, Israel pursued, with varying degrees of success, anti-terrorism cooperation on a bilateral basis, since efforts to achieve comprehensive multilateral arrangements failed. Bilateral efforts concentrated mainly on police work and exchanges of intelligence. But cooperation clearly depended on the origin of the terrorists. Western European governments were more inclined to cooperate when common efforts assisted in the suppression of their domestic terrorists (who were frequently linked to and operating jointly with Palestinian terrorists). There was rather less cooperation in containing Palestinian and Arab terrorism carried out on their territory, but usually not directed against them as host country.[81]

While German authorities have exchanged information with Israel and sometimes have consented to Israeli investigations, including the interrogation of terrorists imprisoned in Germany, these efforts did not lead to the extradition of terrorists to Israel. As for the French, cooperation never expanded beyond the level of police and intelligence assistance into mutual obligation either to try terrorist offenders or to extradite them. Furthermore, Israeli efforts to undermine Palestinian terrorism abroad were torpedoed by "under the table" agreements of Western governments, buying foreign terrorist "cease-fires" and foreign terrorist disengagement in the local sphere in exchange for free transit, non-extradition, and no expulsion of wanted and accused terrorists.[82] Thus, Israel witnessed more cases of terrorists being released than those in which they were prosecuted or extradited.

Israel and the US cooperated closely on counter-terrorism intelligence matters. A 1968 agreement codified intelligence cooperation, but it probably existed, de facto, for many years prior to that.[83] Israeli sources claim that the US bombing of Libya in 1986, as well as the earlier diversion of the Egypt-Air aircraft carrying Abu al-Abbas and the *Achille Lauro* hijackers and the Israeli air strike on Tunis (both in 1985), was made possible by such exchanges of information.[84] American involvement in fighting terrorism in the Middle East commenced in the 1980s after the siege of the US embassy in Teheran. Israeli-American cooperation was accompanied by public statements by leaders of both countries, stressing the need for international cooperation in order to suppress international terrorism. However, some have been critical of the relationship. The arms-for-hostages deal that lay at the heart of the Iran-Contra affair was a joint American-Israeli initiative. It both undermined US counter-terrorism policy and damaged the Reagan presidency, while Israel emerged relatively unscathed.[85]

Intelligence aside, Israeli anti-terrorism efforts abroad usually involved diplomacy, public opinion and propaganda campaigns, and target-hardening measures. On the diplomatic level, within the international organizations, Israel carried out constant efforts aimed at the adoption and implementation of anti-terrorism resolutions. The main endeavors in this regard were conducted at the UN General Assembly. These achieved only modest success in the 1970s, however, because many assembly members were well disposed to the PLO and opposed to Israeli occupation of the West Bank and Gaza. Israel is also active in other international forms, such as UN agencies (e.g. the International Civil Aviation Organization), the Council of Europe, international tourism, and international jurists organizations.[86] Public opinion and public relations initiatives, which were the domain of the Foreign Office, usually emphasized the nature and development of the Arab-Israeli conflict and the Palestinian component of terrorism. For many years though, Israeli public relation efforts were rather modest and later, during the Likud government (1977–1984), counterproductive. Most efforts were defensive, designed to reduce Israel's isolation.

CONCLUSIONS

What was the balance of costs arising from the interaction of Palestinian terrorism and Israeli democracy? When analyzing the Israeli case, it is important to take the following major factors into consideration: first, Israeli democracy and Palestinian terrorism have been affected more by the wider Arab-Israeli conflict than by their mutual interaction. Second, terrorism's impact on Israeli democracy is measured by normative socio-political criteria; the impact of Israeli anti-terrorism methods on Palestinian terrorism is measured by empirical, political, and technical/operational criteria.

Israeli society and Israeli democracy have suffered severe blows in recent years. While formal democracy continues to function, deep wounds have been carved in the liberal ethical commitment to democracy. What sets the Israeli experience apart from that of other democratic states is that the roots undermining democracy lie principally in the occupation of the territories and only to a marginal degree in terrorism as a distinct factor. In other words, it was not the tactic of terrorism and the physical characteristics of this kind of warfare that pushed some frightened Israelis into anti-democratic attitudes and behavior in the 1980s and 1990s. Rather, it was the prospect of a political solution, the possible establishment of a Palestinian state on the West Bank, and the threat of such a state to the utopian ideal of a Greater Erez-Israel. In this context, terrorism was only a catalyst; it kept the "flame of fear" burning, but did not bring it about and did not control it. That said, "Israeli society seems to tolerate casualties inflicted by terrorist strikes less than those caused by other sources. [Yet], this is not a uniquely Israeli phenomenon and is in fact demonstrated as well in other countries which face terrorism."[87]

The impact of the measures undertaken against terrorism must be weighed against the operational goals of the terrorists, their political structure, and the physical threat challenging Israel. In all cases, Israeli countermeasures kept domestic anti-Israeli terrorism including terrorism from the territories to a minimum. The attempts to launch terrorist assaults failed more often than they succeeded, many of them being discovered and prevented beforehand. The exhaustive means the Israelis employed reduced considerably the terrorists' range of options. Consequently, most of the spectacular terrorist assaults were carried out abroad or were launched into Israel from across its borders. In other words, Israel succeeded in diverting the battle front out of the country into foreign territory. Thus, the terrorists were caught in the middle, being pressured by Israel on the one hand and by the neighboring countries, Jordan and Syria, on the other. By contrast, countering terrorism within the occupied territories imposed a much heavier moral and ethical burden on Israeli society than that arising from countering international terrorism.

From the political perspective, however, Israel only partially achieved its goals. Success in terms of politically isolating the PLO was short-lived and was a function of time, rather than of Israeli efforts. From 1967 until the 1973 war, Israel profited from the fact that the occupation of the territories had not yet become counterproductive in international public opinion. However, the combination of the "David versus Goliath" image of the 1967 war and the perception of Israel as the victim of terrorism lasted only a short time. In the meantime, in spite of successful Israeli operational countermeasures and highly publicized atrocities and failures, Palestinian international terrorism managed to gain important political credibility and influence. Moreover, in these achievements can be seen the original sources of the *Intifada* in the territories. The present insurrection is nurtured, at least in part, by the PLO's success in building and consolidating such a huge organization with (until recently) vast funds that is well connected throughout the Arab world and, on the other, by an international community well disposed to support the organization's motives and goals.[88] In this specific geopolitical setting, terrorism has been instrumental in advancing the political goals of the Palestinian movement. These political benefits, gained initially by terrorism, could not be taken away from the Palestinians by any one of the effective Israeli anti-terrorism measures. Nevertheless, it was only when the PLO formally *abandoned* its armed struggle that it was able to capitalize on those political benefits, by means of the 1993 agreement with Israel. But the more important question for this study is this: Was Palestinian terrorism instrumental in undermining Israeli democracy?

It is impossible to isolate terrorism from the wider Arab-Israeli conflict, which still is the most important issue on the Israeli domestic and foreign policy agendas.

This section, therefore, will attempt to highlight those issues in which terrorism seemed to be more significant than other factors.

First, terrorism was perpetrated by those opposed to Israel's existence and was directed toward its annihilation. However, the Israeli *perception* of the threat was disproportionate to the *objective reality* of the threat.[89] Israelis perceived terrorism not in terms of violations of human rights in peacetime, as do other Western democracies, but rather in terms of the continuous, vicious cycle of war in which Israel has been involved since independence.[90] The use of a military means against terrorism was explained in exactly this way: Terrorism is part of the warfare conducted against Israel, and it can and should be dealt with and deterred by military means.

Second, this view, combined with the fact that Israeli anti-terrorism measures succeeded in keeping Israel nearly immune to terrorism, produced several consequences. First, anti-terrorist measures within Israel did not jeopardize fundamental *Israeli* civil rights. Second, the major endeavors against terrorism were carried out either in the territories or across the border, within the framework of regular army operational activity, so the burden was not felt in everyday life. It was integrated within the overall defense mission and was not perceived specifically as a "terrorism burden." Yet it was this very approach that produced the corrosive effects, arising from the aerial bombardment reprisals against terrorist bases in the midst of civilian populations. It was the first crack in the Israeli commitment to democracy and democratic balance in society. It implied that Israeli citizens had abdicated responsibility for controlling their government and for limiting the use of excessive and inappropriate means to fight terrorism.

Third, the Lebanon War caused a relaxation of democratic inhibitions. The army's Lebanese experience spilled over into its behavior within the territories. Anti-terrorism measures occasionally and informally changed into excessive, oppressive actions, which hurt the innocent. Soldiers experienced erosion of morale arising from the commitment to conduct "policing" functions in the territories, rather than fulfilling their traditional mission of protecting the country against external threats. Over time, a psychological defense barrier has developed to counter the negative self-image. It has caused apathy and disinterest on the one hand and unsatisfied rage on the other, both of which are destructive in a liberal society.[91] Moreover, the Lebanon War and the massacre at Sabra and Shatila shook Israeli society, politicians and ordinary citizens alike. The war, which started *ostensibly* as an anti-terrorist reprisal operation, caused a profound rift in the Israeli consensus concerning terrorism and how to counter it. Thus, the value of certain anti-terrorism measures joined the issues dividing Israeli society. It struck the conscience (and political positions) of Israeli politicians so deeply that they agreed to the 1985 hostage-prisoner exchange, which undermined the fundamental Israeli anti-terrorism principle of non-negotiation.

Finally, Jewish Israeli terrorism reappeared in 1980. The facts that four years were needed to unravel the organization and that an impressive and active lobby pleaded for the underground members' amnesty indicated an erosion of Israel's steadfast liberal negation of terrorism. Indeed, Israeli populist support for Jewish terrorism clearly reflected the fact that the Israeli anti-terrorism consensus had become divided into sharply opposing attitudes regarding the morality of terrorism.[92] Furthermore, the threat of further Jewish counter-terrorism pushed the authorities to withdraw from some basic democratic norms in their fight against Palestinian terrorism, for instance, by inflicting collective punishments *before* initiating legal due process.[93] Thus, the experience in Lebanon and the occupied territories gave terrorism the means to gnaw at Israeli democracy.

This let loose an avalanche of consequences concerning terrorism in general. Jewish settlers in the territories carried out vigilante attacks under the specious guise of self-defense. Perhaps the most troubling aspect of this kind of terrorism is the fact that the perpetrators felt they did not have to fear the authorities; even the judiciary appeared to be tolerant.[94] In short, the vigilantes perceived themselves to be behaving within a consensual atmosphere. This was one of the most significant blows to Israeli democracy.

It was not only the judiciary that found itself unprepared to deal with vigilante counter-terrorism. The military voice, Israel's credibility "insurance," also began stuttering. Uneasiness and dissonance in self-image started to influence its announcements. The army's confusion and consternation, its inability to control and prevent civilian vigilantism, was reflected in the ambiguous and inconsistent army press releases when such events occurred in the areas under military control.[95]

Terrorism became an issue that politicians exploited to arouse false consensus whenever they feared political dissent on crucial and important issues. Touching primordial anxieties, terrorism was manipulated politically to unrealistic dimensions in order to divert attention from a realistic evaluation of Israel's problems. It was transformed into a linguistic means for political purposes, devoid of any proper relevance to the real meaning of the term. Stigmatizing the enemy simply by applying the satanic attribute of "terrorism" legitimized and mobilized support for the use of excessive anti-terrorist emergency means, operationally as well as politically.[96] Indeed, passage of the law prohibiting contact with the PLO on grounds that such contact meant compliance with a terrorist organization was another link in the chain of anti-democratic measures. It clearly imposed limitations on the freedom of expression and thought and signified a regression from Israel's liberal-democratic achievements, even though it has been impossible to enforce.[97]

Ironically, the manipulation of terrorism for political purposes actually served to amplify the terrorizing effects of such attacks. Politicians, seeing terrorists everywhere and in anybody, played into the hands of the terrorists. By misusing the term *terrorism* or perverting the proportions of the phenomenon, particularly immediately after an attack, politicians have succeeded in occasionally causing mob violence, which otherwise has been uncommon in Israeli society. For example, after the attempted murder of two teachers in Afula in 1985, Knesset Vice-President Meir Cohen-Avidav visited the town and incited the Jewish residents against Arab citizens and workers from the territories.[98] Such incidents, however rare, illustrate the fragility of the social fabric and the fertility of the ground for the populist exploitation of the fear of terrorism.

The erosion has taken place subtly, and during the first few years after the 1967 war, it occurred unconsciously, without premeditation. Nonetheless, the Landau Report revealed how far that version had gone. Apart from highlighting once again the need for a comprehensive anti-terrorism policy and the importance of defining the authoritative capacity to take responsibility, it revealed the tip of a growing and unjust iceberg, forming under the constraints and tensions caused by the challenge of terrorism.

The report was very controversial. Indeed, it was an obstacle course, its authors anxious to avoid all of the pitfalls leading to destabilization and the undermining of democracy. According to Judge Landau, the point of equilibrium between national security requirements and civil rights is the "modest measure of physical pressure" permitted during investigation.[99] Some have argued that because of its hesitancy and its legitimization, indeed its quasi-legalization, of the unavoidable grey zone on the margins of democracy, the report should not have been written.[100] On the other hand, there were the critics who saw its value in the fact that the committee was willing to confront this fundamental intellectual and ethical question: How can an enlightened democratic society defend itself against cruel terrorist attacks and maintain its commitment to liberal values and the principle of the rule of law? One of the merits of the report was the fact that it "humanized" the enemy. It recognized his/her basic human rights in spite of the fact that terrorists disregard the law and deprive their victims of their rights. The work of the committee elevated the moral and ethical considerations to a level equal to the vital and existential security needs. The interesting conclusion is that "the same moral imperative, which obliges the *Shabak* people to see in the captive enemy a human being deserving basic protection of his human rights, also grants them the permission to do to the enemy, within the boundaries of law, deeds which otherwise would have been considered criminal."[101]

Writing in 1987, Yeheskel Dror concluded that some serious fissures had split Israeli unity and decisiveness against terrorism. He suggested that Israel reappraise its overall pattern of responsibility for fighting terrorism. Dror especially emphasized staff work to develop and to moderate counter-terrorism strategies and recommended that these strategies be combined with a renewed security (defense) doctrine. The operational responsibility for carrying out the various methods deserved reappraisal, too. Establishing a "rear command" concerning terrorism should be considered as part of a broader authority responsible for the civilian population during wartime and mass catastrophes. No less important is deciding who, on the political level, should be responsible for fighting terrorism. Another aspect Dror felt required attention and improvement concerns the immediate harm caused by terrorism, namely, the mass psychological repercussions, which are, of course, the very raison d'être of terrorism. It is essential to develop an overall strategy to deal with these effects, as well as to mobilize countermeasures that would defuse emotional overreaction and intensifying hatred. This is especially important in view of the emergence of Islamic-motivated terrorism, which could mobilize more people (not only Palestinians) on the more emotive and idealistic grounds of Islamic revolution. Dror insisted that civilian immunity and capability to endure long periods of terrorism receive high-level attention in order to prepare for the possibility of types of public traumas never known before. Continuous innovation and preparation of public will are essential, since effective counter-terrorism measures may cause terrorists to adopt new and unforeseen tactics, thus extending the cycle of violence and response indefinitely.[102] In light of the violent events that have occurred since the 1993 agreement, and the emotional responses they have generated, Dror's suggestions were remarkably prescient, and remain relevant.

Combatting terrorism will accompany Israel's development and consolidation for many years to come. It is, therefore, indispensable that Israel develop a strategy of fighting terrorism, which, on the one hand, is linked to and forms an integral part of its overall security doctrine and, on the other, reflects the political dimension of the struggle, and thus remains anchored to the fundamental human and democratic values cherished by Israeli society.

NOTES

1. Quoted in *Davar*, 4 September 1987, p. 17 [author's translation].

2. The groups are described in US Defense Intelligence Agency, *Terrorist Group Profiles* (Washington, D.C.: US Government Printing Office, 1988), pp. 3–30; for a history of the PLO, see Helena Cobban, *The Palestinian Liberation Organization: People, Power, Politics* (Cambridge: Cambridge University Press, 1984).

3. Klaus Wasmund, "The Political Socialization of West German Terrorists," in Peter H. Merkl, ed., *Political Violence and Terror: Motifs and Motivations* (Berkeley: University of California Press, 1986), pp. 220–21; Robert C. Meade, Jr., *Red Brigades: The Story of Italian Terrorism* (New York: St. Martin's Press, 1990), pp. 221–22, 224; Jillian Becker, *The PLO: The Rise and Fall of the Palestine Liberation Organization* (London: Weidenfeld and Nicolson, 1984), pp. 106–107, 189–93.

4. "Special Double Issue—The Middle East in Documents," *Middle East Focus* 6, nos. 2 and 3 (July/September 1983), p. 22.

5. Yehoshafat Harkabi, *The Palestinian Covenant and Its Meaning* (Totowa, N.J.: Valentine, Mitchell and Co., 1979), pp. 119–31.

6. *Contemporary Mideast Backgrounder*, no. 251 (Jerusalem: Media Analysis Center, October 1988).

7. Zvi Lanir, "The PLO's Conception of the 'Armed Struggle' in the Test of the 'Peace for Galilee' War," *Ma'arachot*, no. 284 (September 1982), pp. 10–23.

8. Eliezer Ben-Rafael, *Israel-Palestine: A Guerrilla Conflict in International Politics* (New York: Greenwood Press, 1987), p. 135.

9. Ibid., pp. 137–52.

10. Gabriel Ben-Dor, "The Strategy of Terrorism in the Arab-Israeli Conflict: The Case of Palestinian Guerrillas," in Yair Evron, ed., *International Violence: Terrorism, Surprise and Control* (Jerusalem: Hebrew University of Jerusalem, Leonard Davis Institute, 1979), p. 139.

11. Quoted in Ibid., pp. 139–40.

12. Alain Frachon, "Murder of Collaborators Could Tarnish Intifada," *Le Monde*, 11–12 June 1989, reprinted in *Manchester Guardian Weekly*, 18 June 1989. See also *Globe and Mail* (Toronto), 30 May 1989 and 9 September 1989.

13. Ariel Merari, et al., "The Palestinian *Intifada*: An Analysis of a Popular Uprising After Seven Months," *Terrorism and Political Violence* 1, no. 2 (April 1989), pp. 191–92; see also Edy Kaufman, "Israeli Perceptions of the Palestinians' 'Limited Violence' in the *Intifada*," *Terrorism and Political Violence* 3, no. 4 (Winter 1991), pp. 10–11, 15–17 (especially Table 2), 26. Both articles tend to confirm the predominance of the *Intifada's* insurrectionary character.

14. Ben-Dor, "The Strategy of Terrorism," pp. 140–41.

15. Cobban, *The Palestinian Liberation Organization*, pp. 81–93.

16. Ibid., pp. 94–96.

17. Ibid., pp. 120–27, 135–36.

18. Emile F. Saliyeh, *The PLO After the Lebanon War* (Boulder, Colo.: Westview Press, 1986), pp. 139–75.

19. Marius Deeb, *Militant Islamic Movements in Lebanon: Origins, Social Basis, and Ideology*, Occasional Papers Series (Washington, D.C.: Georgetown University, Center for Contemporary Arab Studies, November 1986), p. 17; Chris P. Ioannides, "The PLO and the Islamic Revolution in Iran," in Augustus Richard Norton and Martin H. Greenberg, *The International Relations of the Palestine Liberation Organization* (Carbondale and Edwardsville, Ill.: Southern Illinois University Press, 1989), pp. 91–95.

20. Lanir, "The PLO's Conception of the 'Armed Struggle'"; and Ben-Rafael, *Israel-Palestine*, pp. 25–43, 99–134.

21. M. Graeme Bannerman, "Arabs and Israelis: Slow Walk Toward Peace," *Foreign Affairs* 72, no. 1 (1993), pp. 148–49, 153; see "Text of Declaration of Principles on Interim Self-Government Arrangements," *Dispatch Supplement* 4, no. 4 (Washington, D.C.: US Department of State, September 1993), pp. 2–6.

22. Yeheskel Dror, "Terrorism in a Split World," *Bamahane* [IDF weekly], 22 July 1987, p. 16; Yeheskel Dror, "International Terrorism, Situation Assessment," *Sekira Hodshit* [IDF monthly] 32, no. 11–12 (1985) pp. 37–46. See also David K. Shipler, *Arab and Jew: Wounded Spirits in a Promised Land* (New York: Viking/Penguin, 1986), pp. 79–137, 181–83, 191, 199, 215.

23. Noemi Gal-Or, *The Jewish Underground: Our Terrorism* (Tel Aviv: Hakibbutz Hameuchad, n.d.); Kaufman, "Israeli Perceptions," pp. 7, 22.

24. Dror, "Terrorism in a Split World."

25. Hanan Alon, *Countering Palestinian Terrorism in Israel: Toward a Policy Analysis of Countermeasures* (Santa Monica, Calif.: Rand Corporation, 1980), p. 91.

26. Ibid., pp. 91–92.

27. Ben-Dor, "The Strategy of Terrorism," pp. 141–42.

28. Ehud Shprinzak, *Every Man Whatsoever Is Right in His Own Eyes: Illegalism in Israeli Society* (Tel Aviv: Sifriat Poalim, 1986), p. 174.

29. Jehuda Reinharz, ed., *Living with Anti-Semitism: Modern Jewish Responses* (London: Brandeis University Press, 1987), p. 472 and n.14.

30. *Haaretz*, 8 July 1985, p. 7.

31. *Haaretz*, Mussaf Shabat, February 1978, pp. 8–9; Yitshak Rabin, "An International Agency Against Terrorism," in Benjamin Netanyahu, ed., *Terrorism: How the West Can Win* (New York: Farrar, Straus, and Giroux, 1986), pp. 182–85.

32. *Haaretz*, 8 July 1985, p. 7; Alon, *Countering Palestinian Terrorism*, p. 181.

33. Alon, *Countering Palestinian Terrorism*, p. 182.

34. Ibid.; *Haaretz*, 8 July 1985.

35. For instance, European Community embargoes on Israel during the Lebanon War, 1982–1984, and after the Tunis air raid in 1986. See also *Haaretz*, 4 October 1985, p. 11.

36. Noemi Gal-Or, "The Israeli Defense Forces and Unconventional Warfare: The Palestinian Factor and Israeli National Security Doctrine," *Terrorism and Political Violence* 2, no. 2 (Summer, 1990), pp. 212–26.

37. Noemi Gal-Or, "Tolerating Terrorism in Israel," in Noemi Gal-Or, ed., *Tolerating Terrorism in the West: An International Survey* (London: Routledge, 1991), pp. 59–60, 75–82, 85–89; Ian S. Lustick, *For the Land and the Lord: Jewish Fundamentalism in Israel* (New York: Council on Foreign Relations, 1988), pp. 11–12, 65–69. See also Haggai Segal, *Dear Brothers* (Jerusalem: Keter, 1987), p. 283; Edward F. Mickolus, Todd Sandler, and Jean M. Murdock, *International Terrorism in the 1980s: A Chronology of Events,* vol. 2 (Ames: Iowa State University Press, 1989), pp. 202–203; *Haaretz*, 22 May 1985, p. 7.

38. Amitzur Ilan, *Bernadotte in Palestine, 1948: A Study in Contemporary Knight Errantry* (London: Macmillan, 1989), pp. 193-222, 228; "Prevention of Terrorism Decree no. 33, for the year 1948," in Robert Gideon, ed., *State of Israel Laws*, vol. 16 (Tel Aviv: Gideon Publishers Ltd., n.d.), pp. 8959–8963.

39. S. S. Feler, "The Law Amendment of Prevention of Terrorism Decree," *Davar*, 8 August 1986, p. 17.

40. *Haaretz*, 7 August 1985, p. 7; David A. Charters, *The British Army and Jewish Insurgency in Palestine 1945–47* (London: Macmillan, 1989), p. 87.

41. *Haaretz*, 14 October 1987, p. 11, and 2 December 1987, p. 9.

42. Moshe Drori, *The Legislation in the Area of Judea and Samaria* (Jerusalem: Hebrew University of Jerusalem, Faculty of Law, Harry Sacher Institute for Legislative Research and Comparative Law, 1975), p. 171.

43. *Haaretz*, 30 July 1985, p. 2, and 18 October 1985, p. 12. On the case of Abu Daoud, see Noemi Gal-Or, *International Cooperation to Suppress Terrorism* (New York: St. Martin's Press, 1985), pp. 71–72; and Chapter 5 of this volume.

44. *Haaretz*, 30 July 1985, p. 2.

45. *The Rule of Law in the Areas Administered by Israel* (Tel Aviv: Israel National Section of the International Commission of Jurists, 1981), pp. 25–27. *Haaretz*, 8 February 1988, p. 3.

46. Drori, *The Legislation*, pp. 94–95, 156–57, 159; *Haaretz*, 17 February 1986, p. 9; *The Rule of Law*, pp. 67–72, 87.

47. Mickolus, Sandler, and Murdock, *International Terrorism* vol. 2, pp. 202–203. See also *Haaretz*, 22 May 1985, p. 7; 23 May 1985, p. 3; and 9 June 1985, p. 9.

48. See Mickolus, Sandler, and Murdock, *International Terrorism*, pp. 219–24; *Globe and Mail*, 10 September 1985. Some of those released in the May 1985 exchange committed new lethal attacks. *Haaretz*, 17 February 1987, p. 11.

49. Quoted in Ben-Rafael, *Israel-Palestine*, p. 105.

50. Ibid., p. 70; *Haaretz*, 21 September 1987, p. 9; Dan Raviv and Yossi Melman, *Every Spy a Prince: The Complete History of Israel's Intelligence Community* (Boston: Houghton

Mifflin, 1990), pp. 170–74, describes *Shabak*'s (or *Shin Bet's*) methods in the territories.

51. *Haaretz*, 6 November 1987, p. 16; *Koteret Rashit*, no. 182 (28 May 1986), pp. 8–9, and no. 183 (4 June 1986), pp. 16–17.

52. *Investigation Committee Concerning Investigation Methods of the General Security Service in Matters of Hostile Terrorism Activity—The Complete Report*, reprinted in *Haaretz*, 1 November 1988, pp. 13–17.

53. *Haaretz*, 1 November 1987, p. 9, and 9 November 1987, p. 11.

54. *Globe and Mail*, 5 February 1993.

55. Ben-Rafael, *Israel-Palestine*, pp. 69–72, 111, points at the effectiveness and success of the preventive task of the intelligence services; see also Ian Black and Benny Morris, *Israel's Secret Wars: A History of Israel's Intelligence Services* (New York: Grove Weidenfeld, 1991), pp. 236–37, 243–59, 263–64, 266–69, 279–80.

56. The JAMAM was first used successfully in March 1988, rescuing the passengers of a hijacked bus. Although it was present during previous assaults, the army was introduced to end these events. *Haaretz*, 8 March 1988, p. 3.

57. *Haaretz*, 29 December 1985, p. 7, and 14 February 1986, p. 3.

58. Stuart A. Cohen and Efraim Inbar, "Varieties of Counter-insurgency Activities: Israel's Military Operations Against the Palestinians, 1948–90," *Small Wars and Insurgencies* 2, no. 1 (April 1991), pp. 45–46. See also *The Rule of Law*, pp. 68–69, 72–73, 87. The undercover squads were officially revealed on Israeli TV in June 1991.

59. Some cases in which settlers, under the guise of guard duties, were suspected of having killed Palestinians were dealt with secretly. *Haaretz*, 11 December 1986, p. 1, 2; 14 October 1987, p. 7, and 3 November 1987, p. 15. Such killings may be more organized—as, for example, those claimed by the individuals or group calling themselves the *Sicarii*. See *Globe and Mail*, 28 April 1989, p. 5.

60. *Haaretz*, 11 July 1986, p. 1, and 14 December 1987, p. 3.

61. See Alon, *Countering Palestinian Terrorism*, pp. 68–71, 76–81.

62. Ben-Rafael, *Israel-Palestine*, pp. 99–100: Lanir, "The PLO's Conception of the 'Armed Struggle'"; Uri Milstein, *The History of the Israel Paratroopers (From the War of Independence to the Lebanon War)*, 3 vols. (Tel Aviv: Schalgi Ltd., 1985). On the political, strategic, institutional, and doctrinal sources of Israeli offensive strategy, see Ariel Levite, *Offense and Defense in Israeli Military Doctrine* (Boulder, Colo.: Westview Press, 1990), pp. 10–14, 27–62.

63. Alon, *Countering Palestinian Terrorism*, pp. 70, 77–81; Cohen and Inbar, "Varieties of Counter-insurgency Activities," pp. 48–50, 53–56.

64. Lanir, "The PLO's Conception of the 'Armed Struggle,'" p. 16; Cohen and Inbar, "Varieties of Counter-insurgency Activities," pp. 47–48.

65. Bruce Hoffman, *Commando Raids: 1946–1983*, no. N-2316-USDP (Santa Monica, Calif.: Rand Corp., October 1985), p. 38.

66. Colonel Benny Michelsohn, "Operation 'TOFET' (INFERNO): Fighting East of the Jordan River March 1968," in Jean Pariseau, ed., *Acta No. 14 Proceedings of the 14th International Military History Colloquium, Montreal 1988*, vol. 2 (Ottawa: International Commission of Military History, 1989), pp. 788–817.

67. Gal-Or, "The Israeli Defense Forces and Unconventional Warfare," pp. 216–17, 222–24.

68. In 1987, former Defense Minister and current Prime Minister Yitshak Rabin maintained that terrorism, not being war for the very existence of the state, should cost the

minimum human price. Therefore, air strikes are "cheaper" than land operations. *Maariv Shabat*, 23 October 1987, p. 5.

69. *Haaretz*, 4 October 1985, p. 11, and 3 September 1987, p. 11.

70. Raymond Tanter and Lisa Kaufman, "Terror and Reprisal: Process and Choice," in Evron, *International Violence,* p. 203–30 (emphasis in the original text)

71. Ben-Rafael, *Israel-Palestine*, p. 84. On the other hand, the Christian-dominated South Lebanon Army of Major Hadad began to operate, building up a buffer zone between the PLO forces and the Israeli border.

72. Cohen and Inbar, "Varieties of Counter-insurgency Activities," pp. 53, 56.

73. Gal-Or, *International Cooperation*, pp. 231–73.

74. On Mossad's use of lethal force in anti-terrorist efforts, see Black and Morris, *Israel's Secret Wars*, pp. 272–77, 527–28; note that the PLO did not blame Israel for Abu Iyad's death. Shlomo Gazit and Michael Handel, "Intelligence Warfare Against Terrorism Organizations," *Maarachot* [IDF monthly], no. 278 (January/February 1981), pp. 10–14; "Cutting Arafat's Sea Link," *Newsweek*, 1 December 1986, p. 46; *Globe and Mail*, 18 April 1988; *Washington Post*, 21 April 1988; *Los Angeles Times*, 22 April 1988. George Jonas, *Vengeance* (Toronto: Lester and Orpen Dennys, 1984), which purports to be a firsthand account of the actions of a Mossad assassination team, should be read with caution.

75. See Chapter 3 in this volume.

76. Alon, *Countering Palestinian Terrorism*, pp. 76–77. "Blurring" means that all along the border, several times a day, the army marks fresh double or triple parallel lines in the sand and later follows these lines to discover footprints or any other traces of infiltrators.

77. Itamar Rabinovitch, *The War for Lebanon, 1970–1985*, rev. ed. (Ithaca, N.Y.: Cornell University Press, 1985), pp. 107, 109–10, 112, 197.

78. International law permits the interrogation of vessel crews outside the country's territorial waters. *Maariv Shabat*, 13 November 1987, p. 1; Chaim Stav, "Danger from the Deep: Terrorism and Piracy on the High Seas," *Terrorism Update*, no. 92 (January 1988).

79. On 25 February 1994, a Jewish settler opposed to the Israeli-PLO autonomy agreement shot and killed some thirty Arabs in a mosque in Hebron. In response *Hamas* carried out a series of bombing and other attacks in Israel itself, causing at least fourteen deaths, and wounding about 75 people. See *Globe and Mail*, 7 April 1994, 14 April 1994, and 19 April 1994.

80. Alon, *Countering Palestinian Terrorism*, p. 81.

81. Gal-Or, *International Cooperation*, pp. 189–205; Noemi Gal-Or, "Suppressing Terrorism: Problems of European-Israeli Cooperation," in Ilan Greilsammer and Joseph H. H. Weiler, eds., *Europe and Israel: Troubled Neighbours* (Berlin: Walter de Gruyter, 1988), pp. 313–37.

82. Gal-Or, *International Cooperation*, pp. 231–73. See Chapters 4 and 5 in this volume.

83. *Haaretz*, 23 June 1985, p. 7.

84. *Haaretz*, 23 June 1985, p. 7, and 31 December 1987, p. 11.

85. See, for example, Helena Cobban, "The U.S.-Israeli Relationship in the Reagan Era," *Conflict Quarterly* 9, no. 2 (Spring 1989), pp. 6, 8, 13, 16–17, 21; David C. Martin and John Walcott, *Best Laid Plans: The Inside Story of America's War Against Terrorism* (New York: Harper and Row, 1988), pp. 192–93, 228–32, 327–28; Patricia Ann O'Connor, ed., *The Iran-Contra Puzzle* (Washington, D.C.: Congressional Quarterly Inc., 1987), pp. 43–45.

86. *Haaretz*, 2 July 1986, p. 3, and 24 September 1986, p. 3.

87. Alon, *Countering Palestinian Terrorism*, p. 93.

88. Ben-Rafael, *Israel-Palestine*, pp. 134–35. See *Der Spiegel*, 28 October 1985, pp. 175–78; see also James Adams, *The Financing of Terror* (London: New English Library, 1986), pp. 55–59, 64–66, 84–89, 93, 94, 96–125; "Who Pays Arafat?" *U.S. News and World Report*, 26 April 1993, pp. 46–52; David McDowall, *Palestine and Israel: The Uprising and Beyond* (Berkeley: University of California Press, 1989), pp. 31–36.

89. Alon, *Countering Palestinian Terrorism*, p. 180; Kaufman, "Israeli Perceptions," pp. 6–8, 11, 13, 16–18.

90. Harkabi, *The Palestinian Covenant*, pp. 119–31.

91. David Grossman, *Yellow Wind* (Tel Aviv: Hakibbutz Hameuchad, 1987), p. 172. See also Gunther E. Rothenberg, "Israeli Defence Forces and Low Intensity Operations," in David A. Charters and Maurice Tugwell, eds., *Armies in Low-intensity Conflict: A Comparative Analysis* (London: Brassey's, 1989), pp. 70–72, on the effects of the Lebanon War and duty in the territories on the morale and performance of the IDF. See also *Haaretz*, 5 March 1987, p. 9.

92. Gal-Or, "Tolerating Terrorism in Israel," pp. 59–92. By 1991, all of the Underground had completed their sentences.

93. *Haaretz*, 30 October 1984, p. 9, and 11 July 1985, p. 7.

94. *Haaretz*, 30 October 1984, p. 9; Gal-Or, "Tolerating Terrorism in Israel," pp. 82–84.

95. *Haaretz*, 15 December 1986, p. 9.

96. For example, Israeli leaders refer to Arafat solely as "Chief of Terrorists" or "Chief of Murderers" and not "Head of the PLO." *Haaretz*, 13 October 1985, p. 12. See also Kaufman, "Israeli Perceptions," pp. 19–21.

97. *Haaretz*, 2 August 1985, p. 11.

98. *Haaretz*, 29 July 1985, p. 7, and 1 August 1985, p. 1.

99. Judge Landau, speech given on the occasion of the anniversary of Jaffee Center for Strategic Studies, Tel Aviv, 13 January 1988.

100. *Haaretz*, 4 November 1987, p. 9.

101. *Haaretz*, 8 November 1987, p. 9 [author's translation].

102. Yeheskel Dror, "The Necessity of a Rear Command," *Bamahane* [IDF weekly], 22 July 1987, p. 28.

7

The United States' Response to International Terrorism

J. Brent Wilson

INTRODUCTION

The Clinton administration was barely one month old when a bomb explosion at the World Trade Center in New York killed 6 persons and injured up to 1,000 more, on 26 February 1993.[1] Police quickly arrested a number of suspects, whose behavior initially suggested an amateur effort.[2] But what the bomb and the alleged perpetrators seemed to lack in sophistication was more than matched by their potential significance. Their suspected links to an Islamic fundamentalist cleric who actively opposes the Egyptian government transformed a domestic event into the first *major* international terrorist incident on the US mainland.[3] That the suspected bomb team members were arrested quickly can be attributed in part to their carelessness, but also to efficient police work and the counter-terrorism mechanisms put in place over several decades. The aim of this chapter is to explain how and why those mechanisms came to be and what impact they have had on American democracy. Beginning in the early 1970s and concluding with the final year of the Bush presidency, it highlights key periods, events, and decisions in the development of the American approach to countering international terrorism. As the World Trade Center bombing indicates, the story is still unfolding. Primary sources are few, and the secondary literature is often subjective and self-serving. So what follows should be considered a preliminary assessment.

NATURE AND DIMENSIONS OF THE THREAT

Terrorism is not new to Americans, but international terrorism incidents have been relatively rare in the US. This immunity is the result of several factors, including geographic separation from the main sources of terrorism, the absence of systematic anti-state violence in American political culture, and the countermeasures discussed in this chapter. At no time was the stability of the US ever jeopardized by domestic or international terrorism.[4] Nevertheless, American citizens and US interests have been the frequent targets of terrorism overseas. Moreover, responding to international terrorism has created diplomatic problems for the US. Before the late 1960s, international terrorism was carried out by ethnic or separatist groups, such as the Basques. Their targets were confined to small geographic areas, and attacks were generally very selective. However, in the early 1970s, more "ideological" terrorist groups, such as the left-wing Red Brigades in Italy and the Red Army Faction in West Germany, sought out "imperialist" targets in Western Europe.[5] By 1970, Palestinian groups, such as the Popular Front for the Liberation of Palestine (PFLP), were emerging as a dangerous threat. The anti-imperialist ideology shared by some of these groups, particularly the Red Army Faction and PFLP, also brought them together in more functional ways, including joint training and combined terrorist attacks.

Until 1979, US government personnel and installations were attacked infrequently. The seizure of the US embassy and its diplomatic personnel in Teheran in 1979 by Iranian students and the Revolutionary Guard altered the pattern of attacks. By 1980, abductions and assaults on US diplomats outnumbered incidents involving businessmen.[6] Americans made desirable targets for terrorists for several reasons. First, they were highly visible all over the world, as diplomats, businessmen, armed forces personnel, and tourists and, therefore, were accessible. Second, the high concentration of media in the United States guaranteed the perpetrators widespread exposure. Third, the US is a representative democracy, and because democratic states respond to public pressure, they were seen as vulnerable to terrorist coercion. Similarly, democratic states such as the US were viewed as the chief obstacles to the political objectives of many terrorist groups. Thus, US targets had symbolic value to the terrorists. Finally, until the mid-1980s, attacking Americans entailed little cost, since the government lacked a coherent policy for combatting terrorism.[7]

By 1979, other trends were emerging that led to increased frequency and effectiveness. First was state-sponsored terrorism. Although states had been assisting terrorist groups, such as radical factions within the Palestine Liberation Organization (PLO),[8] since the late 1960s, direct state involvement became more significant in the early 1980s following the Iranian seizure of the US embassy and the Libyan government's assassination campaign against expatriate dissidents living in Europe.[9] Consequently, the US began to identify such states as threats. In part, state sponsorship accounted for a rapid increase in the number of incidents in the Middle East, which by 1985 became the region most troubled by international terrorism. A wide variety of groups received state support, including radical Shiite groups in the Middle East, Africa, and Western Europe; radical Palestinians; Latin American insurgents; European separatists; and the Japanese Red Army.[10]

The other source of terrorism from 1980 onward was the regional influence of the Islamic fundamentalist revolution in Iran. Its pan-Islamic appeal, its call for militancy and martyrdom, and its identification of the US as a syn imperialism—exemplified by the seizure of the US embassy in Teheran—pi. an inspiration for like-minded individuals and groups elsewhere in the region, especially in Lebanon. In 1983, Lebanese Shiite Muslim fundamentalist groups with close ties to Iran, such as *Hizb'Allah* (sometimes called Islamic Jihad), began attacking American targets in Lebanon. The 1983 bombings of the US embassy and the Marine barracks in Beirut cost 305 American lives. This was followed by a series of kidnappings from 1984 to 1988, including CIA head of station William Buckley. By 1985, after the hijacking of TWA Flight 847, it had become apparent that Iran, and not Syria or Libya, was the instigator of much of the terrorism in the Middle East, although the other two states were not entirely innocent. The extent of Iran's involvement in the taking of hostages in Lebanon was not made clear until early 1992, after the last American hostage, Terry Anderson, had been released. According to the *Washington Post*, the Iranian revolutionary government paid for both the upkeep and the release of Western hostages and exerted a high degree of control over their fate; all negotiations leading to release took place in Teheran.[11]

According to the US government, Latin American states such as Cuba and Sandinista Nicaragua were also active supporters of terrorists, both internationally and within the region. Because of their political and economic influence, Americans and their interests, especially oil companies, became the targets of terrorist groups such as the *Sendero Luminoso* in Peru and the National Liberation Army in Colombia, who tried to disrupt foreign investment in order to create economic chaos and destabilize the government. More recently, however, terrorism in this region has become complicated by the interaction of terrorists, arms dealers, and drug traffickers, especially in Peru and Colombia. In 1989, although Latin America experienced only 24 percent of the total number of incidents worldwide, 64 percent of all attacks on American citizens and property occurred in this region.[12] In 1992, Latin America recorded the highest number of international terrorist incidents for the fourth year running.[13]

The form of terrorist attacks took on a pattern at the outset and remained consistent throughout. Most attacks were bombings, followed by arson and armed attacks. Hostage-takings, kidnappings, and hijackings fluctuated in their frequency. In 1985, sixty American citizens were seized, thirteen through kidnapping. However, the number of Americans who were kidnapped decreased markedly in the last few years of the 1980s. At the outset, the most frequent US targets were businesses and businessmen. Terrorists switched to government, diplomatic, and military targets between 1980 and 1983. These attacks ranged from individual incidents, such as the kidnapping of Brigadier General James Dozier in Italy in December 1981 and the shooting of Lieutenant Colonel Charles Ray in Paris in January 1982, to massive attacks, such as the destruction of the Marine barracks in Beirut. From 1984, the main targets again became business facilities and personnel, tourists, and non-official targets, such as educators and administrators at overseas universities, probably because of tighter security at diplomatic installations. Nevertheless, attacks on US officials, although they were less frequent, still guaranteed widespread attention, as was shown by the kidnapping of Lieutenant Colonel William Higgins in 1988 and his subsequent "execution."

The death and casualty toll from terrorist attacks generally matched the numerical rise and decline of incidents. However, some years stand out as being particularly costly because of major terrorist "spectaculars." For instance, the bombings in Beirut in 1983 resulted in more than 300 deaths and 170 other casualties. Similarly, the downing of Pan Am Flight 103 in December 1988 led to the deaths of 189 Americans. However, many incidents had either no casualties or very few. Nevertheless, some of these less-lethal events gained notoriety because of the circumstances surrounding the incidents. These would include the killings of Robert Stethem and Leon Klinghoffer during the TWA Flight 847 and *Achille Lauro* hijackings, respectively, which received widespread press coverage. Many of the American dead and wounded have been categorized as "incidental" casualties, meaning they were unlucky bystanders at attacks in which persons or facilities of other nationalities were the principal targets. Among this category would be the five Americans killed and fifteen injured during the attack by Abu Nidal Organization terrorists on the El Al ticket counter at the Rome airport in December 1985.

COMBATTING THE THREAT: THE US RESPONSE

Policy Setting

The US government over time worked out an elaborate framework and array of organizations to implement counter-terrorism policies. At its head is the executive branch, which plays a vital role through the president and the National Security Council (NSC). The president's influence in counter-terrorism is twofold. First, he formulates policy and initiates legislation, and so must place the issue in its proper order of foreign policy priorities, as well as ensure continuity and consistency of policies. He also directs executive agencies to take steps to develop and implement policy and to perform certain acts. Second, because terrorist incidents can become crisis situations, the president frequently becomes personally involved in particular incidents as they unfold and can be responsible for many of the critical decisions. Therefore, the president can become a key player in the government's response. However, the president is not a solitary actor in this regard; congressional, cabinet, and NSC bureaucratic politics both enhance and constrain the president's freedom of action.[14]

After the Munich massacre in September 1972, the Nixon administration began developing an apparatus for dealing with terrorism. The first of the institutional foundations on which future counter-terrorist policy was based was the Cabinet Committee to Combat Terrorism. Its primary task was to coordinate among the government agencies ongoing activity for the prevention of terrorism. However, the committee met only once, in October 1972, to endorse initiatives already taken or decided. Therefore, the main responsibility for coordinating policy fell to the committee's working group. At the outset, it consisted of senior representatives from the various departments or agencies represented on the committee, but within a few years, it had expanded to include eleven additional members, which—in conjunction with other problems—reduced its effectiveness.[15]

In late 1977, President Jimmy Carter abolished the inactive cabinet committee and gave responsibility for coordinating the anti-terrorist program to a more elaborate framework, which divided responsibilities between crisis response and policy development and coordination. The Special Coordination Committee (SCC) of the NSC supervised the senior interagency group discussed below and assisted the president in crisis management of specific incidents requiring highest-level decisions. Otherwise, the response was based on the lead agency concept. This concept dictated that international incidents were the responsibility of the State Department, aircraft hijackings were primarily the responsibility of the Federal Aviation Administration (FAA), and domestic incidents that came under federal jurisdiction were left to the Department of Justice and the Federal Bureau of Investigation (FBI). If interagency policy disputes arose, the agencies were to convene under NSC staff leadership to resolve them.[16]

Long-range policy planning, operational coordination, and information exchange were the responsibility of the Executive Committee on Terrorism (ECT), the senior interagency group. The ECT consisted of representatives from the Departments of State, Defense (DoD), Justice, Treasury, Transportation, and Energy; the Central Intelligence Agency (CIA); and the NSC. Its work was supported by a working group. However, over time the working group became too large—eventually it included over thirty agencies—and it had to be streamlined into several committees.[17]

Early in the Reagan years, Secretary of State Alexander Haig undertook a review of the apparatus and made changes. In 1982, an Interdepartmental Group on Terrorism (IG/T) replaced the ECT, and the working group was eliminated. The IG/T added two new members to the former ECT roster (the vice-president and the Drug Enforcement Administration) and was intended to provide a forum in which the departments and agencies concerned could share ideas and "make recommendations on policy and programs."[18] As before, however, the lead agency for countering international terrorism was the Department of State. The department's role was to formulate policy, draw up emergency plans, and administer various programs. It also coordinated activities with other departments and agencies, Congress, and the media. In the event of a crisis, the State Department was to take charge of the US response by organizing a task force. Through its Office of Security, it was also responsible for embassy security. Its Threat Analysis Group attempted to identify terrorist "hotspots."[19] Primary responsibility was allocated to the State Department for several reasons. First, US policy has been based on the understanding that the roots of terrorism fall within the domain of politics, especially international relations. Moreover, the US has tended to view terrorism as low-intensity warfare[20] and to consider its first line of defense as lying overseas. Therefore, solving the problem requires the assistance and cooperation of other countries, especially in Europe—hence, the role of diplomacy, and of the State Department.

That said, the State Department did not set up the Office for Combatting Terrorism (OCT) until the summer of 1976. Until then, efforts were headed by a special assistant for combatting terrorism and deputy to the secretary of state. The position had a rather low priority; it changed hands seven times in seven years and was seen as a dead-end position. It was not until Anthony C. E. Quainton was appointed in 1978 and stayed until 1981 that it achieved any continuity or power— he had the rank of ambassador and reported to the deputy secretary.[21]

The State Department's organization for countering terrorism underwent major change in the early 1980s under Secretary Haig, who gave terrorism a much higher profile. In February 1982, the OCT was reconstituted and given wider responsibility. Planning and policy (OCT) and response (Office of Security) were brought under the same head, and the new director was given an ambassadorial rank equal to the assistant secretary and placed in a direct reporting position to the undersecretary for management. In other words, the State Department integrated its activities to enhance its ability to respond to the threat.[22]

However, this structure did not stand for long. Two years later, the OCT added Emergency Planning to its title and expanded its mandate to include coordinating intelligence, administering the Anti-Terrorism Assistance (ATA) Program, and ensuring the adequacy of emergency plans at overseas missions. Then, in 1985, the Report of the Secretary of State's Advisory Panel on Overseas Security (the Inman Report) brought about another radical restructuring of the department's counter-terrorism branch. This included the establishment of a new Bureau of Diplomatic Security and the Office of Ambassador-at-large for Counter-Terrorism. Diplomatic Security became responsible for protective security for diplomatic personnel and facilities abroad. The responsibilities of the ambassador-at-large for counter-terrorism included reporting directly to the secretary of state; chairing the IG/T; managing a research program designed to anticipate new terrorist tactics and to develop new, practical ways to identify, track, and apprehend terrorists; and meeting regularly with counterparts in other countries to foster cooperation and coordinate actions.[23]

As of the fall of 1989, the State Department's counter-terrorism effort was organized into three levels. First, policy oversight and management of terrorism-related issues were coordinated by the State Department through the Policy Coordinating Committee on Terrorism, which was chaired by the coordinator for counter-terrorism. It included representatives at the assistant secretary level from eleven agencies and departments with terrorism-related responsibilities. Second, the department had a crisis management structure capable of responding to specific events by forming a task force that would remain in contact with crisis teams at the White House and the Pentagon and in the intelligence community. This structure also would be used to stay in touch with missions overseas in order to gather information, monitor the crisis, and coordinate a response. In addition it would be used to develop policy options, keep in touch with victims' families, brief Congress, and interact with the media. Finally, the department contributed to specially trained teams that assist embassies, as well as foreign governments, in responding to crises. In 1993, however, the State Department underwent a wholesale reorganization. A new Bureau of Narcotics, Terrorism, and Crime absorbed the counter-terrorism responsibilities of the Bureau of Diplomatic Security, and the coordinator for counter-terrorism was promoted to the deputy assistant secretary level in the new bureau. This change undoubtedly reflected the perception that the distinctions between ordinary organized crime and political crime had become blurred in recent years.[24]

The Department of Transportation's FAA is the agency responsible for aviation safety. The FAA first became involved in terrorism in 1970, following the PFLP hijackings, when President Richard Nixon created the Federal Sky Marshal program, which placed armed US Marshals on international flights. This proved effective and was terminated in 1974 when the threat abated. The FAA also developed a profile for terrorist hijackers that helped to identify threats. It held exercises and trained domestic flight crews in conjunction with the FBI, and it provided technical assistance and training in civil aviation security to foreign carriers, both in the US as part of the ATA Program and overseas. Over time the threat from hijackings has been almost eliminated. However, terrorists again changed tactics, and sabotage replaced hijackings as the most serious threat to aviation safety, as was shown dramatically in December 1988 with the destruction of Pan Am Flight 103. The FAA, criticized for its handling of the Pan Am incident, was urged to devote more resources to anticipating changing threats to aviation security.[25]

The Immigration and Naturalization Service (INS) of the Department of Justice—"the agency with primary responsibility for determining the admissibility of persons attempting entry into the U.S. and maintaining the integrity of [US] borders—is [the] country's first line of defense against terrorist incursions."[26] The INS works closely with other departments and agencies (e.g. State Department, CIA, FBI), as well as with its overseas counterparts through informal channels with the TREVI Group, to identify and apprehend terrorists trying to enter the US surreptitiously using false travel documents.

The Justice Department is primarily responsible for the prosecution of cases involving terrorists. As the government's chief federal law enforcement arm, the FBI is directly involved in combatting terrorism as the lead agency for domestic terrorism. Naturally, both approach international terrorism from a law enforcement perspective. The FBI generally favors the application of criminal laws, rather than diplomatic, economic, and military methods, as the government's most effective weapon against terrorism.[27] For many years, The FBI had the authority to investigate terrorist crimes against American citizens overseas. But it was not until the mid-1980s that Congress enacted legislation that gave the FBI the procedures needed to do so and to exercise extraterritorial jurisdiction by apprehending suspects and returning them to the US for trial.[28]

In this context, the FBI has carried out investigations of numerous incidents worldwide, with the support of the host governments, in cases such as the bombing of Pan Am Flight 103. It assisted foreign law enforcement agencies in apprehending and prosecuting terrorists, including Mohammed Ali Hamadei, a participant in the TWA Flight 847 hijacking, who was arrested and tried in West Germany.[29] The FBI has also worked closely with Interpol, the international network of national central bureaus that exchange intelligence in order to assist law enforcement agencies in the detection and deterrence of international crime and criminals.[30]

The FBI has also actively pursued suspects abroad on its own. In its most notable such operation to date, the FBI in 1987 arrested overseas the Lebanese Amal militiaman Fawaz Younis, who was accused of participating in the 1985 hijacking of a Jordanian airliner with at least two Americans on board. They returned him to the United States where he stood trial for conspiracy to commit air piracy, hostage-taking, and hijacking a commercial airliner. Younis was convicted in March 1989 and sentenced to thirty years in prison.[31]

Several agencies from the intelligence community play a part in countering terrorism through the collection, analysis and interpretation, and dissemination of intelligence to the appropriate national and international organizations. They include the National Security Agency (NSA) and the National Reconnaissance Office, which provide signals intelligence and overhead reconnaissance, respectively; the Defense Intelligence Agency (DIA); and the Bureau of Intelligence and Research of the State Department. The CIA, as the principal agency responsible for intelligence gathering abroad, is the backbone of US anti- and counter-terrorist intelligence efforts.[32] More will be said of this later. Likewise, the DoD organizations for conducting military counter-terrorism operations will be discussed later in this chapter.

Finally, the legislative branch also plays a role in combatting terrorism. Congress partly fulfills its role through control and oversight of the budget; it exercises its authority in this regard by approving and funding agency programs. The Senate ratifies all treaties. Since the early 1970s, Congress has become more involved in oversight of foreign affairs, including intelligence gathering and measures to combat terrorism. It exercises its influence through various committees, notably the House Committee on Foreign Affairs and the Senate Judiciary Committee. Periodically, these committees convened, sometimes jointly, to review counter-terrorism policy. Congress's particular concerns have been diplomatic security and protection of American citizens abroad. It was also responsible for the oversight of existing laws and the promulgation of new legislation. Since the early 1970s, Congress has initiated and passed several major pieces of legislation concerning terrorism, which will be discussed shortly.

The enactment of special legislation and the use of the intelligence community to respond to terrorism raised the possibility that US laws and the rights of US citizens could be compromised. Congressional committees oversee the intelligence services in an effort to prevent or minimize transgressions. In addition, the House Judiciary Committee can call on the General Accounting Office (GAO) to review the safeguards taken by organizations (such as the US National Central Bureau of the Justice Department) to protect the privacy rights of Americans as provided in the Privacy Act of 1974.[33] Some observers have suggested that Congress was poorly equipped to carry out its responsibilities. However, the Congress has proved to be a useful forum for the education of the public and the discussion of the problem, and for the formation of a bipartisan consensus on how to combat terrorism.[34]

Although such a consensus exists between Congress and the White House over efforts to combat terrorism, disagreements have arisen over specific measures. Approval of a new extradition treaty with the United Kingdom (UK) was held up by the Senate, which came under much pressure from the Irish-American lobby to block ratification in 1986. Similarly, the White House has encountered trouble obtaining resources to implement its programs at times. For instance, it was unable to obtain sufficient funding to carry out the recommendations of the Inman Report regarding the strengthening of embassies and overseas facilities. Later, it had difficulty obtaining money for the counter-terrorism research and development program.[35] Relations between the legislative and the executive branches were aggravated by the Iran-Contra scandal, which seriously damaged bipartisan cooperation.

The structure and function of the organizations involved affected the ability of the US government to develop and implement an effective counter-terrorism strategy. Consequently, close cooperation and smooth operation sometimes were absent from the US structure. First, there were difficulties arising from bureaucratic behavior, especially assignment of priorities. Some agencies did not see terrorism as being relevant to their central roles and missions. The State Department, for instance, initially saw terrorism essentially as a Middle Eastern problem and not part of its main mission—East–West relations. So it did not establish the OCT until 1976. The Carter NSC was criticized for failing to assign a high priority to terrorism, although the reorganization in 1977—creating the SCC Executive Committee and its working group—suggests otherwise. Finally, DoD's focus on strategic forces, rapid deployment, NATO coordination, sea power projection, and manpower shortages precluded an early commitment to counter-terrorism.[36]

Second, interagency friction hampered cooperation. In the early 1970s, it appears that the working group was free of interagency battling. However, friction developed later between the State Department and some of the other departments and agencies with anti-terrorist responsibilities. Among these "turf battles" was the State Department's clash with the Justice Department over chairmanship of the ECT, which hindered policy development. Similarly, the FBI and the Los Angeles Police Department engaged in a prolonged dispute over responsibility for counter-terrorism security for the 1984 Olympic Games.[37]

The third problem area was the lack of central direction. The Reagan adminstration saw the need for improvement in the structure of agencies and departments, especially after the Dozier kidnapping, when the "tangled chain of command" became very obvious.[38] However, in spite of several reorganizations (or perhaps because of them), in the mid-1980s, some suggested that the US structure still lacked focus. During the 1985 joint hearings the Senate Judiciary Committee and House Committee on Foreign Affairs concluded that the US still had no comprehensive counter-terrorism policy, except for agreement on non-negotiation with terrorists. The hearings also concluded that the major reasons for this were that the proliferation of agencies made coordination and cooperation more difficult, lines of authority were vague, responsibilities were uncertain, and accountability was impossible. Strategies were undeveloped because decision-makers responded to each new crisis in an ad hoc way, unrelated to previous experience.[39]

After the TWA Flight 847 incident, President Reagan created a panel chaired by Vice-President George Bush to review US counter-terrorist efforts. The task force report concluded that the system in place was sound, but that it needed fine tuning and a higher priority, with a more action-oriented approach, and made several recommendations for improvements to the organizational structure. According to Bush, implementation of their recommendations brought together the various parts of the government to agree to broad rules for action, settled festering problems of jurisdiction, resolved policy issues regarding the seriousness of the terrorist threat and the range of actions appropriate to dealing with it, and set issues in the context of a broader strategy.[40]

Nevertheless, the effectiveness of the structure remains open to question. It has been argued that the Iran-Contra scandal showed that the organization still lacked a formal structure with adequate support.[41] Some analysts maintain that the frequent major restructuring of the organizational chart "demonstrates and reinforces the image of confusion and inadequacy."[42] They point to the lead agency concept as a source of this confusion. For instance, while the State Department is the lead agency for international incidents outside the US, according to Oliver Revell (the FBI's deputy assistant director for investigations), it is the FBI that has

the only responsibility for the criminal investigation of terrorist incidents wherever they occur. So the State Department does not control or direct our criminal investigations, but they have the lead liaison and coordination for the non-investigative responsibilities. When an incident occurs then that lead ceases as far as the criminal investigation and it is a matter wholly within our . . . jurisdiction. And we work with and coordinate with State to facilitate the investigation. But the criminal investigation of a terrorist act is a matter that is totally within the purview of the FBI for investigations and the Justice Department for prosecution, not the State Department. . . . So the lead agency . . . is not the agency solely responsible, it is the agency that has the coordination responsibility, and within that there are a number of other functioning entities that have primary responsibilities.[43]

Since all acts of terrorism are defined by US law as crimes, this delineation of jurisdictions gives the FBI a far greater role in combatting international terrorism overseas than the lead agency concept suggests. It also underlines the point that terrorism is a very complex problem, and that no one agency possesses all of the resources needed to combat it.[44]

Evolution of Policy

The US began developing a policy for countering acts of international terrorism in late 1969 in response to the increase in airline hijackings. Over most of the period since then, American anti-terrorist policy has been based on several principles. First, the US should reject terrorism on any basis, since it is a criminal activity that no political cause could justify. The government acknowledged that some international issues require attention, but legitimate political objectives should be pursued through the appropriate means. Second, the US should demonstrate leadership by example and diplomacy in attempting to find collective solutions to problems. Third, the US should seek effective prosecution and punishment of terrorists and be willing to use all legal measures to accomplish these tasks. Fourth, the US should use every available resource to gain the safe return of Americans held hostage. However, after conceding to terrorist demands in a few early incidents, in 1970 the policy became less accommodating. Daniel Mitrione, an American advisor to the Uruguayan police, was seized by Tupamaro guerrillas in July 1970. After the Uruguayan government—with the public support of Washington—refused to comply with terrorist demands to release 150 prisoners, the Tupamaros killed Mitrione. The "no deals" approach was reinforced in September 1970 with the PFLP's multiple hijackings of airliners to Dawson's Field, Jordan; the US demanded unconditional release of the hostages, some of whom were Americans.

Following this incident, the US formally adopted a no-concessions policy, where it refused to pay ransom, release prisoners, or change policies in order to resolve terrorist incidents. Otherwise, the US reasoned, it would lead to an increase in terrorist incidents and put hundreds of American nationals at risk. For the same reasons, it opposed other foreign governments, individuals, and companies doing so. The policy also had the effect of relieving ambassadors overseas of the burden of becoming involved in hostage negotiations. The final principle was that terrorists should be tried within the country where the incident occurred or extradited to the appropriate country. As well, the US endorsed and initiated multilateral conventions against international terrorism, designed to strengthen deterrence of terrorist acts by raising the costs and risks of undertaking them.[45]

The Ford and Carter administrations' anti-terrorism policy differed little from the principles established by President Nixon. The Carter administration enhanced existing policy in two cases: First, it would prepare for anti-terrorism operations in response to specific acts of terrorism. Second, to better predict incidents and support the above measures, it would increase intelligence and counter-intelligence capabilities.[46]

The Reagan administration looked on international terrorism as a serious threat from the outset; on 27 January 1981, President Reagan promised "swift and effective retribution" for terrorist attacks.[47] Subsequently, it became a dominant foreign policy issue for the administration.[48] The reasons for this new priority were frequently expressed, at least by senior members of the executive branch, in terms common to American foreign policy statements. For instance, according to Vice-President Bush, "As a stable and prosperous country, a society Abraham Lincoln called 'the last, best hope on earth,' the United States has a duty to help freedom loving and democratic countries throughout the world, especially in our own hemisphere, combat terrorism."[49]

The bombing of the US embassy and the Marine barracks in Beirut in 1983 began a key period in the development of US policy. The Reagan policy became more proactive in April 1984 when it codified its counter-terrorism strategy with National Security Decision Directive (NSDD) No. 138. This new policy guidance statement marked an important development in the evolution of the American counter-terrorism program. Reagan's new policy was based on three solid pillars. First, the government would stand firm against terrorists and not make concessions, pay ransom, pardon convicted terrorists, or make deals. Second, state sponsorship of terrorism was a menace to all nations, and the US was prepared to take the lead in putting pressure on these states by penalizing them for their actions. Finally, the US would promote cooperation among states on practical measures to identify, track down, arrest, prosecute, and punish terrorists through the imposition of the rule of law.[50]

The policy emphasized the need to understand the aims and strategies of terrorists in order to deal with them more effectively. In the administration's view, terrorists were criminals who had targeted democracies, which they believed were vulnerable to their methods. Terrorists sought to change or interrupt policies they opposed, including the peaceful resolution of international problems, particularly through hostage-taking. One should not become sympathetic toward them; policies of refuge and asylum for those who claimed political motivations for their acts were "outdated." The government must refuse to make concessions; "behavior rewarded is behavior repeated" became a catch-phrase of the State Department.[51] In short, there was no justification for terrorism, and it should be seen as a threat to national security.

In order to foster the correct environment for combatting terrorism, therefore, the administration set about "educating" the public about the realities of terrorism, as defined by the administration. According to Deputy Secretary of State John Whitehead: "Over the years, too many of us have accepted uncritically certain very misleading views about the nature of terrorism, views which disarm us intellectually and strengthen our adversaries. For any counterterrorism policy to be effective, these conceptions must be dispelled."[52] Representatives of the administration, including the secretary of state and the ambassador at large-for-terrorism, engaged in this public relations initiative and spoke frequently to a wide audience. They attempted to explode what they considered to be the myths of terrorism, including the beliefs that all terrorists are madmen and that vigorous action only aggravates the problem.

The new policy also recognized the need for timely and accurate intelligence about terrorists, their plans, and their capabilities as "a fundamental underpinning" of the policy. Following the Long Commission Report (on the bombing of the Marine barracks in Beirut), it was recognized that identifying terrorists was difficult. Technical means, like electronic or satellite intercepts, were of limited value; frequently, agents were needed on the ground. However, penetrating organizations, especially those supported by states or based on local clans or families, was difficult. The pooling of intelligence with other governments, especially to deter incidents, was encouraged.[53]

Furthermore, the administration saw the need to strengthen security measures, especially through target-hardening at US facilities overseas. Airline safety was also a source of major concern. However, the administration also recognized that the primary legal, political, moral, and practical responsibilities for dealing with terrorism abroad rested with foreign governments. Therefore, it needed to get other nations to do more to fight terrorism. The government's more proactive counter-terrorism policy was supposed to encourage international cooperation and to permit unilateral actions if such cooperation proved ineffective.

This aspect of the policy required the US to go on the offensive to disrupt terrorist operations, destroy networks, and bring terrorists to justice through the application of the rule of law. This action program would raise the costs and reduce the rewards to terrorists. The main targets were states sponsoring terrorism. The government would expose the links between these countries and terrorists and then break them.[54]

In summary, this new policy represented a broad-front approach taken on at least three levels. First were multilateral actions, including the use of regional multilateral and international declarations, statements, agreements, and treaties. Second were intensified bilateral relationships with friendly governments. Closer contact at this level would streamline international legal procedures, particularly the strengthening of extradition treaties, in order to ensure that terrorists were brought to justice and to promote closer cooperation among law enforcement agencies. Third were unilateral measures, including implementation of economic sanctions and military actions to prevent or deter possible terrorist actions and to rescue hostages.[55]

The program designed to implement the policy consisted of at least five major components: overt and covert intelligence operations to predict, deter, and respond to incidents; diplomatic efforts to foster international cooperation; economic steps to increase pressure on regimes aiding or abetting terrorism; legal efforts to tighten US criminal statutes to increase the penalties for attacking Americans; and, finally, military operations to punish those responsible for attacks.[56]

Some questioned the wisdom of certain elements of the US policy. It has been pointed out that the no-concessions policy is based on the supposition that terrorists are like criminals, seeking some kind of reward, whereas terrorism is undertaken for a variety of reasons, some of which have nothing to do with ransom. Some have also argued that countries that had been more accommodating had not experienced markedly greater numbers of attacks. Therefore, they argued, this approach needed reformulation. Others have suggested that the Reagan administration overinflated terrorism's significance, and that the high-profile and large apparatus dedicated to countering it created the perception that the goals of the terrorists were succeeding.[57]

Until November 1991, when the Pan Am Flight 103 bombing investigation led to the indictment of two Libyan officials, many questioned President Reagan's focus on Libya. This focus encountered resistance, particularly from professional foreign service personnel at the State Department, who worried that it would undercut US policy in the Middle East and North Africa. Over time it became apparent that a wide gulf existed between the professionals and the White House, partly as a result of the ideological bent of the administration, which turned the struggle against terrorism into a moral issue as well as part of the East-West conflict (by linking the Soviet Union to the spread of international terrorism). Such criticisms also arose in part because much of the policy developed by the Reagan administration was initiated by the NSC, not the bureaucracy. It was widely held that Reagan White House advisors ignored the advice of the professionals, especially those from the State Department.[58] Consequently, some critics claimed that President Reagan's counter-terrorism policy rested on unsound assumptions.

American policy did not change significantly under the Bush administration.[59] However, the end of the Cold War and the onset of the recession, coupled with a significant decline in the number of incidents,[60] served to de-politicize the issue. The administration's firm adherence to the no-concessions policy during Iraq's mass hostage-taking in 1990 was not seriously challenged, even by media and public pressure to "do something."[61]

Legislation

During the period under study, the US enacted several pieces of special legislation to improve the effectiveness of its anti-terrorism program at both the state and the federal levels. This was, in part, an attempt to tighten up their criminal statutes to make prosecution easier. In 1974, Congress passed Public Law 93-366, which included the Antihijacking Act and the Air Transportation Security Act, giving the FAA authority over aircraft terrorism. Likewise, in 1976, it passed Public Law 94-467, the Act for the Prevention and Punishment of Crimes Against Internationally Protected Persons in order to ratify and give force in US law to the 1973 United Nations (UN) Convention. As a result of the 1984 Act to Combat International Terrorism, the Department of Justice and the FBI became more directly involved in investigating and prosecuting terrorists who commit crimes against Americans abroad. This allowed the US to issue arrest warrants and extradition requests for the hijackers of TWA Flight 847 and the *Achille Lauro*.

The Omnibus Anti-terrorism Act of 1986, also known as the "long arm of the law" statute, made terrorist acts against Americans abroad a federal crime and permitted arrest overseas and trial in US courts. Fawaz Younis was apprehended in 1987 under the terms of this act. The Anti-terrorism and Arms Export Amendments Act of 1989 prohibited the export of military equipment or munitions to any state supporting international terrorism. The same year the US ratified two treaties that extended the "prosecute or extradite" principle to attacks on civilian airports and shipping. Prompted by the *Achille Lauro* hijacking and the Rome and Vienna airport attacks, these agreements were still awaiting implementing legislation in 1993.[62]

Negotiations

Despite its policy of no concessions, the US negotiated with terrorists on several occasions. In 1979, after its Teheran embassy was taken, the US tried to negotiate release of the hostages. Ultimately, they were released through a settlement mediated by Algeria.[63] In June 1985, once the passengers had been removed from the hijacked TWA flight and were hidden in Beirut, a military rescue became impossible, and negotiation was the only option left. The US opened talks with the terrorists through Nabbi Berri (the leader of the Lebanese Shiite Amal militia), as well as Israel and Syria. The result was that the passenger hostages were released; Israel, in turn, released 735 Shiites (captured in Lebanon) in two batches, but denied publicly that there was any "deal" that linked the passenger and prisoner releases.[64]

However, the most egregious departure from the US's no negotiations policy was getting under way just as the TWA crisis came to an end. President Reagan was under considerable public pressure, particularly from the hostages' families, to "do something" that would lead to the release of the eight American hostages held in Lebanon by the Islamic Jihad. At the same time, the administration wished to develop a diplomatic "opening" to Iran in order to pre-empt possible Soviet gains in the event of instability there. The initiative, which linked the possible release of hostages to a revival of American-Iranian relations by means of arms sales, seems to have come from the Israeli government three days after the end of the TWA incident. The proposal generated considerable controversy within the administration. Nevertheless, the deal was approved, and between August 1985 and November 1986, Israel and the US sold and delivered more than 2,000 missiles to Iran. The negotiations and sales were handled covertly by members of the NSC staff through a number of "shady" Israeli and Iranian middlemen. But all of this yielded only three American hostages before the deal was exposed in a Beirut magazine in November 1986. Criticism of the arms-for-hostages trade was compounded by revelations that funds paid by Iran were diverted secretly and illegally to support the US-backed Contra rebels in Nicaragua.[65] The unraveling of the scandal did considerable damage to the Reagan presidency and to the credibility of US anti-terrorism policy among American allies, whom the US had urged not to negotiate with terrorists.

Intelligence

The United States has used its intelligence agencies and their capabilities to counter terrorism, but prior to the 1980s their role was essentially passive. That began to change early in the Reagan administration, which made revitalization of the intelligence apparatus a priority. One of the catalysts for change was the failed Iranian hostage rescue mission. The intelligence community faced serious problems supporting this operation. The CIA did not have a stay-behind capability after the embassy was lost and so had difficulty gathering information on the ground. So the NSA and the CIA passed on information gathered by other means. However, relations between the CIA and the military force were not good. Colonel Charlie Beckwith, commander of the rescue assault team, was critical of the CIA's efforts, and the military eventually inserted their own personnel into Teheran to gather intelligence.[66]

Some of the intelligence community's difficulties may have stemmed from long-term problems. According to some critics, it was focused too narrowly on gathering intelligence on Soviet military forces. Similarly, it was accused of a propensity to identify the Soviet Union as the chief culprit in international terrorism. The community was also suffering from the effects of the Carter cutbacks and other legal restrictions.[67]

In order to revitalize the capabilities of the intelligence community, the Reagan administration lifted restrictions that had hampered the collection of intelligence and ordered a review of intelligence on terrorism. Subsequently, the CIA received more funding. Steps were taken to intensify the collection, analysis, and dissemination of information at home and abroad and to pool intelligence from all sources through the creation of fusion centers. A computer network was set up, linking all analysts working on terrorism in all government agencies. The administration also promoted the creation and training of FBI and CIA para-military teams that could assist embassies overseas during crises. With NSDD No. 138 in 1984, the president directed the intelligence community to adopt a more proactive approach. The CIA was to take more aggressive measures to deny terrorists a base in the US, to carry out covert/overt actions abroad designed to bring pressure on governments supporting terrorism to terminate their aid, and to mount deception and disinformation operations, as well as operations intended to create friction and conflict within and between terrorist groups. Furthermore, in 1985, President Reagan issued an intelligence finding authorizing the CIA to hunt down and apprehend terrorists. In order to carry out this task, the CIA created a new Counter-terrorism Center consisting of analysts and covert operations specialists.[68]

The Reagan administration believed that improvements in the intelligence apparatus were effective. It asserted that intelligence cooperation with European states had helped to reduce terrorism in Western Europe by one-third since 1985 and had prevented more than 200 attacks between 1985 and 1988.[69] However, some critics maintained that the intelligence community's capabilities were still inadequate. The fact that the hostage crisis in Lebanon continued to the end of 1991, and the US still did not know where they were or exactly who was holding them, showed the limitations of US intelligence.[70] Indeed, the US faced some of its most serious intelligence-gathering challenges in Lebanon. Once the US's Beirut embassy was destroyed in 1983, the CIA's intelligence capability was impeded by the loss of senior controllers and analysts. As well, the CIA had lost some of its network when the PLO was evacuated the previous summer. As a result, it was unable to identify who was responsible for the various incidents. There was a wide difference of opinion, for instance, over Syria's role in the embassy bombing. Perhaps even more serious, once the Marines arrived, they did not receive good local intelligence about the terrorist threat. For instance, the FBI's report on the embassy bombing was not circulated to the Marines.[71] However, former Director of Central Intelligence Stansfield Turner maintains that it was unreasonable to expect the CIA to have anticipated the threat in Lebanon far enough in advance to have placed an agent in every terrorist organization:

Spies cannot be recruited overnight. A suitable candidate must be identified, his friendship and trust nurtured over weeks and months until he is willing to work for us, an opportunity found to insert him in the organizations we want to learn about, and enough time allowed him to gain the trust of that organization. In Lebanon the CIA would have had to elevate terrorism to a very high priority perhaps a year or more before the actual attack. There were many terrorist groups to infiltrate, and the one that carried out the attack may well have come into Lebanon from Iran only a few months before the attack. And terrorist groups are usually composed of fanatics who are not easily fooled by impostors. All this is not to say that the CIA should not have been trying to place agents in Lebanon or that it could not have done better. It is to say that even had it had the presence to make an all out effort, its chances of success were low.[72]

The perils of operating in the Byzantine world of Lebanese politics without reliable intelligence again became tragically apparent in March 1985. The CIA had provided counter-terrorist training to Lebanese intelligence officers in the hope that they might penetrate the Shiite terrorist cells responsible for the kidnappings of Americans in order to gain information. Instead, they attempted to blow up Sheik Fadlallah, the spiritual leader of the *Hizb'Allah*. Naturally, the CIA was blamed for the attack, which missed the sheik, but killed eighty others, once its covert training plan was exposed.[73]

Given the limitations of published sources, the foregoing can hardly be considered definitive. However, it does *suggest* a mixed record of success, a conclusion consistent with most intelligence activities.

Military and Para-military Activities

Until 1978, the DoD treated countering terrorism as a "back burner" issue, while it attended to its other concerns. It was not until January 1978 that the DoD set up a steering committee on terrorism; however, it became inactive early in the Reagan administration.[74]

After the Munich affair (1972) and the Mayaguez disaster (1975), a small group of officers and DoD officials had become alert to the need for a counter-terrorist capability. However, nothing concrete was done at this point, mainly because terrorism was not seen as a serious threat. Then the Hanafi incident in Washington in March 1977 demonstrated that the US lacked the capability to use force against terrorism. But it was not until the Mogadishu hijacking (October 1977), which demonstrated the value of a highly trained rescue assault force, that President Carter directed the DoD to establish a counter-terrorist unit. Drawn from the Army Special Forces and activated in November 1977, it became known as Delta Force. It became operational two years later.[75]

The military's counter-terrorism doctrine was set within the context of special operations, which could be either overt or clandestine. Their character had been guided by National Security Action Memorandum No. 57, formulated by the Kennedy administration after the Bay of Pigs debacle, which in theory gave the DoD priority over the CIA in large-scale covert para-military operations. However, traditionally, the military has been wary of covert operations, and during the Reagan years, Defense Secretary Caspar Weinberger continued to distance the military from CIA covert operations, believing it to be dangerous to engage in operations that had undefined political goals.[76] Moreover, until 1977, the idea of creating another "elite" force had faced opposition from the conservative, mainstream military establishment. There has never been fondness for special forces, or even an understanding of unconventional warfare, in the US military, whose traditional mission and focus have been conventional conflict. The need to form a special force sounded like an admission of failure; it would mean additional expense and would drain the best troops from regular units. Finally, intraservice rivalries among the Special Forces and the Army Rangers led to a turf fight, which was not resolved in favor of Delta Force until August 1978.[77]

Delta Force also encountered certain difficulties during its training and preparation. First, the account of its commander, Colonel Charlie Beckwith, leaves the impression that they knew very little about terrorism during this formative period. Perhaps more important, their methods were based on the Mogadishu scenario, where the unit had permission to enter a "friendly" country. In fact, in their first major operation (the attempted rescue in Iran in April 1980), Delta Force faced a hostile setting. For this and other reasons, by 1979 when Delta Force became fully operational, it had neither a viable strategy nor a strong support mechanism. Many of the arrangements were ad hoc and were complicated by bureaucratic infighting.[78] In 1980 the US mounted Operation EAGLE CLAW to rescue the American hostages being held in Teheran. Led by Delta Force, the mission involved a large multiservice team in a complex airborne/overland rescue assault and extraction operation. In the end, the mission had to be aborted because several helicopters became inoperable. During the withdrawal from the initial landing point inside Iran, US aircraft collided, resulting in the deaths of several military personnel who had to be left behind.[79]

In the wake of the disaster, the Joint Chiefs of Staff (JCS) commissioned a Special Operations Review Group to examine the failure. The review group's report found that the immediate cause of the failure was too few helicopters. Another cause was excessive operational security, the result of which was that the plan was not rigorously examined. Participants became too swept up in the determination to rescue the hostages, and caution was cast aside. However, the basic problem with the mission was the organization, which was made up of disparate elements of the armed forces. Too many details were left out of the planning of this complex operation. In short, it was too ad hoc. Some critics concluded from this that the US was physically and psychologically unprepared to fight terrorism. It was asserted that President Carter's cuts in the Pentagon's budget had left military personnel unable to do their jobs effectively, and, still bearing the scars of Vietnam, they had lost their nerve and demonstrated incompetence.[80]

One result of the review group's Report was that in late 1980 the DoD established a new counter-terrorism force, the Joint Special Operations Command (JSOC). A permanent, self-contained multiservice formation, which incorporated Delta Force along with other Special Forces units, JSOC was supposed to eliminate the ad hoc approach to counter-terrorism operations by bringing all of the deployable units and their supporting assets under a single command and by coordinating their training and other preparations. In 1984, the Joint Special Operations Agency (JSOA) was established at the Pentagon in order to coordinate planning, budgeting, doctrine, training standards, and readiness for JSOC at the highest level. It was the contact point between JSOC and the Joint Chiefs of Staff— a clear indication of JSOC's status and the high priority being given to military counter-terrorism efforts. JSOA was also JSOC's conduit for intelligence from nation-level agencies.[81]

During the early 1980s, the nature of JSOC's work changed considerably. Instead of engaging directly in operations, it began advising the security forces of other countries on rescue missions and other counter-terrorism measures. Nevertheless, JSOC units were used in operational roles. For instance, during the *Achille Lauro* hijacking, troops from Delta Force and Seal Team 6 were deployed, although the hijackers surrendered before a rescue could be mounted. However, the Seals were used in the subsequent operation to seize the fleeing hijackers; they surrounded the Egyptian aircraft carrying the terrorists at Sigonella air base in Sicily. The Seals in turn found themselves surrounded by Italian police, and a brief, but tense, standoff ensued until the police arrested the terrorists.[82]

Although the Reagan administration attempted to revitalize Special Operations Forces (SOF) capabilities by increasing their size and budgets, interservice rivalry continued to hamper the program. In addition, it appeared that the US military generally did not understand the terrorist phenomenon, and its planning of military operations overseas was poor.[83] While these criticisms may have been legitimate when they were first made, the performance of the SOF in the Gulf War suggests that perhaps most of these problems have been overcome.

At times, conventional US military forces also became involved in counter-terrorist operations. In the wake of the bombing of the Marine headquarters in Beirut, the US used fighters and the 16-inch guns of the battleship *New Jersey* to hit targets in the Shouf Mountains. Navy fighters were also used to apprehend the hijackers of the *Achille Lauro* and, in 1986, to carry out operations designed to strike at terrorist targets in Libya.

The April 1986 air raid on Libya, known as Operation EL DORADO CANYON, offers insights into the difficulties the armed forces faced in operations against terrorists. The *La Belle* disco bombing in Berlin provoked an intense debate in Washington over how the US should strike back; those who favored the use of force, including Secretary of State George Shultz, were opposed by those who were more reluctant to take military action, including Vice-President Bush, Defense Secretary Weinberger, the CIA, and the JCS. The advocates of proactive military measures prevailed, and the result was the raid on Libya in mid-April.[84]

The operational effectiveness of these military measures is the subject of much debate. Analysts have pointed to the serious failure of some operations, including the 1980 hostage rescue attempt. Other operations, such as the interception of the *Achille Lauro* hijackers, were more successfully militarily, while the Libyan bombing raid had mixed results. In the latter case, the US was essentially using military force to send a political message. Consequently, the targets attacked during the Libyan raid were not all vulnerable to the capabilities of the aircraft. In the aftermath it was determined that the air raid had done relatively little damage and Qaddafi had not been undermined.[85] This case demonstrates the difficulty of bringing conventional military force to bear on terrorism. Frequently, the demands are outside the capacity of the military, and when it is employed, it can be a blunt instrument when what was needed was surgical precision.

If the operational effectiveness of military forces has been variable, the long-term political effects of military actions remain even more problematic. The Reagan administration claimed that the raid on Libya led to a marked, if temporary, reduction in Libyan state-sponsored terrorism.[86] Equally important, it spurred the European governments to realize that international terrorism posed a serious threat of escalation of conflict and galvanized them into intensifying their own anti-terrorist efforts. Subsequently, several governments followed the US lead by imposing political, economic, and security measures against Libya, including sanctions, the expulsion of Libyan diplomats and the increased coordination of international police operations. Robert B. Oakley, Ambassador-at-large for Counter-terrorism claimed that the effects of the raid led to the 1986 Tokyo summit declaration, which he described as "an unprecedented collective effort to combat terrorism."[87] It was in this sense that Secretary Shultz could legitimately declare that "the American bombing raid on Libya opened a new chapter in the international fight against terrorism,"[88] while Oakley's successor, Paul Bremer described it as the watershed event in the world's struggle against terrorism.[89]

American military actions have drawn criticism, however. The interception of the Egyptian airliner by Navy fighters during the *Achille Lauro* incident has been described as "'hijacking' the hijackers."[90] It also caused the temporary alienation of Egypt from the US, and the fall of the pro-US government in Italy. Opposition to the attack on Libya was even more pointed. The European Parliament condemned it as a "flagrant violation of international law" and approved an emergency resolution that stated the attack was a danger to international security and peace.[91]

The US policy of unilateral military action raised serious questions about the legitimacy and legality of reprisals. Some argue that the use of military force discredits US policy, as it is seen to be engaging in unacceptable behavior, which will only strengthen the enemy and provoke even more terror by contributing to a cycle of escalation. In Marc Celmer's words, "retaliatory strikes are a demonstration of a nation's frustration with a problem it cannot handle."[92] As the Egyptian interception and the Libyan raid showed, military actions can also aggravate relations with friendly states. In short, according to some, a policy of reprisal had little legitimacy, was of dubious legality, raised grave risks, and its costs outweighed any short-term success that may have been gained.[93]

The Reagan administration rejected these arguments completely. With the escalation of tensions with Libya, the US came to see the crisis as a matter of self-defense rather than one of retaliation, which could violate international law. In this line of argument, the US relied on article 51 of the UN Charter, which ensures a country's inherent right to self-defense. In 1986, Deputy Secretary of State Whitehead stated:

the UN Charter is not a suicide pact. Article 51 explicitly allows the right of self-defense. It is absurd to argue that international law prohibits us from acting in our own self-defense. On the contrary, there is ample legal authority for the view that a state which supports terrorist or subversive attacks against another state or which supports terrorist planning within its own territory is responsible for such attacks. Such conduct can amount to an ongoing armed aggression against the other state in international law.[94]

This argument was important because the US had to make sure that its actions looked legitimate in the eyes of the rest of the world, especially those of the European allies. But the effectiveness and legitimacy of reprisals remain open to debate.

Target-Hardening

Since the mid-1970s, the FAA has worked with the International Civil Aviation Organization (ICAO) to improve minimum security standards at domestic and foreign airports. American representatives sat on committees and panels that reviewed those standards and made recommendations for improvements, including amendments to earlier agreements. For instance, in 1988–1989, the US signed and ratified a protocol that supplements and extends the legal "prosecute or extradite" framework of the 1971 Montreal Convention. Prompted by several acts of terrorism at international airports, including the attacks at the Rome and Vienna airports, it addresses acts of violence committed at airports serving international civil aviation, even where such acts do not endanger the safety of aircraft in flight.[95]

The bombing of the Pan Am flight had a major impact on efforts to improve aviation security, and the ICAO has been the forum for new measures. In early 1989, the US and Britain called for new ways to improve security procedures in order to counter the shift to aircraft sabotage. A special meeting of the ICAO Council in February called for the drafting of an international convention requiring all nations to include taggants in all newly manufactured plastic explosives in order to make detection easier. This convention was completed in 1991 and signed by more than fifty countries. In June 1989, the ICAO also adopted a no-takeoff policy for hijacked aircraft. Originally proposed by the US and the UK, this policy commits ICAO members to prevent the takeoff of hijacked aircraft unless the lives of the passengers are threatened.[96]

In 1985, Congress passed the International Security and Development Cooperation Act, which included the Foreign Airport Security Act. This established an airport assessment program, which is implemented by the State Department and the FAA. Under these provisions, the FAA inspects and assesses security measures at foreign airports served by US carriers or from which other carriers fly directly to US destinations. If problems identified by the FAA go uncorrected, it will issue a travel advisory through the State Department,[97] as was done in 1985 against the Athens airport. The threat of lost business compelled some foreign airports to upgrade their safety standards.

Beginning in the 1970s, the State Department physically strengthened its embassies periodically and heightened the security awareness of personnel. For instance, after the embassy bombing in Beirut, the US took measures to protect diplomatic premises from large bombs. The only way to keep the sites safe was to keep such bombs as far away as possible through the use of roadblocks. However, in 1985, the Inman Report was critical of the department's approach to security, stating that it suffered from chronic understaffing in the Security Office, from insufficient funds, and from an inadequate command structure. As a result, the State Department established a Diplomatic Security Bureau and initiated a program of construction, including more than sixty new embassies and consulates, incorporating special features such as reinforced window structures that would rectify such problems as buildings fronting on busy streets and extensive glass facades. The program also provided for more security officers, secure communications equipment, residential security improvements, and armored vehicles. Although Congress approved only about half of the required funds, and the GAO criticized the program as inefficient, Secretary Shultz believed that these efforts paid off in terms of reduced vulnerability.[98]

In the late 1980s, the State Department became responsible for coordinating and funding an interagency counter-terrorism research and development program to deal with the new explosives technology that was having an impact on the struggle between terrorists and governments. Not easily detected, these explosives made certain targets, especially aircraft, more vulnerable to sabotage. Effective countermeasures depend on the development and application of even newer technology. Recent developments, like the thermal neutron analyzer, have increased the effectiveness of airport security, although the threat has not yet been eliminated. The government also saw the need to anticipate the next stage of escalation in order to prevent and deter terrorists. Under this program, priority has been given to the development of high-technology "sniffers" (capable of detecting nitrogen vapors in explosives) that can be installed at high-threat diplomatic posts and at airports, as well as to the development of devices capable of detecting chemical and/or biological agents in closed containers.[99]

International Cooperation

It is an axiom of US policy that the problem of international terrorism will be solved through long-term, cooperative, international action that will increase the possibility of preventing terrorism or that will competently handle and resolve incidents in a way that denies terrorists the benefits of their actions. At different times, the US has attempted to use international diplomacy and initiatives to combat terrorism. These measures range from international claims to diplomatic protests and quiet diplomacy.[100]

The US has tried to build a deterrent against terrorism by developing international legal conventions. It actively supported the drafting of the 1973 UN Convention on the protection of diplomatic personnel and other official persons and the punishment of attacks against them. Other efforts were less successful. In September 1972, in response to the Munich massacre, the US tabled at the UN a draft convention on the prevention and punishment of terrorism and a draft resolution that, among other things, called for a conference to consider the adoption of the proposed convention. However, the international community was divided over the definition and causes of terrorism and how it should be dealt with, and the convention met with opposition from a coalition of Third World and Communist states, some of whom feared that it could interfere with national liberation movements. It was passed over in favor of Resolution 3034, which the US did not support because it did not address measures that could be taken to prevent terrorism.[101]

Following that setback, the US continued the multilateral approach by trying to persuade the international community to deal with specific acts of terrorism, such as hijackings, rather than pressing for an all-encompassing convention. As a major commercial aviation country, the US gave priority to air terrorism, being signatory to three anti-hijacking accords. Some analysts concluded that these conventions were not a very effective constraint on terrorism, since many countries are not a party to them and they lacked "teeth." To address these concerns, the US has tried to strengthen these accords with supplementary agreements to "prosecute or extradite" hijackers, to extend the no-takeoff policy, and to apply sanctions to any country that provides safe haven to hijackers.[102]

After the *Achille Lauro* incident, the US developed greater concern for security standards for ships and ports. In March 1988, acting on a 1986 US resolution, the US and twenty-two other countries signed the Rome Convention and protocol, negotiated under the auspices of the International Maritime Organization, which filled a gap in international law by ensuring that states will have jurisdiction to prosecute or extradite individuals who commit acts of terrorism on or against vessels and fixed platforms on the high seas. The US saw this agreement as a major step forward in reducing the vulnerability of travelers to some forms of terrorism.[103]

Since the late 1970s, the US has also adopted a regional approach as an alternative to the multilateral approach, through regional declarations based on Western Europe and the other industrialized democracies.[104] The other major forum is the Summit Seven. Its first policy statement was the Declaration on Hijacking made at the Bonn Economic Summit in 1978, which the US saw as a major step forward in international cooperation. Between 1979 and 1987, the group adopted seven more declarations or statements on terrorism. These expressed consensus on major principles regarding terrorism, but because they lacked specific provisions and enforcement mechanisms to ensure compliance, it is difficult to measure their effectiveness. The declaration of the 1987 Venice summit expanded the scope of the Bonn agreement on hijacking to declare that the summit nations would take joint action to suspend air services if any state does not honor its international obligation to prosecute or extradite persons who commit any act of terrorism against civil aviation.

But it was the May 1986 Tokyo declaration, formulated shortly after the US bombing of Libya, that was the most sought-after and comprehensive declaration to date. The Reagan administration was seeking and achieved a unified hard line against states aiding terrorists, particularly Libya. Unlike the earlier documents, the Tokyo declaration outlined specific anti-terrorist measures, including "limits on the size of diplomatic delegations of governments [identified as supporters of] terrorism, more stringent extradition arrangements, and refusal to permit entry of any person expelled from another country for terrorist activities."[105]

The leading summit partners also joined forces to apply pressure to Syria, after it became evident that the Syrian government had been involved in the attempted bombing of an Israeli airliner at Heathrow Airport in April 1986. In October, the US and Britain, and several other countries, withdrew their ambassadors from Damascus in order to express disapproval and to pressure Syria by isolating it diplomatically. The campaign was relaxed in June 1987 after Syria expelled the Abu Nidal group in order to improve the chances of advancing Middle Eastern peace plans. However, Syria remains on the American list of supporters of terrorism, even though Syria and the US were de facto "allies" during the 1991 Gulf War and Syria continues to contribute positively to the Middle East peace process.[106]

The Reagan administration tried to improve bilateral relations through increased contact with friendly governments. These meetings led to better exchanges of intelligence, more frequent high-level communications, cooperative efforts in counter-terrorism technology, and improved judicial and military cooperation, such as American participation in the TREVI Group. The US also changed its extradition treaties with a number of countries to prevent terrorists from escaping justice by taking advantage of legal protection intended for refugees seeking political asylum. The supplementary extradition treaty with Britain, for instance, was designed to prevent Irish terrorists accused of crimes in the UK from finding refuge in the US, something they had been able to do by calling their actions political acts. President Reagan supported his friend and ally British Prime Minister Thatcher in this effort, since allowing claims of political motivation and exception would undermine efforts to pressure other countries to extradite terrorists to the US.[107]

Central to these international agreements was the subject of "extradition or prosecution" and acceptance of this duty by other nations. In the absence of universality, however, the US tried to negotiate bilateral agreements. Yet this approach, too, has limitations. Some nations extended political asylum to terrorists and refused extradition if the offenses were seen as political in nature. Greece, for example, refused to extradite a member of the 19 May group who was arrested in 1988 for the bombing of a Pan Am airliner over the Pacific in October 1982. That said, the US and its allies had some success in this regard. Between 1986 and 1988, over forty significant terrorists were arrested and convicted. The US saw these not just as convictions, but also as a positive sign of increased international cooperation, since the actions were sometimes undertaken by countries whose interests had not been the primary targets of the terrorists.[108]

Nevertheless, international law also has its limitations. It has proven impossible to extend it to some perpetrators, such as national leaders like Muammar Qaddafi of Libya. Nor is international cooperation always effective. Some countries resented pressure to act from the US. Others, such as Italy and France, with their own "special relationships" in the Middle East, preferred to act leniently or arrive at accommodations with the terrorists, rather than adopting effective measures to counter them.

Therefore, especially during the Reagan years, the US, has also acted unilaterally by using more aggressive "self-help" measures, such as the use of the armed forces discussed earlier. In general, the Reagan administration's diplomatic style displayed a "marked propensity for unilateralism."[109] This approach arose in part from the belief that the European allies acted in bad faith by "cutting deals" with terrorists or their sponsors and in part from a belief that the US needed to show stronger leadership on the world stage, especially in efforts to counter international terrorism. The unilateral measures included economic sanctions and export controls. For example, under the Export Administration Act of 1979, the US placed trading restrictions on countries determined by the secretary of state to have supported acts of international terrorism. To date, seven countries—North Korea, South Yemen, Syria, Libya, Iran, Cuba, and Iraq (removed in 1982 and reinstated in 1990)—have been so listed. These controls were strengthened further by the Anti-terrorism and Arms Export Amendments Act of 1989.[110]

Libya and its leader, Muammar Qaddafi, have been a longstanding problem for the US. During the Carter administration, the policy was either to ignore him or to try to strengthen his neighbors against his subversion. In 1981, Reagan took a tougher unilateral line, especially after the clash between American and Libyan aircraft over the Gulf of Sidra, the assassination of Egyptian President Anwar Sadat, and rumors of Libyan hit teams operating in the US. In response to the shooting of a Libyan dissident in Colorado in May 1981, the US closed the Libyan diplomatic mission in Washington and expelled its diplomats. In December 1981, the administration also imposed a trade embargo and a boycott on Libyan oil imports, as well as invalidating US passports for travel to Libya (in order to prevent American oil workers from becoming hostages there). After the attacks on the Rome and Vienna airports in December 1985 (the perpetrators of which carried passports stolen by the Libyan government), Libya became the prime target of the US counter-terrorism program.

In January 1986, using the International Emergency Economic Powers Act, the government halted all US business activity with Libya, seized Libyan assets in the country, ordered the remaining Americans out of Libya, and called on its allies to join in a campaign of collective pressure on Libya to deter Qaddafi from supporting terrorism. To be completely effective, the US needed the cooperation of its European allies. However, it received little support until April 1986 when the Libyan bombing of the *La Belle* disco in West Berlin led to the US raid and prompted joint European/American measures against Libya. In 1992, in response to Libya's refusal to hand over for trial the two intelligence officers accused of bombing Pan Am Flight 103, the UN Security Council imposed a wide range of economic sanctions on Libya[111]—a collective response that obviates the requirement for any further unilateral American action for the time being.

The US also acted unilaterally by arresting Fawaz Younis in 1987 under the extraterritorial jurisdiction provided by the 1986 "long-arm" legislation. This case was the focus of much criticism. Some analysts worried that overseas arrests could violate international law. Others asserted that Younis was "a small fry" among terrorists whose conviction would not deter other terrorists, while some said that the facts of the case were too murky to risk a negative ruling against this legislation. Still others questioned the cost—in excess of $1 million—of capturing and trying one individual. However, Oliver Revell, who directed the operation, maintains that it sent a clear message to terrorists that they were not immune to arrest. Younis was convicted of air piracy in March 1989.[112]

The State Department has developed several other programs for countering terrorism. The department believes that the ATA Program, which Congress approved in November 1983 has been among the more effective. It is designed to help relatively inexperienced friendly governments counter terrorism by training their police and security personnel (at US facilities) in anti-terrorism policy, crisis management, hostage and barricade negotiations, airport security, and bomb disposal methods. According to the State Department, this program contributes to the security of US citizens and facilities overseas, particularly through the strengthening of the capabilities of police forces in the host nations; builds more effective relationships between US policy-makers and regional security officers and their foreign counterparts; and fosters a respect for the rule of law and human rights among the trainees. By the end of 1992, the US had trained some 14,000 persons from seventy-five countries under the auspices of the ATA Program.[113]

The State Department also administers the Rewards Program, authorized by the 1984 Act to Combat International Terrorism, that was designed to make terrorists more vulnerable to discovery. Under this program, the department offers rewards for information leading to the prosecution of terrorists for specific acts. In late 1989, it was expanded to include payment of up to $2 million for information leading to the prevention, frustration, or favorable resolution of a terrorist attack against US citizens or property overseas. The program has been widely publicized abroad in a number of languages.[114]

CONCLUSIONS

American efforts to combat terrorism may yet have a lasting impact in two spheres under study: the democratic nature of the US itself and the problem of international terrorism. First, if a prime objective of terrorists is to provoke the government into adopting costly and time-consuming security measures that restrict freedoms and disrupt normal life on the domestic front, then they have had some success. Security searches are the norm at US airports; moreover, Americans no longer travel as freely overseas as they once did.[115] During the 1991 Gulf War, Iraqi threats to use terrorism against coalition states prompted increased security at sites in Washington and elsewhere in the US and caused the US to withdraw some personnel from diplomatic missions overseas. Several American airlines suspended flights to the Middle East.[116]

Americans have also been affected by terrorism in a broader, more collective way. According to one source, after the 1979–1980 Iranian crisis and the aborted rescue mission, "the nation's humiliation was total."[117] The prospects for the hostages worsened, and President Carter's political position was seriously weakened. For fourteen months, US foreign policy was paralyzed and it cost Carter the presidency. The perception that Americans were helpless against terrorists helped to get tough-talking Ronald Reagan elected president, but even he could not easily reverse the sense of malaise. By January 1984, the US presence in Lebanon had lost public support, partly as a result of casualties inflicted by terrorists.[118]

If terrorism has affected American political culture, what impact has it had on American democratic values? In a 1986 address to the Brookings Institution, Deputy Secretary of State John Whitehead pointed out that terrorism is largely directed against democracies, since they oppose those who seek to impose their will and values on others by force. Terrorism, he said, not only challenges America's fundamental strategic interests, but also threatens the country's most basic values, including the rule of law and the peaceful resolution of disputes. Whitehead went on to say that the US has not only the right, but also the obligation to defend its citizens against terrorism and could not rule out the use of armed force:[119] "Our morality must be a source of strength not paralysis. Otherwise, we will be surrendering the world's future to those who are most brutal, most unscrupulous, and most hostile to everything we believe in."[120] Whitehead's speech, and similar ones by other senior officials, represented a major public relations effort by the Reagan administration to politicize the terrorism issue. The strategy was to make clear the risks posed by terrorism and to garner public support for the war on terrorism by couching it in terms of "motherhood" values and issues the American people would understand.

However, such rhetoric notwithstanding, it is apparent that at no time did terrorism jeopardize the stability of the nation. Moreover, despite the myriad actions taken by the government to combat terrorism, there were few instances where these measures impinged on the rights and values of the nation, or groups within it. One controversial case was the FBI's investigation of CISPES (Committee in Solidarity with the People of El Salvador), which was suspected—but cleared— of supporting the Salvadoran guerrillas, whom the Reagan administration had labeled as "terrorists."[121] During the Gulf War, the fear of Iraqi-sponsored terrorism prompted a countrywide FBI search for Iraqi visitors whose visas had expired, leading to charges of harassment of Arab Americans. The mayor of Detroit, succumbing to media-fed hysteria, declared an anti-terrorist state of emergency and requested National Guard troops to protect vital services.[122]

If terrorism has had a minimal impact on the US, then what effect has US policy had on terrorism? The foregoing suggests that the US has had a mixed record of success. Critics, like Celmer, assert that the Reagan administration's policies and actions had no positive impact on the deterrence, prevention, or suppression of international terrorism. They did not create a greater degree of safety for Americans traveling and living abroad. As well, incidents such as the attack on Libya, the hostage crisis in Lebanon, and the Iran-Contra affair demonstrated the continued unpreparedness of the crisis management program and the inadequacy of contingency planning, and they have soured relations abroad.[123]

How accurate is this assessment? Recent statistics indicate a significant decrease in incidents. Aircraft hijackings are at their lowest levels ever, largely as a result of more effective airline and airport security. However, a single major incident, like the destruction of the Pan Am flight, can quickly alter perceptions of the threat. The rule of law is being extended to terrorists by many nations, and terrorists are going to jail in greater numbers, due in large part to improved police procedures and a redefinition of terrorism as a crime. Some of these trends have their roots in policies initiated by the United States.

Since 1987, state-sponsored terrorism has declined or become better concealed. Some state sponsors of terrorism have shown some changed behavior. Syrian involvement was not detected in any major activity between 1986 and 1992. However, both Syria and the Syrian-occupied Bekka Valley in Lebanon continued to be used as sanctuaries by a number of terrorist groups, including the PFLP–GC. Libya ostensibly became more cautious and circumspect, but, in 1991, it was charged with direct complicity in the Pan Am Flight 103 bombing and continued to provide sanctuary to Abu Nidal into the 1990s, in spite of Libyan claims to the contrary. Iran still shows a willingness to use terrorism selectively as a legitimate tool to achieve foreign policy goals, especially through radical Shiite groups in Lebanon. Therefore, although strides have been made, state sponsorship of terrorism has not been eradicated, which is perhaps the best that can be expected.[124]

Equally, there is little doubt that other nations, especially in Europe, began to take more effective measures to counter terrorism after the unilateral American action in 1986. As the result of what Paul Bremer has described as a "sea change" in international attitudes toward terrorism, governments became tougher in their outlook, and more of the global debate focused on the criminal effects of terrorism, not its causes. The US claimed a large measure of the credit for this initiative, pointing to the raid on Libya as the prime catalyst. It also claimed to have made "remarkable" progress in thwarting potential attacks.[125]

However, some of this success has been qualified. To some extent, the decline in aircraft hijackings has been replaced by sabotage. The US experienced little success on the issue of Western hostages in Lebanon until after the end of the 1991 Gulf War. Their release came about not because the US applied effective counter-terrorism policies, but rather because in the changed atmosphere of the post-war Middle East, the hostages had outlived their usefulness.

Moreover, American success entailed certain costs. There is little doubt that American relations with European nations were more tense in 1986 and early 1987, largely as a result of the Libyan raid. The Iran-Contra scandal certainly contributed to the troubles by shaking European confidence in the Reagan administration. Revelations that a small group of individuals was determining foreign policy issues, some of which were of deep concern to American allies, without reference to the president, the State Department, or the Congress demonstrated a serious flaw in the decision-making process and undermined the administration's credibility as a reliable partner. The effects were made worse by the appearance that the US had violated its no-concessions policy, which it had so adamantly advocated. This outraged some European governments and called into question the dependability of the US in dealing with the Middle East question. It confirmed the belief of some governments, particularly France, that they were correct in making their own hostage deals.[126]

At first, the administration tried to downplay the effects of the scandal, but by late 1988, it was admitting that it had dealt a blow to US prestige. The Bush administration, however, believed that by early 1989 the US had restored strong bipartisan support for the policy of no concessions, especially among the American people.[127] And while some Europeans clearly retained lingering doubts about the Iran-Contra affair, the success of American efforts in forging the multinational coalition during the Persian Gulf crisis and War—and in sustaining the momentum for a comprehensive peace process—suggests that the Bush administration's assessment was correct. If Iran-Contra has not been forgotten, with the Clinton presidency under way, at least it is no longer a foreign policy burden.

There are a number of reasons for this mixed success. First, the American response was massive, as it attempted to bring the full resources of government to bear. Yet, at times, the apparatus was too cumbersome, and too many details were left out. The crisis management organization lacked interagency cooperation, which hampered both the planning and the execution of counter-terrorism measures.

Second, in the past there *was* a tendency to look for quick solutions. Pressure to "do something" about the hostages in Lebanon helped to lead the Reagan administration into the Iran-Contra affair. This prompted some observers to conclude that the US has neither the stomach nor the attention span for waging war on terrorism.[128] By the end of the 1980s, however, statements by government officials suggested that they had learned the need for patience. In 1986, Ambassador Oakley noted that "fighting terrorism is a long-term effort which will draw on the best within us," and three years later his successor stated that "There are no simple knock-out punches," and that "terrorists continue to try to find new 'weak links' in the security chain which they can exploit. There are no quick fixes in this business."[129]

Finally, difficulties stemmed from the way Americans perceive terrorism. Like Israel, they have tended to see it as a form of warfare that had to be met with military force, a perception that has produced some negative consequences. Similarly, the tendency of the Reagan administration to confuse the war on terrorism with the war on communism clouded the issue. Perceptions about terrorism planted fears in the Reagan administration that led the US to take steps not in its own best interest. This raises the question of the appropriateness of the Reagan administration's response to international terrorism. Was it measured and in the best interests of the US, or was it an overreaction that contributed to international disruption and gave the terrorists what they wanted?

One must, in the end, question how significant terrorism was as a foreign policy issue for the Reagan administration. By the end of the second term, it had become clear that the most pressing issues had been relations with the Soviets, the struggle against communism, arms control, and the strategic defense initiative. During the Reagan years, terrorism was, to a certain extent, peripheral; occasionally, it deflected the government from its main tasks when serious incidents occurred.[130] The World Trade Center bombing notwithstanding, today international terrorism appears even less central to American foreign policy. The 1993 reorganization of State Department responsibilities for terrorism merely serves to confirm that view.

NOTES

1. *New York Times*, 27 February 1993. Five died in the initial blast, and one died later of injuries sustained.

2. The first suspect was arrested after trying to claim the rental deposit on the van believed to contain the bomb. *New York Times*, 5 March 1993.

3. *Globe and Mail* (Toronto), 6 March 1993.

4. Statement of Ambassador Robert B. Oakley, 16 June 1986, in *Department of State Bulletin* (August 1986), pp. 1–2.

5. Dennis Pluchinsky, "Political Terrorism in Western Europe: Some Themes and Variations," in Yonah Alexander and Kenneth A. Myers, eds., *Terrorism in Europe* (New York: St. Martin's Press, 1982), pp. 43–46, 51.

6. US Central Intelligence Agency (CIA), National Foreign Assessment Center, *Patterns of International Terrorism: 1980* (Washington, D.C.: US Central Intelligence Agency, June 1981), p. 5.

7. Edward A. Lynch, "International Terrorism: The Search for a Policy," *Terrorism: An International Journal* 9, no. 1 (1987), pp. 11–13.

8. Secret documents of the Soviet Communist Party Central Committee and the KGB, published in *Moscow News*, no. 25 (17 June 1992), reveal a covert Soviet transfer of weapons and munitions to the PFLP in 1975.

9. See James Adams, *The Financing of Terror* (London: New English Library, 1986); CIA, *Patterns of International Terrorism: 1980*, p. iii; Diane Tueller Pritchett, "The Syrian Strategy on Terrorism, 1971–1977," *Conflict Quarterly* 8, no. 3 (Summer 1988), pp. 27–48.

10. *Patterns of Global Terrorism: 1989* (Washington, D.C.: US Department of State, April 1990), p. 43.

11. *Washington Post*, 19 January 1992.

12. *Patterns of Global Terrorism: 1989*, pp. 43, 46. For a critique of US policy toward Cuba and Nicaragua, see Piero Gleijeses, "The Reagan Doctrine and Central America," *Current History* 85, no. 515 (December 1986), pp. 401 404, 435 37.

13. *Patterns of Global Terrorism: 1992*, pp. 1, 9–12, 58. On the narcotics/insurgency relationship in Peru, see Gabriela Tarazona-Sevillano, *Sendero Luminoso and the Threat of Narcoterrorism* (New York: Praeger/Center for Strategic and International Studies, 1990), pp. 29–54.

14. Marc A. Celmer, *Terrorism, U.S. Strategy, and Reagan Policies* (Westport, Conn.: Greenwood Press, 1987), pp. 59–60; William Regis Farrell, *The U.S. Government Response to Terrorism: In Search of an Effective Strategy* (Boulder, Colo.: Westview Press, 1982), p. 124. See also Carnes Lord, *The Presidency and the Management of National Security* (New York: Free Press, 1988), pp. 3–8, 15–17, 20–33, and chaps. 2, 3.

15. Celmer, *Terrorism*, pp. 17–19; Farrell, *The U.S. Government Response*, pp. 32–33. Among the bodies initially represented were the NSC, the State Department, the Department of Defense (DoD), the CIA, and the Federal Bureau of Investigation (FBI).

16. Celmer, *Terrorism*, pp. 19–20; James B. Motley, *U.S. Strategy to Counter Domestic Political Terrorism* (Washington, D.C.: National Defense University Press, 1983), pp. 34–38.

17. G. Davidson Smith, *Combating Terrorism* (London: Routledge, 1990), pp. 115–116; Motley, *U.S. Strategy*, pp. 35, 37, 38.

18. Celmer, *Terrorism*, p. 23.

19. Ibid., pp. 29–33.

20. Ibid., p. 8.

21. Farrell, *The U.S. Government Response*, p. 98; Davidson Smith, *Combating Terrorism*, pp. 114–15.

22. Celmer, *Terrorism*, p. 31; Davidson Smith, *Combating Terrorism*, pp. 117–18.

23. *Report of the Secretary of State's Advisory Panel on Overseas Security* (US Department of State, June 1985); see also Celmer, *Terrorism*, p. 37; Davidson Smith, *Combating Terrorism*, pp. 119–20.

24. Ambassador Morris D. Busby, "Cooperation in Countering Terrorism," *Department of State Bulletin* (December 1989), p. 48; US Department of State, "Department of State Reorganization," *Dispatch* 4, no. 6 (8 February 1993), p. 70.

25. Brian Michael Jenkins, "The Terrorist Threat to Commercial Aviation," *TVI Report* 9, no. 3 (1990), pp. 1–6; L. Paul Bremer, "Terrorism: Its Evolving Nature," *Current Policy*, no. 1151 (9 February 1989), pp. 3–5; *Report of the President's Commission on Aviation Security and Terrorism* (Washington, D.C.: US Government Printing Office, 15 May 1990), pp. 3–67.

26. Alan C. Nelson, "Preventing the Entry of International Terrorists," *Police Chief* 56, no. 3 (March 1989), pp. 50–52.

27. Oliver B. Revell, "International Terrorism in the United States," *Police Chief* 56, no. 3 (March 1989), p. 19.

28. Extraterritorial jurisdiction over specific crimes was extended by the Comprehensive Crime Control Act of 1984 and the Omnibus Diplomatic Security and Antiterrorism Act of 1986. See, D. F. Martell, "FBI's Expanding Role in International Terrorism Investigations," *FBI Law Enforcement Bulletin* 56, no. 11 (October 1987), pp. 28–32. In June 1989, the Justice Department authorized the FBI to arrest in foreign countries (without the consent of the country concerned) persons charged under US laws. *Manchester Guardian Weekly*, 22 October 1989.

29. In November 1991, following a lengthy investigation, the US and Britain jointly indicted two Libyan intelligence officers for the bombing of Pan Am Flight 103. "Fact Sheet: Additional Information on the Bombing of Pan Am Flight 103," *Dispatch* 2, no. 46 (18 November 1991), pp. 854–58; on the Hamadei case, see Chapter 3 of this volume.

30. *Counterterrorism: Role of Interpol and the U.S. National Central Bureau* (Washington, D.C.: US General Accounting Office, June 1987), p. 3.

31. *Washington Post*, 18 September 1987, p. 1; *Los Angeles Times*, 15 March 1989, p. 1.

32. On the role of intelligence in combating terrorism, see David A. Charters, "Counterterrorism Intelligence: Sources, Methods, Process and Problems," in David A. Charters, ed., *Democratic Responses to International Terrorism*, (Dobbs Ferry, N.Y.: Transnational Publishers, 1991), pp. 227–66. On the CIA's role, see Executive Order No. 11905, 18 February 1976, item no. 640, "The U.S. Intelligence Community," National Security Archive Microfiche Collection (copy in Centre for Conflict Studies, University of New Brunswick).

33. *Counterterrorism*, pp. 3–4.

34. Lynch, *International Terrorism*, p. 3; Lord, *The Presidency*, pp. 7–8, 146.

35. Davidson Smith, *Combating Terrorism*, p. 110; Testimony of Secretary of State Before the Senate Budget Committee in *Department of State Bulletin* (March 1987), p. 13; Morris Busby, "Counter-terrorism in the 1990s," *Current Policy* no. 1243 (3 January 1990), p. 3; US Congress, Office of Technology Assessment, *Technology Against Terrorism: The Federal Effort* (Washington, D.C.: US Government Printing Office, July 1991), pp. 4–7.

36. Farrell, *The U.S. Government Response*, pp. 114, 121; Davidson Smith, *Combating Terrorism*, p. 54.

37. Farrell, *The U.S. Government Response*, pp. 112, 123–24; Davidson Smith, *Combating Terrorism*, pp. 54, 73, 111, 146, 182.

38. Military commands disputed jurisdiction; the DoD was at odds with the State Department, while the CIA was not fully involved. David C. Martin and John Walcott, *Best Laid Plans: The Inside Story of America's War Against Terrorism* (New York: Harper and Row, 1988), p. 63.

39. Celmer, *Terrorism*, p. 24; See Lynch, *International Terrorism*, pp. 2–3, for a more thorough discussion of the hearings and their findings.

40. *Public Report of the Vice-President's Task Force on Combatting Terrorism* (Washington, D.C.: US Government Printing Office, February 1986); Statement by Vice-President George Bush, 26 January 1987, in *Department of State Bulletin* (April 1987), p. 4.

41. Lord, *The Presidency*, pp. 3, 81–82; Davidson Smith, *Combating Terrorism*, pp. 119–20.

42. Celmer, *Terrorism*, p. 37.

43. Author's interview with Oliver Revell, 6 February 1990.

44. Celmer, *Terrorism*, p. 48.

45. Principles cited in testimony before Senate Judiciary Committee, 1975, by the State Department coordinator for combatting terrorism, reprinted in Farrell, *The U.S. Government Response*, pp. 33–34.

46. Farrell, *The U.S. Government Response*, pp. 34–35.

47. Quoted in Ibid., p. 91.

48. Celmer, *Terrorism*, p. 113.

49. George Bush, "Untiring Against Terrorism," 20 January 1987, in *Department of State Bulletin* (April 1987), p. 4. On the foreign policy concerns and style of the Reagan administration, see Robert Tucker, "Reagan's Foreign Policy," *Foreign Affairs* 68, no. 1 (1989), pp. 1–27.

50. Statement of Ambassador Robert B. Oakley, in *Department of State Bulletin* (August 1986), p. 3; Celmer, *Terrorism*, p. 24.

51. Statement of Ambassador Oakley, in *Department of State Bulletin* (August 1986), p. 12; see also L. Paul Bremer, "Essential Ingredients in the Fight Against Terrorism," in *Department of State Bulletin* (July 1988), p. 64.

52. John C. Whitehead, "Terrorism: The Challenge and the Response," in *Department of State Bulletin*, (February 1987), p. 72.

53. Celmer, *Terrorism*, p. 13.

54. George Shultz, "The Struggle Against Terrorism," in *Department of State Bulletin*, (April 1988), pp. 35–38.

55. Celmer, *Terrorism*, p. 13.

56. John F. Guilmartin, Jr., "Terrorism: Political Challenge and Military Response," in William R. Snyder and James Brown, eds., *Defense Policy in the Reagan Administration* (Washington, D.C.: National Defense University Press, 1988), pp. 115–42.

57. Ernest Evans, *Calling a Truce to Terror: The American Response to International Terror* (Westport, Conn.: Greenwood Press, 1979), pp. 82–90; Farrell, *The U.S. Government Response*, p. 90; Celmer, *Terrorism*, pp. 113–14; Davidson Smith, *Combating Terrorism*, pp. 63–64, 156, 234.

58. Martin and Walcott, *Best Laid Plans*, pp. 88–89, 96, 101; Celmer, *Terrorism*, pp. 5, 114; see also "Fact Sheet: Additional Information on the Bombing of Pan Am Flight 103," pp. 854–57.

59. On the counter-terrorism policy of the Bush administration, see Robert C. Kingston, "The American Approach to Combatting Terrorism," *Terrorism and Political Violence* 4, no. 3 (Autumn 1992), pp. 102–103.

60. *Patterns of Global Terrorism: 1992*, pp. 1, 57.

61. Lawrence Freedman and Efraim Karsh, *The Gulf Conflict, 1990–1991: Diplomacy and War in the New World Order* (Princeton, N.J.: Princeton University Press, 1993), pp. 134–41, 154–57, 201, 222–23, 263.

62. Brent L. Smith, "Antiterrorism Legislation in the United States: Problems and Implications," *Terrorism: An International Journal* 7, no. 2 (1984), pp. 213–31; Brent L. Smith, "State Anti-terrorism Legislation in the United States: A Review of Statutory Utilization," *Conflict Quarterly* 7, no. 1 (Winter 1988), pp. 29–47. See also US Library of Congress, Congressional Research Service, *International Terrorism: A Compilation of Major Laws, Treaties, Agreements and Executive Documents* (Washington, D.C.: US Government Printing Office, August 1987); Public Law 101–222, Anti-terrorism and Arms Export Amendments Act of 1989; and Laurence Pope, "Department's Efforts to Combat International Terrorism," *Dispatch* 4, no. 17 (26 April 1993), p. 301.

63. Warren Christopher and Paul H. Kreisberg, *American Hostages in Iran: The Conduct of a Crisis* (New York: Council on Foreign Relations, 1985), pp. 3–4, 209, 214–17, 224–28, 293–324.

64. Martin and Walcott, *The Best Laid Plans*, pp. 186–98.

65. Patricia Ann O'Connor, ed. *The Iran-Contra Puzzle* (Washington, D.C.: Congressional Quarterly, Inc., 1987), pp. 15, 18–19, 22–27, 34, 43–45, 48–52.

66. Paul B. Ryan, *The Iranian Rescue Mission: Why It Failed* (Annapolis, Md.: US Naval Institute Press, 1985), pp. 34–35.

67. Martin and Walcott, *Best Laid Plans*, p. 47. See also Richard D. Crabtree, "U.S. Policy for Countering Terrorism: The Intelligence Dimension," *Conflict Quarterly* 6, no. 1 (Winter, 1986), pp. 5–17; Celmer, *Terrorism*, p. 91.

68. Martin and Walcott, *Best Laid Plans*, pp. 156–57, 321, 344–45; Celmer, *Terrorism*, pp. 24, 63, 85.

69. Bremer, "Essential Ingredients," p. 63.

70. Celmer, *Terrorism*, p. 88.

71. Martin and Walcott, *Best Laid Plans*, pp. 105–106. See also, Charters, "Counter-terrorism Intelligence," pp. 257–58; and Glenn Hastedt, "Intelligence Failure and Terrorism: The Attack on the Marines in Beirut," *Conflict Quarterly* 8, no. 2 (Spring 1988), pp. 7–22.

72. Stansfield Turner, *Secrecy and Democracy: The CIA in Transition* (Boston: Houghton Mifflin, 1985), pp. 207–208.

73. The TWA hijackers reportedly said that Navy diver Robert Stethem was killed to avenge the bombing. Martin and Walcott, *Best Laid Plans*, pp. 219–20.

74. Farrell, *The U.S. Government Response*, p. 108.

75. Celmer, *Terrorism*, pp. 66–67; Martin and Walcott, *Best Laid Plans*, p. 38.

76. Interview with Colonel Rod Paschall, former commander of Delta Force, 7 February 1990; Celmer, *Terrorism*, p. 64.

77. Guilmartin, "Terrorism," p. 136. See also Celmer, *Terrorism*, p. 67; Martin and Walcott, *Best Laid Plans*, p. 37; and Colonel Charlie A. Beckwith, *Delta Force* (New York: Harcourt, Brace, Jovanovich, 1983), pp. 102, 118–19, 127.

78. Beckwith, *Delta Force*, pp. 133–37, 140–41, 143–46, 155–59, 169–70, 181–86, 188.

79. Ryan, *The Iranian Rescue Mission*, pp. 1–2, 63–94.

80. Special Operations Review Group, *Rescue Mission Report* (Washington, D.C.: US Department of Defense, August 1980), pp. 51–53; Celmer, *Terrorism*, p. 68.

81. Celmer, *Terrorism*, p. 71. See also Farrell, *The U.S. Government Response*, p. 65; Martin and Walcott, *Best Laid Plans*, p. 60; and Steven Emerson, *Secret Warriors: Inside the Covert Military Operations of the Reagan Era* (New York: Putnam, 1988), p. 202.

82. Interview with Colonel Rod Paschall; Guilmartin, "Terrorism," pp. 128–29; Martin and Walcott, *Best Laid Plans*, pp. 249–54.

83. Noel Koch, "Objecting to Reality: The Struggle to Restore U.S. Special Operations Forces," in Loren B. Thompson, ed., *Low-intensity Conflict: The Pattern of Warfare in the Modern World* (Lexington, Mass.: Lexington Books, 1989), pp. 51–75; see also Guilmartin, "Terrorism," pp. 134–36; Celmer, *Terrorism*, p. 74.

84. Brian L. Davis, *Qadaffi, Terrorism, and the Origins of the U.S. Attack on Libya* (New York: Praeger, 1990), pp. 62–65.

85. Celmer, *Terrorism*, p. 66; Martin and Walcott, *Best Laid Plans*, p. 313.

86. Involvement in terrorism declined from nineteen incidents in 1986 to only three in 1990. US Department of State, *Libya's Continuing Responsibility for Terrorism* (Washington, D.C.: Department of State, November 1991), p. 9.

87. Quoted in statement of Ambassador Robert B. Oakley, (August 1986), p. 4; James M. Markham, "Europe's Anti-Terrorism Tied to U.S. Libya Raids," *New York Times*, 14 April 1987, p. 8.

88. Shultz, "The Struggle Against Terrorism," p. 37.

89. Bremer, "Essential Ingredients," p. 64.

90. Antonio Cassese, *Terrorism, Politics and Law: The Achille Lauro Affair* (Princeton, N.J.: Princeton University Press, 1989), p. 129.

91. Quoted in *Globe and Mail*, 18 April 1986; Martin and Walcott, *Best Laid Plans*, p. 257.

92. Celmer, *Terrorism*, p. 66.

93. Evans, *Calling a Truce*, pp. 51–52, 121–22.

94. Whitehead, "Terrorism: The Challenge and the Response," p. 72.

95. *Patterns of Global Terrorism: 1988*, p. 6; Pope, "Department's Efforts," p. 301.

96. *Report of the President's Commission on Aviation Security and Terrorism*, pp. 171, 175–76; Pope, "Department's Efforts."

97. *Report of the President's Commission on Aviation Security and Terrorism*, pp. 28–29.

98. US Department of State, *Report of the Secretary of State's Advisory Panel on Overseas Security*; Davidson Smith, *Combating Terrorism*, pp. 119–20; Shultz, "The Struggle Against Terrorism," p. 37. See also Andrew Selth, *Against Every Human Law: The Terrorist Threat to Diplomacy* (Rushcutter's Bay: Australian National University Press, 1988), p. 59.

99. See L. Paul Bremer III, "High Technology Terrorism," in *Department of State*

Bulletin (July 1988), pp. 65–67; *Report of the President's Commission on Aviation Security and Terrorism*, pp. 63–67; US Congress, *Technology Against Terrorism*, pp. 5, 7–12, 35, 91–99.

100. John F. Murphy, *State Support of International Terrorism: Legal, Political and Economic Dimensions* (Boulder, Colo.: Westview Press, 1989), chap. 4.

101. Celmer, *Terrorism*, pp. 97–98, 100–101; Selth, *Against Every Human Law*, p. 71.

102. Farrell, *The U.S. Government Response*, pp. 8–10; John F. Murphy, *Punishing International Terrorists: The Legal Framework for Policy Initiatives* (Totowa, N.J.: Rowman and Allanheld, 1985), pp. 16–21, 30, 108–16. See also, *Report of the President's Commission on Aviation Security and Terrorism*, pp. 37, 170–71, 175–76; and Pope, "Department's Efforts."

103. See Jeffrey D. Simon, "The Implications of the Achille Lauro Hijacking for the Maritime Community," *TVI Report* 7, no. 1 (1986), pp. 20–24; Robert G. Moore, "The Price of Admiralty: Regulatory Responses to the Threat of Maritime Terrorism," *TVI Report* 7, no. 1 (1986), pp. 27–30; "The Price of Admiralty II," *TVI Report* 7, no. 2 (1987), pp. 16–20; and Natalino Ronzitti, ed., *Maritime Terrorism and International Law* (Dordrecht, The Netherlands: Martinus Nijhoff, 1990), pp. 69–96 and App. I, II.

104. See Geoffrey M. Levitt, *Democracies Against Terrorism: The Western Response to State-supported Terrorism* (New York: Praeger, 1988), pp. 96–98; and José Luis Nunes and Lawrence J. Smith, co-rapporteurs, *Sub-committee on Terrorism: Final Report,* (North Atlantic Assembly Papers, Brussels: North Atlantic Assembly, January 1989), p. 28.

105. Celmer, *Terrorism*, pp. 104–5; Levitt, *Democracies Against Terrorism*, pp. 106–108, (appendix comprising the texts of the declarations); Selth, *Against Every Human Law*, pp. 69–70.

106. *Patterns of Global Terrorism 1990*, pp. 35–36; Freedman and Karsh, *The Gulf Conflict*, pp. 95–97.

107. Davidson Smith, *Combating Terrorism*, pp. 215–23; after a prolonged, controversial case, Provisional Irish Republican Army fugitive Joe Doherty was extradited from the US to the UK in 1992. See Martin Dillon, *Joe Doherty, the IRA and the Special Relationship* (London: Hutchinson, 1992); and *Washington Post*, 16 January 1992.

108. Radio address by President Ronald Reagan, "International Terrorism," 31 May 1986, in *Department of State Bulletin* (September 1986), p. 23; Shultz, "The Struggle Against Terrorism," p. 38.

109. Robert Tucker, "Reagan's Foreign Policy," *Foreign Affairs* 68, no. 1 (1989), p. 5.

110. Celmer, *Terrorism*, pp. 40, 58 n.51; Murphy, *State Support of International Terrorism*, p. 69; Pope, "Department's Efforts," p. 300.

111. Martin and Walcott, *Best Laid Plans*, pp. 275–76; *Patterns of International Terrorism: 1992*, p. 2.

112. Martin and Walcott, *Best Laid Plans*, p. 345; *Los Angeles Times*, 15 March 1989, p. 1; Interview with Oliver Revell.

113. See L. Paul Bremer III, "U.S. Antiterrorism Assistance Program," in *Department of State Bulletin* (June 1988), pp. 63–64; Pope, "Department's Efforts," pp. 300–301.

114. US Library of Congress, *International Terrorism*, pp. 45–47; Secretary of State James Baker, "Rewards for Terrorism Information Program," *Dispatch* 1, no. 8 (22 October 1990), pp. 208–209.

115. In 1986, the State Department estimated that European and Middle Eastern

countries on the Mediterranean rim lost over $1 billion in anticipated revenue from canceled tourism in 1985. Statement of Ambassador Robert B. Oakley, (August 1986), p. 10.

116. "Terror: Iraq's Second Front," *Newsweek*, 28 January 1991, p. 50; *New York Times*, 8 February 1991, p. A8.

117. Martin and Walcott, *Best Laid Plans*, p. 29.

118. Ibid., pp. 42, 148.

119. Whitehead, "Terrorism: The Challenge and the Response," pp. 71, 72.

120. Ibid., pp. 72–73.

121. See *Washington Post*, 13 February 1987; and *Newsweek*, 8 February 1988. On the FBI's guidelines for such investigations, see the series of 1983 Justice Department memoranda, items 390–93, "U.S. Intelligence Community," National Security Archive Microfiche Collection, copies in Centre for Conflict Studies Library, University of New Brunswick.

122. *Globe and Mail*, 18 January 1991, p. A8; *Maclean's*, 28 January 1991, p. 24.

123. Celmer, *Terrorism*, pp. 113–14.

124. Ibid., pp. 46–47.

125. L. Paul Bremer, "Countering Terrorism in the 1980s and 1990s," in *Department of State Bulletin* (February 1989), pp. 61–62. The US claimed that in 1985 at least 120 attacks were foiled overseas. Statement of Ambassador Robert B. Oakley, (August 1986), p. 4.

126. *Washington Times*, 9 February 1987, p. 6. See Michael Howard, "A European Perspective on the Reagan Years," *Foreign Affairs* 66, no. 3 (1988), pp. 483–86; Paul Johnson, "Europe and the Reagan Years," *Foreign Affairs* 68, no. 1 (1989), p. 36. See also Chapter 5 in this volume.

127. Bremer, "Countering Terrorism in the 1980s and 1990s," (February 1989), p. 61.

128. Martin and Walcott, *Best Laid Plans*, p. 312.

129. See Ambassador Robert B. Oakley, "International Terrorism," 16 June 1986, in *Department of State Bulletin*, (August 1986) p. 5; Bremer, "Essential Ingredients," p. 64, and Bremer, "Terrorism: Its Evolving Nature," p. 74.

130. As Oliver Revell pointed out, the NSC meets on many national security issues, and "terrorism is probably one of the issues that it meets least frequently on, unless there is an ongoing crisis." Interview with Oliver Revell.

8

Conclusions: Security and Liberty in Balance—Countering Terrorism in the Democratic Context

David A. Charters

In his opening chapter, Grant Wardlaw identified the central problem for democracies engaged in countering terrorism: "constructing rational, appropriate, and consistent countermeasures that deal with the threat without fundamentally undermining or changing the democratic practices and traditions that the measures are designed to protect."[1] He went on to enunciate a number of general principles of democratic counter-terrorism "strategy": a definition of terrorism agreed on and understood by government and its polity that clearly delimits what is and is not terrorism (and thus determines which events require a counter-terrorism response), sophisticated analysis to distinguish between types and levels of terrorist threats, flexible policy, policy language that matches words to deeds in a consistent and credible manner, a realization (by government and the public) that there are no simple solutions or ideal outcomes, and well-trained and -prepared counter-terrorism machinery that functions without paralyzing government or deeply implicating the persons and prestige of high office in the outcome of decision-making and its consequences. These are by no means the only criteria for assessing the value of counter-terrorism policies in a democratic context. They are, however, important ones and will be examined further as this concluding assessment develops.

THE FINDINGS

What International Terrorism Accomplished

Writing in 1986, Walter Laqueur observed that, in the future, historians might legitimately conclude that the terrorist problem had been "oversold," perhaps deliberately. The historian would note that the rhetoric of political leaders vastly outstripped the scale of the problem and the resources applied in efforts to contain it.[2] Conventional wars have almost always been more deadly, and highway accidents in a single year in the United States have regularly killed more people than international terrorism. The murder rate in several major American cities exceeds that of the Northern Ireland conflict by a wide margin. Yet neither traffic deaths nor urban murders have been subjected to the kind of overheated rhetoric that has characterized political discourse on terrorism.

The evidence presented in this volume might tend to lend weight to such a "revisionist" interpretation of the history of international terrorism. To the extent that distinctions can be drawn between international and domestic terrorism, the latter was a more serious problem in Britain, Italy, and West Germany and was at least a comparable threat in France. In these and other states, international terrorism inflicted minimal numbers of casualties and only modest damage to the infrastructure of the state. Only the United States suffered a significant number of fatalities (about 450) from international terrorism in the 1980s, and most of those from just three incidents—the bombings of the US embassy and the Marine barracks in Beirut and of Pan Am Flight 103. In most cases, it was little more than a nuisance factor, horrifying in its immediate casualty effects and aggravating in its ability to complicate domestic and foreign politics, but neither sustained nor powerful enough to undermine the foundations of the state. In Israel's case, however, international terrorism was a "threat multiplier," insufficient *alone* to shake the state, but one factor among many that worked their corrosive influence on the fabric of Israeli democracy. Thus, the first significant finding is that *by itself international terrorism was not a serious threat to the fundamental stability and functioning of democratic states.*

Yet this conclusion should not be seen as an attempt to trivialize the significance of international terrorism. As Laqueur points out, terrorism's impact cannot be measured solely in terms of the number of casualties inflicted.[3] Nor is the undermining of the state the only measure of success. Even those terrorist groups whose ultimate objective is some kind of new social order have short-term and intermediate goals that they view as necessary and desirable; the nature of success, then, lies in bending the state to their will in fulfilling those goals. Forcing the state to respond is the key, for as Nicholas O. Berry asserts, "terrorism is efficacious only if the target makes it so."[4] There were at least three responses that international terrorists could elicit from their targets that would be harmful to democracy: First, forcing a government to modify or abandon its policies and courses of action in favor of those dictated by the terrorists (this involves the removal of a portion of the power of democratically elected representatives and its replacement by a degree of coercive power wielded by the terrorists); second, changing attitudes of the population in favor of less democratic means of government, and finally, persuading governments to introduce countermeasures that undermine democratic practices and human rights. To what extent was international terrorism able to elicit these responses?

First, all but one state (the UK) modified its policies or courses of action in order to accommodate or negotiate deals with international terrorists. France was the most consistent in this regard, with very negative consequences for the French population, whose lives were placed in jeopardy. In the mid-1980s, the United

States and Israel changed what previously had been firm policies against meeting terrorist demands and entered into negotiations. The political consequences of these actions were very damaging to the governments concerned, as they undercut laws as well as longstanding policies. In Israel, the decision compounded an already difficult crisis of attitude—moral, legal, and functional—about how best to respond to terrorism, including the domestic Israeli variety. In the United States, the Iran-Contra affair shook the authority of the presidency in a manner reminiscent of the Watergate scandal. Temporarily, at least, it disrupted interdepartmental cooperation and undermined allied confidence in the administration's competence and commitment to countering international terrorism.

Second, public attitudes were changed in favor of applying harsher—and less democratic—countermeasures against terrorists. However, in at least three of the countries studied—the UK, Italy, and West Germany—domestic terrorism was already a significant factor, and the borderline between domestic and international terrorism was somewhat indistinct. In such cases, it is unlikely that the public drew clear distinctions between domestic and international terrorism in either calling for or acquiescing in tougher countermeasures. So a clear link is difficult to establish. It is much clearer in the cases of France and Israel, where the threat of international terrorism overshadowed the domestic one. Yet, even here, assertions must be qualified with respect to Israel because of its unique siege mentality brought on by the permanent state of war with its neighbors. Israel's attitudes toward and responses to international terrorism cannot be separated from its wider security concerns. Only in the United States were attitudes not modified noticeably in favor of harsher measures *inside* the country. Undoubtedly, this can be attributed to the fact that the internal domestic and international terrorist threats were minimal. However, *international* terrorism against US citizens and institutions *abroad* produced a very different reaction; in these instances, many Americans—from the president down—favored the use of severe measures (including armed force) *outside* the country against international terrorists and their alleged sponsors.

Finally, most countries introduced countermeasures that impinged to a greater or lesser degree on democratic practices and civil liberties. But, in most cases, new powers were introduced to deal with domestic, *not* international, terrorism. This was clearly the case in the US, the UK, West Germany, and Italy. Similar powers in Israel actually predated the creation of the state, and the first new legislation in this regard was introduced to counter a domestic Israeli group, albeit after their attack on a foreign target. Only the restrictions introduced by France seemed clearly directed at external terrorist threats and these were open to subjective interpretation; as a result, residents or citizens of France who *appeared to be foreigners* could be subjected to official harassment until their innocence was clearly established. In the United States, a few state governments introduced anti-terrorist legislation, but these laws have seldom been used; prosecutions tend to be brought under existing criminal law. The laws passed by Congress applicable to federal authorities were intended to expand their powers in operating *overseas*, not in the US itself. This is not to suggest that powers were never abused or rights violated, merely that if so, they were not the result of *new* laws, restrictions, or countermeasures.

Obviously, these laws and countermeasures had some impact on democratic practices and civil liberties, matters that go to the heart of the rationale of this study. Before addressing those issues, however, this chapter will examine the effectiveness of the anti-terrorism policies and actions undertaken by the states concerned.

Effectiveness of Anti-terrorism Policies and Countermeasures

In theory, assessing the effectiveness of anti-terrorism policies and actions should be relatively easy. A number of obvious criteria could serve as empirical "yardsticks" against which effectiveness could be judged:

1. The rate of terrorist incidents in the country concerned;

2. The number of casualties resulting from terrorism;

3. The number of terrorists captured, convicted, and jailed as a result of due process, and *not replaced* in the terrorist group; and

4. The number of terrorists "neutralized" as a result of attrition (i.e., killed or wounded), and *not replaced*.

By this model, if categories 1 and 2 declined as 3 and 4 increased, then the relative security of national territory and of nationals and installations overseas would be enhanced. Anti-terrorist policies and actions would then be judged as successful and, therefore, effective.

In reality, however, it is not so easy to make such judgments. First, it is possible for the rate of incidents to decline while the number of casualties increases. This has happened with respect to attacks on civil aviation.[5] If this occurs, can any effectiveness be claimed? Second, terrorist activities may decline for reasons that have little to do with countermeasures, but rather are related to changing dynamics (political or social) within the group. The fact that this occurs after certain countermeasures have been applied might be coincidental, without any clear cause-and-effect relationship. The disintegration of the Armenian Secret Army for the Liberation of Armenia from 1983 may be a case in point. Third, the social milieu that gave rise to terrorism and subsequently nourished it may change—and not necessarily as a result of government policies. In such changed circumstances, terrorists might conclude that terrorism is either unnecessary or so unwelcome that erstwhile supporters abandon the "cause" and the movement.[6] In short, terrorism may simply go "out of fashion."[7]

Returning to the question of the countermeasures themselves, however, it remains difficult to make exact assessments of both individual initiatives and collective efforts. Certain activities are unmeasurable because of lack of data. For example, how many terrorist operations were aborted at the planning stage after the would-be perpetrators reconnoitred the target and concluded that it could not be attacked or, if it could, that the cost-benefit trade-off was not worthwhile? Terrorist groups have told us little about these instances. How many terrorist operations were prevented by preemptive action? Governments and security forces rarely discuss this form of activity, yet it is clear that it occurs.[8] Both of these circumstances are examples of effective countermeasures; a terrorist attack that does *not* occur for the reasons cited above represents a counter-terrorism *success*. But it is difficult to prove a negative—and impossible in the absence of data. Therefore, such cases are not included in the assessment of the measures employed by the countries in this study. Yet even assessing verifiable activities is not easy. As Christopher Hewitt observes, if terrorism declines when two measures are used simultaneously, "which policy is responsible for the decline?"[9] He prefaces his own conclusions on effectiveness with a cautionary note: "It would be satisfying to report that we had identified a number of policies that were consistently successful in reducing terrorism, but such is not the case. Instead what our research suggests is that some policies do not work at all, and some policies are successful in certain situations but not in others."[10] The findings of this study tend to support Hewitt's thesis.

Certain countermeasures—international cooperation, target-hardening, the increased use of intelligence resources, and the creation of specialized military and para-military counter-terrorism units—were common to all of the countries studied. As noted earlier, almost all entered into negotiations with terrorists or their sponsors at one time or another. The greatest diversity was in crisis management and contingency planning. It was virtually non-existent in Italy and apparently remains largely decentralized in West Germany. The other countries had crisis management/contingency planning resources of varying types and quality.

Given the limitations of trying to assess effectiveness, what can be said about the performance of these policies and countermeasures? First, all governments except that of the UK applied flexible policies, but *negotiations and making "deals" with international terrorists were largely ineffective*. Terrorists usually regarded deals as temporary tactical ploys, not as permanent prohibitions against the use of violence. They returned to terrorism as soon as they felt circumstances warranted. While such arrangements sometimes yielded a temporary gain for the government, such as the release of hostages, it was often at a cost, in lives or money, then or later. There were exceptions to this rule: Italy's "understanding" with the Palestine Liberation Organization (PLO) kept Italy relatively free of Palestinian terrorism for a prolonged period. But Italy's immunity ended with the splits in the PLO after their evacuation from Beirut in 1982. Moreover, extreme factions, such as Abu Nidal's, operated where they chose—including Italy—regardless of any understandings.

Second, *international cooperation produced positive results, particularly on functional matters, such as the exchange of intelligence and criminal investigation data. Multilateral and bilateral arrangements between agencies*, exemplified by the TREVI Group and shared access to Germany's Federal Criminal Office (BKA) computer files, *were most effective*. Such links enhanced the ability of police forces and security/intelligence services to conduct investigations, share evidence, make arrests, and gain convictions. The Anglo-American Pan Am Flight 103 investigation, the Hamadei case, and the investigation of the Committee of Solidarity with Arab and Middle East Political Prisoners demonstrated the benefits of transnational cooperation between police and security services.

That said, there were some limits on the effectiveness of cooperation. Difficulties arose at the level of multilateral government-to-government collaboration over major policy issues, such as the application of sanctions and the question of extradition. It was at this level that national interest and sovereignty hindered cooperation. For example, France's blind pursuit of narrowly defined national self-interest in foreign policy and on the domestic front (the asylum-extradition issue) impeded the effectiveness of international cooperation, with negative consequences for its own population and those of its neighbors. But France was not alone in this regard. Because of its partial diplomatic isolation arising from the conflict in the Middle East, Israel tended to take unilateral initiatives, which sometimes had negative effects elsewhere.

So, too, did the United States, but for different reasons. Thus, although the US both contributed to and benefited from international cooperation, the gains were periodically offset by the unintended effects of unilateral actions, such as the interception of the *Achille Lauro* hijackers and the bombing of Libya. These differences of national policy and approach also tended to undermine collective efforts in the realm of sanctions. While near unity was achieved on sanctions against Syria in late 1986, there was no such collective will with respect to Libya until 1992. Indeed, the failure of the US to persuade its allies to follow its lead on the Libyan issue probably contributed to the unilateral US attack in April 1986. No more successful were efforts to cut off airline service to states alleged to be supporting international terrorism. Such isolation was never complete and rarely lasted more than a few weeks. (The ban on Libyan air traffic imposed by the United Nations may be the sole exception.)

To summarize, then, even if international cooperation did not produce *all* that was hoped of it, it was generally beneficial in important, if low-profile, areas. However, the failure of any one country to cooperate tended to undermine the counter-terrorism efforts of the rest. In short, unilateralism in any form created problems, not solutions.

Third, not surprisingly, *the effective management of responses to discrete terrorist incidents was most likely in those countries that had created and maintained permanent crisis management facilities.* Only two states, Israel and the UK, were effective in this respect. It is probably not coincidental that these two states were confronted by protracted domestic insurgencies and had implemented the most comprehensive "packages" of counter-terrorism measures. Elsewhere, crisis management was marked by politicization—the interference of senior political leaders either in the organization of crisis management or in its implementation during an actual crisis. The other problem was ad hocracy. In fact, the two were almost invariably linked. France, Italy, and the United States were plagued by both, to different degrees and under different circumstances.

In the American case, politicization was notable during the Teheran hostage crisis and in the Iran-Contra affair (in the latter case, existing structures were deliberately bypassed). The ad hoc element manifested itself in the "tinkering" to which the US crisis management structures were constantly subjected. To a considerable extent, this was a product of politicization; each administration tried to put its own stamp on the crisis management system, with the result that it was almost always being reorganized. Consequently, the American system, like its French and Italian counterparts, was not effective. It seems fair to conclude, then, that crisis management will succeed only if there is continuity and stability in personnel, organization, and procedures, altered solely by testing and experience, not by bureaucratic tinkering.

Each of the cases emphasized the importance of intelligence, but also illustrated the difficulty of examining the subject of intelligence itself. There were insufficient data from which to draw firm conclusions about the performance of individual security/intelligence services or to make comparative assessments. Nevertheless, certain observations stand out. As Arie Ofri notes, terrorism can be seen as a form of surprise attack.[11] In this respect, the findings of this study are consistent with those of studies of intelligence and surprise in other countries: *Even capable intelligence services are unable to prevent all terrorist attacks.*[12] But without the warning and security provided by intelligence, many *more* attacks would have succeeded. Therefore, *intelligence was crucial to minimizing the threat from international terrorism, even if it could not eliminate the risk altogether.*

These observations, and the reasons for them—the difficulties of collecting and assessing intelligence about clandestine terrorist groups and the problems of interagency duplication and conflict—are consistent with other studies of counter-terrorism intelligence.[13] Indeed, these cases emphasize the point that, just as the boundaries between domestic and international terrorism—and the responses to them—are often artificial, the institutional and jurisdictional boundaries between domestic and foreign intelligence services, and between them and the police, may be just as artificial when applied to counter-terrorism intelligence work. They would appear to reinforce the argument for allocating (or dividing) the task functionally, rather than institutionally.[14]

The majority of governments did develop definitions of terrorism that incorporated some of the basic characteristics of the phenomenon, even if they were not as rigorous as academic definitions. But it is by no means certain that the lack of definitional clarity significantly hampered the ability of every government to respond effectively. Nor is it clear that such definitions were understood by the informed public in the countries concerned, or that this made a great deal of difference. The exception in this regard was the United States, where debate on the matter was most wide-ranging, both inside and outside of government. Yet the debate did little to clarify the issue and, in fact, may have actually muddied the waters. Both official and academic definitions of terrorism tended to blur the distinctions between terrorism and other forms of conflict, and buzzwords such as narco-terrorism, when used out of context, still preclude clear thinking and hamper interagency policy-making.

Given its definitional problems, it is not surprising that the quality of American threat analysis was not as good as that of several other countries. The Italians probably had the most sophisticated conception of the problem, which set international terrorism in the context of Italian foreign policy and drew distinctions among the different origins, objectives, and targets of such terrorism. If their assessments were less finely nuanced from a political perspective, British and German intelligence nonetheless appeared to have gauged the *level* of threat with reasonable accuracy. Not so the French, who grossly underestimated the risk, or the Israelis and the Americans, who tended to inflate the threat to the state. The US annual calculated *totals* of international terrorist incidents were not necessarily wrong (or more inaccurate than other estimates). Rather, they tended to highlight attacks on US persons and installations and reflected the Reagan administration's preoccupation with the Soviet threat. This accorded international terrorism the status of a national security issue and created a sense of urgency and imminent danger that the problem probably did not deserve. If this observation is correct, then it may explain the administration's desire to take offensive military action against a "grave threat" that was, at least in part, of its own making. In short, *skewed analysis produced skewed policy*.

Every country studied introduced some means of target-hardening, with varying degrees of success. For example, improvements in airport security in Europe and North America in the early 1970s dramatically reduced airliner hijacking, although this did not eliminate it completely. Hijackers simply switched to less secure airports, often in the Third World. In the 1980s, terrorists circumvented existing security procedures and technologies by changing tactics; they carried out armed assaults at airports and placed virtually undetectable bombs on board aircraft. Likewise, the seizure of embassies in the 1970s led to tighter security in the 1980s. This, in turn, caused terrorists to switch targets and tactics.

These observations illustrate several points about target-hardening; first, it was essentially reactive, a response to a series of attacks. Rarely was it applied in a proactive sense, that is, in anticipation of terrorist attacks or of changes in their modus operandi. This probably reflects a limitation of security/intelligence already noted above: the inability to prevent surprise attack.

Second, terrorism and target-hardening were two parts of a dynamic process; improvements or changes in the tactics or the technology of one produced a response in the other. Governments and terrorists tried to find ways of nullifying the effectiveness of each other's respective methods and technologies. Yet terrorists consistently worked with a limited repertoire of tactics and technologies in the 1970s and 1980s, showing themselves to be conservative, rather than innovative.[15] Moreover, the response resources available to government, the security forces, and business vastly outstripped those of terrorists. These two facts help to explain why international terrorists only rarely were able to deliver serious attacks, why it was difficult for them to sustain success for a prolonged period, and, hence, why they were unable to pose a serious threat to the stability of states.

Third, given the nature of the threat and the limits of target-hardening countermeasures, the effectiveness of these countermeasures may have been more apparent than real; the deterrent effect is hard to prove. If, as a result of target-hardening, terrorists switch tactics or targets in order to continue attacks, they have been stymied temporarily, but not deterred. Nonetheless, even a temporary respite from attack may be beneficial for public morale. So *the psychological impact of target-hardening*, even if it is reactive and the nature of the threat changes later, *may be as important as the barrier effect.*

Finally, the limits of target-hardening highlight a fundamental point: *Democratic states cannot provide total security from terrorist attack while maintaining the open society that is the essence of democracy.* Even Israel, which is closer to a garrison state than the other democracies, has been unable to prevent all attacks on its territory or on its installations and representatives abroad. Yet to make no effort at target-hardening, or a totally inadequate one—as France did—is totally irresponsible and morally unjustifiable in view of the human cost.

Each of the subject countries created special forces or modified existing units to carry out special anti-terrorist missions, usually oriented to the rescue of hostages. Five of the six countries used these forces for such rescue operations, and four of the five were successful. Because of the narrow focus of their missions, these units were used infrequently. When they were used, however, the outcome was rarely in doubt; international terrorists were no match for well-trained, well-led professional soldiers or para-military police in properly planned rescue assault operations.

Military and para-military forces were used for other missions related to counter-terrorism, with a more mixed record of success. Israeli land and sea patrols were largely effective in either preventing terrorists from getting into Israel or capturing them if they did penetrate the country. The Italian *Carabinieri*, on the other hand, were not effective when used for large-scale search and protective duties; their procedures were not oriented to dealing with a clandestine enemy. France, Israel, and the United States used their military forces to conduct reprisal raids against states or groups believed to be responsible for terrorist attacks, again with mixed results. French and American reprisals in Lebanon in 1983 had no measurable effect on Shiite terrorists then or subsequently. The US raid on Libya in April 1986 apparently did persuade Qaddafi to reduce his (detectable) involvement in supporting international terrorism against the United States, if only temporarily. In the 1980s, the Israelis regularly used reprisals—usually in the form of air strikes—which had an *attrition* effect in terms of inflicting casualties, but no noticeable *deterrent* effect on the Palestinian groups whose attacks on Israel, or on Israeli forces in Lebanon, had caused the reprisals. In fact, such reprisals may have helped to sustain commitment to the Palestinian cause and to encourage recruitment to the militant groups, thereby offsetting the attrition effect. Moreover, both the

US and Israel found that the imprecision of reprisals, and the resultant collateral casualties and damage, caused controversy and brought criticism from those nations that were otherwise allied in the struggle against international terrorism. The apparent disproportion of scale between the terrorist attack and an air raid tended to undercut the moral high ground of the democracies that used the reprisal strategy, making it easy for critics to blur the distinctions between democracies and terrorists, between just causes and unjust means.[16] In short, *the political and moral costs of reprisals were usually greater than their deterrent or attrition effects*.

Similar points could be made regarding two other types of military operation described in this volume: the air interception of the *Achille Lauro* hijackers and the killing of the would-be Irish Republican Army bombers in Gibraltar by Britain's Special Air Service Regiment (SAS). The latter eliminated a potentially significant bomb threat, while the former delivered terrorist fugitives into custody in the country where they could be (and were) prosecuted legitimately and successfully. Both the operations were executed flawlessly and demonstrated the reach and the power of the professional armed forces of the state. However, both had undesirable political consequences and were legally and morally controversial. The Gibraltar operation, in particular, *appeared* to violate the principles of due process, whether or not that was the case in fact. Yet appearances *are* important; in democracies, justice must be seen to be done, and the Gibraltar operation left much to be desired in that regard.

The evidence from the case studies, therefore, suggests that *in responding to international terrorism, the most effective role for military/para-military forces is the hostage rescue assault. It is morally defensible; is clearly defined; can be conducted within a legal, constitutional framework; and, finally, is likely to succeed.*

From the perspective of effectiveness, how did these states measure up against Wardlaw's criteria? As the foregoing suggests, the record is a mixed one. Only two countries, the UK and West Germany, demonstrated satisfactory overall performance of institutions; rational, appropriate, and consistent countermeasures; *and* effectiveness against international terrorism. While the performance of Italy's institutions of government and law enforcement was much less efficient, Italy's basic policy approach was sound (within Italy's terms of reference) and produced results satisfactory to Italy—if not always satisfactory to others. The French response was poor; it was hampered by inconsistent and inappropriate policies and inadequate performance by many national institutions. While the consequences were deadly for many French citizens, they were not fatal to the state. But the credibility of national leaders was undermined by the difference between words and deeds.

Israeli performance was impressive until the late 1970s, but deteriorated thereafter—once Israel was drawn into the Lebanese civil war. Although Israeli territory remains relatively free of international terrorism, until recently its diplomatic and military responses moved it further from resolution of the fundamental crisis that gives rise to terrorism and transformed counter-terrorism into a higher form of warfare that perpetuated terrorism and carried risks of escalation to interstate conflict. Finally, the United States suffered from inconsistencies of policy, of political rhetoric, and of both capabilities and accomplishments. With a few exceptions, institutional performance was inadequate. Like Israel, US territory was relatively free of international terrorist attacks, but a tendency to aggressive, unilateral countermeasures abroad (also like Israel) demonstrated only marginal effectiveness at high political cost.

Impact of Countermeasures on Democratic Processes and Civil Liberties

The impact of these countermeasures on the democratic structures, processes, and character of the states concerned is of fundamental importance. It has already been shown that international terrorism did not threaten the basic stability of these states, but that—in concert with domestic terrorism—it contributed to a public mood that favored harsher countermeasures. Most of the *special* measures introduced, however, arose from the various domestic terrorist threats these states faced.

Moreover, the evidence suggests that there was little consistency in either the promulgation or the application of anti-democratic powers and countermeasures. Indeed, some comfort might be taken from the fact that, for all the fulsome political "tub thumping" about the need to "stamp out terrorism," *there was no wholesale rush to restrict freedoms for the sake of greater security from terrorism.* Only two states (the UK and Israel) introduced the full range of encroaching powers; the United States added none at all.

The power most commonly expanded was that of search and arrest (by five countries: the UK, West Germany, Italy, France, and Israel). Periods of detention before charge was extended by four countries: the UK, Italy, France, and Israel. Likewise, four countries—the UK, West Germany, Italy, and Israel—proscribed terrorist organizations. Only the UK and France added new deportation powers to deal with international terrorism. Such powers already existed in most countries with respect to ordinary criminal offenses, but were invariably difficult to enforce (in, for example, France and the United States) in cases where the offense appeared to have a political dimension. Italy and West Germany placed restrictions on the actions of lawyers representing suspected terrorists. Only Italy legally mandated the expansion of intrusive means of investigation; elsewhere, such powers were used under existing legislation, by administrative procedures, or simply as custom dictated (as in the UK until 1989, when the Security Service finally was given a formal mandate by legislation).

The principle that justice must be *seen* to be done may be a cliché, but it is nonetheless of fundamental importance in a liberal democracy. It was partly eroded in West Germany, Italy, Israel, and the UK. In the first two, the lawyer-client relationship was subjected to some restrictions. These were imposed in instances where the lawyers were themselves suspected of involvement in political violence or were implicated in efforts to assist their clients in escaping custody (for example, by smuggling weapons into prison). The UK and Israel modified their court procedures: The former introduced non-jury courts, while the latter used military courts to hear certain cases. However, two points must be made in this regard: First, these changes were introduced to deal with *domestic* political violence and were not applied to international terrorists. Second, they were subject to spatial selectivity[17] in their application; that is, they were used only in certain areas—Northern Ireland and Israel's occupied territories (the West Bank and the Gaza Strip). These facts serve to highlight an important observation: the harshest and most comprehensive regimes of counter-terrorism powers were introduced (or retained) by those states threatened either by sustained serious terrorist insurgency (the UK vis-à-vis Northern Ireland) or by a combination of threatened and actual war, of domestic and international terrorism (Israel). In other words, *international terrorism alone was not usually sufficient cause to bring about the introduction of counter-terrorism measures that encroached on democratic processes and civil liberties.*

That said, it is important to note that erosion of democracy and liberty did not take place solely within the ambit of special legislation or administrative measures. Indeed, the violations that occurred outside the realm of law and administrative power were often more serious. Moreover, these activities posed unique problems of accountability and ethics. The issue of intrusive investigation powers has already been noted; the BKA's effort to computerize data collected on terrorists was grossly disproportionate to the terrorist problem, the data base contained incorrect data on people, and the result was a clear violation of the right to privacy. In the United States, the case involving the Committee in Solidarity with the People of El Salvador refocused attention on a perennial problem: that security forces are unable or unwilling to distinguish between legitimate dissent and political extremism or subversion. Police malfeasance appears to have been at the root of two miscarriages of justice in the UK, in which apparently innocent people were jailed for bombings (at Guildford and Birmingham) they did not commit. The cases raise questions about the integrity and accountability of police personnel and about the integrity and impartiality of the courts. When such questions arise, there are indeed grounds for concern about the protection of civil liberties in an otherwise democratic state.

But it is the use of violence by agents of the state that raises the most troubling questions. In the British context, concerns arose about the use of lethal force by the SAS, instead of arrest by the police, to resolve two international terrorist situations: the Iranian embassy siege and the Gibraltar incident. While few questioned the SAS's methods in the first situation because the terrorists posed obvious and immediate risks to their hostages, in the latter case the immediate threat to lives was less certain. Nonetheless, the SAS made no effort to apprehend the terrorists by non-lethal means, but rather killed them in a manner that suggested a premeditated plan of extrajudicial execution. Although the SAS was cleared of wrongdoing, the operation very clearly strayed into a grey area of dubious legality and morality.

In Israel, excesses by at least one branch of the security forces were even more serious. Not only did the *Shabak* kill two terrorists and try to cover it up by shifting the blame to the army, but also used torture to extract confessions from alleged terrorists and then deliberately misled the courts about this by introducing false evidence. Summary executions, torture, falsification of evidence, and cover-ups are the weapons of state terror, the very antithesis of democracy and human rights.

It is no coincidence that these situations arise in Britain and Israel. In both cases, the use of security forces and the excesses that ensued could be attributed to the spillover effect of their involvement in protracted low-intensity conflict elsewhere in territory under their control: Northern Ireland and the occupied territories. The operational culture of those wars was incompatible with the normal political culture of the democracies that exists outside of those combat zones. Yet the protracted nature of those conflicts was gradually transforming the democracies by blurring the distinctions between them and the otherwise clearly defined theaters of war, and between the conflict methods that were acceptable in each. In Israel, the transformation has been more prolonged, more influential, and more corrosive of democratic values to the extent that some Israelis were prepared to draw distinctions between "good" and "bad" terrorism, an indication of complete moral confusion.

SIGNIFICANCE OF THE FINDINGS

These findings challenge the often strongly held notion that democratic states could or would be extinguished either by international terrorism itself or by the response to it. At least among the countries studied, neither fate has occurred. If international terrorism did not prove to be the major destabilizing threat to liberal democracies that many suggested, neither did the responses of those states realize the worst fears regarding the demise of civil liberties. Even where special powers were introduced, democracy was not extinguished; draconian powers did not lead to draconian practice. However imperfectly, democratic checks and balances worked. So it seems fair to conclude that combatting international terrorism does not commit a democracy to a suicide pact; *an acceptable degree of effectiveness is compatible with a wide measure of liberty*. Indeed, there is a curious, but significant, irony in these findings. The World Trade Center bombing and related plots notwithstanding, the most open, and thus supposedly the most vulnerable democracy, the United States, was the one whose domestic security was least threatened by international terrorism. The US faced more serious threats to people and installations abroad.

On the other hand, the findings with respect to Britain and Israel tend to support the contention that protracted domestic (or, in Israel's case, quasi-domestic) terrorism is more likely to lead to anti-democratic practices and the erosion of civil liberties. The relevance of this to the problem of responding to international terrorism is threefold: First, *attitudes* are important. The psychological climate of public opinion in the political culture affected by terrorism will not only shape specific response measures, but also determine how far the public is prepared to go in accepting anti-democratic measures and even to tolerate vigilantism and/or excess by the security forces. Terrorism creates fear, individually and collectively; the desire to escape from a climate of fear into greater security is a natural reaction. Herein lies the source of creeping authoritarianism. In the context of countering terrorism in a democracy, there is much truth to be found in Franklin D. Roosevelt's warning, "The only thing we have to fear is fear itself."[18]

This suggests that, from a civil liberties perspective, fear-reduction measures may be as beneficial, and as important and necessary, as those designed to reduce, contain, or eliminate the physical threat of the terrorists. Such fear-reduction measures might include both effective crisis management, which is seen as keeping threats under control, and limited target-hardening measures (such as those found at airports), when they can be justified by the actual level of threat. However, a great deal depends on the way the threat is presented in public, political, and media discourse. Without minimizing or glossing over genuine threats, every effort should be made to reduce the level of "hype" about the power of terrorism and to place greater emphasis on the limits and failures of terrorism and on the successes against it. This could be facilitated by the publication and discussion of objective assessments regarding the types and levels of terrorist threats. Thus, even if incidents occur, the elements of shock and surprise—the key ingredients of fear—could be reduced, along with the likelihood of public demands for excessive countermeasures.[19]

The second point arising from the British and Israeli experiences is that excesses are as likely to arise within the ambit of executive and administrative agencies as from special legislated powers. The implication of this is the need to strengthen checks and balances with two additional provisions: institutionalized, but independent, oversight and enforcement mechanisms. This would ensure that excesses are either prevented or, if not, then detected, terminated, and punished. Assuring that justice is done and that it applies equally to agents as well as opponents of the state will help to preserve fundamental principles of democracy.

Finally, the British and Israeli examples indicate that, since the overlap of domestic and international terrorism erodes the distinctions between the two, it is difficult to compartmentalize the responses to the respective problems. Yet the experiences of other countries—the US and Italy—suggest that some compartmentalization is desirable from the civil liberties perspective. Treating international terrorism mainly as a foreign policy responsibility, rather than one of domestic law enforcement, may provide a higher degree of assurance that democratic liberties will be protected. This conclusion is strengthened by the findings on effectiveness, which showed positive results from bilateral and multilateral cooperation, at least in certain functional areas.

Moreover, because of the national situations in which domestic and international terrorism arose, most of the countries studied were unable to isolate the two types of terrorism completely. This brings the focus back to the character of the political culture of those countries. While there were obvious commonalities of experience and response, there were distinct differences as well, differences that could not be traced merely to different levels of terrorist threat. Rather, they had their origins in features unique to each individual political culture: Britain's historical Irish problem; Israel's siege situation; Italy's Mediterranean foreign policy; and the US's quasi-imperial global presence, its contradictory Middle East policies, and the permanent state of flux that characterizes its administrative and executive structures. Each state assigned a different level of priority to the terrorist problem, in relation to other issues confronting it. While international terrorism often commanded attention well out of proportion to its importance, that attention, as Laqueur observed, rarely translated into high-priority programs. Even the Reagan administration, more fixated than its allies on the terrorist issue, devoted more time and resources to problems such as US-Soviet relations, the defense budget, and the national deficit. Moreover, each state applied its counter-terrorism resources in ways that reflected the national political culture, and that put national interests first. In sum, political culture, more than any other factor, shaped—and continues to shape—democratic responses to the challenge of international terrorism. Herein lies the final commonality in the comparative study—the commonality of uniqueness of national responses.

This says a great deal about the kinds of achievements that can be expected realistically as efforts against international terrorism continue. It suggests that in spite of the end of the Cold War, and the transition to a more unified Europe, even the most promising dimension of counter-terrorism—international cooperation—will continue to be hampered by competing and conflicting national interests and occasional unilateral gestures. In 1989 the tally of international terrorism incidents registered its first significant decline after more than a decade of apparently inexorable growth. With the exception of a brief "spike" in 1991 related to the Gulf War, this pattern continued through 1992, suggesting a long-term trend. However, the world remains volatile, and political violence remains endemic in certain regions. So even if 1989 was a watershed or a turning point in the campaign against international terrorism, it is clear that we have not seen the end of the phenomenon. Given the limitations that competing political cultures impose on transnational cooperative efforts, the leaders of liberal democracies confront a significant challenge: to demonstrate the patience to sustain a commitment both to democratic values and to incremental successes against terrorism over the long haul and to avoid the temptation and perils of seeking a panacea in the apparent quick fix. These leaders will be most helpful in this regard if they lower expectations by conditioning the public to accept the notion of a long struggle, occasional setbacks, and perhaps something less than total victory, for it is too soon to claim victory. In this respect, a cautionary note, sounded more than fifty years ago by Sir Winston

Churchill, probably sets the most appropriate tone:

Now this is not the end. It is not even the beginning of the end. But is, perhaps, the end of the beginning.[20]

NOTES

1. See Chapter 1 of this volume.
2. Walter Laqueur, "Reflections on Terrorism," *Foreign Affairs* 65, no. 1 (Fall 1986), pp. 86–87.
3. Ibid., p. 87.
4. Nicholas O. Berry, "Theories on the Efficacy of Terrorism," *Conflict Quarterly* 7, no. 1 (Winter 1987), p. 17.
5. Between June 1985 and September 1989, only four bombings aboard airliners claimed a total of 885 lives. See James Ott, "FAA Security Panel Examines Means of Improving Defense Against Terrorists," *Aviation Week and Space Technology*, 13 November 1989, p. 76.
6. Martha Crenshaw, "How Terrorism Declines," *Terrorism and Political Violence* 3, no. 1 (Spring 1991), pp. 80–87.
7. Jeffrey Ian Ross and Ted Robert Gurr, in "Why Terrorism Subsides: A Comparative Study of Canada and the United States," *Comparative Politics* 21, no. 4 (July 1989), p. 413, suggests this happened in Quebec after the 1970 October Crisis.
8. In 1988, the State Department claimed that increased intelligence gathering and exchange had prevented 200 terrorist attacks during the previous three years, but few details were provided, so the claim is unverifiable. L. Paul Bremer, "Essential Ingredients in the Fight Against Terrorism," in *Department of State Bulletin* (July 1988), p. 63.
9. Christopher Hewitt, *The Effectiveness of Anti-terrorist Policies* (Lanham, Md.: University Press of America, 1984), p. 90.
10. Ibid., p. 92.
11. Arie Ofri, "Intelligence and Counterterrorism," *Orbis* 28, no. 1 (Spring 1984), p. 46.
12. See, for example, Richard K. Betts, *Surprise Attack: Lessons for Defense Planning* (Washington, D.C.: Brookings Institution, 1982).
13. See David A. Charters, "Counterterrorism Intelligence: Sources, Methods, Process and Problems," in David A. Charters, ed., *Democratic Responses to International Terrorism* (Dobbs Ferry, N.Y.: Transnational Publishers, 1991), pp. 236–66.
14. A. Stuart Farson, "Criminal Intelligence vs. Security Intelligence: a Reevaluation of the Police Role in the Response to Terrorism," in Charters, ed., *Democratic Responses to International Terrorism*, pp. 191–226.
15. Jeffrey Ian Ross, "The Nature of Contemporary International Terrorism," in Charters, ed., *Democratic Responses to International Terrorism*, p. 32.
16. Ronald D. Crelinsten and Alex P. Schmid, "Western Responses to Terrorism: A Twenty-five Year Balance Sheet," *Terrorism and Political Violence* 4, no. 4 (Winter 1992), pp. 315–22.
17. On the concept of spatial selectivity, see Randall W. Heather, "The British Army in Northern Ireland, 1969–1972," (M.A. thesis, University of New Brunswick, 1986), pp. 46–48, 206–207.

18. First Inaugural Address, 4 March 1933, cited in Emily Morison Beck, ed., *[Bartlett's] Familiar Quotations*, 15th ed. (Boston: Little, Brown, 1980), p. 779.

19. Crelinsten and Schmid, "Western Responses," pp. 323–25.

20. Speech at Lord Mayor's Day Luncheon, 10 November 1942 (following victory by British and Allied forces at El Alamein), cited in Beck, ed., *[Bartlett's] Familiar Quotations*, p. 746.

Selected Bibliography

The literature on terrorism is extensive, comprising in excess of 6,000 items. What follows is a *selected* bibliography of major studies, collections, and research tools published since 1980. The reader is encouraged to consult the bibliographies and research guides cited below and the notes in the chapters of this volume for further sources.

BIBLIOGRAPHIES, CHRONOLOGIES, COMPILATIONS, AND RESEARCH GUIDES

Beanlands, Bruce, and James Deacon. *Counter-terrorism Bibliography.* Ottawa: Solicitor General of Canada, 1988.

Burns, Richard D. *The Secret Wars: A Guide to Sources in English.* Vol. 3, *International Terrorism, 1968–1980.* Santa Barbara, Calif.: ABC-CLIO, 1980.

Friedlander, Robert A. *Terrorism: Documents of International and Local Control.* 6 vols. New York: Oceana Publications, 1979–1992.

Gardela, Karen, and Bruce Hoffman. *The Rand Chronology of International Terrorism.* Santa Monica, Calif.: Rand Corp., 1990–date.

Jaffee Center for Strategic Studies. *INTER [A Review of] International Terrorism [1984–date].* Ramat Aviv: Tel Aviv University, 1985–date. [various authors, especially Anat Kurz and Ariel Merari].

Janke, Peter. *Guerrilla and Terrorist Organisations: A World Directory.* Brighton, England: Harvester Press, 1983.

Lakos, Amos. *International Terrorism: A Bibliography.* Boulder, Colo.: Westview Press, 1986.

—, *Terrorism, 1980–1990: A Bibliography.* Boulder, Colo.: Westview Press, 1991. Mickolus, Edward F. *Terrorism, 1988–1991: A Chronology of*

Events and A Selectively Annotated Bibliography. Westport, Conn.:
     Greenwood Press, 1993.

Mickolus, Edward F., with Peter A. Flemming. *Terrorism, 1980–1987: A Se-
     lectively Annotated Bibliography.* Westport, Conn.: Greenwood Press,
     1988.

Mickolus, Edward F., Todd Sandler and Jean M. Murdock. *International Ter-
     rorism in the 1980s: A Chronology of Events.* 2 vols. Ames: Iowa State
     University Press, 1989 [covers 1980–1987].

Newton, Michael, and Judy Ann Newton. *Terrorism in the United States and
     Europe, 1800–1959.* New York: Garland Publishing, 1988.

Norton, Augustus R., and Martin H. Greenberg. *International Terrorism: An
     Annotated Bibliography and Research Guide.* Boulder, Colo.: Westview
     Press, 1980.

Ontiveros, Suzanne Robitaille, ed. *Global Terrorism: A Historical Bibliography.*
     Santa Barbara, Calif.: ABC-CLIO, 1986.

Picard, Robert G., and Rhonda S. Sheets, comps. *Terrorism and the News Media
     Research Bibliography.* Boston: Terrorism and the News Media Re-
     search Project, Emerson College, 1986.

Revolutionary and Dissident Movements: An International Guide. 3 eds. Detroit:
     Gale Research Company/Longman (UK), 1983–1991 [various editors].

Schmid, Alex P., Albert J. Jongman, *Political Terrorism: A New Guide to Actors,
     Authors, Concepts, Data Bases, Theories, and Literature.* New
     Brunswick, N.J.: Transaction Books 1988.

Thackrah, John Richard. *Encyclopedia of Terrorism and Political Violence.*
     London: Routledge and Kegan Paul, 1987.

US Defense Intelligence Agency. *Terrorist Group Profiles.* Washington, D.C.:
     US Government Printing Office, December 1988.

US Department of State. *Patterns of Global [International] Terrorism.* Wash-
     ington, D.C.: US Department of State, 1982 – date.

US Library of Congress, Congressional Research Service. *International Ter-
     rorism: A Compilation of Major Laws, Treaties, Agreements and
     Executive Documents. Report Prepared for the Committee on Foreign
     Affairs, U.S. House of Representatives.* Washington, D.C.: US Govern-
     ment Printing Office, 1987.

BOOKS AND MONOGRAPHS

Adams, James. *The Financing of Terror.* London: New English Library, 1986.

Alexander, Yonah, and Kenneth A. Myers, eds. *Terrorism in Europe.* New York:
     St. Martin's Press, 1982.

Aston, Clive. *A Contemporary Crisis: Political Hostage-Taking and the Experience
     of Western Europe.* Westport, Conn.: Greenwood Press, 1982.

Canada. Senate. *Report of the Senate Special Committee on Terrorism and the
     Public Safety.* Ottawa: Supply and Services, June 1987.

—. Senate. *Report of the Second Special Committee of the Senate on Terrorism and Public Safety.* Ottawa: Supply and Services, June 1989.

Cassese, Antonio. *Terrorism, Politics and Law: The Achille Lauro Affair.* Princeton, N.J.: Princeton University Press, 1989.

Chaliand, Gerard. *Terrorism: From Popular Struggle to Media Spectacle.* London: Saqi Books, 1987.

Charters, David A., ed. *Democratic Responses to International Terrorism.* Dobbs Ferry, N.Y.: Transnational Publishers, 1991.

Crenshaw, Martha. *Terrorism and International Cooperation.* Occasional Papers Series, no. 11. New York: Institute for East-West Security Studies, 1989.

—, ed. *Terrorism, Legitimacy, and Power: the Consequences of Political Violence.* Middletown, Conn.: Wesleyan University Press, 1983.

Davidson Smith, G. *Combating Terrorism.* London: Routledge, 1990.

Falk, Richard. *Revolutionaries and Functionaries: The Dual Face of Terrorism.* New York: E.P. Dutton, 1988.

Ford, Franklin. *Political Murder: From Tyrannicide to Terrorism.* Cambridge: Harvard University Press, 1985.

Freedman, Lawrence, et al. *Terrorism and International Order.* London: Routledge and Kegan Paul, 1986.

Frey, R. G., and Christopher W. Morris. *Violence, Terrorism, and Justice.* Cambridge: Cambridge University Press, 1991.

Gal-Or, Noemi. *International Cooperation to Suppress Terrorism.* New York: St. Martin's Press, 1985.

—. *Tolerating Terrorism in the West: An International Survey.* London: Routledge, 1991.

Hevener, Natalie Kaufman, ed. *Diplomacy in a Dangerous World: Protection for Diplomats Under International Law.* Boulder, Colo.: Westview Press, 1986.

Hewitt, Christopher. *The Effectiveness of Anti-terrorist Policies.* Lanham, Md.: University Press of America, 1984.

Hoffman, Bruce, and Jennifer Morrison Taw. *A Strategic Framework for Countering Terrorism and Insurgency.* No. N–3506–DOS. Santa Monica, Calif.: Rand Corp., 1992.

Jenkins, Brian Michael. *New Modes of Conflict.* No. R–3009-DNA. Santa Monica, Calif.: Rand Corp., 1983.

Kegley, Charles W., Jr. *International Terrorism: Characteristics, Causes, Controls.* New York: St. Martin's Press, 1990.

Laqueur, Walter. *The Age of Terrorism.* Boston: Little, Brown, 1987.

Levitt, Geoffrey M. *Democracies Against Terror: The Western Response to State-supported Terrorism.* Washington Papers, no. 134. New York: Praeger; Washington, D.C.: Center for Strategic and International Studies, 1988.

Livingstone, Neil C. *The War Against Terrorism.* Lexington, Mass.: Lexington Books, 1982.

—, and Terrell E. Arnold, eds. *Fighting Back: Winning the War Against Terrorism.* Lexington, Mass.: Lexington Books, 1986.

Lodge, Juliet, ed. *The Threat of Terrorism.* Boulder, Colo.: Westview Press, 1988.

Long, David E. *The Anatomy of Terrorism.* New York: Free Press, 1990.

Merkl, Peter H., ed. *Political Violence and Terror: Motifs and Motivations.* Berkeley: University of California Press, 1986.

Miller, Abraham H. *Terrorism and Hostage Negotiations.* Boulder, Colo.: Westview Press, 1980.

—, ed. *Terrorism, the Media and the Law.* Dobbs Ferry, N.Y.: Transnational Publishers, 1982.

Murphy, John F. *Punishing International Terrorists: the Legal Framework for Policy Initiatives.* Totowa, N.J.: Rowman and Allanheld, 1985.

—. *State Support of International Terrorism: Legal, Political and Economic Dimensions.* Boulder, CO: Westview Press, 1989.

O'Sullivan, Noel, ed. *Terrorism, Ideology and Revolution: The Origins of Modern Political Violence.* Boulder, Colo.: Westview Press, 1986.

Rapoport, David C., ed. *Inside Terrorist Organizations.* London: Frank Cass, 1988.

—, and Yonah Alexander, eds. *The Morality of Terrorism: Religious and Secular Justifications.* 2d ed. New York: Columbia University Press, 1989.

Reich, Walter, ed. *Origins of Terrorism: Psychologies, Ideologies, Theologies and States of Mind.* Cambridge: Cambridge University Press, 1990.

Ronzitti, Natalino. *Maritime Terrorism and International Law.* Dordrecht, The Netherlands: Martinus Nijhoff, 1990.

—. *Rescuing Nationals Abroad Through Military Coercion and Intervention on Grounds of Humanity.* London: Sage Publications, 1982.

Rubin, Barry, ed. *Terrorism and Politics.* New York: St. Martin's Press, 1991.

Schmid, Alex P., and Janny de Graaf. *Violence as Communication: Insurgent Terrorism and the Western News Media.* London: Sage Publications, 1982.

Sederberg, Peter C. *Terrorist Myths: Illusion, Rhetoric and Reality.* Englewood Cliffs, N.J.: Prentice-Hall, 1989.

Selth, Andrew. *Against Every Human Law: The Terrorist Threat to Diplomacy.* Rushcutters Bay, Australia: Pergamon, 1988.

Slann, Martin, and Bernard Schechterman, eds. *Multidimensional Terrorism.* Boulder, Colo.: Lynne Rienner Publishers, 1987.

Slater, Robert O., and Michael Stohl, eds. *Current Perspectives on International Terrorism.* London: Macmillan, 1988.

Stohl, Michael, ed. *The Politics of Terrorism.* 3d ed. New York: Marcel Dekker, 1988.

—, and George A. Lopez, eds. *The State as Terrorist: the Dynamics of Governmental Violence and Repression.* Westport, Conn.: Greenwood Press, 1984.

Taylor, Maxwell. *The Fanatics: A Behavioral Approach to Political Violence.* London: Brassey's 1991.

—. *The Terrorist.* London: Brassey's, 1988.

Wardlaw, Grant. *Political Terrorism: Theory, Tactics and Counter-measures.* 2d ed. Cambridge: Cambridge University Press, 1989.

Weinberg, Leonard, and Paul B. Davis. *Introduction to Political Terrorism.* Hightstown, N.J.:McGraw-Hill, 1988.

Wilkinson, Paul. *Terrorism and the Liberal State.* 2d ed. London: Macmillan, 1986.

—, and A. M. Stewart, eds. *Contemporary Research on Terrorism.* Aberdeen, UK: Aberdeen University Press, 1987.

Wolf, John B. *Fear of Fear: A Survey of Terrorist Operations and Controls in Open Societies.* New York: Plenum Press, 1981.

PERIODICALS

Several periodicals are devoted exclusively to the study of terrorism or publish articles on the subject on a frequent basis. These include the following:

Conflict Quarterly. Centre for Conflict Studies, University of New Brunswick, Canada. 1980–1994.

Studies in Conflict and Terrorism. Crane Russak, Washington, D.C. 1992–date (succeeds *Terrorism: An International Journal*).

Terrorism and Political Violence. Frank Cass, London, UK. 1989–date.

Terrorism: An International Journal. Crane Russak, Washington, D.C. 1977–1991.

TVI Report. TVI Inc., Beverly Hills, Calif., 1979–date (up to 1985 *TVI Journal*).

Violence and Terrorism—Annual Editions. Dushkin Publishing Group, Guilford, Conn. 1990–date.

Index

Contributors

David A. Charters. Director of the Centre for Conflict Studies and Associate Professor of History at the University of New Brunswick, Fredericton.

Robert H. Evans. Director, The Bologna Center of the Johns Hopkins University School of Advanced International Studies, Baltimore.

Noemi Gal-Or. Visiting Professor, Department of History, University of British Columbia, Vancouver.

Michael M. Harrison. Late Associate Director, Programme for Strategic and International Studies, Graduate Institute of International Studies, Geneva, Switzerland.

Stephen M. Sobieck. Assistant Professor, International Relations, California State University, Long Beach.

Grant Wardlaw. Consultant, Attorney General's Department, Government of Australia.

Bruce W. Warner. Strategic Analyst, Ministry of the Solicitor-General, Canada

J. Brent Wilson. Senior Researcher, Centre for Conflict Studies, University of New Brunswick, Fredericton.

ISBN 0-313-28964-6

90000>

EAN

9 780313 289644

HARDCOVER BAR CODE